Free Market Fairness

Free Market Fairness

JOHN TOMASI

PRINCETON UNIVERSITY PRESS

PRINCETON AND OXFORD

Library of Congress Cataloging-in-Publication Data

Tomasi, John, 1961–
    Free market fairness / John Tomasi.
        p. cm.
    Includes bibliographical references and index.
    ISBN 978-0-691-14446-7 (hbk.)
    1. Liberalism. 2. Equality. 3. Liberty. 4. Capitalism. 5. Free enterprise.
I. Title.
    JC574.T657 2012
    330.12'2—dc23
                        2011037125

British Library Cataloging-in-Publication Data is available
This book has been composed in Palatino LT Std
Printed on acid-free paper. ∞
Printed in the United States of America
1 3 5 7 9 10 8 6 4 2

Capitalismus sine stercore tauri.

Contents

Acknowledgments

Many colleagues, students, and friends helped me write this book, including: Sahar Akhtar, Larry Alexander, Richard Arneson, Bas van der Bassan, Anthony Bedami, Zack Beauchamp, Barbara Buckinx, Steve Calabresi, Yvonne Chiu, Tom Christiano, Mark Cladis, Ross Corbett, Dina Egge, Michael Frazer, Bill Galston, Jerry Gaus, Scott Gerber, Alex Gourevitch, Charles Griswold, Leigh Jenco, Kate Johnson, Laura Joyce, Mark Koyama, Chandran Kukathas, Mark LeBar, Hugh Lazenby, Helene Landemore, Brink Lindsey, Loren Lomasky, Roderick Long, Minh Ly, Matthew Lyddon, John McCormick, David McIlroy, Eric Mack, Jim Morone, Emily Nacol, Jan Narveson, Michael Novak, Carlos Ormachea, Carmen Pavel, Philip Pettit, John Phillips, Jeppe von Platz, Dennis Rasmussen, Danny Shapiro, Paul Starr, Annie Stilz, Jason Swadley, Adam Tebble, George Thomas, Scott Turcotte, Chad Van Schoelandt, Debra Satz, Doug Den Uyl, Keven Vallier, Andrew Volmert, Steve Wall, Greg Weiner, Dan Wewers, Will Wilkinson, and Matt Zwolinkski.

Among the many who sent written comments, several merit separate thanks: Samuel Freeman, David Schmidtz, Steve Macedo, Richard Arneson, Jacob Levy, Tom Spragens, Danny Shapiro, and two anonymous reviewers for the Press. I have special debts to Freeman and Schmidtz. From different political perspectives, Sam and Dave encouraged this project from the start. That has long seemed significant to me.

Brown University is a special place to think and write about political philosophy. I thank my colleagues David Estlund, Sharon Krause, Corey Brettschneider, and Charles Larmore for their suggestions and friendship. The postdoctoral fellows in Brown's Political Theory Project have been a source of energy and ideas. Keith Hankins and Jason Swadley, PhD candidates at the University of Arizona and Brown respectively, were diligent and creative research assistants. Jason Brennan has been my neighbor in the Political Theory Project throughout the years I wrote this book. I understand the state of our discipline far better because of my daily conversations with Jay. More than colleagues, Jay and I have been intellectual coconspirators: classical liberals who see the need for change. I thank him.

I gave many public presentations on this work. Several stand out: the Manhattan Institute's 2007 Hayek Lecture delivered at the Princeton Club in New York; the 2008 Bradley Lecture at the American Enterprise Institute; a conference in Princeton on "Liberal Libertarians" organized by Doug Massey; and a 2009 American Political Science Association (APSA) panel in Toronto (chaired by Steve Macedo) on "Libertarianism: Can There Be a Moral Defense?" I benefited from book workshops at the University of Arizona, at Brown University, at the Institute for Humane Studies' Social Change Workshop for graduate students and, especially, from a lively group that discussed a near final version at the Grande Colonial Hotel in La Jolla, California, in January of 2011: Arneson, Schmidtz, Wilkinson, Long, Alexander, Macedo, Shapiro, Wall, LeBar, Stilz, Hankins, and Wolinski. Thank you.

Ian Malcolm had faith in this unlikely project from the beginning. I thank Rob Tempio for picking it up and carrying it through.

The epigraph is the slogan of a famous study group founded by my former teacher, G. A. Cohen—slightly adapted.

Finally, I thank my family, Amy, Peter and Lydia. I dedicate this book to my mother and my father, and their American dream.

Introduction

Some of my best friends are libertarians. But by this I do not mean the usual thing: that these people are my friends *even though* they are libertarians. And while I do not quite mean the opposite, that would bring us somewhat closer to the truth. The mere fact that someone is a libertarian is enough to dispose me to befriend them. This is because I find libertarianism a profoundly attractive political view.

I use the term *libertarianism* here in the popular, colloquial sense, meaning that cluster of political views associated with the "right-wing" of liberal democratic polities. In various ways, and for various reasons, theorists in this broad tradition support the idea of limited government and wide private freedom, most notably in economic affairs. Classical liberals, economic liberals, anarcho-capitalists, right-libertarians, or (as some insist) *real* liberals—for now, I use the term *libertarian* to refer to them all.

For me, the main attraction of this broad libertarian tradition is its emphasis on property rights. All liberals value the civil and political rights of individuals: the right to a fair trial, freedom of expression, political participation, personal autonomy, and so on. But libertarians are distinct in asserting that the economic rights of capitalism— the right to start a business, personally negotiate the terms of one's employment, or decide how to spend (or save) the income one earns—are essential parts of freedom too.

I like this aspect of libertarianism. At its best I see the libertarian defense of property rights as springing from an attractive ideal of political agency. Possessing some particular bundle of material goods, for libertarians, is not nearly so important as possessing those goods because of one's own actions and choices. When we are free, we are aware of ourselves as central causes of the lives we lead. It is not just captains of industry or heroes of Ayn Rand novels who define themselves through their accomplishments in the economic realm. Many ordinary people—middle-class parents, single moms, entry-level workers—become who they are, and express who they hope to be, by the personal choices they make regarding work, saving, and spending. These are areas in which people earn esteem from others and feel a proper pride for things they themselves do. In economic affairs, libertarians insist, it is not merely the outcome that matters: the process must be considered too. Diminishing personal agency in economic affairs—no matter how lofty the social goal—drains vital blood from a person's life. When private economic freedoms are curtailed, libertarians claim, people become in some important sense less free. People in this tradition also emphasize property rights for instrumental reasons: property rights are linked to other basic rights, promote the creation of social wealth, encourage personal responsibility, and mitigate the dangers of concentrated political power. But the libertarian claim that property rights protect freedom has always seemed most important to me.

I am also drawn to the libertarian idea of "spontaneous order." Sometimes social goals are most effectively pursued directly; for example, by the creation of a governmental program guaranteeing the delivery of some needed good or service. But libertarian thinkers emphasize that at other times—perhaps most times—social goals are best pursued indirectly. A commercial market is a paradigm of spontaneous order. The production of the most ordinary commercial good—a lowly pencil—requires the mobilization of a staggeringly complex system of actors: foresters, miners, sailors, metallurgists, chemists, gluers, accountants, and more. As Leonard Read observes, there may be literally *"not a single person on the face of this earth"* who knows how to make a pencil.[1] Yet pencils are produced. These complex productive systems typically were not planned: they evolved. They are products of human action but not of human design. Friedrich Hayek argues that a free society is best thought of as a spontaneous order in which people should be allowed to pursue their own goals on the basis of information available only to themselves. Along with the moral ideal of private economic liberty, I find the libertarian emphasis on spontaneous order deeply attractive.

Like many people around the world, I associate these libertarian ideas with the United States of America. America is not the only country with a culture that celebrates capitalism. Further, as a matter of historical fact, America has many times failed to affirm these capitalistic freedoms—and has also violated other basic liberal values, sometimes egregiously. Nonetheless, there seems to be a special connection between libertarianism and the aspirations of ordinary Americans. The American dream posits America as a land of entrepreneurs. Writing in the 1790s, the Federalist leader Gouverneur

Morris proudly referred to his countrymen as "the first-born children of the commercial age."[2] America, on this vision, is a land of opportunities—not a place of guarantees. The Declaration of Independence states that people have a right, not to happiness, but to the *pursuit* thereof. This land of opportunity exposes people to risks of failure and by that very fact offers them a chance for accomplishments genuinely their own. Dean Alfange's poem, "An American's Creed," includes these lines: "I do not wish to be a kept citizen, / Humbled and dulled, / By having the state look after me. / I want to take the calculated risk, / To dream and to build, / To fail and to succeed."[3] Whatever life they lead, on this vision, Americans can take pride in knowing that their life is significantly one of their own creation.

We may well debate whether Americans continue to affirm these traditional values of individual responsibility and causal self-authorship. We might even debate whether they should. Personally, I like this "American" vision of social life. It gives shape to the two philosophical ideas I mentioned earlier: the idea of private economic freedom and the idea of society as a spontaneous order. I am drawn to the libertarian tradition, and to many libertarians, for all these reasons.

However, I am a professional academic working in the shadow of the twentieth century. This means that most of my friends are not libertarians. Most of my professional friends and colleagues, by far, are left liberals.[4] New liberals, modern liberals, liberal democratic theorists, prioritarians, sufficientarians, egalitarians of various stripes, or—at their most enthusiastic—high liberals; for now I use the term *left liberals* to refer to them all. Speaking generally, left liberals are skeptical of the moral significance of private economic liberty. They are skeptical also of distributions of goods that result from the exercise of those capitalist freedoms. Left liberals think distributive issues are better brought under the control of deliberative bodies, and that a central function of government is to ensure that citizens have access to a wide range of social services—education, health care, social security, and the like.

Because of my convictions about the importance of private economic liberty, you might guess that I have moral qualms about the institutional orientation of left liberalism. Nonetheless, there are ideas within the left liberal tradition I find attractive too.

In recent decades, many left liberal theorists have adopted a certain view about political justification. If a set of political and economic institutions is to be just and legitimate, those institutions must be justifiable to the citizens who are to live within them. According to John Rawls, the problem of political justification is to be settled "by working out a problem of deliberation."[5] Anarcho-capitalists such as Murray Rothbard argue that state institutions are justified only if they gain the literal consent of every person subject to them.[6] By contrast, philosophers in the deliberative tradition emphasize the idea of moral acceptability. To be justified, institutions must pass a test of acceptability to citizens understood as beings who, in their moral nature, wish to live together on terms that all can accept. According to Rawls and many other philosophers on the left, this deliberative or "democratic" approach is closely connected to a further idea: the idea of social, or distributive, justice.

Against the libertarians and traditional classical liberals, left liberals insist that the concept "justice" applies to more than mere individual actions. Instead, the social order as a whole—the pattern in which goods and opportunities are distributed or, better, the set of institutions that generate such patterns—can properly be described as just or unjust. Social justice requires more than the protection of the formal rights of citizens. In Rawls's elegant phrase, justice requires that citizens "share one another's fate."[7] Institutions must be arranged so people can look upon the special skills and talents of their fellow citizens not as weapons to be feared but as in some sense a common bounty. There are many formulations of the distributional requirements of social justice within the left-liberal tradition. Here is a general formulation that will do for now: justice requires that institutions be designed so that the benefits they help produce are enjoyed by all citizens, including the least fortunate. Everyone is the author of a life, and the storyline of that life is fantastically important to each person. We honor the importance of self-authorship when we insist that our institutions leave no one behind. Like the deliberative approach to political justification, I find this idea of social justice compelling.

My simultaneous attraction to libertarian ideas and to left-liberal ones often makes things awkward for me. Thinkers I admire reject each other's core commitments. Hayek, for example, rejects social justice as a moral standard.[8] Within the context of a spontaneously ordered society, Hayek says the phrase "social justice" is a piece of incoherent nonsense—like the phrase "a moral stone." From the other side, Rawls rejects the idea that the economic rights of capitalism have any essential connection to liberty. Market distributions, unless corrected, are unjust: they reflect accidents of birth and endowment that are "arbitrary from the moral point of view." Because of the way some libertarians emphasize property rights, Rawls says they should not even be recognized as holding a properly liberal position.[9] Morally, institutionally, and dispositionally, it seems, my two sets of friends do not mix.

In this book, I introduce a liberal research program that I call market democracy. Market democracy is a deliberative form of liberalism that is sensitive to the moral insights of libertarianism. Market democracy combines the four ideas I just mentioned: (1) capitalistic economic freedoms as vital aspects of liberty, (2) society as a spontaneous order, (3) just and legitimate political institutions as acceptable to all who make their lives among them, (4) social justice as the ultimate standard of political evaluation. Here is a simple way to begin thinking about this view: market democracy affirms capitalistic economic liberties as first-order requirements of social justice.

Market democracy takes a fundamentally deliberative approach to the problem of political justification. It sees society as a fair system of social cooperation. Within such a society, citizens are committed to supporting political and economic institutions that their fellow citizens can join them in supporting, regardless of their particular social or economic status. Being "democratic" in this sense, market democracy affirms a robustly substantive conception of equality as a requirement of liberal justice. Yet market democracy approaches social justice in an unusual way: signally, by affirming a powerful set of private economic liberties as among the basic rights of liberal citizens. Market democracy does not assert the importance of private economic liberty merely on instrumental grounds (for example, because such liberties are expected to lead to economic efficiency) or even from the idea that a society based on such liberties might satisfy some hoped-for distributional ideal (for example, as in the empirical claim that capitalism benefits the poor). Instead, market democracy affirms the moral importance of private economic liberty primarily on *deliberative* grounds: market democracy sees the affirmation of private economic liberty as a requirement of democratic legitimacy itself.

I hope the market democratic approach will be of interest to anyone who, like me, finds the four ideas I mentioned a moment ago attractive, and who wishes to see how they might be brought together into a unified philosophical framework. As my argument for market democracy unfolds, I offer more precise interpretations of those four ideas: private economic liberty, spontaneous order, deliberative justification, and social justice. As I begin specifying how I interpret those ideas and begin adjusting them so that they might fit together, I anticipate that some thinkers from each tradition will object to the interpretations I adopt.

For example, consider the first idea I mentioned, the idea that the economic rights of capitalism have intrinsic or fundamental moral value. Traditionally, thinkers in the market-liberal tradition have interpreted this to mean that economic liberties should be treated on a par with the civil and political liberties of citizens. Economic rights, like civil and political ones, are basic rights. Recently, though, some thinkers in this tradition have adopted a stronger thesis. They interpret the intrinsic value of capitalistic rights to mean that economic rights are *more basic* than other rights. At the limit, civil and political rights are not merely less weighty than property rights: such rights are themselves *types of* property rights.[10] Property rights, on this view, are moral absolutes. The stronger interpretation would require the enforcement of almost any contract citizens enter into— for example, contracts for voluntary slavery or the transfer of vital bodily organs. The weaker interpretation of economic liberties would not: it affirms the inalienability of certain basic rights and liberties, including those protecting bodily integrity, and asserts that private economic rights must be protected *along with* the other basic rights and liberties. This is a significant dispute within the free market tradition. Indeed, within the technical literature, the term "libertarian" is sometimes reserved to mark the position of those who take the stronger/absolutist interpretation, with all others then being cast as (mere) "classical liberals."

In any case, market democracy adopts the weaker of these two theses regarding the intrinsic value of property rights. Market democracy views the economic rights of capitalism as *on a par* with the other basic rights and liberties. Property rights are component parts of a multifaceted, liberty-protecting scheme. Like freedoms of speech and religion, the economic freedoms of citizens merit foundational protection. Property rights, while basic, are not moral absolutes. The right to free speech does not empower theater-goers to shout "Fire!", just as economic rights of capitalism do not allow for completely unregulated economic action. In this sense, I suppose, the market democratic claim about the intrinsic value of property rights might be described more precisely as "classical liberal" rather than "libertarian." Libertarians who are skeptical of the classical liberal approach to economic liberty will be skeptical of market democracy.

Similarly, consider the idea of spontaneous order. Thinkers within the tradition of free market liberalism use the theory of spontaneous order in different ways. Sometimes, spontaneous order is used in what I shall call an ontological sense. A society either *is* a spontaneous order or it *is not* one. Normative implications are then drawn (or blocked from being drawn) by an analysis of this ontological fact. For example, if a society *is* a spontaneous order, then it is sometimes claimed that whatever rules, norms, and distributions result from spontaneous processes are justified by that very fact. There is no external standard by which the products of spontaneous forces might be evaluated.

Other times, however, the idea of spontaneous order is used to denote, not a state of affairs, but a strategy of social construction. In pursuit of desired ends we face the choice of employing spontaneous orders or other types of order—typically, orders that are more direct or planned. Market democracy rejects the ontological use of spontaneous order theory. It affirms spontaneous order as a strategy of social construction. In this too, market democracy does not seek to please everyone in the free market tradition.

From the other ideological side, consider the idea of social justice. There is a vast literature debating the requirements of social justice. Some think the phrase "social justice" is a standard for evaluating the particular distributions of goods within a society at any particular time. They see a demand for "social justice" as a demand for immediate state action to correct that distribution so that it matches the ideal.

By contrast, market democracy sees social justice as a standard that applies holistically. Social justice is a property not of particular distributions, but of social institutions taken as a whole. As such, a demand for social justice does not necessarily call for (or allow) immediate state action to adjust or "correct" particular distributions. Social justice requires that one take a longer view. It is a standard that tells us what sort of macroinstitutional forms we should work toward.

Market democracy is built from the general formulation of social justice I mentioned a moment ago: along with securing a set of basic liberties for all citizens, justice requires that we prefer social institutions designed to benefit the poor. By affirming such institutions, we express our commitment to respect citizens of every class as free and equal moral beings. This is not the only formulation of social justice within the liberal tradition, and even this formulation can be interpreted in myriad ways. For my purposes, we should distinguish two rival interpretations of social justice.

One interpretation of social justice emphasizes the value of equality. A society in which people's holdings are more equal is, by that fact, better than a society in which people's holdings are less equal.[11] This interpretation is often concerned with the political standing of people throughout the various domains of their lives: preferring, for example, that workplaces be democratically controlled. We benefit the poor by working toward institutions that make the holdings, opportunities, and statuses across society more equal. This approach, which sees equality itself as a value, has been called "egalitarian."[12]

The pursuit of equality, however, may result in a situation where everyone has less than they might otherwise have had. Other theorists, therefore, interpret the requirement of benefiting the poor in a different way. They think equality of holdings and statuses is a goal only if the lives of people, and the lives of the poor in particular, would be improved by the pursuit of that goal. Their concern is not with equality per se but with the holdings of the poor. We benefit the poor by choosing social institutions that generate the largest possible bundle of goods under their personal control (even if, in doing so, some other citizens may personally control still larger bundles of goods). Because of its focus on the absolute holdings of poor people, we might call this general approach "humanitarian" (this approach is sometimes called "prioritarian").

Market democracy affirms a humanitarian interpretation of social justice rather than an egalitarian one. The basic rights of all citizens in place, social institutions should be designed so that the members of the poorest class personally control the largest possible bundle of goods (say, wealth and income). Anyone committed to an egalitarian interpretation of social justice will be unhappy with market democracy.

Liberalism has long been divided between a "free market" tradition and a "democratic" one: the former based on a concern for private economic liberty, the latter on a concern for social justice. Market democracy is erected atop footings sunk deep in each tradition. Because it is built up from those footings, it may seem market democracy aims to bridge—and thereby close—that historical divide. I do not think of market democracy this way. It is not a compromise, or middle place, between the left-liberal tradition and the libertarian one. It is not animated by an ambition to bring together or somehow reconcile these two traditions—for example, by somehow dissolving the differences between them. Nor, certainly, is it an attempt to co-opt the ideals of one tradition to advance the agenda of the other. Instead, market democracy is a genuine hybrid. It results from a sincere attempt to combine appealing ideas from two great liberal traditions. Market democracy is a view that stands on its own and that, I hope, will prove attractive in its own right. Its attractions endure whether or not it induces any partisan to "switch sides."

There is a different approach to fusionism that I wish to mention so that I might put it firmly aside. This approach is built from the following idea: libertarians and left liberals share the same moral commitments—such as concern for the poor—and differ merely about an empirical question: Which set of institutions, (roughly) free market ones or (roughly) big government ones, best honor or help secure those shared moral commitments?[13]

Fusionist views of this sort are not market democratic in my sense. Such views seek to skim above the moral debates between libertarians and left liberals. They see the differences between the two traditions as mere differences of empirical fact. As a result, this form of fusionism avoids the hard question of whether the moral ideas I mentioned might be brought together into a coherent philosophical framework. That alone disqualifies such approaches from counting as market democratic. But such views also worry me even on their own terms. For, despite their fusionist aspirations, they require that vital moral insights, most notably from the libertarian side, be jettisoned or left to straggle along behind in weak and attenuated form.

After all, what would it mean for libertarians to affirm the same moral commitments of the left liberals? Two things. First, it would mean that libertarians would join the left liberals in affirming the same list of basic rights and liberties that are held by all citizens. Second, it would require that libertarians accept the left liberal account of what it means to show proper concern for the poor. Both requirements are problematic.

Consider the first. As I mentioned, libertarians have long insisted that wide-ranging private economic liberties are among the most sacred and inviolable rights of free citizens. By contrast, paragons of left liberalism such as Rawls recognize only a spare list of economic liberties as basic. For the Rawlsians, the question of whether the list of constitutionally protected rights should be "thickened up" so as to include, for example, the right to own private productive property is one that must be decided in light of historical, cultural, and economic conditions. Maybe liberalism will call for a socialist economy; maybe it will allow some kind of private market. Should libertarians join the left liberals in that approach to basic rights and liberties? If they do, in what sense do they remain libertarians at all?

The second requirement is equally problematic. Let's accept that libertarians can join left liberals in being concerned for the poor. Let's even accept (as I shall soon argue) that libertarians should join them in expressing that concern in terms of a commitment to social justice. Let's even accept, as I shall also argue, that libertarians should affirm the same formal conception of social justice as the left liberals: when considering a variety of institutional forms, social justice requires that we prefer the one that, while fully respecting the basic rights and liberties common to all citizens, brings about the greatest benefits to the poor.

To traditional libertarians, this may already seem like a lot to concede. But the approach I just mentioned would require libertarians to go a step further still. It would require libertarians to allow the left liberals to decide what goods or states of affairs properly count as "benefiting" the poor. For reasons already sketched, there is no a priori reason to think libertarians should be ready to agree with the left liberals about which goods or states of affairs are most valuable to the poor.

I think of market democracy not as a single interpretation of liberalism but as a general research program. We have a wealth of competing conceptions of social justice developed by political philosophers on the liberal left. But none of these conceptions affirm extensive systems of property as basic rights. Nor do any of them give a central place to spontaneous order in the way classical liberals and libertarians do. In evaluating outcomes, these conceptions put comparatively little moral weight on thicker, context-dependent questions about how those outcomes come about—questions that libertarians, at their best, make central.

If we are wealthy (surfeit?) with left liberal theories of social justice, we are impoverished with respect to libertarian or "right liberal" theories of that sort. As a research program, market democracy encourages scholars to consider whether any, or all, of the existing (leftist) conceptions of social justice might be adjusted so as to recognize a wide array of private economic freedoms as basic rights and to adopt principles of spontaneous order in pursuit of their various distributional goals. Market democracy encourages scholars to seek other ways to combine these "un-combinables"—private economic freedom and social justice—too.

To make this proposal plausible, I mean to work out a market democratic interpretation of a uniquely prominent conception of liberal justice: the view Rawls calls justice as fairness. I focus on Rawls's view for several reasons. First, the general formulation of justice as fairness that Rawls provides is rich and complex enough to be interpreted in a great variety of ways. Many theorists have made careers by developing such interpretations. Most all those interpretations of justice as fairness, like Rawls's own, have clustered comfortably on the left. However, there are interpretative possibilities on the right as well. Indeed, one of these interpretive possibilities comes very close to capturing my own political convictions.

I believe that liberal citizens have powerful claims of freedom across the economic realms of working, consuming, and owning. Once these economic freedoms are protected on a par with the other basic rights of liberal citizens, then justice requires that we seek social institutions that most improve the position of the poor (interpreted in humanitarian terms). Viewed through an ideal theoretic lens that I shall describe, there is a range of free market institutions that satisfies that distributive condition. That is a highly simplified account of the interpretation of justice as fairness that I shall be defending. I call it *free market fairness*.

Market democracy is a broad and complex research program. A complete exposition of market democracy, or even of all the component requirements of the particular view I call free market fairness, is beyond the scope of this book. I hope simply to introduce the market democratic approach and make plausible the particular reading of it—free market fairness—that I find most attractive. In that sense, this book is a primer on market democracy.

Nonetheless, this book aims to be disruptive. Left liberalism is the reigning ideology of the academic elite. My mentors in graduate school, my professional colleagues, the deans at my university, the students in my classes—most all of them roll out their blankets someplace or other within this broad left-liberal camp. Within those academic circles—my circles—the political prescriptions of left liberalism are so widely accepted that they have come to define what can only be described as the "moral status quo." Members of this academic elite want political change. Yet when asked to indicate what change they seek, most point in the same general direction.

Perhaps there is nothing worrying about this conformity of opinion. After all, one task of philosophy is to seek the truth. The moral consensus within the contemporary academy may merely demonstrate that the assertions of the left-liberal paradigm are true. In that case, it would be fitting that contemporary academics continue to add new layers of scholarship atop the assumptions of left liberalism— even if the effect of their efforts is to deepen and harden the academically dominant view. However, another time-honored role of philosophy has been to challenge status quos—including even status quos of its own creation. This role is particularly important when it comes to philosophizing about politics. For in the domain of political philosophy, as Hegel observed, the owl of Minerva has a worrying habit of arriving only at dusk.[14]

A major theme of this book is that the academic consensus around left liberalism does indeed indicate the arrival of a kind of dusk. Left liberalism developed in the twentieth century in part because of a sense that our world had changed in important ways from the world of Adam Smith, James Madison, David Ricardo, and other classical liberals. The advent of industrial capitalism was not a necessary condition for the development of the liberal conception of social justice. In principle at least, philosophers could have developed that ideal a priori, without any new empirical observations. Yet philosophers, as real people, necessarily inhabit particular historical and economic epochs. Features of those epochs, or at least the beliefs philosophers have about the nature of those epochs, often serve as stimulants. Observations about our particular social world often stir us to rethink inherited ideals in new and unexpected ways.

The idea of social justice, I suggest, developed in response to tectonic economic shifts philosophers observed around them during the early stages of industrial capitalism. But the world has not stopped changing. One of the most profound changes within western liberal democracies over the past century or so has been another phenomenon associated with capitalism: economic growth. So slowly and steadily as to be almost imperceptible, western societies have grown spectacularly wealthier in just the last few generations. Compounding has quietly made us rich. Citizens in the United States today find themselves roughly eight times wealthier than their grandparents. During that period, the inflation-adjusted wages of unskilled workers doubled, then more than doubled again.[15] As *The Times* of London wryly notes: "Today's supermarket customers eat considerably better than the Queen ate 50 years ago."[16] The growth of social wealth has profound consequences—most notably for the way people think about their economic liberties.

Early thinkers in the left-liberal tradition expected the development of capitalism to render private economic liberties increasingly less important to people. In an era of mass production, the right to individually negotiate the terms of employment might plausibly be claimed to render people vulnerable rather than to make them free. As western societies have grown wealthier, however, something surprising has occurred: ordinary citizens are assigning *more* value to private economic freedom rather than less.

Political parties increasingly feel the tremors of this shift. A campaign to repeal the "death tax"—an inheritance tax that would apply only to the wealthiest 2 percent of the population—wins broad support not just among the rich but also among the working class.[17] A proposal to apply a "luxury tax" to purely cosmetic medical procedures—the so-called Botax—meets a groundswell of opposition not just from industry lobbyists but from ordinary, middle-class folk.[18] Pollsters find poor citizens prefer policies that increase economic growth over those that redistribute wealth.[19] A prominent left-liberal political theorist describes as "dismaying and galling" his experience of driving up to the comfortable homes of his fellow Democratic precinct workers past trailer parks festooned with signs supporting lower taxes and reductions in government spending.[20]

Naturally, these facts can read in different ways: perhaps these people are greedy, ignorant, and easily misled (as well as vain). Another reading—one with tantalizing philosophical possibilities—is this: as societies grow wealthier, citizens sometimes assign *greater* value to their private economic freedoms. Of course, no matter how one decides to read the facts I just mentioned, the path along which political philosophy develops cannot be set by the opinions and attitudes of ordinary people. Political philosophy is not conducted by opinion poll.[21] Nonetheless, facts such as these can stimulate philosophical developments. They do this by suggesting new possibilities for philosophers to ponder.

At the same time that citizens in some societies seem to be placing new value on their economic liberties, the ideal of social justice is also gaining power. The threads from which the various theories of social justice are woven reach deep into the moral consciences of liberal citizens. Americans of diverse financial positions and political viewpoints, for example, converge on the idea that all citizens—including the poorest class—should have a real opportunity to improve their circumstances over the course of their lives.[22] Equality of opportunity, substantive as well as formal, has become part of the fabric of western constitutional democracies. The twentieth-century formulations of social justice, however, diminish (or reject) the moral value of the economic liberties of capitalism. The inherited social justice paradigm rests on the assumption that property rights are *not* among the sacred and inviolable rights of liberal citizens. Add this dogma to the growing popular support for economic freedom, and something has to give.

What must give, I suggest, is the moral status quo. For too long we have relied on a static map of the ideological terrain of liberal political thought. That map places classical liberalism and left liberalism in rival camps, with the left-liberal camp firmly (and exclusively) entrenched on the moral high ground. This map has encouraged even leading philosophers to take pinched and ungenerous views of the positions of their rivals. More important, this map restricts the intellectual flexibility of contemporary thinkers—scholars and students and citizens alike. This map encourages even people of good will to believe that certain inherited ideological boundaries cannot be crossed. Libertarianism *or* left liberalism. Capitalism *or* democracy. Free markets *or* fairness. One side or the other, everyone must choose.

Market democracy encourages the drawing of new maps—ones that depict the main moral insights of liberalism as mobile rather than fixed. Liberals of good faith need not choose between two camps—classical liberal on one side, high liberal on the other. Market democracy is my attempt to show how the board pieces of liberalism might be arranged in a new and different way.

This book has eight chapters. I begin with an intellectual history of liberalism, with some reference to the history of actual liberal societies, most notably the United States. To motivate the search for market democracy, chapters 1 and 2 describe how the currently dominant left-liberal paradigm displaced the earlier classical liberal one. I explain how the intellectual dominance of left liberalism hangs heavily on a single peg: the claim that private economic liberties are morally less important than the other traditional rights and liberties of liberalism. In chapter 3, I suggest that the peg supporting that high liberalism thesis may be more fragile than its defenders realize, focusing on populist responses to the fact of economic growth. The center of this book, conceptually as well as positionally, is chapter 4. In that chapter I introduce the hybrid approach to liberal theory building I call market democracy. Market democracy, in all its variants, combines a concern for private individual economic liberty with a commitment to social justice. As such, market democracy offers an alternative to classical liberalism and to high liberalism alike, at least as those views are traditionally conceived. The rest of the book elaborates market democracy. Most notably, I develop my own preferred market democratic view: free market fairness. I seek to make that view attractive to open-minded defenders of the two great rival liberal traditions: chapters 5 and 6 are directed to classical liberals and libertarians, chapters 7 and 8 to high liberals of the political left. I conclude with some thoughts about free market fairness and its relation to traditional American values.

A note on terminology. As we have already seen, schools of liberal thought are often labeled differently in popular and scholarly discourse. Even among scholars, labels are often used in different ways and are demarcated by different sets of criteria.[23] Allow me to stipulate how I shall be using some major terms in this book.

Henceforth, I reserve the term *libertarian* for use in the technical sense mentioned above, to denote a family of liberal views that gives exceptionally high priority to the economic liberties of capitalism. The main division I shall be discussing is that between *classical liberalism* (of which libertarianism as defined above is but a species) and

the tradition of views that its own proponents call *high liberalism*.
Classical liberalism is the liberalism of Adam Smith, David Hume,
F. A. Hayek, and of libertarians such as Robert Nozick; high lib-
eralism, that of John Stuart Mill, T. H. Green, John Rawls, Ronald
Dworkin, Martha Nussbaum, Thomas Nagel, Joshua Cohen, Will
Kymlicka, Amy Gutmann, and a great many other contemporary
scholars. I demarcate these two liberal schools in terms of their *sub-
stantive moral commitments*. In particular, classical liberals affirm what
I shall call a *thick* conception of economic liberty; high liberals, a *thin*
conception.[24]

Most liberals agree that some rights and liberties are more important or "basic" than others. Basic liberties merit a high degree of political protection, often by being entrenched as constitutional rights.
Along with civil liberties, such as the right to a fair trial, and political liberties, such as the right to vote, all liberals include some economic liberties on their lists of basic liberties. These liberties protect
independent economic activity and so guarantee citizens a range
of decision-making power with respect to economic questions that
touch the cores of their lives.

But liberals differ about the economic liberties they consider
basic. On thick conceptions of economic liberty, the wide-ranging
economic liberties traditionally associated with capitalist economies
are affirmed as basic rights. Wide individual freedom of economic
contract and powerful rights to the private ownership of productive property are prominent features of the thick conception of economic liberty. On thin conceptions, by contrast, less weight is given
to private economic liberty generally, and the list of basic economic
liberties itself is narrower. Rather than wide freedom of economic
contract, for example, that list might include only a limited right to
free occupational choice. A thin conception may include a right to
own personal property but may not include the right to own productive property. At the limit, the high liberal tradition includes forms
of liberalism embedded in a socialist economy—possibly with the
private ownership of productive property being outlawed altogether.

Continuing with this approach of demarcating liberal schools in
terms of their treatment of economic liberty, I shall henceforth treat
libertarianism as a variant within the classical liberal tradition.[25] As
classical liberals, libertarians affirm a thick conception of economic
liberty. But while traditional classical liberals affirm a general right of

economic liberty as being on a par with the other traditional liberal rights and liberties, libertarians affirm those economic liberties as the weightiest of all rights, and possibly even as moral absolutes. For example, while many classical liberals advocate limited tax-funded support for education and a safety net, the libertarian approach typically rules out such programs.

My way of distinguishing classical and high liberalism, by focusing on whether a view affirms a thick or a thin conception of basic economic liberties, is not the only method, or even the most common method, of distinguishing these two traditions. Samuel Freeman, who coined the term "high liberalism," demarcates these two schools not in terms of their substantive moral commitments but by their justificatory foundations. On Freeman's reading, most classical liberals emphasize private economic liberties primarily because they believe such liberties are instrumentally valuable: economic liberties create wealth and so are conducive to overall happiness (though classical liberals sometimes draw upon ideas of natural rights too). High liberals, by contrast, give the economic liberties of capitalism only a smaller role because they are concerned first and foremost with respecting citizens as free and equal self-governing agents. Thus Freeman, following Rawls, calls classical liberalism the "liberalism of happiness" and high liberalism the "liberalism of freedom."[26] However, this way of demarcating the classical and high liberal traditions prejudges precisely the questions I wish to open.

Is the best defense of private property given in libertarian terms of efficiency, natural law, or self-ownership? Do we really respect individuals as free and equal self-governing agents by restricting their economic liberty? Is a commitment to private property compatible with a commitment to the poor? Is deliberative democracy a vehicle that can only make left turns? Is high liberalism the *highest* form of liberalism? These are questions this book will pursue.

Free Market Fairness

CHAPTER 1
Classical Liberalism

Property and Equality

Liberalism has a complicated history. If asked to draw a quick sketch, however, most contemporary theorists would find the main lines of liberal thought easy enough to depict. Liberalism passed through two great, evolutionary stages. There was an early "classical" stage that emphasized private property. It claimed that people are respected as equals if the law treats them all the same, regardless of material inequalities that might emerge between them. The classical view was eventually displaced by modern, "high" liberalism. As the masterworks of the High Renaissance represent the culmination of a creative movement begun by early Renaissance artists, so high liberals see their political view as the fulfillment of a normative ideal first discussed, but only partially understood, by classical liberal thinkers: the ideal of political equality. Thus while classical liberalism was founded on a formal conception of equality, high liberalism develops the idea of equality into a substantive moral ideal. High liberalism affirms social justice as the ultimate standard of institutional evaluation and, perhaps as a consequence, relegates private economic liberty to a secondary place. High liberalism, on this telling, is an unambiguous moral advance over the early liberal view.

If I were set to work on the task of sketching liberalism's history, my picture would also depict two great schools of thought, with the (self-described) "high liberal" school emerging after the (temporally) "classical" one. However, my picture would depict the lines of moral advancement and regression between the two schools as decidedly mixed. Along the dimension of equality, for example, my drawing would depict the substantive ideal of equality developed by high liberals as a moral improvement over the purely formal classical liberal ideal. Regarding the protection of the basic liberties of citizens, however, my drawing would depict the classical liberal respect for private economic liberty as appropriate and the high liberal neglect of such liberty as a significant moral defect. In terms of the relative moral standing of the two views, therefore, my drawing would feature big arrows pointing in opposite directions.

I discuss classical liberalism in this chapter, high liberalism in the next. While not presented quite in stick-figure terms, my account will be simple, broad stroked, and intentionally stylized. Most histories of liberalism emphasize the role of religious conflict. I mention such conflicts barely at all. This is because my aim is to describe the origins of a conflict *within* liberal thinking—the conflict between those who see liberalism as a doctrine of limited government power and wide individual economic freedom, and those who see it as a doctrine calling for extensive direct government involvement in the lives of citizens, most notably in economic affairs. In particular, I hope to show the power of the stage-evolutionary interpretation of liberal history that dominates contemporary academic discourse, the one that depicts the latter view as morally superior to the former one. So I shall focus on the key adaptive mechanisms that allowed the high liberal view to propagate and become widely hailed as fit. The history of ideas I provide will be interspersed with references to events within actual liberal societies. I do this in order to draw attention to a line of ambiguity that runs through this evolutionary tale: an ambiguity about the moral value of economic liberty.

As an intellectual movement, the start of the liberal revolution is usually traced to 1689, the year John Locke published his *Second Treatise of Government*.[1] Locke was writing against two strong undercurrents of English social life: first, the lingering psychological eddies of feudalism, with its ideal of social order based on status and rank; second, a stream of worries springing from the recent attempts by a series of English kings to establish themselves as absolute monarchs. To appreciate Locke's contribution to liberal thought, we must first dip into those background currents.

Under the Norman system of feudalism, political power was concentrated in the person of the king. Members of other strata were connected to the king either by oaths or by station of birth.[2] A large class of serfs could own no property. They worked the land and paid tithes to a small class of barons who, in turn, were tied by pledges of fealty to the king. Power was highly personal in nature. People experienced life not as free and equal citizens but as embedded members of hereditary groups. One's place of residence, occupation, and even the particulars of family life were typically assigned on the basis of social rank. Far from affirming equality and freedom, the feudal order was grounded on differentiation and constraint. The central function of the political system was to preserve the peace and stability of this hierarchical order.

Of course, the particulars of feudal life did not conform neatly to this idealized form. In England, there were stirrings of political freedom almost from the start of the Norman period, typically dated to Battle of Hastings in 1066. In 1101, less than fifty years after Hastings, William's son, Henry I, assented to the Charter of Liberty, which proved to be the first in a long line of such charters. These charters, the most important of which was the Magna Carta of 1215, represented a strong and building set of restraints on royal power by means of law. Secure rights of property, held against the king, were among the most important checks provided by the Magna Carta.[3]

The Great Charters defined property rights relations between the king and barons.[4] By extension, they also provided an early platform for the development of a system of rules governing the daily interactions of English subjects. Many of these rules, known as the common law, concerned ordinary commercial transactions. Reforms introduced by Henry II allowed the common law gradually to displace idiosyncratic customs of feudal and county courts, bringing more uniformity to the experience of English subjects. By defining rights of holding and rules of exchange, the common law carved out relatively secure areas for private interpersonal action. By securing claims to property, these precepts enabled people to better assess the risks and rewards of ventures they might consider launching with one another. Common law made the social world increasingly navigable to individuals in their everyday lives.[5]

The main struts of the status-based legal framework of Norman feudalism remained in place during this period, though they were sinking ever lower now. Status-preserving features of that framework, such as the doctrines of primogeniture and entailment, continued to impose differential horizons on people's life-prospects.[6] Still, through the fifteenth and sixteenth centuries ordinary Englishmen grew ever more accustomed to directing their own affairs and living within social structures created by their own actions. Increasingly, they saw the system of common law as a cultural inheritance. The liberties protected by common law came to be seen as the birthright of every English subject. Slowly, over centuries, changes in the circumstances of life were outpacing the dogmas of the old order.[7]

The depth of these changes was dramatically sounded during the seventeenth century, when a series of English kings attempted to establish themselves as absolute monarchs: first James I and his son Charles I, and later James II. Under absolutism, a monarch asserts authority over all aspects of political life without any constitutional checks on his power. Claiming to hold sovereign authority directly from God, these kings asserted that none of their subjects—including those subjects who served in parliamentary bodies—had any right to limit royal power.[8] All political authority, all land and property was by divine right vested in the person of the king, and he could grant monopoly rights and levy taxes as he saw fit.

By this time, however, the idea of the "rights of Englishmen" and the tradition of parliamentary democracy were too strongly rooted to permit the movement toward absolutism. People resented the royal monopolies and preferred a more open system of competition based on merit.[9] Taxes levied by Charles without the consent of Parliament, in particular his infamous "ship money" scheme, met bitter opposition. The attempts by James and Charles to establish absolutist rule in England led to the English Civil Wars (1642–49), capped by the execution of Charles on January 30, 1649. A few decades later, an attempt by James II to establish an absolutist monarchy led to the Glorious Revolution of 1688, effectively ending absolutist ambitions in England.

English monarchs were now understood to hold their authority only by the consent of a representative assembly. The passage of the 1689 Bill of Rights codified these important changes. As a matter of established law, English monarchs henceforth lacked the authority to levy taxes, make appointments, or maintain a standing army except with the permission of Parliament. People had a right to petition the monarch; rights to freedom of speech and assembly were first exercised. England had become a constitutional monarchy.

Locke was writing in the period immediately downstream from these events. He was aware that many of his fellow citizens were close to accepting "the dangerous belief that 'all government in the world is merely the product of force and violence.'"[10] By beginning his argument with an account of man's condition in the state of nature, Locke sought to present the possibility of legitimate government in a more hopeful way.

State-of-nature arguments are heuristic devices. To glimpse the true nature of persons, we filter out the culturally specific assumptions about people's stations and roles that muddy our moral vision. Considered in their natural state, Locke argued, people are born free and equal as children of God. They are free in that they need permission from no other person to act. They are equal in that there is no natural political authority of one person over another.[11] People are also by nature needful. They must cooperatively interact with the raw, God-given bounty around them in order to fill their stomachs, shelter their bodies, and flourish as children of God. The political problem facing people was a common and public one: how might they devise a form of government appropriate to the condition of freedom, equality, and need into which people by nature find themselves?

Locke found the beginnings of an answer to this question in his doctrine of self-ownership. Owning themselves, people own their labor too. By mixing their labor with things in the world, people develop ownership relations with those things. For Locke, property is part of the natural fabric of the universe. Because some people work harder and more effectively than others, inequalities of holding are also part of that fabric. In the early stages of social development, these inequalities will be limited by the requirement that no one takes any more than they can use before it spoils.[12] The invention of money amplifies the degree of inequality while increasing the productivity of labor. Since people accept the custom of money, they accept those greater inequalities too.[13] On Locke's telling, the process of property acquisition that generates an increase of wealth also supports a growth in the population, even as productive land becomes scarce. To escape these "inconveniencies," Locke says people agree to establish a civil society and government.

Legitimate government must be founded on the consent of those to be governed. People who are free and equal, however, would not consent to be governed by a legal order that forced some, by birth, into lives of bondage or submission. Nor would they accept that they were born into a position of submission to a divinely appointed king. The status-based feudal system, like the claims of the absolute monarchs, had implied just that. Against these ideas, Locke insisted that governments are legitimate only when they preserve the natural free-dom of all citizens, no matter their parentage or place of birth. Governments did not exist merely to enforce order. So too, government was not a device for enhancing the glory or wealth of any hereditary class, whether aristocrat or king. Political power, Locke suggested, was a public rather than a private power. The only legitimate function of government was the equal protection of the natural rights to life, liberty, and property. "The great and chief end, therefore, of Men's uniting into commonwealths, and putting themselves under government, is the Preservation of their Property."[14]

Later writers hailed property as the institutional pivot of this new political system. David Hume, for example, set out "three fundamental laws of nature," all of which concerned the protection of economic liberty. Those laws protected the "stability of possession," the free transfer of property by consent, and a guarantee that promises and contracts be performed.[15] Hume saw the protection of economic freedom as fundamental to the welfare of society as a whole. He wrote: "Tis on the strict observance of those three laws, that the peace and security of human society entirely depend; nor is there any possibility of establishing a good correspondence among men, where these are neglected. Society is absolutely necessary for the well-being of men; and these are as necessary to the support of society." Property supports society *and* human well-being.

The contrast with the feudal and absolutist conceptions of social order is stark. Those schemes see social order as something that must be imposed from the top down onto society. By contrast, the development of a relatively autonomous economic sphere opens the possibility of more complex social orders. With a secure system of property rights, individuals and associations are free to interact peacefully in pursuit of diverse goals and ideals. Rather than being a product of conscious control, social order emerges spontaneously from the cooperation and competition of ordinary citizens.

Market Society

If Locke provided the moral foundations for liberalism, Adam Smith explained the feature of this new political order that was most radical and, to many, most mysterious. If economic life were freed from direct political control, Smith explained, the result would be prosperity at a level hitherto unimagined. Throughout the medieval era, prices of goods and services were set with an eye to doing justice—at least, justice in the eyes of those in positions of privilege.[16] Local leaders and church authorities had substantial power to set the prices at which commodities could be bought and sold. Laws against usury allowed the Church and a small number of politically connected bankers to earn monopoly rents.[17] Under absolutism the monarch claimed the authority, in principle at least, to be able to determine the distribution of goods and opportunities across the society.

The quasi-market system that had slowly emerged increasingly freed prices from direct political control and instead matched supply to demand. Smith described key mechanisms that made this motor run—the principle of the division of labor, for example. Most important for our purposes, Smith suggested that this system of free, unplanned pricing might work in a way that created general prosperity. By separating the economic and political spheres, the new order sought to break up the old systems of patronage and concentrated power. It brought reforms allowing individuals and associations to control their destinies in economic affairs and thus determine the shape of their own lives.

According to what Smith called "the system of natural liberty," governmental activity should be limited to three areas: national defense, the provision of a limited range of public goods, and the exact administration of justice.[18] It is the conception of justice that most strikingly differentiated this new system of liberty from the system of royal patronage it sought to displace. As with Locke, the essence of this emerging "liberal" program lay in the idea that the purpose of the state is to protect the freedom of citizens equally. The proper way for the state to accomplish this goal is to limit the range of its own activities.

This liberal program came to include religious toleration, freedom of speech and of association, freedoms of private life (such as freedoms regarding movement, occupation, and marriage) and, above all, economic freedoms such as the right to the private ownership of productive property and the right freely to enter into contracts. The liberal conception of justice required that the state restrain itself from impinging on the freedom of the citizens in all these areas.[19] Prices were allowed to reflect facts about supply and demand. Distributions of goods and services would not be determined by fiat but, increasingly, by the choices of parties interacting in the marketplace. According to Smith, "little else is requisite to carry a state to the highest degree of opulence from the lowest barbarism but peace, easy taxes, and a tolerable administration of justice: all the rest brought about by the natural course of events."[20]

Smith, like Hume, saw commercial society as a kind of natural or spontaneous order. He wrote: "Every man thus lives by exchanging, or becomes in some measure a merchant, and the society itself grows to be what is properly a commercial society."[21] The propensity to barter and truck is part of human nature. This propensity springs most immediately from people's concern for their own well-being and the well-being of those closest to them. But this propensity is enhanced by people's inchoate awareness that trading is also beneficial to one's trading partners and, by extension, to the society as a whole.

Of course, this system was not "natural" in a literal sense. The cultural conventions and legal processes that make it possible for people to engage in commercial activities were social in origin. Indeed, that whole system had evolved slowly as the product of countless instances of people exercising and developing their commercial capacities. In turn, those norms and rules made possible the exercise of these capacities. Still a new and seemingly more "natural" form of social order was the result. As Joyce Appleby puts it: "The new economic relations were undirected but patterned, uncoerced but orderly, free but predictable. They began to resemble—in men's minds at least—the operation of systems in the physical universe."[22]

For Smith, the system of natural liberty was natural in a moral sense as well. Under the old system, people's place in the economic order was determined by their birth rank and political connections. By contrast, the commercial society was predicated on the idea of careers open to talents. Positions should be open to all, with people coming to occupy their various places in the economic order on the basis of their hard work, ambition, and talent. Latent talents would be more fully harnessed than in a system of political preferment. Distributions of wealth and position would reflect the natural facts of difference between people, even while serving to enrich the society as a whole.

Smith did not imagine that this liberal program would solve all of humanity's problems, or that it would result in a social order with even rough equality of possession. Smith writes, "The rich and opulent merchant who does nothing but give a few directions, lives in a far greater state of luxury and ease . . . than his clerks, who do all the business." The clerks too live better than the artisans, Smith notes, who in turn live better than the poor laborer on whose efforts the whole system relies: "Thus he who as it were supports the whole frame of society and furnishes the means of the convenience and ease of all the rest is possessed of a very small share and is buried in obscurity. He bears on his shoulders the whole of mankind, and unable to sustain the load is buried by the weight of it and thrust down into the lowest parts of the earth."[23] Smith adamantly rejected the view, common in his day, that the working poor had fundamentally different capacities than those in more fortunate classes. The street porter and the philosopher were not by nature so different as the latter liked to think. Smith thought social institutions might be arranged to provide all citizens the chance to better their position.[24]

Smith was convinced that the surest way to improve the condition of the poor over time was by creating the conditions of a flourishing free market in which the productive resources of a nation—material, technological, and human—might be developed and exercised. Smith's attack on mercantilism—a system by which economic rules were enacted to enrich preferred constituencies rather than to enhance overall productivity—was based on these concerns.[25] Smith saw productivity as a social good. It was this idea that led Smith to advocate the carefully bounded social welfare programs that have so long been part of the classical liberal tradition. Tax-supported schooling, especially for children of the laboring poor, was the most important of these. Smith advocated a variety of other programs—taxes on house rents and road taxes on luxury vehicles—designed, in part, to redistribute wealth from the rich to the poor.[26]

For Smith, the key to prosperity was to limit the discretionary power of government in economic affairs. In economic matters, the proper role of government is to specify and enforce a set of economic liberties that make possible a system of free markets. Those market conditions should be designed and maintained so as to achieve maximal efficiency and productive output. Ultimately, though, Smith believed that the wealth of a nation is not measured by the quantity of goods produced, but rather in the quality of life and happiness of the citizenry as a whole. He writes, "That state is properly opulent in which opulence is easily come at, or in which a little labour, properly and judiciously employed, is capable of procuring any man a great abundance of all the necessaries and conveniences of life. . . . National opulence is the opulence of the whole people."[27] The system of economic liberty, Smith argues, is the surest way to achieve a social order that would be wealthy in this humane sense. Smith was by no means a strict consequentialist: he saw moral right and economic efficiency as working together.

This idea that justice could be achieved mainly through the restraint of government activity was but a reflection of Locke's basic contention that all people are by nature "equal and independent." Liberalism grew from reasoning about natural rights. In order to respect the natural rights of all citizens, the state must not grant advantages or impose legal restrictions on the basis of class, hereditary status, or personal connections. It took time for the full implications of this revolutionary doctrine to be worked out. On the economic front, formal equality generated pressure against vestigial feudal practices: the royal conferment of monopolies, for example, and the estate-securing practices such as primogeniture. Politically, formal equality served as a ground for criticizing peerages and other forms of hereditary political authority and would later ground calls for universal suffrage and, eventually, for political equality of citizens from all classes, genders, and races. These reforms, hard-won products of political struggles over many generations, were mere windings out of the Lockean idea that people are by nature free and equal.

With the writings of Locke and Smith and others in their school, a new ideal of social order appears in the political imagination of the West: an order of law-governed flux. Under this ideal, a central task of government is to provide a secure set of laws protecting property and exchange, laws equally applicable to all and known in advance to be more or less fixed. Within the stable frame of strong but limited government, however, all else is change. Social order—the character and orientation of human commitments, expectations, and desires—is constantly recreating itself from within. Patterns of distribution within the social world are not a reflection of anyone's intention or design, but emerge as the unplanned and ever-changing product of choices individuals make in pursuit of their goals and ends.[28]

This liberal ideal of commercial society did more than challenge the established political and social traditions of the day: it challenged the notion of tradition itself. No longer would the social world be structured according to legally enforced patterns passed down from one generation to the next, or indeed according to any predetermined patterns. Henceforth, order would be the ever-changing product of human freedom under conditions of economic freedom and formal legal equality.

The system of natural liberty proved to be a potent solvent against the gummed-up social hierarchies of seventeenth- and eighteenth-century Europe. The historian T. S. Ashton describes the effects of this liberal program in England during the late eighteenth and early nineteenth centuries: "Many old privileges and monopolies were swept away, and legislative impediments to enterprise removed. The State came to play a less active, the individual and the voluntary association a more active, part in affairs. Ideas of innovation and progress undermined traditional sanctions: men began to look forward, rather than backward, and their thoughts as to the nature and purpose of social life were transformed."[29] Commercial freedom was the outboard motor of this process, leaving the old ideals of hierarchy and control churning in its wake.

America

Actual societies never conform neatly to philosophical ideals: when adopted as a governing ideal, the chalk of political philosophy must always write across the rough slate of historical particularities.[30] Nonetheless, to add nuance to our philosophical sketch of classical liberalism, let's pause to consider an example. The political ideas of Locke, Smith, and Hume came together dramatically with the founding of the American republic. While contemporary America has moved far from the classical liberal ideal, the early decades of the early republic offer us an intriguing glimpse of classical liberal ideas in action.

Revolutionary America was not purely Lockean or Smithian. The legal institution of slavery is the most egregious "particularity" separating the historical reality of this society from any philosophical ideal, classical liberal or otherwise. Further, the founders' vision of America, while self-consciously Lockean, included significant republican elements.[31] Like the monarchical system in England, the republican vision of some founders relied on an ideal of aristocracy, though one based more on talent than birth. To founders such as George Washington and Alexander Hamilton, America was to be a hierarchy based on merit, where merit denoted the disinterested rule of the civically virtuous. The greatest threat to liberty, all parties agreed, came from the tendency of governments to grow and consolidate their power against the interests of ordinary citizens. But in America, Washington and Hamilton opined, the surest defense of the liberty of the many was the virtue of the few. Within a decade, however, a more radical transformation was underway. Confounding the expectations of the patricians of the revolutionary generation, Americans rapidly coalesced around a more democratic ideal of a classless society. Equality rather than virtue became the imperative of the American republic. Most surprising were the institutional and moral tools by which Americans pursued equality. For rather than relying on an aristocratic ideal of disinterested virtue, Americans sought equality through the more common and populist idea of commercial society. "Property must be secured or liberty cannot exist," John Adams said in 1790.[32] Property and an insistence on what Hume had called "stability of possession" became central to the American ideal of classlessness.

On the republican conception affirmed by many of the founders, liberty meant virtuous self-government.[33] By 1800, however, that ideal was rapidly displaced by a Jeffersonian ideal of freedom. This new ideal focused on the equal legal standing of individuals, especially in economic affairs. Freedom involved the equal right of people to make their own way in the world.

Commercial society is essential to this ideal of equal liberty. A speech by Samuel Latham Mitchell in the 1790s explains: "All citizens are acknowledged equal as to their rights, and the only inequality subsisting is that which arises from office, talents or wealth. But as the road lay open for everyone to aspire to these, it is by the exercise of one or more of his rights that a man acquires these means of affluence." In this Jeffersonian vision, opportunity was the latch that connected the boxcars of equality and freedom. As the safeguard of liberty and the foundation of civil society, the institution of property was to hold all those ideas together and make them run.[34]

The idea of property as a bulwark against tyranny had long been a staple of the classical liberal political tradition. This sentiment was captured by the early American description of property rights as "the guardian of every other right."[35] Assertions about the importance of property rights were noncontroversial, with debates focused on the question of how best to protect such rights and, to a lesser degree, on questions about their exact parameters. Many state constitutions included language that explicitly affirmed the importance of property. Before the decision to add the Bill of Rights, however, the framers' main strategy was to protect property through a network of counterbalancing institutional devices to limit overweening governmental power. Their constitutional tradition saw unrestrained democracy as the greatest threat to settled rights of property. Populist calls to seize and redistribute wealth were viewed as siren songs: unjust, impracticable, and ultimately destructive to the society as a whole. Separation of powers and the elaborate system of checks placed on legislative action were seen as ramparts against democratic threats to property.[36]

By 1787 James Madison had closely studied Adam Smith's revolutionary work *The Wealth of Nations*. Throughout the constitutional debates, Madison was among the strongest advocates of explicit protections for the economic liberties of private citizens.[37] Indeed, Madison gave property ownership a central place in the statement of political theory he proposed as an introduction to the constitution: "That government is instituted, and ought to be exercised for the benefit of the people; which consists in the enjoyment of life and liberty, with the right of acquiring and using property, and generally of pursuing and obtaining happiness and safety."[38]

The founding generation was vigilant against the consolidation of state power, an event they would view as the "Europeanization" of their fledgling American republic. They stoutly defended economic liberty for that reason. The Fifth Amendment, for example, contains two main elements: a set of procedural safeguards regarding criminal trials and a strong and explicit set of property right guarantees. It states, in part, that no person may be "deprived of life, liberty, or property, without due process of law, nor shall private property be taken for public use, without just compensation."[39] The due process clause has roots running back to the Magna Carta of 1215. In protecting citizens against the arbitrary seizure of their property, that clause erects a hurdle that any government agency would henceforth need to leap. The takings clause places limits on the power of eminent domain, an ancient prerogative by which the governing power may seize property for a pressing public purpose. In time there would be controversies over the meaning and strength of both these clauses. At the founding, though, its was widely understood that the Fifth Amendment set out a general right protecting economic freedom, much as the First Amendment sets out a general right protecting religious freedom.[40] In this way, as constitutional historian James W. Ely Jr. comments, "The Fifth Amendment explicitly incorporated into the Constitution the Lockean conception that protection of property is a chief aim of government."[41] The aim of government is to protect the natural rights of citizens. Property rights are among the most important of these.

Although emphasizing the importance of economic liberty, the American founders were not property rights absolutists. The framers would have been dumbstruck by the idea, common among some later libertarians, that property must never be impinged, regulated, or taxed by government in any way.[42] Instead, the framers thought government could intervene in the economic sphere for a variety of social purposes. For example, like earlier thinkers in the liberal tradition, most leaders in the American republic favored public support of education. The main debates concerned whether that public support should occur at the national or state level.[43] The Constitution, through its doctrine of enumerated powers, grants substantial power to the federal government in other economic areas as well: the power to levy taxes in order to pay war debts (and thus improve America's access to foreign credit markets), to make laws regarding copyrights and patents, to establish the rules and terms of bankruptcy, to impose protectionist tariffs on foreign goods, and, perhaps most important of all, to regulate interstate commerce for certain purposes. Clearly, the framers did not regard property rights as moral absolutes.

The founders were also concerned to protect civil and political rights along with economic rights. The federal constitution and the state constitutions were careful to protect civil rights: the right to a fair trial, and protections against unreasonable searches and seizures, for example. A variety of political rights—the right of property owners to vote, and freedom of the press—were also basic. Regarding some non-economic rights, the novel character of the American regime called for even stronger protections than those set out among "the hereditary rights of Englishmen." Madison argued that the American version of representative government—one completely devoid of hereditary positions of power—called for more robust political debates and thus for stronger press protections than that provided under English common law (a difference between the American and British protections of speech that extends to this day).[44] Americans of this generation saw civil, economic and political rights as working together in a mutually supporting system. The elements of the system would often need to be balanced and shaped to fit together, but, taken as a whole, it was seen as necessary to preserve the social conditions in which all citizens might enjoy the blessings of liberty.[45]

As we saw a moment ago, Federalists such as Washington imagined America as a hierarchical republic based on a civic conception of merit. What emerged in America, for those recognized as citizens at least, was something quite different. America became more democratic precisely by becoming more commercial. The American society of white male landholders, though "classless" among that group, was still differentiated in important ways: at any given time, some citizens and their families would be wealthier than others. But these differentiations relied on a new conception of merit. Instead of merit referring to the disinterested virtue of a few leaders—the natural aristocracy—merit was redefined in populist, commercial terms. Among patricians, the need to work had long denoted low status: leisure was more highly valued than work. The Americans reversed this, prizing invention and productivity and condemning idleness. Individuals would rise and fall based on their levels of ambition, hard work, and good fortune. However great one family's success, and however terrible another's failure, there was nothing fixed about that state of affairs. The road of social and economic aspiration was open. For those recognized as citizens at least, America of that period has aptly been described as "a brave new world of freedom and equality."[46]

The capacity of early American political institutions to produce this brave new world was conditioned by the cultural, demographic, and economic characteristics of that time and place. The economy was essentially agrarian. Land was plentiful. The population was growing. Wages were high. Workplaces were small and personal. Ambition was celebrated. Opportunity abounded. Additionally, the injustice of slavery boosted the economy. All combined, Americans of this period soon enjoyed the highest standard living in the world.

In 1776 the American Declaration of Independence startled the world with its assertion that all men are by nature equal.[47] By the early 1800s America startled the world again with the unique cultural interpretation it developed of that grand ideal. Rather than relying on the virtue of a natural aristocracy, America developed a conception of equality founded on the "humdrum interests of ordinary money-making."[48] Gordon Wood has aptly described this American conception of equality as based upon "the democratization of ambition."[49] Within this social system, people have no need to impress great aristocrats and no reason to fear them. Society is a system of self-interested cooperation. In such a society, people could celebrate the talents and ambitions of their fellow citizens as they went about the busy task of building a better and more prosperous social world. There is a deep populism in the public philosophy of this period. Free labor, hard work, rugged independence, attention to things near rather than things far—these are not the virtues of elites, but the stuff of ordinary people living ordinary lives.[50] Justice is distribution according to hard work, pluck, and skill.

The Americans themselves, and many European commentators, looked upon this new society with marvel.[51] Despite the imperfections and manifest contradictions of early America, many glimpsed there the shape of a new and unexpected ideal. This was an ideal of equality based on commercial exchanges between legal equals.[52] Jefferson's America, with its emphasis on commerce and formal equality, did not achieve the ideal of a classless society. But it powerfully illuminates that ideal.

Hayek

The first fully modern formulations of classical liberalism would come only long after the Jeffersonian vision of America had faded away. To find those formulations, we need to skip ahead a century and a half, into the middle and later years of the twentieth century. In that period, the classical liberal political tradition was revived in the writtings of Ludwig von Mises, Milton Friedman, and especially, F. A. Hayek.[53] While there are important differences between the views of all these thinkers, I shall focus on Hayek's theory as an exemplar of the classical liberal view.

For Hayek, freedom is a matter of individuals using their own knowledge to pursue their own purposes.[54] A free society stands in constant danger of erosion into something very different: a form of order in which some common goal or standard, however attractive in theory, is imposed on all the members of society. The imperative of pursuing that common goal requires an abridgement of the freedom of individuals to pursue their chosen ends and stunts their capacity even to conceive of goals of their own. Ultimately, the pursuit of that common goal may destroy the very sources of wealth on which the pursuit of social goals, of any type, depend.

Hayek thinks the distinction between these two very different visions of society is obscured by an ambiguity in our use of the term *law*. There is a form of law rooted in the English and Scottish traditions that Hayek calls *nomos*. For Hayek, *nomos* is "grown" law. The English common law developed incrementally as judges settled whatever disputes that arose as people pursued their diverse plans. Hayek describes law of this sort as a multipurpose tool. Rather than being consciously crafted to produce some outcome, the rules of nomos have a general character that makes them useful for the pursuit of diverse goals. These rules are justified only because they have proven useful over time to help people pursue their goals. It is these rules that "form the basis of the spontaneous order of society at large."[55]

Hayek contrasts nomos with what he calls *thesis*, or "made" law. Thesis refers in particular to laws made by legislative bodies with the intention of producing some particular desired outcome in the (erstwhile) spontaneous order. Where nomos denotes laws of general applicability, thesis refers to sets of commands that are to be executed by specific people for specific purposes. Rather than emerging in response to the needs of individuals to have their disputes adjudicated, thesis refers to commands intended to produce some antecedently known outcome. While nomos, or the law of liberty, "[is] derived from the conditions of a spontaneous order which made has not made," thesis, the rule of organization laid down by authority, "serve[s] the deliberate building of an organization serving specific purposes." Hayek says that *nomoi* are discovered, not consciously made. These rules evolve naturally, rather than being invented by the designing mind of some self-consciously organizing agent.

Because the creation of nomos does not require (or indeed make room for) a conscious organizing agent, Hayek refers to nomos as purpose-independent law. Purpose-independent laws are useful to people in pursuing diverse purposes known only to each of them. Hayek's enthusiasm for emergent processes may lead us to think he advocates a purely evolutionary view about the validity of these laws. On that view, spontaneous processes ipso facto consecrate their products, whatever those products might be. However, this could not be Hayek's view.[56] For Hayek, purpose-independent law has a meta-purpose: the value of that law lies in its ability to preserve and extend the order of a free society. "In a free society the general good consists principally in the facilitation of the pursuit of unknown individual purposes." So Hayek's concern for freedom generates a standard by which we might evaluate rules and social institutions more generally. Rules and institutions should create the conditions that increase the likelihood that each can achieve their own ends.[57]

Knowledge is always central to Hayek. Information is dispersed across society and is difficult (if not impossible) to "collect."[58] Hayek writes: "The peculiar character of the problem of a rational economic order is determined precisely by the fact that the knowledge of the circumstances of which we must make use never exists in concentrated or integrated form, but solely as the dispersed bits of incomplete and frequently contradictory knowledge which all the separate individuals possess." Because of this characteristic of knowledge, Hayek argues that the best way to create those conditions in which each has the best chance of using their own knowledge to achieve their own ends is by protecting private property. According to Hayek, "civilization begins when the individual in pursuit of his ends can make use of more knowledge than he himself acquired and when he can transcend the boundaries of his ignorance by profiting from knowledge that he himself does not possess."[59]

Like many in the classical liberal tradition, Hayek uses the term "property" loosely to denote not only material things but also the broader idea from Locke of the "life, liberty and estates" of every individual. These laws of property are paradigms of what Hayek calls nomos: they are general, multipurpose instruments that coordinate the activities and expectations of people pursing diverse goals in such a way that the overall system offers each the greatest chance of having their expectations satisfied. Laws increase predictability, telling us what facts we can count on and thereby increasing knowledge.[60]

For Hayek, the protection of freedom and the achievement of economic efficiency go together. The economic problem of society is "how to secure the best use of resources known to any of the members of society, for ends whose relative importance only these individuals know."[61] Rules of property are tools that empower individuals to make the best use of local knowledge available only to themselves, thus maximizing the chances that resources will be put to use in ways that allow people to realize their goals. Property rules draw the clear boundaries that people need if they are to use their own knowledge in pursuit of their own ends without colliding with others. Hayek describes property as "the only solution we have yet discovered to the problem of reconciling individual freedom with the absence of conflict." Thus, "law, liberty, and property are an inseparable trinity."[62]

Like others in this tradition, Hayek sees classical liberalism as resting on an ideal of formal equality.[63] Coercion is justifiable only to secure obedience to universal rules of just conduct. The ideal of formal equality was being threatened by an ideal of "substantive" equality, which sought to use coercion to enforce social legislation designed to benefit certain preferred groups. According to Hayek, however, "equal treatment . . . has nothing to do with the question of whether the application of such general rules in a particular situation may lead to *results* which are more favorable to some groups than to the others: justice is not concerned with the results of the various transactions but only with whether the transactions themselves are fair."[64]

Hayek's commitment to formal equality leads him to reject all forms of "social legislation" in pursuit of social or distributive justice. The concept of justice applies to transactions not outcomes. Justice cannot possibly serve as a process-independent standard of evaluation of distributions that result from transactions. The pursuit of social justice requires that authorities consciously redirect resources from certain groups toward other preferred groups. This ideal requires the steady transformation of a society from a free spontaneous order to more planned organizational form, a change that can be achieved only by the displacement of the nomoi of grown private law with the more particularistic, command-oriented public legislative law of thesis. The transition of a spontaneous order into an "organization" destroys the sources of social wealth and induces citizens to play ever more passive roles. "This pursuit of 'social justice' made it necessary for governments to treat the citizen and his property as an object of administration with the aim of securing particular results for particular groups."[65] The protection of property rights, on which Hayek sees the prosperity of the entire social system resting, is incompatible with the "will-o-the-wisp" of social justice.

We begin to find tensions with Hayek's work here, however, and these tensions run throughout the classical liberal tradition. Hayek's first commitment is to securing the conditions in which all have the best chance of pursing goals and aims of their own. While he rejects the ideal of "social justice," Hayek is frank in his assessment of specific areas in which *thesis*-like interventions might be permissible, perhaps in service to that overarching goal. While emphasizing the importance of property rights, Hayek follows others in this tradition by refusing to treat such rights as moral absolutes trumping every other concern. Like early liberals such as Smith, as well as his own contemporaries such as Milton Friedman, Hayek thinks taxes may be imposed for the public support of education. Similarly, he argues for a social safety net for the unemployed—"an assured minimum income, a floor below which nobody need descend"—as well as public support for orphans and a range of other social service programs for those who fall into extreme want.[66] Hayek sees the family as an essential mechanism for the transmission of values that make possible the development of one's abilities and talents—including one's ability to benefit from schooling. Regarding a secure family environment, Hayek says: "There can be no doubt that those who are either wholly deprived of this benefit, or grew up in unfavorable conditions are gravely handicapped; and few will question that it will be desirable that some public institution should so far as possible assist such unfortunate children when relatives and neighbors fail."[67] While insisting that justice requires that democracies be guided by general principles, Hayek even accepts the idea of (mildly) progressive taxation to fund these programs.[68]

Hayek saw the rise of the administrative state as a grave threat to freedom. Less often noted, though, is that Hayek, especially in his early writing, was also critical of market-absolutist positions. It is worth quoting him at length: "no government in modern times has ever confined itself to the 'individualist minimum' which has occasionally been described, nor has such confinement of governmental activity been advocated by the 'orthodox' classical economists. All governments have made provision for the indigent, unfortunate, and disabled and have concerned themselves with questions of health and the dissemination of knowledge." Hayek continues: "There is little reason why the government should not also play some role, or even take the initiative, in such areas as social insurance and education, or temporarily subsidize certain experimental developments. Our problem here is not so much the aims as the methods of government action."[69] In his later work, Hayek becomes increasingly skeptical that governments could become involved in some of these areas without quickly becoming overinvolved. But this flexibility is a significant feature of Hayek's political work.[70]

Given Hayek's commitment to market-based processes of spontaneous order, it may seem surprising that he advocates tax-funded support for programs such as these. After all, on a purely evolutionary view, the question of how much should be spent on schooling within a society would appear to be very like the question of how much should be spent on shoes, cornstarch, or any other commodity in that society. In all such cases, we might expect Hayek to say that such questions should be answered through a discovery process: just prices, like just distributions, are determined by the choices individuals make within institutions designed to allow them to make use of the information each possesses in service to their own ends.[71] But instead, like many other classical liberals, Hayek sometimes advocates direct interventions in the market in pursuit of particular social ends that are somehow identifiable independently of that discovery procedure.

What's more, and again like others in the classical liberal tradition, there is a certain looseness with which Hayek explains his reasons for taking these positions. Regarding the minimum income, for example, Hayek writes as though he cannot decide how best to justify such programs: "Such service functions of the government [to provide for the weak or needy] a wealthy community may decide to provide for a minority—either on moral grounds or as an insurance against contingencies that may affect anybody." After noting that any taxes needed to pay for such programs can be levied according to uniform principles, Hayek adds simply that such programs "need not lead to a restriction of freedom, or conflict with the rule of law."[72] We know that Hayek rejects the ideal of social justice, so we know that he could not see the selected social service programs as being requirements of that standard. Sometimes he appears to invoke a consequentialist standard: tax-raising coercion by the state to support social service programs, he tells us, "can never be justified in terms of the interests of the immediate beneficiary . . . but only in terms of the general benefits which may be enjoyed by all citizens."[73] Like many others before him, Hayek leaves us to guess at his precise reasons for advocating these familiar features of the classical liberal political program. We return to this point in the following section.

Classical Liberalism

Allow me to summarize the essential features of classical liberalism. When I speak of the classical liberal tradition, I mean a tradition of liberal thought committed to (1) a thick conception of economic liberty grounded mainly in consequentialist considerations, (2) a formal conception of equality that sees the outcome of free market exchanges as largely definitive of justice, and (3) a limited but important state role in tax-funded education and social service programs. Let me say a few words about each of these ideas, beginning with the idea of thick economic liberty.

While classical liberals emphasize the importance of "property," I shall henceforth use the category "economic liberty" instead. As religious liberties protect the independence of citizens with respect to religious questions, so economic liberties preserve their independence regarding a range of economic issues in their lives.

James Nickel helpfully divides these myriad economic issues into four (partially overlapping) categories of liberty protection: liberties of labor, transacting, holding, and using.[74] Regarding the economic liberty of *labor*, Nickel says: "This is the liberty to employ one's body and time in productive activity that one has chosen or accepted, and under arrangements that one has chosen or accepted." The liberty of *transacting* allows individuals to engage in free economic activity: "This is the freedom to manage one's economic affairs at the individual and household levels and on larger scales as well." Transacting involves the liberty to trade in the marketplace, to create things for sale, and to save and invest. It also covers the freedom of individuals and groups to start, run, and close down businesses such as factories, shops, farms, and commercial enterprises of many sorts. The economic liberty of *holding* concerns freedom in the realm of several properties. "This category covers legitimate ways of acquiring and holding productive property, using and developing property for commercial and productive purposes, and property transactions such as investing, buying, selling, trading and giving." Finally, there is a range of liberties concerning *using*. "This is the liberty to make use of legitimately acquired resources for consumption and production." The liberty of using protects the freedom of citizens to buy, use, and consume natural resources, consumer goods, and services. On the commercial level, this liberty protects production-related consumption (such as deciding which parts to use, or which power sources to purchase). On the domestic level, it protects a range of personal, economic decision making, including questions about what to eat and drink, what to wear, what type of housing to have, and a wide range of services—including what forms of entertainment, of cultural experience, and perhaps what educational experiences and which health care services—one might choose to purchase. To simplify, I will sometimes refer to the economic liberties as concerning liberties of *working* and of *owning*.

Most legal systems include some degree of protection for each of these categories of economic liberty. However, systems differ dramatically in the way they specify the activities that are to be protected in each category. Significantly, systems also differ in the degree of importance they assign to such protections when they conflict with other social goals and values.[75]

Classical liberals, as we have seen, affirm what we might call a thick conception of economic liberty. They tend to interpret each category of private economic liberty as having a wide scope. Regarding the liberties of holding (or "owning"), for example, classical liberals affirm not only right to ownership of personal property (as guaranteed even by most socialist systems) but rights to the private ownership of productive property as well. People should be free to start small businesses, join in large capital ventures with others, and generally to establish economic entities of a great variety of kinds (including, if they wish, worker-directed cooperatives). Closely connected, classical liberals typically interpret the economic liberty of labor to include a wide freedom of individuals to negotiate personally the terms of their employment (including both wage rates and number of hours to be worked). Classical liberals interpret the economic liberty of transacting to include the right of individuals to decide for themselves how much to save for retirement, how much to invest in health care, and to make decisions about many other issues of long-term financial planning.

Further, classical liberals see these wide-ranging economic liberties as being especially weighty compared to other social values. They see economic liberties as having a political status comparable to that of the other traditional liberal rights and liberties, such as liberties of speech and association. But classical liberals do not treat economic liberties as moral absolutes or as in any way more basic than the other fundamental rights and liberties. While important, such liberties do not trump every other social concern.

First, classical liberals accept that even the most weighty economic liberties can sometimes be curtailed or regulated in order to preserve other foundational liberties, and sometimes for other important social purposes as well. For example, classical liberals would not think the state should enforce contracts that alienate citizens from their other basic rights and liberties (for example, an economic contract that required some form of religious devotion). Second, classical liberals traditionally grant that governments have some (carefully limited) powers of eminent domain. They also recognize governments as having the power to act so as to maintain free and competitive markets; for example, by regulating or breaking up monopolies of scarce resources, or by forbidding various forms of collusion and price fixing.

Socialists sometimes define the economic liberties differently. For them, economic liberty involves the right to participate in collective decision making about the uses of socially owned property.[76] There are complicated issues here, but speaking generally, classical liberals are skeptical of this socialist conception. They see the socialist approach as involving a form of *political* liberty rather than one of economic liberty. Imagine a conception of religious liberty under which each citizen was given a say about what religious practices would henceforth be required by all members of the community. Rather than protecting individual freedom in the area of religion, such a system would violate religious liberty by making religious decisions subject to collective decisions. Similarly, classical liberals see the socialist conception as giving primacy to collective decision making in the economic affairs, rather than protecting independent economic decision making and activity.[77] When I speak of thick economic liberty, I shall mean economic liberty in the classical liberal sense.

Classical liberals vary in the way they justify their platform of thick economic liberty. Locke's most famous argument for property rights rests on the idea of self-ownership, and Adam Smith sometimes speaks of these liberties as natural rights. But Locke and Smith also emphasize the social utility of property rights. As Locke puts it, "labor puts the difference of value on every thing" and allows us to make the best use of God's creation. For Hayek, economic liberties empower individuals to make use of knowledge available only to themselves, thus greatly increasing economic productivity. Economic liberties create a culture that values hard work and personal responsibility. A secure system of economic liberty helps create the conditions in which social resources will be put to their most efficient uses, thus benefiting society as a whole.

The ideal of formal equality follows directly from this idea. Under a system of preferment and patronage, such as mercantilism, economic relations are constrained by the biases and interests of the politically powerful. If, instead, careers are left open to talent, workers are free to change professions as they like and to market their services to others upon whatever terms they mutually agree. Commercial enterprises have wide freedom to seek out willing trade partners without the constraint or permission of third parties. On the individual level, a person's lineage or religion would no longer be the fundamental determinant of their economic prospects. Economic liberties give people an equal right to compete for positions on the basis of their talents and ambitions, empowering each of them to become more fully the authors of their own lives. As an ideal, equality requires that no individual or group face legal restrictions on their ambitions or life plans that are based on the prejudices (or self-interest) of others. Everyone should have an equal right to participate and compete.

Because economic liberties promote economic development and protect the freedom of individuals in these ways, classical liberals see the distributions that emerge from market exchanges as morally just. People may acquire holdings through nonmarket mechanisms, as with inheritances and gifts. They may also legitimately be taxed in order to pay for the provision of public goods and other necessary costs of government, including a general police power. But for classical liberals, market mechanisms, operating against a background of a secure set of economic liberties, provide the ultimate standard for justice in a free society.[78]

At the same time, classical liberals see a limited but important role for the state in the provision of social services to the most needy. Classical liberals typically advocate public support for education and the provision of a social safety net, though the rationales for these programs are often not made completely clear.

In any case, classical liberals see their platform of thick economic liberty as providing a bulwark preventing these limited programs from expanding and colonizing the social network more widely. Economic liberty enhances freedom, promotes prosperity, and provides a rampart against the constant threat of centralizing governmental power. For classical liberals, economic liberty and political equality are fundamentally fused.

CHAPTER 2

High Liberalism

Property or Equality

While Americans were pursuing the classical liberal ideal, a different ideal of equality was emerging on the European continent. Like the Americans, revolutionists in France dreamed of establishing a classless society. However, the Europeans did not dream of a commercial republic where legally equal citizens would be differentiated only by hard work and natural talent. Leading members of the French Revolution saw the rejection of monarchism as opening a more radical possibility: a substantive conception of equality based on an equal sharing of material goods.

In a speech to the French National Convention in 1793, a leading revolutionary figure named Armand de la Meuse provided a neat formulation of this idea: "there cannot be . . . a more dangerous, absurd, and immoral contradiction than political equality without social and economic equality."[1] La Muese's colleague, Gracchus Babeuf, drew out the radical implications of this idea. By nature, Babeuf declared, every person has "an equal right to the enjoyment of all wealth." Speaking of people's equal right to social wealth, Babeuf declared: "the aim of society is to defend this equality, often attacked by the strong and the wicked in the state of nature, and to increase, by the co-operation of all, this enjoyment."[2] Babeuf's formulation is extreme, but still we find in this rhetoric a vision of liberal equality very different from the classical liberal one. On this ideal, property rights are not guardians of equality but obstacles to its achievement.

This worry about property rights extends back at least to Rousseau. In his *Discourse on the Origins of Inequality*, Rousseau suggests that Locke and the other state-of-nature theorists do not provide a true picture of man's natural condition. On Rousseau's mythopoeic telling, the real starting place of human history was not merely pre-political, as Locke had claimed, but also presocial, prelinguistic, and even prepsychological. Human history antedates people's gaining an awareness of self. In this, their true natural state, people lived spontaneously and thus were perfectly free and happy.

For Rousseau, culture is corrupting. It fastens chains upon natural freedom. Political society must be seen in this light. Hobbes, a protoliberal, had argued that the state was necessary to save people from the all-against-all war that Hobbes says rages in the state of nature. Locke, more gently, sees the state as required to remedy certain "inconveniencies" that people faced in that natural prepolitical condition. But Hobbes and Locke both see the arrival of the state as an unambiguous moral improvement. Rousseau, by contrast, argues that laws often *cause* the very disorders they are then called upon to restrain.[3]

Rousseau sees this unhappy cycle as swirling most dangerously around laws securing economic liberty. Laws protecting property and freedom of contract do not really protect people from domination. Commercial society instead forces people into relations of bondage and inequality. According to Rousseau, "inequality, being almost nonexistent in the state of Nature, owes its force and growth to the development of our faculties and the progress of the human Mind, and finally becomes stable and legitimate by the establishment of property and Laws."[4] Commercial society, far from offering a new world of freedom and equality, is yet another way of fixing in place a social world that is essentially vertical, adversarial, and unfree.[5]

The hammer of Rousseau's critique would be swung more boldly by Karl Marx. Like Rousseau, Marx suggests that the liberal guarantee of merely legal equality provides no guarantee that the liberal social world will not be marked by fixed and enduring class divisions, divisions based on people's standing in the economic order.[6] People's material holdings—the money and goods they have—affect their life prospects at least as much as they affect their political status. It is a farce, Marx claims, to call people in such a society "equally free" merely because of the legal equality of status granted to them by courts. The liberal ideal is internally inconsistent: the formal equality of liberalism is a mask behind which hides a society as exploitative as any in the history of mankind. Liberalism, on any of its classical formulations at least, has no resources to recognize enduring material inequalities as a problem. Indeed, Marx describes liberalism as the latest in the long historical line of status-based social orders.[7]

Under the force of such critiques, and drawn by ideals of material egalitarianism, many abandoned liberalism altogether for socialism or communism. Others retained their commitment to central liberal ideas (such as the importance of individual freedom) but sought to take on board some of the concerns of liberalism's critics. A shift began to occur in the consciousness of many liberals.

John Stuart Mill is a central figure in this process. Earlier liberals had seen economic liberty as a crucial component of equal freedom. Economic liberties have intrinsic value: they carve out a sphere of protection that allows people to become responsible authors of their own lives. Economic liberties are instrumentally valuable too: the protection of such liberties helps generate a social world of variety and abundance. When Mill surveys the traditional list of liberal liberties, however, he singles out the economic liberties for relegation to a distinctly secondary place.

Mill's official argument for treating the economic liberties in this exceptional way is based on his distinction between two spheres of human activity. In the sphere of liberty are activities that primarily concern only the individual, or if they involve other people they do so only with their free consent and participation. This is the sphere of individual liberty.[8] The other sphere, that of coercion, concerns activities that directly affect other people. Society does have a direct interest is these activities and so may properly exercise coercion there to promote the common good. While Mill sees freedoms of speech and assembly, conscious and religion, and other activities central to become the author of one's own life as self-regarding activities, he insists that economic activities are other-regarding: "trade is a social act."

As commentators such as Daniel Jacobson have noted, however, speech and assembly would also appear to be acts that affect others.[9] So we need to look deeper to understand why Mill singles out economic liberty in this way. Mill's moral and political philosophy rests ultimately on a perfectionist ideal of the person. Mill sees *individuality* as capturing something close to the moral essence of personhood. While a self-proclaimed utilitarian, Mill emphasizes that he means "utility in the largest sense, grounded on the permanent interests of man as a progressive being."[10] Chief among those interests is that of developing a life plan to suit one's character. By creating such a plan, people express their distinctive sense of what is valuable and worth doing in life. By developing and pursing such a plan, people develop their higher capacities of reasoning, develop intimate connections with others, and enhance their moral sensitivities. Mill saw intellectual pursuits as central to a well-lived life, but he famously claimed to be open to experimentation. So Mill readily acknowledged that there might be a wide range of activities and life plans in which people find meaning and develop themselves as individuals.

However, Mill did not see how activities in the economic sphere could contribute to individuality in his sense. Freedoms of thought and association are important to forming and carrying out a life worthy of man as a progressive being. But Mill does not see economic liberties—the freedom to hold productive property, or to enter into economic contracts—as playing any central role in this process. Starting a business, holding a job, seeking a promotion, being a breadwinner for one's family, saving for the future—these are roles that economic necessity may require people to play from time to time. But none of these activities is constitutive of liberty.[11] Economic life provides barren soil for the development of individuality. Progressive beings do not need economic liberty in order to "pursue their own good their own way." For Mill, economic liberties are instrumentally valuable: "property is only a means to an end, not itself the end."[12]

Mill's doubts about the intrinsic moral value of economic activity did not wholly cut him off from the laissez-faire political positions of his father, James Mill, and David Ricardo. Mill is best thought of as a mixed figure, one grounded in classical liberal principles who began a long slow turn of liberalism in a more collectivist economic direction. Writing in the early stages of industrial capitalism, Mill saw an unregulated economy as creating the social evil of two great classes: a small class of the rich who by their legally sanctioned control of capital would live off the labor of the many. In that state of affairs, the workplace is a forum of moral degradation. In a free market economy, Mill says, "the rich regard the poor as, by a kind of natural law, their servants and dependents."[13] The workers, for their part, develop only feelings of resentment as they work. The wage relationship is intrinsically undesirable. Rather than promoting the kind of self-respect that makes self-authorship possible, wage labor reduces people to a condition of conformity and deference.

Mill's most famous contribution to economics is his distinction between questions about the production of goods and questions about their distribution. While the former depend on relatively fixed "natural" rules, Mill saw the latter as more thoroughly a social creation. Since Mill saw the institutions of distribution as socially created, he argued that society could and should adjust those distributive institutions to desired ends. Mill advocated a program of steeply progressive inheritance taxes and an ambitious program of wealth transfer not only to the poor but to the middle classes as well. Leisure rather than productive work would be the emphasis of this society, with a small class of cultivated elites serving as models to others of how to live gracefully and well. Thus Mill describes his ideal society as having "a well-paid and affluent body of labourers; no enormous fortunes, except what were earned and accumulated during a single lifetime; but a much larger body of persons than at present, not only exempt from the coarser toils, but with sufficient leisure, both physical and mental, from mechanical details, to cultivate freely the graces of life, and afford examples of them to the classes less favourably circumstanced for their growth."[14]

Mill became increasingly interested in socialism. He believed the workplace could be reformed so as to do away with the private ownership of productive property and thus liberate workers from the degradation of wage labor. On Mill's preferred model, the workers would come to own and control their firms themselves. Decisions would be made democratically, and profits would be the joint property of all the contributing workers.[15] Real capital production would cease and the economy would enter a "stationary state." Whether or not such regimes might be practical in his day, Mill argued that liberals should recognize this sort of market socialist regime as a moral ideal.

Mill's defense of a "thin" conception of economic liberty begins a great fissure in the history of liberal thought. The transformation of liberalism from a doctrine of strictly limited government to one of more expansive government begins here. Mill is explicit about how his critique of economic liberty changes the wider ideological orientation of liberals: the institutional form for realizing liberal values might not be capitalism or commercial society at all. Property, in Mill's view, has no essential link to liberal freedom. Liberal principles do not necessarily lead to a society grounded in strong private rights of property and to a government of limited economic power.

The Decline of Economic Liberty

The institutions of the early American republic emphasized private property, commercial exchange, and guarantees of formal legal equality. Justice, in that social world, was understood primarily as a property of individuals. Justice is distribution to each according to his talent or desert. A society that provided formal protection to the natural rights of citizens could yield something new in the history of the world: a genuinely free and classless society. Or so many Americans of that era believed.

However, the social and economic conditions on which that belief relied were rapidly changing. Many philosophers saw these changes as requiring a shift in the liberal understanding of justice as well. The first wave of Western industrialization ran roughly from 1750 to 1880. The birth of industrialization brought wealth but also new challenges for ordinary working people. Adam Smith had argued that "the division of labor is limited by the extent of the market."[16] As markets became more global, Smith's prediction was borne out. Instead of the personalized work of farming, people increasingly took up specialized positions in production lines of great manufacturing plants. First in England and later in America, rural, agrarian economies became urban, industrial ones.[17] The economy was further revolutionized by the invention of steam- and machine-based forms of manufacture. Where before families had moved out onto the frontier to stake a claim, the population was now concentrating in cities and other centers of manufacture. The rise of the corporation and the creation in 1890 of a market in corporate stock accelerated these changes. Instead of owning, or working to own, the tools they used each day—horses, plows, fields—people increasingly worked in great factories owned by distant others. Even in America it became less common for people to control the direction and intensity of their productive activities. Increasingly, the conditions of work were decided for people by others. The ideal of formal equality, given full play in these changed economic conditions, generates a social world with a unique set of challenges.[18]

Granted, the equal freedoms of Smith's commercial order were acid to the feudal practices of status-based economic preferment. But what if, in these new conditions, classical liberal institutions generated a hereditary class structure of a different kind? With industrialization, rights to private productive property made possible the amassing of great new fortunes. That same system of property rights generated economic imperatives that concentrated capital in great industries, built and controlled by a small number of private hands. Locke had argued that the essential role of the state is to protect property rights; but what if those property rights predictably, even if not intentionally, generate a society divided by hereditary class distinctions? In this case, the so-called system of natural liberty would turn out to be yet another device by which inequalities of status are coercively imposed upon the people. George Bernard Shaw satirized the classical understanding of liberty as "the right to have tea at the Ritz—for anyone who could afford it."[19]

The idea of social justice developed against this background. Instead of the classical ideal of free markets and formal legal equality, by the start of the twentieth century a group of new liberals advocated a government with wide economic powers to pursue a more substantive ideal of equality. One reason the idea of "substantive" equality has proven attractive is that it seems to evolve naturally from moral ideas that animated the classical liberal thinkers. Indeed, the same reasoning that led classical liberals to reject the feudal idea of hierarchical inequality can be used to explain why new liberals affirm the ideal of substantive equality.

For classical liberals such as Smith and Hume, the rules of a free society are like the rules of a competitive board game. If the game is to treat all the players as equally free and responsible participants, it cannot include rules that impose disabilities on certain participants and bestow advantages on others. Imagine a version of the board game Monopoly that includes additional, token-specific rules: players who find themselves holding the Thimble, Shoe, and Car tokens, let's imagine, are prohibited from purchasing or holding any property.[20] Further, all players with those tokens must give 10 percent of their money to the player holding the Cannon token each time they pass around the board. The player holding the Cannon token has taken an oath of fealty to the Terrier. The Cannon is thus allowed to amass property and money, but holds its wealth only at the pleasure of the Terrier. The Terrier can confiscate property from and levy taxes upon the Cannon, or call upon him for service, at any time. Call this "Feudal Monopoly."

Feudal Monopoly violates the classical liberal principle of formal equality because it varies the rules by status. In a society based on equal freedom, as in a traditional game of Monopoly, the same rules must apply equally to all players. This requirement springs directly from the ideal of voluntarism in human affairs. After all, once people learned the rules of Feudal Monopoly, it would be difficult to find any who would be willing to sit down and play it. Similarly, it would be implausible to expect people to give their consent to enter into a society organized along feudal lines.

Classical Liberal Monopoly therefore sweeps away all token-specific rules. It requires that the same rules apply equally to all players. With formal equality in place, the distributions that emerge will largely reflect the talent and ambition the players exhibit as they play the game. Under this "system of natural liberty," each will receive his due. Under formal equality, classical liberals argued, people can enjoy the benefits of social cooperation. By enforcing this system, the state will have discharged its responsibility to treat all citizens as "free and equal children of God."

For the new liberals, however, formal equality of opportunity does not go far enough. In the first place, people come into the world with very different natural abilities—physical traits, intellectual aptitudes, and emotional dispositions. Differences of family life and station can amplify the effects of these genetic advantages and disabilities. No one can be said to have earned these initial advantages: for the most part, people are simply born with them. The system of formal equality of opportunity seeks to remove status-based arbitrariness from the social world. But that system leaves in place the arbitrary advantages of birth and family circumstance. Under Classical Liberal Monopoly, the same rules apply equally to all players but, we might say, players start the game with very different amounts of money. Classical liberals accept this as "natural," but the new liberals see it as unfair. The stain of that unfairness would not be lifted merely by the requirement that once that game had begun, those differently endowed players must all abide by the same set of formal rules. The reasons classical liberals give for Feudal Monopoly's unfairness apply with equal force against Classical Liberal Monopoly too. Both systems allow distributions to arise on the basis of features that seem arbitrary.[21]

Modern liberals advocate a substantive conception of equality to address this concern. While classical liberals thought of justice as applying mainly to the actions of individuals, these self-styled "new liberals" suggested that social outcomes, and even the shape of distributions over a society as a whole, might properly be described as just or unjust.[22] Justice requires that we consider the actual availability of goods and opportunities to citizens. Social justice requires more than formal equality of opportunity: it requires that people have access to the goods they need to make their freedoms valuable. According to modern liberals, social or distributive justice is a natural development from the Lockean idea of respecting citizens as free and equal children of God.

This change in the philosophical standard of liberalism was accelerated by changes in people's wider understanding of society and the laws of economics. The case for classical liberalism had long been cast in broadly consequentialist terms: free markets, against a background of secure economic liberties, would tend to bring about economically efficient distribution of goods and services.[23] The Great Crash of 1929 shook many people's confidence in that classical liberal claim. At the same time, the work of John Maynard Keynes seemed to provide a scientific basis to the growing confidence in the efficiency of more direct government control of the economy. Famously, Keynes argued that the new tools of social science made full employment a realistic policy objective. Less noticed, Keynes argued that large government programs for the redistribution of wealth, far from leading to inefficiencies, would stimulate consumption and thus enhance the growth of capital: institutions that pursue social justice are good for the economy.[24] In a line that captured the spirit of the time, newly elected American president Franklin D. Roosevelt declared in 1932: "the day of enlightened administration has arrived."[25]

The rise of social justice was mirrored by the decline of economic liberty. This was true not only philosophically but in the practice of constitutional law as well. During the Antebellum Era, roughly 1791–1861, the Supreme Court followed the classical liberal creed of affirming property rights as among the most important basic rights. Under Chief Justice John Marshall, the Court routinely applied the contract clause to curb the regulatory ambitions of politicians at the state and local level.[26] At the same time, the commerce clause was given a strict construction: it permitted federal regulation of commerce only in clear cases of trade between parties in different states. In a string of property rights cases, the Fifth Amendment guarantee of "due process" was developed into a doctrine requiring substantive protections for the economic liberty of citizens. The adoption of the

Fourteenth Amendment in 1868 strengthened the connection of the constitution to capitalism. As James Ely has noted: "Armed with the due process clause of the Fourteenth Amendment, the Supreme Court emerged as a champion of economic liberty and carefully scrutinized state efforts to regulate business activity."[27] There was a lively awareness among jurists of the time that economic freedoms protected individuals against the danger of special interest (or class-based) legislation. As in the founding era, jurists of the Antebellum period saw property rights as important not only for their role in promoting economic growth but also as essential guardians of individual liberty. A thick conception of economic liberty was still seen as a requirement of liberty and precondition of prosperity.

By the start of the twentieth century, this doctrine of "laissez-faire constitutionalism" was under increasing attack. New social conditions, Progressives argued, required a new political orientation. Old notions of property rights should not be allowed to tie the hands of government experts impartially pursuing important social goals. As Louis Brandeis wrote: "There must be power in the United States and the Nation to remould, through experimentation, our economic practices and institutions to meet changing social and economic needs."[28] The written Constitution seemed to deny government officials this called-for power. Bound to that Constitution, the Supreme Court found itself in growing tension with Progressive programs and ideals. The breaking point came when the Supreme Court, led by stalwarts such as Justice George Sutherland, struck down central elements of Roosevelt's New Deal.[29] However, by the late 1930s, President Roosevelt was able to remake the Court and a new era of constitutionalism was begun.

The most striking feature of the "New Court" was its attitude toward economic liberty. Ownership rights, basic to the founders' idea of liberty, were now sharply distinguished from personal liberties.[30] To impinge on the economic liberty of citizens, the government had only to demonstrate a "rational basis" for a proposed regulation. Economic liberties that had been fundamental to laissez-faire constitutionalism were henceforth relegated to a secondary place.[31] The old doctrine of economic due process was swept away. The interstate commerce clause was interpreted ever more broadly: any economic activity, even a single farmer's decision on how much corn to plant, potentially has some fractional effect on "commerce" and so might henceforth be regulated.[32] The new doctrine of "liberal constitutionalism" cleared a wide path for government action in pursuit of social goals.

The touchstone for this modern liberal approach to governance remains a speech President Roosevelt gave on January 11, 1944, in which he proposed "a second bill of rights."[33] Roosevelt declared that the American Revolution was radically incomplete. The rights enunciated by the framers, with their emphasis on economic liberty and consequent limitations on government power, have "proved inadequate." Experience has taught us that "individual freedom cannot exist without economic security." According to Roosevelt, every American has a right to a decent job; adequate food, shelter and clothing; education, recreation, and quality medical care.[34] Liberal equality requires more than mere equal treatment before the law. It requires that government ensure that citizens receive the support they need to make their freedoms and opportunities real. Liberalism is not a doctrine of limited government power and wide individual economic freedom. It is a doctrine that calls for extensive government involvement in economic affairs, an involvement that touches a wide range of economic activities and that holds citizens of every class—rich, middle, and poor—in a steady embrace.

Rawls

The publication of Rawls's *A Theory of Justice* in 1971 marked a turning point in the development of the modern, or as it became known after Rawls, the "high" liberal tradition. Many thinkers before Rawls had argued that liberalism demanded something more than the classical liberal ideal of formal equality, but the moral justification of that new idea of social justice, as well as its precise content, remained unclear.

Liberal theory, as Rawls saw it, was facing a justificatory dilemma. What is the appropriate moral basis for the rights and other normative principles of liberalism? Utilitarianism is one option. But utilitarianism often generates requirements that liberals find counterintuitive. It might demand, for example, that essential interests of individuals be sacrificed on the altar of the common good. More generally, because of the aggregating tendencies of consequentialist theories, Rawls worries that such theories fail to honor each person as an independent moral agent worthy of respect. Alternatively, one might seek to develop political principles by a direct appeal to moral intuitions. However, people often find that their own moral intuitions conflict with one another. Lacking any systematic structure, intuitionism provides no way of determining the priority relations among our various moral commitments. In light of these difficulties, the appropriate moral foundation for the new liberal theory of "social justice" remained unclear. As long as that moral foundation was unclear, the requirements of social justice also could be given in only rough, imprecise terms.

In response to these problems, Rawls works out a justificatory theory he calls constructivism. Instead of relying directly on the "jumble" of moral intuitions, or on consequentialist concerns such as maximizing happiness or aggregate wealth, constructivism seeks to identify principles of justice by reasoning directly about the moral requirements of social life. A democratic society, in Rawls's view, is a fair system of cooperation between persons conceived as citizens. Members of that society, in their moral essence as citizens, are free and equal self-governing agents. A theory of justice should set out the requirements that social institutions must satisfy to respect citizens as moral agents engaged in a cooperative venture. Rawls thinks of these as requirements of fairness, and so calls the theory of justice he develops in response to these concerns "justice as fairness." Justice as fairness consists of two main principles: the first sets out basic rights and liberties; the second adds a series of distributional requirements.

Originally, Rawls hoped to identify a unique set of principles of justice, principles that could be derived determinatively from a device he called the original position. This device involved describing parties choosing principles of justice from behind a veil of ignorance. Later, however, Rawls tempered his ambitions and came to see that his hope that people could agree on one set of principles must be abandoned. Rawls realized that the various elements of the original position—the motivations and form of reasoning ascribed to the parties, the specific features of the veil, the range of candidates' conceptions of justice set before them—could reasonably be described in different ways. At best, therefore, the original position generates not one unique set of principles, but rather a range of alternative conceptions of justice.[35]

Still, Rawls's theory succeeds in giving general definitional content to an ideal of distributive justice that had been building within modern liberal circles for a century. Beneath the controversies and technical complications, the distributional requirements of Rawlsian justice rely on a simple idea. This idea, the bottle of champagne that *A Theory of Justice* cracked against the side of the high liberal ship, is this: A system of social cooperation is just only if it improves the lot of all who cooperate. More precisely, a set of institutional arrangements is just only if, along with protecting a set of basic rights and liberties, it is designed to help people produce goods and create opportunities in a way that benefits the members of every social class. Further, if we are making a choice between two sets of arrangements that benefit the least fortunate, justice requires that we prefer the arrangements that bring them the greatest benefits. According to this "difference principle," justice requires that we seek to maximize the benefits to the least well-off.[36]

As we saw earlier with our Monopoly example, modern liberals criticize the classical liberal system of formal equality for allowing seemingly arbitrary factors—lucky circumstances of birth, for example—to influence distributive outcomes. If classical liberals think market outcomes define justice, but those outcomes are influenced by morally arbitrary factors, then the moral status of the classical liberal conception of justice becomes suspect. The modern liberal idea of social justice seeks to address this issue.

How can this be done? It might seem that every distribution be completely *untouched* by arbitrary factors if it is to qualify as fully just. From "the moral point of view," even the most basic features of our experience, our specific genetic endowments and unique family experiences, our personalities, our determination and will, may seem "arbitrary." To fully respect our common personhood, perhaps, every difference is intolerable to high liberals. The demands of social justice are insatiable. Perhaps the role of the state is to ensure that all citizens enjoy exactly the same goods and opportunities. Perhaps fair equality requires absolute material equality—as Gracchus Babeuf declared. Perhaps it requires even more.[37]

To answer these concerns, every version of high liberalism must set principled limits to the demands of justice. Contemporary philosophers working in the high liberal tradition answer this question in diverse ways, but here again Rawls's approach is instructive. First, humans are biologically separate beings. Any theory of justice must respect the norms of personal integrity implied by that fact. Second, across a broad range of socioeconomic conditions, attempts to achieve material equality by "leveling down" the advantaged might decrease the overall stock of goods and opportunities in the society. Such programs might reduce the social benefits that are available to the citizens who were least favored in the first place.

Rawls develops his distributive theory from this last idea. According to justice as fairness, as we have seen, institutions should be arranged so that any inequalities that emerge are advantageous to the least fortunate. This may require the adoption of institutional forms that have the effect of "correcting" undeserved inequalities. There is an interpretation of high liberalism, sometimes called "luck egalitarianism," that sees the correction of those undeserved advantages as the ultimate point of justice.[38] For Rawls, however, the point of justice lies elsewhere. For him, the concern to redress undeserved inequalities is always in service of a deeper ideal.[39] This is the democratic ideal of a society in which people, as citizens, encounter one another as free and equal moral beings. Justice requires that we seek to create a social world in which the moral powers of all citizens might be developed and exercised, including the powers of those who fare least well in the genetic and social lottery.

The idea that people have special moral powers or capacities in their roles as citizens has a long history, with philosophers defining these powers in various ways.[40] Like Rawls, I will follow tradition by distinguishing two central moral capacities. The first is a capacity for what I shall call responsible self-authorship. By this I mean that all healthy adult citizens, regardless of their particular advantages or disadvantages given by birth, have the capacity to develop and act upon a life plan (whether that plan be individual, collective, or otherwise shared). People are life agents and their agency matters. As responsible self-authors, they have the capacity to realistically assess the options before them and, in light of that assessment, to set standards for a life of a sort that each deems worth living.[41] The second power is more obviously social in nature. This is the moral capacity to honor one's fellow citizens as responsible self-authors too. By this I mean that citizens can recognize that their fellow citizens have lives to lead that are fantastically important to each of them. Whenever they call on the coercive force of the law, they need to be careful to do so in a way that fully respects their fellow citizens as self-authors.[42]

Notice that these ideas of responsible self-authorship are compatible with a wide range of life choices. They are compatible also with many different ways of reasoning about what life to pursue. The conception of citizens as responsible self-authors relies on a "thin" conception of the person.

A concern for these capacities of self-authorship provides high liberalism with its justificatory foundation. For high liberals, the distributive requirements of justice are worked out from that ideal of moral personhood rather than from some consequentialist ideal of persons as maximizers, or some intuitionist ideal of persons as bearers of natural rights. For high liberals, the idea that persons are beings with two moral powers gives social justice its point and thus allows us to define its limits.

Confronted with the inevitable genetic and social differences between them, citizens might seek social institutions that give each the fullest chance to develop and exercise their moral capacities of liberal citizenship. The distributive aspect of social justice emphasizes that all classes of citizens are owed this social expression of respect. This does not require "leveling down" the advantages of any class. Nor, certainly, does it entail that citizens see the talents of others as weapons to be feared—sources of suspicion and distrust. Instead, a commitment to social justice directs us to create institutional conditions in which the least advantaged citizens might rejoice in the exceptional talents and abilities of their fellow citizens—corporate executives such as Steve Jobs, authors such as J. K. Rowling, and athletes such as Tom Brady (or Wilt Chamberlain). A society that discouraged such people, or frustrated the exercise of their talents, would be impoverished. Within a just society, the talents and ambitions of people are to be given play in a way that taken as a whole enriches the lives even of those who are benefited least. In this way, citizens might recognize one another as biologically separate but morally equal participants in a great cooperative venture. They know that the basic institutions of their society are arranged in a way that respects the freedom and equality of each.[43] It is in this sense that, in Rawls's phrase, citizens "share one another's fate."

Of course, not every contemporary high liberal shares Rawls's view about the appropriate grounding of social justice. The recent decades have seen an efflorescence of alternative approaches to left liberalism. "Luck egalitarians" such as Ronald Dworkin and Richard Arneson claim that social justice is primarily a response to the moral imperative to provide special assistance to people who suffer from simple bad luck.[44] On the "capabilities approach" developed by Amartya Sen and Martha Nussbaum, by contrast, the appropriate focus of justice is neither utility nor the shares held by citizens (say of income and resources). Instead, basic justice is about whether people are able to develop their functional capabilities, with a focus on the heterogeneous and multidimensional nature of welfare.[45] There are many other left liberal approaches as well.

Still, all high liberal approaches share a rejection of the classical liberal ideal of formal equality. They insist that any morally adequate account of liberal justice must include a substantive distributive component. As high liberal views they also share something else: all these views relegate the private economic liberties of capitalism to a decidedly secondary place.

This feature of high liberalism has received comparatively little scholarly attention. Most debates within the profession concern which left liberal account of social justice is morally most sound. Contemporary high liberals pour their attention into questions about the specification and justification of liberalism's distributive requirements (and related questions about the scope and nature of those requirements over geopolitical space and to various groups of non-nationals). Yet it is this neglected aspect of contemporary scholarship—its denial of the importance of economic liberty—that brings all these streams of thought together and holds them in a common course.

Again, Rawls is illustrative. Rawls's first principle, recall, sets out a list of basic rights and liberties that must be secured before the distributional goals of the second principle may be pursued.[46] (All high liberals assign special weight to these basic rights and liberties, but not all follow Rawls in assigning them "lexical" priority.) In formulating his list of basic rights and liberties, Rawls adopts the familiar high liberal platform of economic exceptionalism. Following Mill, Rawls singles out the economic liberties from the other traditional liberal rights and liberties for relegation to a lower level of protection. While affirming general rights of association and speech as among the basic liberties of citizens, and adding powerful rights of democratic participation, Rawls carefully slivers off only two aspects of economic liberty for inclusion on his first principle list of protections: a right to personal (nonproductive) property and a right to occupational choice.

Under Rawls's scalpel, the traditional liberal right of ownership is pared down so as to exclude ownership rights in productive property (for example, the right to start and run a small business). What remains of this traditional liberal right is merely a right to own personal (nonproductive) property. Instead of a general right protecting freedoms of working, Rawls affirms only a right to free occupational choice. This right is specified so as to exclude rights that enable individuals to participate in wage labor markets (for example, the right of each person to work for a wage and on terms that each chooses or accepts). Freedom of economic contract, a key feature of the free markets championed by classical liberals, is not recognized by Rawls as a basic right.

Rawls offers only a brief positive argument for narrowing the protection of economic liberty. Explaining why his list of basic liberties includes a right to hold private (nonproductive) property, he says: "The role of this liberty is to allow a sufficient material basis for a sense of personal independence and self-respect, both of which are essential for the development and exercise of the two moral powers." Wider conceptions of economic liberty, whether in a capitalistic or socialistic direction, are not basic liberties. Rawls does not offer a formal argument for this position. He simply states that such liberties are not "necessary for the development and exercise of the two moral powers."[47] Again without argument, Rawls notes how the special treatment accorded to the economic liberties distinguishes the high and classical liberal traditions: "Of course, liberties not on the list, for example the right to own certain kinds of property (e.g., means of production) and freedom of contract as understood by the doctrine of laissez-faire are not basic; and so they are not protected by the priority of the first principle."[48]

Rawls seems unable to imagine how the self-respect of people could be tied directly to the exercise of general economic liberty. Mill is not the only liberal precursor here. Writing in 1930, John Maynard Keynes predicted that within one hundred years the economy would have grown by roughly eight times. At that point, Keynes argues, the economic problem would have been solved. With no need for further growth, mankind could at last turn its attention to "the art of life" and away from what Keynes dismissively describes as the "activities of purpose." While the former concerns the "wise and agreeable" occupation of leisure time, the latter concerns projects and dreams of the "strenuous purposeful money makers."

With the arrival of prosperity, Keynes's predicted, a great change would come over our moral system. "We shall be able to rid ourselves of many of the pseudo-moral principles which have hag-ridden us for two hundred years, by which we have exalted some of the most distasteful of human qualities into the position of the highest virtues." Saving for the future, hard work toward the achievement of one's personal financial goals, striving in the hope of improving the station of family, scrimping in the hope of later providing advantages to one's children, all these would be exposed as the (temporarily useful) pathologies they have always been.

Like Mill, Keynes predicted that the arrival of prosperity would make possible a great change in the political structures of liberal societies, among the most important of which would be a great reduction of the legal weight given to private economic liberty. Again like Mill, Keynes saw the value of the economic liberties of capitalism primarily in instrumental terms. Such freedoms are useful only so long as they lead us toward the point at which the economic problem will be solved. "All kinds of social customs and economic practices, affecting the distribution of wealth and of economic rewards and penalties, which we now maintain at all costs, however distasteful and unjust they may be in themselves, because they are tremendously useful in promoting the accumulation of capital, we shall then be free, at last, to discard." From the moral perspective, the sooner we could discard such liberties (or at least diminish the social importance accorded them) the better.[49]

Rawls similarly views the value of private economic activity primarily in instrumental terms. Since only a few carefully tailored economic liberties are recognized as basic, the specification of the economic liberties of citizens—and of the regulations and limitations that might properly be placed on those economic liberties—are left to be determined at later stages by legislators and other governmental officials. Speaking generally, high liberals believe the economic liberties of citizens should be defined and regulated with an eye toward securing important social goals, most notably the distributive requirements of social justice.

High liberals advocate a range of institutions and regime types that might pursue social justice by this strategy. Some high liberals, Ronald Dworkin prominent among them, advocate a mixed economy and a welfare state with transfer programs that extract wealth from the advantaged—say, by a system of taxes on income and savings—and redistribute it to the less advantaged in the form of state-financed social service programs.[50] The economic liberties are defined and regulated so as to achieve the distributive requirements of justice.

Rawls, for his part, thinks justice as fairness requires something more thoroughgoing. Mill, as we saw, advocated a social democratic system of worker-owned cooperatives. To adopt a system of transfer programs, from Mill's perspective, would be "to nibble at the consequences of unjust power, instead of addressing the injustice itself."[51] Similarly, Rawls emphasizes that his famous difference principle is not a principle of reallocation. The difference principle is not simply a metric that tells us the size of the corrections that must be made in the distributions generated by the existing social system, whatever it might be. As Rawls puts it, the difference principle has no "target" or "cut-off point."[52] Instead, the difference principle requires that we reach down and ask questions about the basic system of production. As Rawls says, "The main problem of distributive justice is the choice of the social system."[53] Justice as fairness requires that we ask: what *whole social system* might express the commitment of citizens to live cooperatively as free and equal self-governing agents?[54]

Like most high liberals, Rawls advocates that a variety of new "branches" of government be grafted onto the (comparatively spare) traditional liberal institutional tree. These include: a branch intended to ensure that the price system remains competitive (say, by regulating proposed corporate mergers, or by breaking up excessively large corporations); a branch to bring about full employment (say, by regulating the supply of money, devising an array of make-work programs whether through general or local government, among other methods); a transfer branch charged with adopting measures that guarantee that poor citizens will receive the various resources owed to them as a matter of justice (programs for the provision of food and housing, schooling, along with programs that assure basic health care to all citizens); and a distributive branch designed to break up

concentrations of wealth that would otherwise threaten the achievement of social justice (say, by enacting steeply progressive taxes of
various sorts, whether those taxes be imposed within generations or
between them). Such branches would also need to provide for the
public funding of elections and government programs designed to
assure that citizens receive politically relevant information on an
ongoing basis.[55]

Rawls hypothesizes that two regime types, and these two alone,
realize justice as fairness. He calls his favored regime types "liberal
(democratic) socialism" and "property-owning democracy."[56] The
status of these claims as hypotheses, and the fact that Rawls claims
that these institutional forms "realize" justice, raise interesting questions to which we return below. For now, the important point is that
high liberals, in their various ways, reject the classical liberal ideal
of formal equality. Along with protecting basic rights and liberties,
liberal justice requires that the basic institutional structure of society
be arranged to satisfy some distributional metric. Left liberals see this
as requiring expansive government involvement in the economy and
a narrowing (or elimination) of any private economic liberties that
might hinder the democratic pursuit of these moral aims.

For high liberals, social justice is the ultimate standard of institutional evaluation. Judged by that standard the market-based institutions of classical liberalism do not fare well. Rawls's argument against
classical liberalism is brief: "Laissez-faire capitalism (the system of
natural liberty . . .) secures only formal equality and rejects both the
fair value of the political liberties and fair equality of opportunity.
It aims for economic efficiency and growth constrained only by a
rather low social minimum."[57] If social justice is the evaluative standard, regime types that emphasize the importance of economic liberty
receive low marks. Property is the enemy of social justice.

The Libertarian Moment

The emergence of libertarianism, especially as defended by Robert Nozick, helped fix the advocates of thick economic liberty and
the advocates of social justice into their two irreconcilable camps.[58]
Before Rawls, the best defenses of left liberalism rested either on a
precarious utilitarianism or a jumble of intuitions. Before Nozick,
the advocates of market society were in a similar conundrum. While

certainly not the first libertarian, Nozick offered a philosophical clarification of earlier expressions of that view. According to Samuel Fleishacker: "Nozick is to the libertarianism that preceded him somewhat as Rawls is to the advocates of distributive justice who preceded him: the first person to provide a clear articulation of the position at stake and its implications."[59] Nozick's book came to enjoy canonical status within the academy: courses that included units on free market liberalism invariably focused on Nozick.[60]

Recall that classical liberalism, in its traditional formulation, affirms a thick conception of economic liberty and a formal conception of equality. That conception nonetheless allows the state to impose taxes to support a limited range of social services that the market might not otherwise make available to all citizens. Classical liberals often do a poor job explaining exactly *why* the liberal state can levy taxes to support social services. In defending "interventionist" programs such as these, classical liberals sometimes invoke consequentialist values, such as the need to prevent social strife and thus maintain economic efficiency.[61] But defended on that basis, it then becomes unclear why those interventions, but not others, are justifiable. At other times classical liberals advert to nonconsequentialist concerns—such as natural duties of charity, or intuitively grounded obligations of beneficence—in an attempt to hold together the various parts of their view.[62]

Nozick's theory, by contrast, is presented as a logical deduction from a set of natural property rights. On the standard reading, those rights are grounded in a moral ideal of persons as self-owners. Nozickian libertarianism: (1) affirms a conception of economic liberty that is not merely thick but absolute; (2) defends a formal conception of equality that sees market outcomes as not merely partially but entirely definitive of justice (even when those market exchanges would result in the alienation of other basic rights and liberties); (3) offers a principled rationale for denying the state any authority to tax citizens to provide social services to others.

Compared to classical liberalism, libertarianism has an axiomatic or deductive character. According to Murray Rothbard, "The right of self-ownership and the right to homestead establish the complete set of principles of the libertarian system. The entire libertarian doctrine then becomes a spinning out and application of all the implications of this central doctrine."[63] For Nozick and Rothbard, self-ownership trips the first domino and makes the rest run.

Speaking generally, libertarianism treats economic liberties as the most fundamental liberties or, perhaps, as the only fundamental liberties.[64] Strict libertarians affirm an absolute right to freedom in working—the freedom to labor and to use labor in production. Similarly, they take the idea of self-ownership to generate absolute rights of holding in one's own body. Combined with absolute rights of transaction, these rights of holding allow citizens to control and dispose of one another's bodies and persons in much the same way they might control and dispose of any other good. While classical liberals tend to develop their political prescriptions from their idea of society as a cooperative venture, libertarians are more likely to put rights center stage and defend whatever states of affairs emerge through the voluntary activities of rights holders.

Thus some libertarians reject the traditional liberal doctrine of the inalienability of people's civil and political liberties. Such libertarians would require the state to enforce contracts by which people sold their votes, their right to speak or to practice a religion of their choice. Nozick and Walter Block defend even voluntary slave contracts.[65] Because of the primacy accorded to property rights, libertarianism regards redistributions of market outcomes as morally suspect.[66] Libertarianism of this sort would not allow taxation to support even the provision of a social safety net. Douglas Rasmussen and Douglas Den Uyl explain: "while no systematic state aid for the extremely poor may seem unsympathetic to some, it is the principled approach."[67] Like most libertarians, Nozick rejects the very idea of social or "redistributive" justice. Liberal principles of justice should be historical rather than patterned. Any questions about the justice of distributions in our world are reducible to questions about the justice of prior appropriations, exchanges, and transfers of goods.

With libertarianism, a new and different form of economic exceptionalism demands a place for itself on the liberal agenda. Traditional classical liberals argue for general rights of economic liberty that are to be protected roughly on a par with the other traditional rights and liberties of liberalism. The high liberal platform of economic exceptionalism singles out economic liberties for relegation to a special lower standing. Libertarians also single out the economic liberties for special treatment. But instead of *lowering* the status of the economic liberties, libertarians *elevate* them above all others. Economic liberties become the weightiest of all rights. Indeed, libertarians such as Jan Narveson assert that liberty *is* property.[68]

With the emergence of Nozickian libertarianism, the (messier) classical liberal tradition quietly slipped out of philosophical conversations.[69] Indeed, among high liberals it is a platitude that political philosophy in the liberal tradition was dead or dormant before Rawls published *A Theory of Justice*. It is remarkable, and revealing, that this idea is accepted by so many high liberals even though classical liberals such as Hayek were publishing their major political works precisely during those (supposedly) dormant decades.[70] Libertarians advocate positions that are foreign to the complexity of the classical liberal tradition, as well as to the constitutional structure of even the most promarket liberal societies such as the United States.[71] Nonetheless, especially within philosophy departments, Nozick's libertarianism became the standard-bearer for economic freedom and limited government. For high liberals eager to attack market-based rivals to their view, libertarianism provided a target-rich environment.

High liberals argue that the foundational idea of Nozickian libertarianism—the idea that people stand in a relationship of ownership to themselves—is fundamentally obscure. A political edifice built atop the obscure notion of ownership, however minimal that edifice might be, essentially lacks any foundations.[72] High liberals such as Samuel Freeman also criticize libertarianism for abandoning the traditional liberal doctrine of inalienable rights and for rejecting a tax-funded safety net even for the destitute.[73] From the high liberal perspective, the development and free exercise of the civil and political liberties are essential to people's moral nature. A state that allows those liberties to be bought and sold does not preserve the conditions necessary to the development of the moral powers of citizens: such a state would allow people to abandon their very status as self-authors.[74] In enforcing such contracts, the liberal state would be complicit in that abandonment. Further, high liberals insist that the public provision of a social minimum is needed to guarantee the effective exercise of citizen's basic liberties. People need this minimum so that they might develop the moral capacities they have as citizens. Explaining Rawls's position, Freeman says, "Views such as libertarianism, or those classical liberal views which entirely deny a social minimum, *are* unreasonable, Rawls contends, since a social minimum is necessary to the adequate development and full exercise of the moral powers, and to pursue a rational conception of the good."[75]

In all these ways, high liberals argue that (right) libertarianism falls short from the perspective of basic liberal values. Rawls claims that libertarianism violates the liberal principle of legitimacy and so should not be recognized as being a *liberal* view.[76] Freeman goes further. If strict libertarians treat property rights as moral absolutes, Freeman says their view is strikingly like a view that liberalism historically defined itself against: the doctrine of private political power that is feudalism.[77]

Nozickian libertarianism also finds itself under a concentrated internal attack from liberal egalitarians. "Left libertarians" affirm the principle of self-ownership but note that the political valence of this claim depends upon how one answers a further question: what is the moral disposition of the natural resources with which self-owners are to interact? Against the Nozickians, left libertarians such as Peter Vallentyne, Hillel Steiner, and Michael Otsuka argue that natural resources are commonly owned. If this is correct, then the principle of self-ownership does not generate strong rights of private ownership. The libertarian premise of self-ownership leads to liberal egalitarian conclusions.[78]

I do not mean to suggest that these arguments are decisive against (right) libertarianism. As I mentioned, Nozick was not the first libertarian, nor is his the only available defense of libertarian principles. There are many forms of libertarianism. It is unclear whether the critiques of Rawls and Freeman apply to all (or any) of them. For one thing, high liberals criticize libertarians for relying on the obscure idea of "self-ownership." But the high liberal critique of libertarianism relies upon a claim that is equally obscure: the claim that libertarians affirm property rights as "moral absolutes." This idea is so obscure it is difficult to judge whether any libertarian actually affirms it.[79]

Unlike Rawls, Nozick turned away from political philosophy almost immediately after publishing his masterwork, *Anarchy, State, and Utopia*. (Alan Ryan has likened Nozick to a man who tossed an intellectual hand grenade into a seminar room, and then walked away.[80]) Because Nozick did not continue to defend and elaborate his view, central aspects of his theory remain unclear. For example, Nozick presents himself as the heir to Locke. But Nozick mentions self-ownership so fleetingly that a case could be made that Nozick grounds his rights in some other idea, such as a conception of liberty (understood as noninterference). Further, while Nozick originally defended voluntary slave contracts, there is evidence that he later abandoned this position, accepting instead a form of libertarianism that affirms the traditional liberal doctrine of inalienable rights.[81] In that case, Nozick was shifting away from strict libertarianism and toward what I call a classical liberal position. Such a position, as I have said, would see the economic liberties as being on a moral par with the other basic liberties, rather than being weightier than the rest. As for the left libertarians, it might well be argued that their deep commitments are to liberal egalitarianism rather than to self-ownership.[82]

However those exegetical debates shake out, the mainstream view of libertarianism holds sway: libertarianism is a doctrine that grounds unyielding rights of property in a moral ideal of persons as self-owners. Libertarianism, so conceived, is implacably opposed to any notion of social or "redistributive" justice.

Liberalismus Sapiens Sapiens

With libertarianism installed as the leading philosophical alternative to high liberalism, high liberals sent out a triumvirate of their own to stand against the libertarian one. While libertarians see people as self-owners, high liberals conceive of persons as free and equal self-governing agents, characterized by a moral capacity for responsible self-authorship. High liberals affirm: (1) a thin conception of economic liberty; (2) a substantive conception of equality, requiring that goods be distributed in a way that benefits the least fortunate; and (3) an expansive role for the state in regulating economic affairs in pursuit of the distributional requirements of social justice. Since the substantive conception of equality represents a moral advance over any purely formal one, the high liberal specification of the basic rights of citizens—a specification that diminishes the scope and importance of economic liberty—must also be morally superior. For anyone committed to social justice, therefore, it is with the redistributive institutions of left liberalism that one's allegiance must lay.

Will Kymlicka, in a popular introductory text, spells out this basic lesson: "The standard left-wing critique of liberal justice is that it endorses formal equality, in the form of equal opportunity or equal civil and political liberty, while ignoring material inequalities, in the form of unequal access to resources. This is a valid criticism of libertarianism, given its commitment to formal rights of self-ownership at the expense of substantive self-determination. But contemporary liberal egalitarian theories, like those of Rawls and Dworkin, do not seem vulnerable to that same criticism."[83]

Thomas Nagel speaks for the professional mainstream when he describes high liberalism as something more than a mere alternative to classical liberalism. Instead, the fairness-based conception of justice Rawls inspired is liberalism in its morally evolved form. As Nagel puts it, "Rawls's theory is the latest stage in a long evolution in the content of liberalism that starts from a narrower notion, exemplified by Locke, which focused on personal freedom and political equality." Nagel continues, "That evolution has been due above all to a recognition of the importance of social and economic structures, equally with political and legal institutions in shaping people's lives and a gradual acceptance of social responsibility for their effects."[84] Liberal societies should retain their constitutional pursuit of justice by means of "negative liberties" in areas of speech, association, and religion. They might also continue to provide some constitutional protection for rights of property and freedom of contract, suitably qualified. But, Nagel assures us, the pursuit of social justice in liberal societies henceforth must be conducted by an ambitious array of legislative and administrative measures designed to ensure fair social outcomes: "tax policies and various approaches to social security, employment, disability compensation, child support, education, medical care and so forth."[85] According to high liberals, these are the policies that a commitment to social justice requires.

This, then, is the master story among liberal political philosophers and theorists of our time. Liberal thought passed through two great evolutionary stages. Early liberals pursued justice primarily by means of constitutional measures protecting negative liberties and securing the conditions for the development of commercial society. They advocated this institutional form because, on their conception, justice was a purely formal, or "procedural" concept. High liberals likewise rely upon constitutional protection for the traditional liberal civil freedoms—freedom of speech, association, and religious liberty prominent among them. But these liberals seek a fuller realization of justice by means of political institutions empowered to bring about fair distributions of wealth and power. They advocate this more expansive role for the state because they conceive of justice in substantive, distributive terms. The deep motivational difference between the two evolutionary stages is that while the new institutional ideal allows liberals to express a concern for substantive equality, the classical institutional ideal does not. Under the force of this argument, liberalism developed from a "low," formal-egalitarian stage to a "high," substantive-egalitarian one. *Cro-Magnon* liberalism was replaced by *Liberalismus sapiens sapiens* and then forgotten. After all, for anyone resisting the wisdom of high liberalism, the only philosophically viable alternative is libertarianism: a doctrine whose very standing as a liberal view is under attack.

We can depict the ideological terrain of contemporary liberal thought in a simple table (see Table 1). Across the top row we have the broad school of traditional classical liberals. Paradigmatic thinkers here include historical figures such as Adam Smith and more recent thinkers such as F. A. Hayek, Milton Friedman, and Richard Epstein. The distinctive political commitment of classical liberals is to private economic liberty (and, perhaps as a result, they reject social justice as an ideal). Classical liberals affirm a thick conception of economic liberty and thus advocate a government of strictly limited legislative powers, especially in the economic realm. Many thinkers in this tradition, most notably modern ones such as Epstein, take a broadly econometric, consequentialist, or "end-directed" approach to political justification. Their political position rests on a view of the person as a utilitarian agent or a *happiness maximizer*.

Across the second row we have libertarianism. I think of libertarianism as a species of classical liberalism, with Nozick, Jan Narveson, and Eric Mack serving as philosophical exemplars. As classical liberals, libertarians are committed to private economic liberty and reject the ideal of social or distributive justice. This is the view that has displaced classical liberalism in the minds of most philosophical defenders of high liberalism, and as such is the promarket view that most high liberals consider their primary rival. Libertarians affirm economic liberty as the fundamental ordering principle of political life. They treat economic liberties as the most weighty of all the basic liberties and perhaps even as moral absolutes. As a consequence, libertarians affirm an extremely limited role for government, typically denying the moral legitimacy of taxation even to support a social safety net or education (on its anarcho-capitalist formulation, libertarianism denies any role for the state at all). Libertarians employ foundationalist or "naturalistic" forms of argument. Their political recommendations can be grounded on a variety of bedrock ideas, including various conceptions of natural liberty. In its paradigmatic formulation, libertarianism is founded on an ideal of persons as *self-owners*.

Finally, we have the morally evolved position of the high liberals. Philosophical exemplars of high liberalism include Rawls, Dworkin, Kymlicka, Nagel, Nussbaum, and a host of prominent contemporary philosophers. The distinctive political commitment of high liberals is to a substantive conception of equality. Perhaps as a result, high liberals are skeptical of the moral importance of private economic liberty. Unlike the classical liberals and libertarians, the high liberal ideal of equality leads them to affirm a conception of social or distributive justice. For them, social justice is the "first virtue," or primary ordering principle, of social institutions. High liberals affirm a thin conception of economic liberty. They empower elected officials to manage the economy and craft distributive programs in pursuit of their distributive ideals. High liberals take a deliberative, or "democratic" approach to political argumentation.[86] A political order is just and legitimate only if the basic terms of that order can be justified to all reasonable members. At the base of the view is a morally robust ideal of the person as a *democratic citizen*. High liberals view citizens as social beings who are endowed with moral powers of responsible self-authorship, including the capacity to honor their fellow citizens as responsible self-authors. The role of the liberal state is to promote conditions in which citizens can exercise and develop these moral powers. In their various ways, high liberals advocate expansive state-based programs of economic redistribution (whether within generations or between them) in pursuit of social justice.

Looked at this way, political debates about the moral valence of capitalism spring ultimately from philosophical disputes about the morally most appropriate way to conceive of political personhood. As Samuel Freeman puts it: "If there is any progress to be made in debates about the importance to liberalism of capitalism, robust private property rights, and the essential role of markets in establishing economic justice, it will require awareness and discussion of the different and conflicting ideals of persons and their social relations that liberals implicitly rely upon in the positions we advocate." After all, Freeman concludes, "At issue in these debates is not simply the nature of our economic and social relations, but ultimately the kinds of persons that we are and can come to be."[87]

TABLE 1

School	Politics	Reasoning	Person
Classical Liberal	Economic Liberty	Ends-Directed	Utility Seeker
Libertarian	Economic Liberty	Naturalistic	Self-Owner
High Liberal	Social Justice	Deliberative	Democratic Citizen

High liberals are happy with this picture. Conceiving of people as self-owners or as happiness seekers may prove attractive to some. But high liberals are confident that their ideal of the democratic citizen provides a richer and more normatively inspiring ideal. If ideological disputes among liberals come down to this question, then it is pretty clear which group holds the adaptive advantage. The authority figures of contemporary political philosophy will solemnly undertake the task of transmitting this tale about the history and moral genesis of high liberalism to their students and to the rising generations of academic professionals. The mission of theorists working in the liberal tradition henceforth is to elucidate and better understand the high, egalitarian view, and the moralized conception of the democratic citizen that underlies it. Their challenge is to extend this paradigm to new issue areas—justice within the household and between cultural groups; rights to health care; the theory of just wages and just prices; democratic control of the workplace; the requirements of equal educational opportunities; questions of distributive justice between nations, global material distribution, and more.

Few if any existing societies conform to the ideals set out by high liberalism. An aspirational consensus has built up around the distributional aspects of high liberalism in some European social democracies—Germany, Sweden, and France perhaps. Insofar as that aspirational consensus holds and takes institutional effect, the citizens of those societies are to be applauded. Elsewhere, as in Great Britain and the United States, the main institutional structures of classical liberalism were eroded during the twentieth century.[88] Yet efforts to move those societies more explicitly in a left liberal direction continue to meet stubborn resistance. From a moral perspective, high liberals insist, those traditions of resistance must be attacked and broken. The choice served up by contemporary political philosophy, after all, is clear. The friends of high liberalism are the friends of social justice. Anyone who maintains an allegiance to a thicker notion of private economic liberty is clinging to an outmoded ideal. That feature of the old liberalism was left behind in order to make room for the distributive concerns of the new liberalism. The evolutionary course of liberal thought allows us no other way to think of these issues.

CHAPTER 3

Thinking the Unthinkable

The Great Fact: Economic Growth

The phrase "thinking the unthinkable" was made notorious by members of the New Labour movement in Britain during the 1990s.[1] Labour's power base had long been the British working class. Labour's political strategy was founded on the assumption that its leftist platform—high tax rates on corporations and wealthy individuals, wide social service programs, and even a call for the full public ownership of productive capital—would be attractive to the British working poor. However, as ever-greater numbers of working people found themselves rising into the middle class, Labour's political base increasingly defected. For the Labour leaders, thinking the unthinkable was above all an exercise in practical political strategy. In calling for a rethinking of even the most basic planks of their platform—such as the call for nationalization of productive resources—New Labour leaders such as Tony Blair were seeking a path to restore their party to political relevance. Any philosopher listening attentively to this process, however, could not help but hear a deeper sort of rethinking being set underway. This was a rethinking of the political and normative significance of the most important feature of twentieth-century life in western democracies: the fact of rising wealth.

Economic growth is making liberal democracies rich. When economists speak of growth, they mean "a *per capita* long run rise in income."[2] The growth experienced by western liberal societies is a recent phenomenon. Viewed historically, this phenomenon is also unique. John Maynard Keynes observes: "From the earliest times of which we have a record—back, say, to two thousand years before Christ—down to the beginning of the eighteenth century, there was no very great change in the standard of life of the average man living in the civilized centres of the earth. Ups and downs, certainly.

Visitations of plague, famine, and war. Golden intervals. But no progressive, violent change."[3] Economist Robert Fogel observes: "it took four thousand years to go from the invention of the plow to figuring out how to hitch a plow up to a horse. And it took 65 years to go from the first flight in a heavier-than-air machine to landing a man on the moon."[4] Growth, in its standard economic sense, began only with the development of market society. Angus Maddison, the great collector of data on economic growth, estimates the average rate of growth of America since 1820 at 2 percent per annum. Over decades, this small but steady rise in income has transformed the lives of ordinary Americans.

Sometimes the changes produced by growth peek out in expected ways. In 2009, one year into a major economic crisis, the *New York Times* ran a story about the hardships being endured by middle- and lower-class people, many of whom were out of work. The story included some curious features. For example, it described the struggles of Pamela Lampley, a forty-year-old mother of three from Dillon, South Carolina. Since losing her job, Ms. Lampley and her family were trying to get by on the salary earned by her husband, who is a machinist. According to the *Times*, Ms. Lampley "feels devastated because they cannot afford to buy their son a laptop to take to college and she cannot give her son money for the movies." Also featured was Cathy Nixon, a thirty-nine-year-old mother of four from Ohio. As a result of losing her job, the story explained, Ms. Nixon was now "unable to afford summer camp and baseball activities for her children, despite scrimping on the basics." The challenges of unemployment—psychological as well as financial—are real and I do not discount them. Still, after a hundred years of growth, even a Great Recession seems to have a different feel.[5]

On the standard economic calculation, Americans today find themselves some eight times wealthier than their ancestors in 1900—a stunning change of affairs.[6] Even that eightfold figure, however, may lead us to underestimate the social significance of growth. Economists find it convenient to measure growth in monetary terms: the inflation adjusted rate of change in *per capita* GDP, for example. But as economic historian Deirdre McCloskey argues, if we are interested in the effects of economic growth on the life experience of people, we need some different measure. Along with the traditional monetary standards, McCloskey suggests that we consider what she calls "*real* national income per head." By real income, McCloskey means "the stuff per person we have—the pounds of bread or the number of haircuts, backs and sides—not the mere dollars or yen."[7]

Some aspects of "real" growth in McCloskey's sense can be quantified fairly easily. Fogel estimates that the average American family in 1875 spent 74 percent of its income on food, clothing, and shelter; compared to the mere 13 percent spent in 1995.[8] According to Michael Cox and Richard Alm, a three-minute phone call across the United States in 1950 cost ninety hours of common labor. By 1999 the cost had fallen to a minute and a half. Cox and Alm also calculate that Americans had one car per every 4.4 persons in 1938, one per 2.4 in 1960, and one per 1.26 by 2003.[9] Such astonishing figures get us closer to appreciating the magnitude of "real" growth, yet they still leave us short. For example, how do we measure the value of the improved voice quality of those (less expensive) recent phone calls? What is the value of being able to receive an electronic message—say, announcing the birth of a child— while out on a walk rather than after days of sitting by the phone? How do we measure the value of receiving such news not just in the form of a voice on the line but through a high-resolution stream of live video?

Other aspects of growth are even more elusive. What would a phone call announcing the birth of a child across the country have been worth in 1875, before the telephone had been invented? How much would a family member in that era have been willing to pay for a plane ticket to go see that child, or to visit an elderly parent—before there were commercial planes? Andrew Carnegie, for all his wealth, could not buy a cure for the pneumonia that killed his mother— though treatments for pneumonia are readily available today.[10] How do we measure the change in people's experiences that have been generated by growth?

The eightfold change in the (inflation adjusted) *per capita* income of average Americans since 1900 is impressive, but considered in terms of real experience the magnitude of change is far greater. According to McCloskey, "if one accounts at their proper value such novelties as jet travel and vitamin pills and instant messaging, then the factor of material improvement climbs even higher than sixteen—to eighteen, or thirty, or far beyond. No previous episode of enrichment for the average person approaches it, not the China of the Song Dynasty or the Egypt of the New Kingdom, nor the glory of Greece or the grandeur of Rome." McCloskey refers to this phenomenon of recent growth as the Great Fact. She notes that no competent economist, regardless of ideology, denies it.[11] McCloskey suggests that the fundamental achievement of modern growth is that it has given ordinary people "the scope to do more."[12]

Populism, Probability, and Political Philosophy

High liberalism has its roots in the Millian idea that economic liberties are less important to the moral development of individuals than their personal or political liberties. The rise of wealth was expected to make that moral fact ever more widely evident. By the middle of the twentieth century, social reformers such as Richard Titmuss euphorically predicted that increases in productivity made possible by industrialization would effectively end economic scarcity. As societies became increasingly affluent, the progressive political program would arrange things so that citizens could all come to enjoy the benefits of wealth. Societies could in effect turn their attention from dismal, individualist-competitive questions of production to happier, collective-democratic ones of distribution.

As social wealth grew, individuals could increasingly be freed of the burdens of personal economic worry. Liberal governments would continue to provide foundational protection to people's political and civil liberties. Decision making in those areas—what to say, read or write? what religion to practice? with whom to associate and for what purposes?—would still be the stuff of the practical freedom experienced by citizens. But decision making in economic matters—how much of one's daily life to devote to work? at what wages and under what conditions? what percentage of one's income to spend now and what percentage to save for retirement? how much to spend on health care for one's parents and how much on the education of one's children?—had increasingly been handed over to the collective. As societies become wealthy, Progressives believed, welfarist (or even socialist) policies would gain ever more popular support.

To the dismay of Titmuss's followers, however, something very close to the opposite occurred. In liberal societies across the world, wealth made many workers *less* enthusiastic about joining unions and other collective bargaining structures. The experience of increasing personal prosperity made working-class citizens in many countries *less* willing to pay taxes in support of state-based service programs. The growth of social wealth made the exercise of personal economic liberty *more* important to many people.

Why are rising incomes accompanied by increasing resistance to taxes in so many liberal countries? Cynics have an easy answer: as people's incomes rise, they become increasingly greedy and self-interested. They resist taxes for that reason. No doubt some people resist taxes simply because they are greedy, but there also seem to be other, more complex moral factors at play. For one thing, as people's incomes rise, they experience an increasing range of personal options about how that income might be spent.[13] Facing this wider range of options, people seem increasingly to find personal meaning in economic decision making. British Labour MP Frank Field expresses this point with startling directness: "The idea that rising tax bills will be hidden by rising real wages has proved to be one of the great fallacies of the post-war period. Rising income levels now offer a growing body of voters the chance for the very first time to make major decisions themselves on the composition of their standard of living. Such opportunities are seized with relish."[14]

Growing prosperity seems to give an ever-wider range of people a sense of power and independence. It encourages a special form of self-esteem that comes when people recognize themselves as central causes of the particular lives they are living—rather than being in any way the ward of others, no matter how well meaning, other-regarding, or wise those others might be. In many countries, ordinary citizens are increasingly resentful about having economic decision-making power taken from them by the planners of the social democratic state. In ways that are difficult fully to understand, *prosperity makes the personal exercise of economic liberty more rather than less valuable to many liberal citizens.*

I will say much more about that idea below. For now, it is worth noting that these populist trends confound the expectations of philosophers, pundits, and politicians alike. Thomas Nagel notes that many Americans believe they have a right to the money they earn from working, and that proposals for taxation must therefore overcome that preexisting right. Nagel calls this view "everyday libertarianism." While deriding this idea as philosophically confused, Nagel notes that many ordinary Americans cling stubbornly to it.[15]

Likewise, Tony Judt notes that polls show that most Americans would like to have their social experience improved. For example, they would like better medical care at lower cost, longer life expectancy, and less crime. However, Judt continues: "When told that these thing are available in Austria, Scandinavia, or the Netherlands, but that they come with higher taxes and an 'interventionary' state, many of those same Americans respond: 'But that is socialism! We do not want the state interfering in our affairs. And above all, we do not wish to pay more taxes.'" Like many pundits from the left, Judt finds this combination of attitudes baffling. He concludes that ordinary Americans suffer from a "curious cognitive dissonance."[16]

In America, many middle- and working-class people are skeptical of redistributive taxation. With only occasional dips, this skepticism has been growing steadily for decades.[17] According to polls cited by Michael Graetz and Ian Shapiro, in 1978 some 30 percent of respondents agreed with the statement that "the government should reduce income differences between rich and poor," and 20 percent disagreed. Twenty years later, only 24 percent agreed with that statement and the number disagreeing rose to 27 percent. In a poll taken in 1997, Graetz and Shapiro note, fully 71 percent Americans agreed that the government should "foster conditions that enable everyone to have a chance to make a high income," but only 22 percent thought government should "redistribute existing wealth." When asked specifically whether "government should work to redistribute income to close the gap between rich and poor," a third agreed. But 64 percent indicated instead that the "government should work to create opportunity, but not distribute wealth."[18]

Consider also the controversy in 2009 over the "Botax." This tax on Botox and other expensive cosmetic enhancements was proposed in the wake of a severe economic downturn as a way to pay for new government health care programs. Although presented as a luxury tax, the Botax was received by the public as an affront to the middle class. According to the American Society of Plastic Surgeons, "about 60% of those planning to have cosmetic medical procedures have an annual household income of $30,000 to $90,000." As one New Jersey plastic surgeon stated, "This tax is not just a luxury tax. This is a tax on the middle class."[19] In the face of widespread opposition, the proposed tax was dropped from the health care bill. National unemployment at the time stood at 10 percent.[20]

The controversy over the estate tax highlights the moral dimensions of these issues. Throughout the twentieth century, America has had a special tax on the estates of the wealthy. During the Clinton and Bush years, popular support for repealing this "death tax" swelled. To block the repeal movement, politicians on the left appealed to people's self-interest—noting that the tax applied only to the top 1 percent or 2 percent of society. To their surprise, though, middle- and working-class people continued to oppose the tax, eventually leading to its repeal. Polling data about people's reasons for opposing the death tax is complicated and, as with most such data, can be read in different ways. Significantly, polls found that large numbers of Americans overestimate their own wealth compared to others and also hold statistically unrealistic beliefs about their own likelihood of becoming rich: 39 percent thought they were in the top 1 percent, or would be soon.[21] Beneath the data, though, most observers see powerful normative beliefs at play. According to Graetz and Shapiro (both of whom support the tax): "What won the day for the forces of repeal was a moral argument based in the great U.S. tradition of hard work and thrift."[22]

Thomas Spragens, who also supports the estate tax, claims that people on the left were incapacitated from offering effective moral arguments of their own in favor of the tax, an incapacitation that Spragens says was caused by "contemporary liberalism's principled disdain for the moral privileging of work."[23] In the estate tax controversy, appeals to self-interest, like moral exhortations about the requirements of social justice, run against a populist stream that finds value in the traditional ideals of hard work and financial ambition. Rather than simply being confused about their own chances of getting rich, ordinary people may oppose the death tax because they value living in a society of the sort that allows anyone, including *people like them*, to rise to great wealth. They resist the tax as a matter of moral principle.

This shift in the moral valence of the economic liberties tracks a deeper change in the nature of capitalism. Before the Industrial Revolution, economic growth was constrained by relatively fixed factors such as the size of the population and the zeal with which rival political systems might induce people to work. Machine-based production shattered those constraints on growth. Machines made possible a new era of self-extending growth, the early form of which became known as industrial capitalism. The logic of industrial capitalism was toward ever more consolidated locations of production—mills producing steel, factories rolling out Ford Model-Ts. This change brought about a steady diminution of the importance of the individual artisan and the individual consumer alike. Individuals were dwarfed by the increasingly large machinery and capital needed for the mass production of uniform goods. This is the stage of capitalism that Mill and Marx criticized in the mid-1800s. Their criticisms of capitalism still resonated with many during the early decades of the 1900s.[24]

By the middle of the twentieth century, however, the nature of capitalist production began to change.[25] For many, this change brought with it another one: a change in the moral valence of private economic liberty. Elements of industrial capitalism such as the extensive division of labor and the pursuit of economies of scale continued to predominate in some parts of the economy—especially regarding heavy industry. However, with rising affluence, a new more complex economy is developing. A central feature of this new economy is an emphasis on personal services and consumer goods. Rather than increasing centralization of production (with the corresponding premium placed on massed capital resources), the new economy increasingly adjusts to the demand from consumers for personalized items. There is a new emphasis on the production of goods with immaterial value, with near zero transaction costs, and increasing product differentiation. Ideas and information are coming to rival capital as the most valued factors of production. In recent decades, most of the largest employment gains have come in occupations that rely on interpersonal skills and emotional intelligence. In sector after sector, the value of imagination and creativity is rising and that of brute efficiency falling. New more flexible forms of workplace management are replacing the rigid, hierarchical structures of the factory system.[26] John Roberts, the renowned professor of business management at Stanford, argued that in this "post-modern" economy, gains to flexibility and creativity are coming to exceed those of coordination and scale.[27]

To take one example, even as late as the 1970s, the corporate culture of IBM was based on hierarchy and a clean-shaven, blue-suited suppression of individuality. Just thirty years later, the workplace cultures of high-technology enterprises such as Apple Inc. or high-flying start-ups such as Google are famous for encouraging creativity and innovation. Within western societies, the old industrial capitalism is being supplanted by more decentralized and micro-market-oriented forms of capitalism.[28] According to Richard Koch and Chris Smith: "We are moving to a world where the individual, autonomous person is central—to the *personalized economy*."

In this new economy, increases in value tend to be the result of innovation driven primarily by creative individuals and teams, rather than simply the product of machines and unskilled workers backed by massed capital. The result is a reunification of personal and economic progress. Provocatively, Koch and Smith continue: "In the long march of history [industrial] capitalism was an aberration, an anomaly. Whereas for 800 years, Europe, and later America, made progress through the expansion and energies of the rising urban middle classes, resulting in economic growth *and* the advance of personal and political freedom, industrial capitalism tore this unity apart. Capitalism brought enormous economic advances, but it also marginalized the individual producer and centralized the economy and society. The personalized economy reverts to the long-term Western trend of advancing wealth and freedom together."[29]

What should be made of these economic and political developments? For politicians and social reformers, the significance of these developments is purely practical. It was Frank Field who coined the New Labour slogan "thinking the unthinkable." Field has suggested that despite the resonance of his slogan, a more accurate description of what he and his fellow New Labourites were about was merely "thinking the workable."[30] The Old Labour platform dismissed the importance of private economic freedom. As the Labour Party's constituency in Britain's working class came increasingly to value their private economic freedoms, Labour leaders faced the choice of falling into irrelevancy or changing their platform. New Labour was concerned about feasibility in the most practical political sense: getting elected into office and staying there.

But how should *philosophers* understand the significance of these developments? Philosophy reaches for the timeless and the true. The philosophical pursuit of truth cannot be constrained, much less settled, by local political trends or popular political polls. Nonetheless, popular opinions sometimes have a relevance to political philosophy that is unlike their relevance to other areas of inquiry. This is a point of utmost importance to the development of the view I call *market democracy*.

To see the unique ways in which popular opinion may be relevant to political philosophy, consider the relevance of popular opinion to other areas of inquiry, for example, mathematics. A well-known probability puzzle is known as the Birthday Problem: "How many people would you need to have in a room to make it more likely than not that two of them have the same birthday?" On reflection, most people make a guess of about 183. Presumably, many nonmathematicians arrive at this answer because they think the correct way to solve the problem is to divide the number of days in a year in half, and then round up. Probability theory, however, demonstrates that the correct answer is much lower: 23.[31] The fact that many untrained people think the answer is around 183 does not give probability theorists any reason to go back and worry about their theorem. With respect to the conclusions of probability theory, the mathematicians have a claim to expertise over common opinion that is absolute. With respect to the conclusions they draw about the moral dimensions of political life, however, the claims to expertise made by political philosophers are more conditional.

Many life experiences have a moral value that can only be appreciated firsthand. Becoming a parent is one example. No matter how they prepare, many new parents report being surprised at the experience—saying, for example, that they never fully understood the love parents have for their children until they became parents themselves. Many life experiences have this quality. Imagine a political science professor named Terry who is strongly committed to a particular presidential candidate (say, one with a strong left liberal agenda). Terry contributes generously to the campaign, writes letters to the local papers, and, on the eve of the election, flies on his own dime to one of the battleground states to go door to door passing out campaign literature. What does it mean to Terry to watch the election results come in and, say, see his candidate achieve a historic victory? Or imagine a college dropout named Amy who has an entry-level job as a pet groomer. Dreaming of owning a business of her own, Amy saves her money, builds a sterling credit rating, wins a bank loan, and finally opens her own pet shop (Amy's Pup-in-the-Tub). What does it mean to Amy to walk into her own shop each morning or, when leaving after a particularly long day, to look back and read her name up on the sign?[32]

The specialized training received by philosophers makes them experts at moving moral concepts around and drawing out the unexpected implications of those concepts. But to understand the moral value of many experiences, a different kind of training is required. That training often consists of living a life in which experiences of the sort in question have a central place.[33] There is no guarantee that the life course that leads one to become a professional philosopher will include many of those kinds of experiences (indeed, it may necessarily preclude some of them). The point is not that people who do political philosophy, in order to do philosophy well, must actually have had experiences of each kind just mentioned—becoming a parent, joining a campaign, or owning a business. The point, rather, is that if one has not had experiences such as these (or if one has personally eschewed the sort of life that might include them), there exists a danger that one might be insufficiently sensitive to the moral role such experiences play in the lives of other people. If many people in one's professional cohort have followed a similar pattern of eschewal, the danger of such distortions may be enhanced.

The conclusions of political philosophy are often built upon assumptions about the relative moral value of the different kinds of experience that might possibly go into a life. When deciding what to include and what to leave off a list of basic liberties, for example, liberal political philosophers necessarily find themselves staking out general claims about the relative moral importance of different domains of activity and experience—civic, political, and economic. But the training philosophers receive in fitting together moral concepts does not itself give any privileged place to the substantive moral assessments professional philosophers make about such issues. Indeed, with respect to many moral judgments, the opinions of the average good citizen may be just as reliable as those of the average professor of philosophy. Sometimes, the moral judgments of average citizens may be *more* reliable.

If the primary moral convictions of large numbers of ordinary people diverge from the moral premises of professional philosophers, the philosophers—unlike the mathematicians—may ipso facto have reason to go back and check their moral premises. On what set of value judgments are my political assumptions based? What evidence do I have for my premises? What are my own biases and how might they affect my confidence in these assumptions? This process might include considering the moral judgments of people with different backgrounds and life experiences than one's own. It might include considering the moral opinions of very large numbers of such people, with greatly diverse experiences and values. While in no way deferring to the political conclusions that such people draw from the particular moral convictions they hold dear, political philosophers may find among those convictions some valuable insights about the strengths and weaknesses of key premises on which their own arguments rely.

I emphasize: this is not an argument for populism about the conclusions of political philosophy (nor, certainly, is it an argument for relativism about its premises). As I explain later in this book, I am sympathetic to the idea, common among Rawlsian high liberals, that there is an ideal theoretic project that is properly conducted largely unconstrained by empirical realities, including the political attitudes that happen to prevail in actual liberal societies. However, we must be careful to keep this idea separate from a very different idea with which it is often elided. This is the idea that once we grant the inability of (mere) feasibility concerns to lower the normative standards of political philosophy, political philosophers, as such, have nothing to learn from the study of those feasibility concerns. This would be a great mistake. Indeed, in the context of the commitment of high liberal political philosophers to identify the requirements of treating people as free and equal citizens, it would be a missed opportunity. Attention to the particular feasibility challenges that are currently roiling actual social democratic regimes may show contemporary philosophers that it is time once again to *raise* liberalism's normative standards.

Economic Liberty and Democratic Legitimacy

High liberals restrict the range of economic liberties they recognize as basic rights. By constraining the private economic freedom of citizens, they make room for expanded governmental activity in pursuit of the distributive requirements of social justice. Even for people committed to social justice, however, there is a moral question about whether it is appropriate to restrict the economic liberties of citizens in this way. The question of whether it is acceptable to single out economic liberty to be specially limited and constrained is a major junction point, perhaps *the* major junction point, within the history of liberal thought. Can the high liberal platform of economic exceptionalism be justified?

Given the importance of this question, it is surprising that high liberal arguments for economic exceptionalism are often presented only obliquely and in an unsustained fashion. Defenses of economic exceptionalism usually take the form of critiques of thick economic freedom. Sometimes such critiques treat libertarianism as the model champion of thick economic liberty, and then treat blows struck against libertarianism as blows against classical liberalism generally. We considered one such critique earlier in this chapter: affirming economic liberty as among the basic liberties is equivalent to affirming economic liberties as moral absolutes. All forms of classical liberalism, including market democracy, collapse into libertarianism. If this were true, the high liberal objections to libertarianism—that it can provide no principled rationale for the provision of a social safety net, and that it requires the state to enforce contracts that alienate other basic liberties—would apply in full force to market democracy.

Whether or not these arguments accurately describe libertarianism, they cannot apply to market democracy. Market democracy rejects the idea that property rights outweigh the other basic liberties or are in any sense moral absolutes. It affirms a thick conception of economic liberty as part of a broader scheme of rights and liberties designed to enable citizens to exercise and develop their moral powers. Market democracy affirms a general right of economic liberty in a way that retains a commitment to the traditional liberal doctrine regarding the inalienability of the other basic rights and liberties. In terms of its substantive moral commitments, market democracy occupies conceptual space that, while akin to libertarianism, is distinct from it. The arguments about "property absolutism" that high liberals direct against libertarians do not apply against market democracy.

Another way high liberals seek to undermine the importance of property rights is to claim that property is a legal convention.[34] The economic liberty of ownership exists as a product of regulatory definitions, rules, and conventions. Now, the idea that property is a legal convention has been widely accepted by classical liberals at least since Hume.[35] Critics of thick economic liberty, however, add a stinger to this idea. If property is a legal convention, this means that claims to ownership are conceptually posterior to the regulatory rules that define and constrain them. So property rights cannot serve as a basis for limiting those regulatory rules. As Liam Murphy and Thomas Nagel put it: "Private property is a legal convention, defined in part by looking at the tax system; therefore, the tax system cannot be evaluated by looking at its impact on private property, conceived as something that has independent existence and validity."[36]

Against the property-absolutist claims of some libertarians, Murphy and Nagel claim that the system of social rules that potentially impacts on property rights is logically prior to those property rights. Thus: "The logical order of priority between taxes and property rights is the reverse of that assumed by libertarians."[37] Murphy and Nagel treat the "everyday libertarian" convictions of ordinary citizens as on a par with the answers such people give to the Birthday Problem: they are baseless, if understandable, confusions. No matter how deep and firmly fixed people's intuitions about the importance of property may be, those intuitions give political philosophers no reason to pause, much less rethink.

Murphy and Nagel direct their argument from legal convention against absolutist conceptions of ownership rights.[38] However, they then proceed as though their critique of pure libertarianism ipso facto rules out classical liberal accounts of ownership as well. Libertarians may well object to the way Murphy and Nagel characterize their view. For my purposes here, let's put that issue aside. For us, the important point is that when applied to nonabsolutist defenses of thick economic liberty, this argument from legal convention quickly loses its force. Indeed, applied against the classical liberal conception of economic liberty I wish to defend, the argument from legal convention is generalizable so as to render it either trivial or circular.

First, lets look at a generalized version of this argument. Consider any legal convention, which we will call X, where X is defined in part by looking at the surrounding systems of rules and regulations that impact on it. According to the argument from legal convention, systems that impact on X cannot be evaluated by asking whether they impact on X (as though X has an independent existence and validity). But now for X, instead of a libertarian conception of property rights, substitute: (1) the right to vote, (2) the right of bodily integrity, or (3) the right to free intellectual development (such as that protected by freedom of the press). I suggest that any of these rights, and many more besides, could equally well be substituted for X. All basic rights and liberties are socially constructed in important ways.

Consider the right to bodily integrity. We cannot know the content of this right except by reference to the surrounding rules that identify when that right is impinged. Is getting bumped in the hallway a violation of the right to bodily integrity? We answer that question only by looking at the complex system of social rules and definitions (such as those that define various forms of assault and battery) that are relevant to this particular right. So too the right to vote must be given definitional content by rules that set out how often elections will be held and determine how they will be structured.

So the observation that "property is a legal convention" does no normative work specific to issues of property (aside from perhaps blocking the pure libertarian claim). We must evaluate systems that impact on economic liberty the same way we evaluate systems that impact on any other "legal conventions." Namely, we must consider the best substantive arguments that can be advanced to tell us what degree of protection from impingement each of those "legal conventions" merits. Whatever "independent existence and validity" the economic liberties have must come from those moral arguments. The strength (or weakness) of those arguments is unaffected by statements about economic freedom's status as a legal convention. With respect to assertions about the legitimacy of restrictions on economic liberty, the claim that such liberties are legal conventions is trivial.

The only way to make the argument from legal convention undermine the importance of thick economic liberty would be to antecedently assume that the moral arguments supporting such liberty are weak or nonexistent. But, again, the observation that "property is a legal convention" does no normative work to support that assumption. With respect to claims about the legitimacy of restrictions on economic liberty, the legal-convention argument about property is circular.

To avoid these problems, high liberals sometimes offer a supplementary argument against economic liberty. This argument seeks to attach the legal-convention critique uniquely to questions of private economic liberty. With economic liberties, this argument goes, a result of their social protection is that large inequalities will emerge between people. These inequalities are far beyond the inequalities that would have occurred in a Hobbesian state of nature. In the state of nature, as Murphy and Nagel point out, "there is little doubt that everyone's level of welfare would be very low and—importantly— roughly equal. We cannot pretend that the differences in ability, personality, and inherited wealth that lead to great inequalities of welfare in an orderly market would have the same effect if there were no government to create and protect legal property rights."[39]

However, this argument also can be generalized with respect to "legal conventions" besides property. Consider freedom of thought, including intellectual freedom. In the state of nature everyone's level of intellectual attainment would be very low and therefore roughly equal. In society, with rules protecting intellectual freedom, differ- ences in intellectual talent, personality, and ambition will lead to much larger inequalities of learning and intellectual accomplishment. Some will devote themselves to the study of arcane problems in phi- losophy (such as the question of what it is like to be a bat).[40] Others may fill their heads with computer game strategies and plots from romantic novels. Whether we are considering economic or intellec- tual liberty, however, the simple fact that social protections magnify inequalities tells us nothing. The important question is the moral one about how we should think about these inequalities. Liberals answer that question first and foremost by examining the moral importance of the activities that give rise to such inequalities in the first place.

There is another argument, this one offered by Rawls, against the affirmation of thick economic liberty—though again this argument is presented only obliquely. Recall that in a democratic society, citizens are committed to act in relation to others on terms they can publically endorse together. Thus one of the central aims of democratic society is to resolve "the impasse . . . as to the way in which social institu- tions are to be arranged if they are to conform to the freedom and equality of citizens as moral persons."[41] However, Rawls says that the choice between the traditional economic liberties of capitalism (such as private ownership of productive property and the freedom of individuals to negotiate the terms of their own employment) and the economic liberties of socialism (which allow only ownership of personal property and a limited freedom of occupational choice) is too controversial to be decided as matters of political justice. Even a philosophically compelling argument, he says, is "most unlikely to convince either side that the other is correct on a question like that of private or social property in the means of production."[42] In the face of these sharply conflicting views, it is unlikely that an overlapping consensus could be reached on this issue. Rawls says the choice between capitalism and socialism must be to left to later stages of justification "when much more information about a society's circumstances and historical traditions is available."[43] In this way, Rawls denies that the economic liberties of capitalism should be recognized as basic rights.

This is curious argument. First, Rawls's plea for neutrality on economic issues fits ill with his own later assertion that socialist regimes (such as liberal democratic socialism) realize liberal justice, while even tepidly capitalist regimes (such welfare state capitalism) violate that standard. Further, as we noted, Rawls bases his ostensible plea for neutrality on this issue on the claim that the choice between socialism and capitalism is too divisive to be settled as a matter of political justice. But such an approach would require that we disfigure the core democratic standard that people should live together on terms that all can accept. People can use the public reason standard in a variety of ways.[44] Within Rawls's system, however, that standard requires merely that we seek consensus among citizens who are politically reasonable, rather than among all citizens regardless of the content of their views.

To see the appeal of this approach, imagine a liberal constitutional democracy within which a large faction of citizens is committed to using the state to impose its preferred religious viewpoint on small factions of citizens holding deviant views. So, as a matter of sociological fact, the status of religious liberty is a matter of controversy in that society. On Rawls's approach to public reason, our commitment to democracy would not allow us (let alone require us) to prescind from philosophical investigations about whether religious liberties should be recognized as among the basic rights of those liberal citizens.

Similarly, even if it were the case that the choice between private and public ownership of productive property was a topic of significant disagreement within the liberal democracies of the West (which it manifestly is not), this sociological fact could not cut off philosophical investigations into the moral standing of thick economic liberty for liberal citizens. With questions of economic liberty, like those of religious liberty, the mere fact of controversy cannot by itself render an issue unfit for public reason arguments. The value pluralism democratic theorists must respect is *reasonable* value pluralism. The mere fact of controversy cannot pull the plug on discussions about the moral requirements of liberal democracy.

So we return to our question: what could justify the high liberal platform of economic exceptionalism? As we have seen, high liberals treat the economic liberties differently from the other traditional liberal freedoms. Rather than including a general right protecting the choice making of citizens in economic affairs, Rawls's list of basic liberties includes only two narrowly crafted economic liberties: a right to own personal (nonproductive) property, and a limited right to occupational choice. To understand the high liberal platform of economic exceptionalism, we need to take a closer look at the moral powers and their relation to the list of basic liberties.

Politics is about coercion. Rules against murder, prohibitions against fraud, and policies about the conduct of elections all require coercive backing. The most basic question philosophers ask about political life concerns the conditions under which the use of such coercion is morally justified. Since Locke, many liberals have given some notion of consent, or justifiability, an important role in legitimating political coercion. The liberal principle of legitimacy is this: the use of political coercion is legitimate only if that coercion is conducted on the basis of principles that can be endorsed by the people subject to that coercion. As Rawls puts it, legitimate political authority requires a "constitution (written or unwritten) the essentials of which all citizens, as reasonable and rational, can endorse in light of their common human reason."[45] The question then arises: under what conditions might this principle of democratic legitimacy be satisfied?

In order to endorse a set of political rules, people must first be capable of assessing those rules. To assess political rules, citizens must exercise powers of judgment known as "moral powers." As responsible self-authors, as I describe people exercising the first of these moral powers, citizens are understood to have the capacity to make a realistic assessment of the life options before them and, in light of that assessment, to choose to pursue some course of life as their own. Without this capacity, citizens would not be able to assess what they believe society ought to allow them to do. The other moral power, in my terms, concerns the capacity people have to recognize their fellow citizens as responsible self-authors too. This involves recognizing that their fellow citizens likewise have lives to lead that are important to them. Since they are capable of recognizing this, citizens are capable of committing themselves to abide by just rules of social conduct. Without this capacity, citizens would be unable to evaluate how well the rules of their society square with their commitment to honor their fellow citizens as responsible self-authors.

If people are to be capable of endorsing the rules that are to govern them, they must be free to exercise and develop their two moral powers. The role of the basic liberties is to protect those powers. In a society without a general right protecting freedom of speech, a ruling party might allow speech on a wide range of topics but forbid speech by their rivals. Denied access to those forms of speech, the citizens would lack important information about the character of their regime and perhaps even about the value of political speech. Without protection of that general liberty, the evaluative capacities of the citizens would be stunted. Even if they acquiesced to the system of governance, their endorsement would not be as robust as the liberal principle of legitimacy requires.[46] Thus, in drawing up a list of basic liberties, we are seeking to identify a set of liberties that "provide[s] the political and social conditions essential for the adequate development and full exercise of the two moral powers."[47] The basic liberties are those liberties that must be protected if citizens are to develop their evaluative horizons, thus making them capable of truly governing themselves.

Formally speaking, therefore, the stipulation and enforcement of a set of basic liberties is a requirement of political legitimacy. But it is important to note that while politics is always about coercion, this does not mean the justification of coercion is the *point* of politics. The liberal commitment to the principle of legitimacy is itself derived from a deeper commitment. At base, high liberals are concerned to respect citizens as free and equal self-governing agents—that is, as members of a cooperative venture who nonetheless have their own lives to lead. It is the commitment to the equal importance of each of those lives that leads liberals to the principle of legitimacy. By insisting that the use of political force be justifiable in principle to all, every person is accounted for as a morally social member.[48] So the imperative to create a social world in which the moral powers of citizens can be fully developed is a requirement of legitimacy. But that imperative springs from the more basic liberal ideal, rooted in the work of Locke, that political institutions must respect people as free and equal moral beings.[49]

Thus basic rights are requirements of democratic legitimacy. For this reason, the list of basic rights has a special status within any liberal schema. The protection of the rights on this list is prior to any other social aim—whether that aim be economic prosperity or even, notably, the lessening of social inequality. Again, democratic theorists can differ about the strength of the priority they assign to basic rights over other social values. Within the orthodox high liberal schema, a basic liberty can only be restricted in order to prevent a more severe restriction of some other basic liberty (or to the scheme of basic liberties as an integrated whole).

The priority assigned to the basic liberties has significant institutional implications. Because the basic liberties are requirements of political legitimacy, high liberals argue that the basic liberties (and the basic liberties alone) should be entrenched in the constitution.[50] The basic liberties are prerequisites for the legitimate exercise of democratic authority. Legislative measures that infringe on those liberties are thus illegitimate. The pursuit of social goals, whether by legislative rule or the exercise of executive prerogative, must not violate the basic rights and liberties enshrined in the constitution.

High liberals claim that some narrowly specified economic liberties should be recognized as basic while other dimensions of economic liberty should be excluded. So high liberals claim that some forms of independent economic activity must be protected if people are fully to develop and exercise their moral powers, while other aspects of personal economic freedom need not be so protected. However, the moral reasoning high liberals use to justify the inclusion of their preferred economic liberties cannot explain why the other aspects of economic liberty must be excluded. On the contrary, the same reasons high liberals offer in support of their preferred economic liberties apply with at least as much force to the aspects of economic freedom they wish to exclude.

Consider freedom of occupational choice. It is easy to see why high liberals affirm this particular economic liberty as a basic right. After all, imagine a society that does not affirm a right to occupational choice. In pursuit of some important social goal, the legislature in this society decides to create a panel of experts (or perhaps a computer program) that assigns an occupation to each citizen. A society organized this way would not respect citizens as "free and equal self-governing agents." People ordinarily spend a large percentage of their time engaged in their occupation. This is one reason why the choice of occupation is often a profound expression of identity: as Aristotle once noted, what we do influences who we are. By choosing which occupation to pursue, we express our values. We say something about what projects we think are worthy of our time, how we value the monetary rewards of work compared to work's other rewards, and about how we balance the value of work with the other parts of our lives.

However, once the right of occupational choice is allowed to be a basic right, it becomes unclear how the other liberties of working can be excluded. Those thicker liberties of working, recall, involve "the liberty to employ one's body and time in productive activity that one has chosen or accepted, and under arrangements that one has chosen or accepted."[51] If the freedom to choose an occupation is essential to the development of the moral powers, the freedom to sell, trade, and donate one's labor looks equally essential for the same reasons. After all, one is defined by one's workplace experience not simply by *what* profession one pursues. One is also defined by *where* one chooses to work, by the *terms* that one seeks and accepts for one's work, by the *number of hours* that one devotes to ones work, and much more besides.

These are not mere details within a person's life. The particular pattern of decisions one makes in response to these questions about working often goes a long way to defining what makes one person's life distinct from the lives of other people. A society that denied individuals the right to make decisions regarding those aspects of their working experience would truncate the ability of those people to be responsible authors of their own lives. Indeed, denied these fuller freedoms of labor, citizens would no longer *be* authors of their own lives. Decisions about matters that affect them intimately would have been taken out of their hands and decided for them by others. The evaluative horizons of those citizens would be narrowed by their experience of life under conditions in which those aspects of liberty were denied. Even if people in such a society acquiesced to these restrictions on their liberty, they would not be in position to endorse the rules of their society in anything like a full or robust manner. Freedom of labor, and to use labor in production, is an essential aspect of a social world that encourages citizens to develop and exercise their moral powers of responsible self-authorship.

A similar argument applies to the economic liberties of ownership. It is easy to see why high liberals affirm that a right to own personal (nonproductive) property is important. Ownership rights to such property can provide a person with personal security: citizens with these rights know they can hold something that cannot be taken away from them. Personal property can include vitally human things such as food, shelter, and clothing. Ownership rights in such things can shelter people from domination by others. The ownership of personal property can also serve as an expression of identity: the things one lives with and attends to on a daily basis help provide moorings to people, providing a kind of stability of life experience through time.

However, rights to the ownership of productive property have many of these same features. The ownership of productive property provides security. Ownership of productive property—say, savings in the form of stocks and bonds—provides individuals and families with a measure of independence. (Permitting citizens to hoard cash, while denying them the right to purchase stocks or other securities, would not be a significant concession to the freedom owed to such citizens.) Ownership rights in productive property are not only important for entrepreneurs. Such rights free ordinary, working-class people from forced dependence on the state and its agents. People who have ownership stakes in productive property are by that very fact able to stand on their own feet and make important life choices. Without such rights, people must depend on the decisions of committees or the outcomes of political campaigns. So the independence and security provided by the right to own productive property is not a mere privilege of economic elites: it is a common experience of citizens in societies where such rights of ownership are affirmed.

Further, just as personal property can be bound up with one's identity, for many people the ownership of productive property plays a profound role in the formation and maintenance of self-authored lives. Sometimes the identity-casting relationships people have to productive property are conspicuously material: as with the way a farmer identifies himself with his field, or the owner of a small business identifies with her shop and its customers and employees (for example, Amy of Amy's Pup-in-the-Tub).

Other times the identity-casting role of ownership is more intellectual, or activity based. Successful investment bankers, for example,
often take an almost professorial approach to their study of financial
trends. Through the roles they play as buyers and sellers of productive property, such people often *become* diligent researchers, creative
analysts, and fiercely independent ("contrarian") thinkers. This is
true of entrepreneurs in other fields as well.

None of this is to deny that people are motivated to work by financial rewards. But rights to the ownership of productive property are
significant to people for reasons that go far beyond the prospect of
personal wealth. Societies that protect the private ownership of productive property as a basic right increase the range of projects, and
the forms of economic relationships, that are available to citizens.[52]
Such societies broaden the evaluative horizons of citizens. The economic liberties make it possible for citizens with diverse values and
interests to more fully develop and exercise the powers they have as
responsible self-authors.

Economic liberty can enhance the freedom of citizens on the output, or consumer, side as well. Many people define themselves by
the financial decisions they make for themselves and their families.
Should everyone in our family pack their own lunches this week so
that we will have money to go to a movie or restaurant together next
weekend? Is it more important to provide our children with separate bedrooms or to add money to college savings accounts opened
in their names? What percentage of my earnings should I spend on
living now, and what percentage should I save for retirement and for
my end-of-life care? Should I take advantage of a sale to purchase a
new television or should I build up my savings in case I lose my job?
How much should we spend on sport, or on home entertainment, or
on culture, or on education, and over what time frame?

Questions about long-term financial planning require that people
think seriously about the relation between the person that each is at
that moment to the person one will become many years in the future.
They call on people to take responsibility now for the person each
will later become. The taking up of these responsibilities is a pas-
sageway from the dependence of childhood (or late adolescence)
into the more challenging and independent world of adulthood.
On Rawls's description, we must respect citizens as beings who are
"capable of adjusting their aims and aspirations in light of what they

can reasonably expect to provide for." Economic decisions call on people to do just this. Such decisions require that people assess their most basic values and, in light of that assessment, set themselves on a course of life that is their own. Economic liberty protects these important aspects of responsible self-authorship. Indeed, among the most important protections needed by responsible self-authors are those that empower individuals to act and to make decisions about the economic aspects of their lives.

Charles Murray writes eloquently about the satisfaction ordinary people gain from work. Paralleling Rawls's discussion of self-respect, Murray says that people need to feel that the things they are doing with their lives are *important*. Murray criticizes the model of the European social democracies on these grounds. Programs for the universal provision of social goods "take the trouble out of life." In doing so, Murray worries, the model "drains too much of the life from life." As a result of one hundred years of economic growth, Murray says that a central problem faced by most citizens in advanced societies is not a lack of material resources but the problem of "how to live *meaningful lives* in an age of plenty and security."[53] By insulating people from economic risks, the European model denies ordinary citizens opportunities to feel the special sense that they have done something genuinely important with their lives. The material benefits of social democracies come with a moral opportunity cost.

Murray describes a man who holds down a janitorial job and thereby supports his family (we could as easily imagine a single mother taking on some difficult job). Such people, Murray suggests, are doing something genuinely important with their lives. Regarding the janitor, Murray states, "He should take deep satisfaction from that, and be praised by his community for doing so." If those same people lived under a system in which they were heavily insulated from economic risks, for example, by being assured that they and their children will be well provided for whether or not they themselves contribute, then that status goes away. "Taking the trouble out of the stuff of life strips people—has already stripped people—of major ways in which human beings look back on their lives and say, 'I made a difference.'"[54] The experience of risk seems to be an essential precondition of the sort of self-respect that liberals value.

We should worry about the high liberal platform of economic exceptionalism for all these reasons. A society that denies people the chance to take up questions of long-term financial planning for themselves, or that restricts the ways in which individuals and families can respond to such questions, thereby diminishes the capacity of citizens to become fully responsible and independent agents. So too a society that limits the freedom of individuals to negotiate the specific terms of their employment, or that makes their ownership of productive property subject to calculations about social expediency, no matter how benevolent their intentions in doing so, thereby creates social conditions in which the moral powers of citizens can be exercised and developed in only a stunted way. Just as respect for the freedom and equality of citizens requires the recognition of religious, associational, and intellectual liberty, respect for citizens requires the recognition of economic liberty as well. As a requirement of liberal legitimacy, and to respect the freedom and independence of all classes of citizens, wide-ranging rights of economic liberty should be recognized as among the basic rights of liberal citizens.

When I say that private economic liberties are among the *basic* rights of liberal citizens, I am not suggesting that these rights will play an equally important role in the self-authorship of every citizen. The private economic liberties may be more central to a process by which our pet-store owner, Amy, develops herself as a responsible self-author than they are in the case of our political scientist, Terry. So the exercise of political liberties may be more central to Terry's life than to Amy's, just as religious liberties may be more important to the self-authorship of a practicing Catholic (or a committed atheist) than to a person who rarely thinks of spiritual questions. Rather, in recognizing these rights as *basic*, we affirm them as components of a fully adequate scheme of rights and liberties. As a set, basic rights allow citizens to develop their capacities of responsible self-authorship without requiring that they all conform to any one view of the good life (or even agree about the relative importance of personal decision making in these different spheres of their lives— political, economic, and religious, for example).[55]

This, precisely, is the problem with the high liberal approach. Rawls makes the protection of private economic liberty a political matter, one to be decided by different liberal societies in different ways in light of cultural conditions. Thus "liberal (democratic) socialism" would allow only rights to personal (nonproductive) property, while a "property-owning democracy" would allow (limited) rights to the private ownership of productive property as well. But this way of accommodating the importance of private economic liberty is unacceptable. Like political liberty (and religious liberty), the protection of private economic freedom is a precondition of citizens' extending their evaluative horizons. In seeking the most appropriate specification of the basic rights and liberties, we seek the specification that most fully allows citizens to develop themselves as responsible self-authors and that also displays the respect they have for their fellow citizens as responsible self-authors. As I have argued, private economic liberties have a special role in protecting citizens as they develop and exercise these moral capacities. The platform of economic exceptionalism renders high liberalism a morally impoverished view.

There is an elephant standing within the theoretical framework of high liberalism. For it is not only classical liberals and libertarians who affirm the fundamental importance of private economic liberty. Like most citizens in contemporary western liberal constitutional democracies, I suspect that most contemporary high liberals would affirm a significantly thicker conception of economic liberty than high liberal paragons such as Mill and Rawls. As Jeremy Waldron admits: "nobody these days seriously imagines an economy either at the national or international level in which private property and markets do not loom large."[56] But if left liberals abandon the canonical high liberal platform of economic exceptionalism, they immediately begin moving away from a social-democratic and toward a more market-democratic interpretation of basic rights. In taking those steps, high liberals do not necessarily have to become full-blown libertarians or classical liberals. They might still claim that some aspects of private economic liberty should be splintered off and denied the protection accorded to the other liberal rights. But then they owe us a moral explanation of how any such narrowing of private economic liberty enhances the status of persons as responsible self-authors. There are reasons why such arguments are unlikely to be forthcoming.

First, any proposal to limit core economic freedoms must not run afoul of the basic liberal concern for the self-respect of citizens. Rawls describes self-respect as having two aspects: a sense of one's own value and a reasonable confidence in one's ability to fulfill one's intentions.[57] With respect to that second aspect, left liberals typically hasten to emphasize that it requires that people be given the material means needed to pursue their goals effectively. But, as we have seen, the mere possession of material means is not sufficient: a person's self-respect is diminished if one is not (and so cannot think of oneself as) the central *cause* of the life one is leading. Having others secure them with "material means" could not provide liberal citizens with that form of self-respect.

There is an analogy with feminism. Before feminism brought about the recognition of women as legal bearers of private economic liberties, women were denied essential preconditions of their self-respect. Having others provide them with all the "gilded material means" in the world could not secure that self-respect for them.[58]

Margaret Holmgren argues that people have a fundamental interest not simply in doing well in life (say, in the sense of possessing certain goods) but in doing well *as a consequence of their own activities*. Indeed, Holmgren sees economic agency as a primary good, a precondition of self-respect. Parties in Rawls's original position therefore "would want to secure for themselves the opportunity to advance by their own efforts."[59] As Holmgren points out, recognizing this interest does not require that it always trumps all other interests people have: in situations where people are simply unable to act for themselves, their needs may well be tended to by others without damage to their self-respect. But in the ordinary course of life, she argues, people do have a fundamental interest in seeing themselves as central causes of the lives they are leading. People respect themselves, in part, because of their genuine achievements. Economic liberties protect this fundamental interest.

Moreover, and significantly, Rawls emphasizes that a condition of the first aspect of self-respect—valuing oneself—is that one be esteemed by others. So Rawls's account of self-respect stresses the importance of status, how we think others value us. Regarding this need for status, crucially, Rawls writes: "the need for status is met by the public recognition of just institutions, together with the full and diverse internal life of the many free communities of interests that the equal liberties allow." Thus, *the basis for self-respect in a just society is not then one's income share but the publicly affirmed distribution of fundamental rights and liberties.*"[60]

And so, with respect to the fundamental economic liberties, market democracy again asks: how can individuals have self-respect if their fellow citizens deny them the right to decide for themselves how many hours they will work each week and under what precise terms and conditions? How can they think of themselves as esteemed by their fellow citizens if those citizens call on the coercive force of the law to impede them in deciding for themselves how much (or little) to save for retirement, the minimum wage they may find acceptable for various forms of work, or to dictate the parameters of the medical care that will be available to them?

In emphasizing the importance of economic liberty for responsible self-authorship, I do not deny the other, more instrumental rationales that classical liberals sometimes offer in defense of property rights and other economic liberties. A robust system of economic liberty—regarding ownership and working—can assist people in making the most efficient use of dispersed knowledge for productive purposes.[61] Economic liberties are "enabling devices" that allow diverse social interests to be peacefully coordinated without recourse to coercive, collective procedures.[62] Property rights can provide bases of resistance against corrupt and oppressive uses of political power.[63] The economic liberties are also linked strongly to many other basic rights, in the sense that "blocking them substantially blocks important parts of other liberties that are widely accepted as basic" (for example, economic liberty is linked to freedoms of religion, communication, association, movement, as well as political liberty).[64]

My primary argument for a thick conception of economic liberty, however, is the moral one. Regardless of the orthodoxies we have inherited, open-minded advocates of deliberative democracy should reject the platform of economic exceptionalism. A thick conception of economic liberty is a requirement of democratic legitimacy.

Endings, and Beginnings, Too

John Rawls died in 2002. Eulogies and obituaries routinely mixed moral praise for Rawls's personal and professional character with moral condemnation for those millions of ordinary Americans who continue to resist Rawls's political prescriptions. Martha Nussbaum's eulogy is emblematic. Here are the closing lines:

America has increasingly moved away from John Rawls. Inequalities have grown, and the electorate seems largely indifferent to them. But our own greed and partiality can hardly diminish the virtues of his distinguished work. Perhaps we can regard the occasion of his death as a challenge to look into ourselves and identify the roots of those selfish passions that eclipse, so much of the time, the vision of the general good. Purity of heart would be to see clearly what has blocked that vision and to act with grace and self-command toward the general good.[65]

If we think of high liberalism as an evolutionary end point, these patterns of evaluation are perfectly appropriate. As liberal societies embarked on more market-oriented approaches to social services, the main reaction of thinkers in the high liberal tradition was not to take these developments as spurs to rethink their basic principles. Instead, their reaction was to hold fast to their inherited moral standards and, gripping those standards, condemn the changes as unjust.

Without mentioning America or Britain by name, Rawls tells us that existing property regimes are "riddled with grave injustices."[66] Rawls, again without mentioning names, says: "Because there exists an ideal property-owning system that would be just [the mixed socialist/capitalist regime that Rawls calls property-owning democracy] does not imply that historical forms are just or even tolerable."[67] So too, Krouse and McPherson take pains to point out: "By comparison with either ideal property-owning democracy or ideal democratic socialism, American society is deeply unjust."[68] On the back cover of Rawls's *Justice as Fairness*, we are told "Rawls is well aware that since the publication of *A Theory of Justice* in 1971, American society has moved farther away from the idea of justice as fairness."

No surprises here. After all, the high liberal orthodoxy assures us that a commitment to social justice requires a commitment to one or another left liberal regime type. To move toward Rawls, America would have to abandon the last remnants of its constitutional commitment to private economic liberty and adopt one of Rawls's preferred institutional forms—property owning democracy, perhaps, or liberal (democratic) socialism. Such regime types regard the economic liberties of individual citizens as fundamentally less important than their civil and political liberties. For anyone committed to social justice, political movements away from "social democracy" and toward limited government must be regarded as unjust. There is only one window cut in the high liberal tower. It offers a clear view over the institutional rooftops of left liberalism, as far as the eye can see.

But what if left liberalism is not the *only* way for a community of citizens to express their commitment to live together as "free and equal self-governing agents"? What if such institutional forms are not even the *best* or *most complete* way to realize the requirements of deliberative equality? I believe that it is time (past time) for political philosophers to venture down from their high liberal tower. They should come down not to abandon that tower and the normative standard it represents. Rather, they should come down simply to listen and learn so that when they go back up they might be in a position to rethink. For high liberals, that process may involve thinking the unthinkable not in a practical or strategic sense. Rather, for high liberals the process of thinking the unthinkable means considering the possibility that the basic moral commitments of late twentieth-century liberal philosophers, while undoubtedly high, were defectively narrow.

The twentieth century brought us the flowering of high liberalism. It sought to enhance the substantive worth of people's civil and political freedoms by downplaying the importance of private economic freedom. But observation of people's practical experience of affluence draws our attention to an exciting new possibility. In conditions of affluence, many people seem to find personal meaning in the exercise of their economic liberties. In terms of developing their moral powers of self-authorship, economic liberties have a value that is much like their freedoms of thought and conscience, the political liberties, and freedom of association. This opens the possibility for a realization of liberal justice that is normatively fuller and more ambitious than that of high liberalism. This liberalism is more complete because it honors the importance of economic liberty while insisting that all citizens, especially the least advantaged, share in the bounty of a free society.

Social democracy was the institutional approach favored by left liberal philosophers. But what should we call this new approach, one that might be morally superior to the social democratic one because it also respects the importance of private economic liberty? I call it *market democracy*.

Chapter 4

Market Democracy

The Conceptual Space

Market democracy is a hybrid. It combines insights from classical liberals such as Hayek with insights from high liberals such as Rawls. Like views in the high liberal tradition, market democracy affirms a robust conception of social justice as the ultimate standard of institutional evaluation. Basic rights and liberties in place, a set of institutions is just only if it works over time to improve the condition of the least well-off citizens. Indeed, to be fully just, those institutions must be affirmed because they are designed to offer greater benefits to the poor than any other alternative set of (rights-protecting) institutions.

Like classical liberal views, however, market democracy affirms a thick conception of economic liberty. It sees a wide-ranging right to economic freedom as among the weightiest rights of citizens. As a consequence of the scope and weight they assign to economic freedom, market democratic regime types strictly limit the scope of legislative authority in economic affairs. Instead, market democracy emphasizes the use of markets in pursuit of social goals. Within market democratic regimes, the distributional requirements of social justice are to be pursued mainly through the forces of spontaneous order.

My purpose in this chapter is to map the conceptual space held by market democracy that I've suggested in previous chapters. Now that we have seen some of the gaps in liberal thought that market democracy tries to fill, it is worth specifying exactly what market democracy is.

Market democracy takes a fundamentally democratic or deliberative approach to the questions of social life. There is a formal conception of democracy according to which a society is "democratic" to the extent that all members have an equal share of fundamental political power. On the approach favored by high liberals, however, the very idea of society carries a moral charge. A society is "democratic" insofar as it protects equal political rights and affirms some substantive conception of social equality among citizens.[1] Society, in its moral essence, is not something private—like a web of commitments spontaneously spun by the decisions of self-owning individuals. Webs of private commitments grow as self-authoring individuals interact voluntarily within the framework of public morality. But it is that public framework that defines the moral character of market democracy.

From a market democratic perspective, market distributions are not simply a natural fact: the particular institutions of every society shape the distributions that the markets there produce. Market democracy sees society as a public thing, the basic institutions of which must be justifiable to the people living under them. Persons are conceived not as disconnected happiness seekers but as democratic citizens. They are moral beings with lives of their own to lead who are simultaneously committed to living with others on terms that even the weakest among them can accept. At base, society is a fair system of cooperation among citizens committed to respecting one another as responsible self-authors.

Market democracy sees these moral ideas of society and personhood as the most appropriate basis for politics. Politics is essentially about creating a framework of rules and institutions that allows citizens to carry out their ambitions in ways that respects the freedom and dignity of all citizens, regardless of their different innate abilities and social starting places. A framework respects people in that way when its institutions are designed to enable all citizens to develop and exercise their "moral powers." Those powers involve the capacity people have to become responsible authors of their own lives, along with their capacity to recognize their fellow citizens as responsible self-authors. Committed to respecting the moral powers of citizenship, and conceiving of society as a public thing, market democracy affirms a substantive conception of equality like that first developed in the high liberal tradition.

Fairness sometimes requires more than formal equality. A game of Monopoly in which some players start with substantially larger amounts of money than others would be unfair. The stain of unfairness would not be lifted merely by the formal requirement that once the game began those differentially endowed players must all abide by the same set of rules. High liberals claim that inequalities in people's talent endowments and family situations raise issues of political morality. Market democracy agrees: undeserved inequalities can generate moral claims within politics.[2] A social world in which the ideal of formal equality was fully implemented might nonetheless turn out to be unfair: along with the forms, the facts matter too. This does not require that society somehow seek to prevent those inequalities from arising in the first place. Nor, certainly, does it require that society seek somehow to equalize the holdings of all citizens. But this recognition does require a specific institutional response. In a just society, institutions and rules should be crafted so that whatever broad patterns of inequality emerge reflect our commitment to respecting all citizens as valued members of a cooperative whole.

Regarding justice in holdings, therefore, market democracy affirms the core ideal of social justice as developed by thinkers such as Rawls. A set of institutional arrangements is just only if, after securing basic rights and liberties, any inequalities that emerge from the activities of citizens turn out to be advantageous even to those who have the smallest bundle of goods.

This is the ideal of reciprocity, or what Rawls formulates as his "difference principle." In a social world of this sort all citizens can celebrate the special talents and skills of their fellow citizens. Even the least fortunate know they are better off in this society because of the productive activities of the most talented and fortunate ones. Together they affirm social and economic structures that make possible cooperation of this sort. In such a society, citizens can look one another in the eye as moral equals, regardless of the native endowments and family circumstances that distinguish them. They respect one another as moral beings with the capacity to assess their life prospects and set their lives on courses chosen by each.

Like views in the classical liberal tradition, however, market democracy affirms the economic liberties of capitalism as basic rights. These include weighty rights of working, transacting, holding, and using. Many libertarians ground their concern for economic liberty on some principle of self-ownership; classical liberal thinkers typically defend economic liberties because of their (hoped-for) positive effects on the economy over time. Market democracy, by contrast, sees a moral ideal of society and personhood as the most appropriate foundation for rights. According to market democracy, a thick conception of economic liberty is needed for citizens to exercise and develop the moral capacities they have as responsible self-authors. This is the core idea of market democracy, and we shall examine the moral case for it in a moment. For now, note that market democracy affirms a thick conception of economic liberty as a requirement of democratic citizenship. Market democracy thus occupies distinct conceptual space within the liberal tradition. To carve out the space, let's contrast market democracy with the strict libertarian interpretation of classical liberalism on one side and the social democratic–left liberal position of high liberalism on the other.

Recall the high liberal critique of libertarianism. For high liberals such as Freeman and Rawls the role of democratic government is to maintain conditions for realizing "a moral ideal of persons as free and equal self-governing agents who have an essential interest in maintaining their freedom, equality and independence." Libertarians such as Nozick and Eric Mack, however, reject that master value. They develop a conception of political life founded on the principle that every individual is a self-owner. Owning themselves, people own their labor and their property. Political norms must be built up from those principles of self-ownership. Because self-ownership is their master value, Freeman argues, strict libertarians treat property rights as moral absolutes. Such libertarians thus care more about property than they do about political equality. For this reason, Freeman argues, libertarianism should not even be counted as a properly liberal view.

However, market democracy is not libertarianism. If strict libertarians see property rights as moral absolutes, market democracy does not think of the economic liberties this way. Market democracy sees the economic liberties of capitalism as working along with the other basic rights and liberties, together functioning as a fully adequate scheme of rights and liberties. Fully adequate to what? Adequate to securing social conditions in which citizens with diverse personal interests and values can exercise their moral powers of citizenship.

Liberals have long argued that personal liberties such as freedom of speech may be regulated or limited to ensure like liberties for others and to protect the scheme of basic liberties as a whole. So too, according to market democracy, the basic economic liberties of individual citizens, such as their right to amass private property or to enter into economic contracts, may properly be regulated and limited in order to maintain other basic liberties.[3] Economic liberties have a range of applications, and some parts of that range may be more essentially linked to self-authorship than other parts. The assertion that economic liberties of transacting should be given protection as constitutional rights, for example, might still allow the liberal state a role in regulating dangerous chemicals. The affirmation of a right to occupational choice is compatible with a regulatory framework that imposes workplace safety standards. But with personal speech as with economic contract, attempts by legislative coalitions to limit the freedom of citizens must pass a high degree of judicial scrutiny. As a matter of institutional design, market democracy affirms that a significant range of economic liberty should be constitutionally entrenched along with the civil and political liberties. Such entrenchment, on the market democratic view, is necessary to secure the social conditions in which people can develop the moral powers they have as free and equal self-governing agents.

High liberals sometimes elide the libertarian and the classical liberal positions on this point. For example, Freeman refers to "Rawls's rejection of the libertarian and classical liberal position that *unrestricted* economic freedoms are among the basic liberties."[4] Even if some libertarians do affirm economic freedoms as absolutes, such a position would be unfamiliar to central figures of the classical liberal tradition such as Smith and Hayek. In any case, market democracy does not affirm unrestricted economic freedoms. Market democracy affirms the economic freedoms of citizens as basic and yet "restricted."[5] Economic liberties are not absolutes, nor are they in any sense "more basic" than people's civil and political liberties. Market democracy is a liberal view that sees a thick conception of economic liberty as working along with civil and political liberty as vital components of a fully adequate scheme.

Within the framework of market democracy, economic liberties of holding can properly be regulated and limited to advance compelling interests of the liberal state. Other aspects of economic liberty can be regulated on similar grounds. Unlike strict libertarians, market democrats can join high liberals as well as classical liberal thinkers such as Milton Friedman, F. A. Hayek, and Richard Epstein, who say that the liberal state should be given the power to provide a social minimum funded by a system of taxation. Further, market democracy recognizes that there can be reasonable disagreement about the proper shape of that social minimum (for example, regarding both the type of taxation system and the type of delivery mechanism—on which see below). For that reason, market democrats might join social democrats in affirming that institutional details about that minimum should be left to be worked out at the legislative stage by democratically elected officials. Unlike the social democrats, however, market democrats assert that legislative proposals in pursuit of the social minimum must pass some heightened degree of judicial scrutiny. In their pursuit of social justice, democratically dominant factions cannot be allowed to impose schemes that wantonly limit the political autonomy of citizens in the economic aspects of their lives. Such schemes would disrupt the fully adequate scheme of basic liberties, thus eroding the conditions necessary for the development and exercise of people's moral powers.

Institutionally, market democracy is more akin to the political systems favored by traditional classical liberals such as Smith, Hayek, and Epstein than it is to systems advocated by libertarians such as Nozick and Mack. In their various ways, those traditional classical liberal thinkers argued that the liberal state has obligations that preclude it from giving *absolute* protection of economic liberty—an unconditional right to property ownership, say, and unregulated freedom of economic contract. Classical liberal thinkers typically saw the liberal state as having a fundamental commitment to protect the religious and political rights of citizens, along with freedom of the press and assembly—rights that citizens were not free to alienate for economic reasons. In the economic realm, classical liberals saw a positive role for the state not just in the provision of public goods proper but also in the provision of a (carefully bounded) range of social service programs. Along with goods such as lighthouses and national defense, classical liberals have traditionally advocated tax-funded support for schooling and a social safety net to assist those most in need. They have also traditionally advocated a restricted role for the state in formulating financial, health, and safety regulations.[6] Some recent thinkers in this classical liberal tradition go further, arguing that the main institutions of the welfare state should be replaced with a direct cash assistance program paid for by taxes (a version of the so-called guaranteed minimum income).[7]

Like social democracy, market democracy affirms a distinction between constitutional essentials (basic liberties) and matters of basic justice. That is, market democracy asserts that the liberal state best pursues the various requirements of liberal justice by means of an institutional division of labor. Some aspects of justice are to be realized by means of the constitutional entrenchment of a set of basic rights and liberties; other aspects of justice are to be placed in the hands of elected officials. However, market democracy demarcates the division of labor in a distinctive way. Unlike social democracy, market democracy emphasizes the importance of economic freedom to the moral well-being of citizens. As made vivid by conditions of affluence that gave birth to the personalized economy, the experience of economic liberty might reasonably be identified as an essential ingredient toward the realization of a Millian ideal of free individuals pursuing their own good their own way. Not all responsible self-authors choose to organize the economic aspects of their lives along the same lines. Restrictions of economic liberty, no matter how lofty the social goal, impose conformity on the life stories that free citizens might otherwise compose. As we will see shortly, this is a central reason why market democracy affirms a thick conception of economic liberty as being on a par with civil and political liberty.

As we have seen, thinkers in the complex and nuanced classical liberal tradition have sometimes done a poor job of explaining exactly *why* they think the liberal state could appropriately enact tax-funded social service programs of various kinds, sometimes saying such programs (but not others) are needed to prevent social strife, or to promote consequentialist values such as economic prosperity. By comparison, the strict libertarian position generates clear lines that many find philosophically satisfying: economic liberties of holding, working, transacting, and using are moral absolutes; the state must enforce any contract that citizens freely devise; taxation to support social service programs is akin to theft.

Why does market democracy insist that economic freedoms should be treated as basic but not absolute? Why does market democracy thus allow taxation in support of a limited range of social service programs? Market democracy affirms these institutional structures as parts of a framework that respects the freedom and equality of all citizens, regardless of social or economic class.

Market democracy, unlike traditional forms of classical liberalism and pure forms of libertarianism alike, is foundationally committed to a robustly reciprocity-based conception of liberal justice. Unlike traditional forms of classical liberalism, market democracy is able to provide a principled rationale for its divergence from pure libertarianism. Let's look more closely at how market democracy generates the boundaries of appropriate state action in economic affairs.

Market democracy attends to what I shall call the *range of self-authorship*.[8] Attention to this range gives us a principled way to pick out political and economic institutions that respect citizens of all classes as free and equal self-governing agents. The idea of a *range* implies a set of parameters, or boundaries, on any candidate set of institutional forms. At points below the lower parameter, we might say, the state intrudes *so little* in the economic realm that the conditions needed for the exercise of responsible self-authorship are not achieved. At points above the upper parameter, the state intrudes *so much* that it truncates the activities of self-authorship. Market democracy identifies just institutions as those that fall within the range of self-authorship.

Consider this range with respect to the economic liberties affirmed by market democracy. At the upper parameter, tax rates and economic regulations can become so burdensome that they impinge upon the responsible self-authorship of citizens. They hinder citizens seeking to carry out economic projects and activities that are central to their life plans. (As we will see shortly, other sorts of government activities, including the service programs of many social democracies, might also truncate economic liberty on this horizon.) At the same time, there is an important parameter at the lower end of the range of self-authorship. Poverty and lack of education may render people incapable of developing their capacities to live as responsible self-authors. In such conditions, a regime that fails to support citizens in times of special need would do too little, and on that ground be unjust. Taken together, these two horizons on the range of self-authorship set principled limits on the redistributory ambitions of the state, while defining a threshold below which no class of citizens should fall.

The parameters of the range of self-authorship can be thought of as existing on a sliding scale. Their placement may vary across different sociological, economic, and cultural-historical settings. The fixing of these parameters across different settings depends ultimately on the account we give about the role of economic liberty in respon-sible self-authorship. We will come to that in a moment. The point here is that the idea of a range of authorship provides another way to understand the distinct conceptual space occupied by market democ-racy. High liberals dispute the placement of the horizon at the high end of our spectrum: they argue that the state should do *more* in the realm of economic distribution, possibly without any limit at all. Lib-ertarians, for their part, dispute the placement at the low end of our spectrum: they insist that the state should have a smaller redistribu-tive role in the economy, or no such role whatsoever.

Out of concern for responsible self-authorship, by contrast, mar-ket democracy insists that lines be drawn on each side. Those two horizons drawn, market democracy occupies the conceptual space in between. It affirms all and only those institutional regimes that seek to create social worlds in which the capacities citizens have for responsible self-authorship—including self-authorship in economic aspects of life—might be exercised and developed.

I began this section by describing market democracy as a hybrid. Our discussion of the range of self-authorship puts us in a better position to understand the depth of this hybridity. A superficial way to create a hybrid might be to combine an institutional view from one school with a set of moral justifications from another. At first glance, market democracy might appear to be hybrid in this sense: market democracy is a "classical liberal" institutional home fit atop a "high liberal" moral foundation. However, market democracy is not a simple-minded attempt to force together the institutional ideals of one tradition and the moral ideals of another, like twisting a square (institutional) peg into a round (justificatory) hole. Nor is market democracy an attempt to defend "right-wing" institutions on the basis of "left-wing" morality. Market democracy is a hybrid in a deeper sense: it is a *justificatory* hybrid. While supporting a broadly classical liberal institutional framework, market democracy combines insights from the classical and liberal traditions *at the level of moral founda-tions.* As such, there is a genuine ambiguity as to whether market democracy is more properly described as a classical liberal view or as a high liberal one.

Throughout this book I have been demarcating various schools of liberal thought in terms of their substantive moral commitments, with special focus on the question of economic liberty. In particular,

I have defined as "classical liberal" those liberal views that affirm a thick conception of economic liberty. Such views affirm a general right of economic freedom as among the basic rights. On this approach, "libertarianism" is one interpretation of classical liberalism, an interpretation marked by the extreme thickness (or absoluteness) accorded to economic liberty. For libertarians, property rights are not simply among the basic rights; they are the most basic of all rights. Views in the "high liberal" tradition, on this schema, recognize only a narrow range of economic decision making as meriting protection as a basic right. High liberals accord the economic rights of capitalism a decidedly secondary place, or reject the idea of capitalism altogether (as with the idealized regime type Rawls defends called "liberal socialism").

If we consider market democracy in terms of its substantive moral commitments, market democracy is a nonlibertarian interpretation of classical liberalism. Unlike views in the high liberal tradition, market democracy affirms capitalistic economic liberties as among the most important rights of citizens; unlike the libertarians, however, market democracy affirms those economic freedoms as on a par with the basic civil and political rights rather than as moral absolutes.

However, there are other criteria by which the various schools of liberal thought might be demarcated, and thus other ways that market democracy might be categorized. Recall that Samuel Freeman, who coined the term "high liberalism," distinguishes schools of liberalism by the nature of their justificatory foundations rather than by their substantive moral commitments. Following Rawls, Freeman interprets traditional classical liberal views as emphasizing economic freedom because they are foundationally committed to maximizing certain values, such as the happiness of citizens. Classical liberalism is based on consequentialism. By contrast, a line of liberal thinking that runs from Mill and Kant to Rawls sees the requirements of public justification, rather than the pursuit of aggregate happiness, as definitive of justice. This is the approach that led Rawls to call classical liberalism the "liberalism of happiness" while referring to his own tradition as the "liberalism of freedom."[9]

Judged by the character of its justificatory foundations, market democracy might reasonably be considered an interpretation of high liberalism. After all, market democracy rejects all versions of the idea that aggregate happiness is the ultimate end of political life. A just society is one whose institutions respect citizens from every social class as free and equal self-governing agents. Market democracy affirms a thick conception of economic freedom, but it does not affirm this conception of economic liberty as a means toward aggregate happiness (as economic freedom might be claimed to do, say, by promoting growth) but as a requirement stemming from its foundational commitment to respect persons as free and equal moral agents: responsible self-authors must be free to make a wide range of decisions in the economic domains of their lives.

Conceived this way, the market democratic approach can claim deep roots in the high liberal tradition.[10] Immanuel Kant is a founding figure of high liberalism, especially if we use that label to describe the moral foundations of his view.[11] Kant's political philosophy, like his moral philosophy, is founded on an ideal of autonomy. Freedom, in the sense of being a chooser of one's own ends, is the fundamental right of every person. By virtue of their common humanity, persons have an equal right to this freedom.[12] But freedom also requires that agents be able to choose the means to their ends. Since we are material beings seeking to exercise our autonomy in a material world, we require "external objects of choice" to pursue our ends. For Kant, secure rights to property emerge as postulates of reason derived from our common nature as independent choosers. Reason also shows that the state is required to convert the provisional rights to property in the state of nature into formal rights backed by law. Property rights, for Kant, are among the most important rights of citizens. Like Mill, Kant is a mixed figure in the history of liberal thought. Because of his emphasis on the moral capacities of citizens and the idea of public authorization of right, Kant can be called an early high liberal. Because of his emphasis on economic liberty and the ideal of formal equality, however, Kant might just as well be described as a classical liberal.[13]

Kant's approach helps highlight the differences between market democracy and the approaches of classical liberals and libertarians working in the Lockean tradition. Following Locke, many libertarians ground property in some concept of self-ownership. On this approach, property rights emerge as a relation of persons to objects in the world; for example, by the process of self-owners mixing their labor with unowned things. Conceived of this way, property rights are strongly prior to the state. The state exists to protect pre-existing rights and so is bounded by those rights.[14]

Market democracy takes a more Kantian approach. Rather than grounding a thick conception of economic liberty on self-ownership, market democracy focuses on the moral ideal of citizens living together as responsible self-authors. Market democracy affirms a wide range of individual freedom regarding economic questions for the same reasons it affirms general liberties with respect to religious and associational questions: a thick conception of economic liberty is a necessary condition of responsible self-authorship. Ownership rights are not so much relations between persons and objects as they are relations between persons as moral agents (Hume likewise thought of property rights primarily as relations between persons).[15] Rights emerge as a social recognition that honoring the capacity of one's fellow citizens to be self-authors requires that one respects fellow citizens' capacity to make choices of their own regarding economic matters. To restrict the capacity of people to make economic choices or, worse, to treat their economic activities merely as a means to the social ends of others, would violate the dignity of such persons and so would be to treat them unjustly. Wide rights to economic liberty, while recognizable without the state, are validated and made fully binding by the political community. For market democracy, the requirements of economic liberty help define the shape and limits of the state, even without being radically prior to it.

Kant's political theory also helps highlight another important difference between market democracy and traditional classical liberal views: while many classical liberals advocate a social safety net funded by taxation, market democracy can provide a rationale for the safety net that is thoroughly principled. (Recall that a rationale for a policy is "thoroughly principled" if the same reasoning that supports the wider features of the view also supports that particular policy.) For Kant, the state exists as a requirement of the free and independent nature of the citizens. As an empirical fact, citizens sometimes fall into conditions of abject poverty. Citizens in that position become dependent on the charity of others and so become unable to participate in the united will needed to authorize public law. Kant advocates a tax-funded safety net: "For reasons of state, the government is therefore authorized to constrain the wealthy to provide the means of sustenance to those who are unable to provide for even their most necessary natural needs."[16]

Market democracy's affirmation of tax-funded social safety net programs follows this pattern. The very status of people as responsible self-authors may be threatened by conditions of extreme need. The state must be empowered to act to protect people's moral status as self-authors. But unlike many traditional classical liberals, market democracy's justification of the safety net is thoroughly principled. After all, the same reasons that market democracy uses to justify the social safety net also justify the market democratic position against the pervasive encroachments on economic liberty allowed by high liberals such as Rawls. Without constitutional guarantees protecting independent economic decision making, people cannot fully exercise their moral powers of self-authorship.

Because I distinguish schools of liberalism in terms of their substantive moral commitments, I think of market democracy as an interpretation of classical liberalism. However, if scholars working in a Rawlsian (or Kantian) framework prefer to classify market democracy as an interpretation of high liberalism, I have no objection. In terms of its substantive moral commitments, we might say, market democracy is classical liberal; in terms of its justificatory foundations, it is high liberal. So market democracy is a hybrid in this sense as well.

Breaking Ice

In chapter 2, I presented a table depicting the major species of liberal thought: classical liberal, libertarian, and high liberal. High liberals see their political view as having emerged through an evolutionary process, a process that demonstrates the moral supremacy of their view. Libertarians and classical liberals, of course, dispute that evolutionary tale. If they do not own themselves, libertarians ask, who does own them? The high liberal suggestion that people should "share one another's fate," or that people should think of their talents as in some sense a common asset, smacks to libertarians and classical liberals alike of a social world in which the talents of some are to be exploited by others. So for their various reasons classical liberals and libertarians consider their moral positions every bit as fit as that of the high liberals. Instead of the high liberal story of evolutionary triumph, a more objective way to describe the state of contemporary liberal scholarship might be in terms of a frozen sea.

Off one coast, we have the two camps of the defenders of private economic liberty: the libertarians and the classical liberals. As we have seen, the distinctive political commitment of classical liberals such as Hayek and Epstein is to private economic liberty. Classical liberals allow taxation to support a limited range of government-provided social goods (education vouchers, a safety net). Their program is based on a conception of the person as a seeker of happiness or utility.

Hunkered down on the ice next to the classical liberals are the libertarians, with anarcho-capitalists such as Murray Rothbard pitching their tents close by. The distinctive political commitment of libertarians is also to private economic liberty, though libertarians tend to treat economic liberties as even more weighty than the classical liberals do ("taxation is theft," they say). Libertarians find their philosophical base in a naturalistic idea of individual liberty or self-ownership.

On the opposite coast, we have the modern or high liberals. This is the comfortable, academically dominant camp. John Rawls is the paradigmatic figure, though if you throw a snowball down the hallway of most any major philosophy or political science department these days you could close your eyes confident that you will hit a high liberal. As we have seen, the distinctive political commitment of high liberals is not to private economic liberty but to social justice. Social institutions should be arranged so as to benefit all members of society, including the poor. High liberals minimize or deny the importance of private economic liberty. After all, such liberties limit the power of government to "spread the wealth around" (whether within generations or between them), which high liberals see as a requirement of social justice. The philosophical base of high liberalism is not a utility seeker or a self-owner but an idea of the person as a democratic citizen. This is a person committed to living with his fellow citizens on terms that all can endorse, regardless of the particular social or economic position each inhabits.

Even this quick topographical sketch can help us understand why the sea between these two coasts thickened and froze. Graduate students attracted to the idea of private economic liberties (wide and powerful rights of private ownership and contract, for example) soon find themselves on dogsleds heading over toward the camps of Hayek and Nozick. As they approach that coast they get to choose whether they are more attracted to Hayekian ends-directed reasoning or the Nozickian foundationalist form. But whichever camp they choose, "social justice" is a phrase they are told they must not speak.

Other students, attracted to the ideal of deliberative justification, find themselves whisked off in the other direction by a high-powered snowmobile. Up, up to the high liberal camp. There they can join the Rawlsians and luck egalitarians such as Ronald Dworkin and the democratic theorists such as Amy Gutmann in warm discussions about the precise nature and requirements of social justice. But in this camp, "private economic liberty" is a phrase only rarely and dismissively heard.

For decades, the residents of these camps have stared at each other across an icy, windswept divide. Occasionally, the defenders of private economic liberty call out to their opponents to abandon the ideal of social justice and come over to join them in affirming one another as self-owners (or utility maximizers). But the advocates of social justice are just as firmly committed to the moral ideal of persons as democratic citizens, beings committed to living among institutions that all might endorse. If they listen to one another at all, neither side is much impressed by the arguments they hear.

Consider the libertarian claim that people are self-owners and the liberal state should protect strong rights of private property and contract for that reason. High liberals reject this premise and conclusion. They ask: Who made the libertarians boss?[17] Property rights are complex, socially elaborated concepts. Whatever scheme of property rights the state enforces, the high liberals say, must be acceptable to all persons making their lives within it. The libertarian's preferred conception of economic liberty may be acceptable to the talented few, but not to the less talented ones against whom it is also to be enforced. High liberals therefore see the libertarian scheme as unjust and illegitimate.

But the libertarian response to the high liberals follows a similar pattern. High liberals argue that the scope and nature of economic liberty should be determined by asking what framework might be acceptable to politically reasonable citizens. But libertarians such as Murray Rothbard ask, who authorized the high liberals to move away from consent to this hypothetical standard of "acceptability"? If people are self-owners, the state is limited to enforcing whatever agreements citizens voluntarily enter into with one another. To enforce a set of rules that limits people's freedom is to treat people and their labor as owned by others. Such a state, libertarians claim, is manifestly coercive and for that very reason unjust.

The groups on the two coasts are anchored to fundamentally different views about the nature of moral personhood. Each knows that the anchors on the other coast are as firmly set as are their own. So for the most part people on both sides just go about their business. They write books and journal articles on topics of interest to others in their own camp; they organize conference panels where they comment on one another's work. But between the two sides, little if anything changes. I call this the *moral status quo*.

Market democracy enters this scene as an icebreaking vessel. Institutionally, market democracy flies the colors of the classical liberal camp. As such, she affirms the basic rights and liberties long championed by liberals of every type: freedom of thought, expression, association, and more. Against the left liberals, though, she also affirms a wide range of private economic liberties—powerful rights of ownership and of individual freedom of contract—as among the weightiest rights. Like traditional classical liberals, she sees the economic freedoms of capitalism as intimately connected to personal freedom: people have a liberty-interest in independent economic activity.

But market democracy has no interest in sitting dock-tied outside the classical liberal camp, locked in wind-worn ice, shouting out arguments across the strait about why high liberals should abandon their camp, trek across the ice, and join those on the other side. Market democracy cares not for "sides." She is a strong-hulled vessel, built to move toward whatever arguments she finds attractive. In terms of fundamental justificatory commitments, market democracy steams away from the camps of the traditional classical liberals, and the traditional libertarians too, rejecting the philosophical underpinning of those views. Breaking a path over to the high liberal side, market democracy affirms the deliberative ideas of personhood and society affirmed by traditional denizens of that camp. Arriving at the high liberal camp, market democracy invites the traditional defenders of high liberalism to look afresh at the moral ideas beneath their own feet.

With the market democratic option before us, debates about private economic liberty and social justice can no longer be scripted as philosophical disagreements about the most appropriate conception of moral personhood. After all, market democracy is based on

Table 2

School	Politics	Reasoning	Person
Classical Liberal	Economic Liberty	Ends-Directed	Utility Seeker
Libertarian	Economic Liberty	Naturalistic	Self-Owner
High Liberal	Social Justice	Deliberative	Democratic Citizen
Market Democracy	**Economic Liberty and Social Justice**	**Deliberative**	**Democratic Citizen**

the same general conception of the person as a democratic citizen affirmed by high liberals. Market democracy urges today's high liberals to examine for themselves certain core assumptions they inherited from earlier, founding figures of the high liberal school. Market democracy appeals to those high liberals in good faith, inviting them to delve more deeply together into the meaning of values they share. As we will see, sincere agreement on the moral nature of political personhood allows for significantly differing viewpoints about the moral valence of capitalism, the requirements of social justice, and about the shape of the liberal state.

Market Democracy as a Research Program

I think of market democracy as a research program. As such, it is compatible with a range of different conceptions of, and approaches to, the democratic ideal of social justice. The exact institutional requirements of market democracy, in turn, will depend on the particular conception of social justice affirmed within the market democratic framework. (To continue our metaphor above: market democracy is not a single icebreaker but a fleet of such vessels, each with a distinctive hull design, a different captain and crew, and, perhaps, its own navigational plan.) I have emphasized one feature that all market democratic interpretations of justice share: they affirm a wide conception of private economic liberties as among the weightiest rights of liberal citizens. But as we have noted, high liberals have widely differing conceptions about the nature and requirements of social justice.

For example, Rawlsians work out justice in terms of fairness; luck egalitarians develop "responsibility sensitive" accounts of distributive justice; advocates of the capabilities approach think of justice in functional terms of people's lived experience. Each of these rival conceptions of social justice generates principles formulated in general terms, so it is possible to interpret the specific requirements of each of these conceptions in a variety of different ways. Because most all these conceptions of social justice have been worked out from a high liberal perspective—that is, a perspective that diminishes the moral significance of private economic liberty—it may seem natural to think the interpretations worked out by the leading advocates of these approaches simply *constitute* those approaches to social justice. Thus whatever range of interpretations of justice as fairness the Rawlsians have worked out ipso facto defines the range of conceptions of justice that may properly be placed under the rubric "justice as fairness." So too with luck egalitarianism, with the capabilities approach, and all the other left liberal approaches to social justice. However, once we see the moral case for including private economic liberties among the basic rights of liberal citizens, we find ourselves needing a broader vocabulary.

I propose that each of the major approaches to social justice developed by high liberals can be interpreted in one of two broadly different ways. On what I will call their *social democratic interpretations*, high liberal theories of social justice are worked out from a starting point that assigns no special weight to private economic freedom. This is the well-worn approach. Thus Rawls, Dworkin, and Nussbaum all have offered what I am calling social democratic interpretations of their respective approaches to social justice. But all these approaches to social justice might instead be given *market democratic interpretations*. From a market democratic perspective, the particular requirements of any given theory of social justice are worked up from a first-order recognition of the moral importance of private economic liberty. As I see it, our profession is rich (surfeit?) with social democratic interpretations of the requirements of social justice. But we are impoverished with respect to the many market democratic interpretations of social justice that might be developed.

Market democracy, as a research program, is neutral as to which approach to social justice is the morally superior one—Rawlsian, luck egalitarian, capabilities-based approaches, or perhaps even republican approaches such as that championed by Philip Pettit. There is nothing inherently incompatible between these forms of social justice and market democracy. Market democracy can accommodate them, and perhaps even make them better. Naturally, people starting from classical liberal premises may develop their own conceptions of social justice—ones based on insights from natural law, for example, or from Hayek's idea of society as a spontaneous order. That suggestion may seem implausible now, but I hope soon to give reason for confidence that classical liberal premises could be used to create a variety of new conceptions of social justice. In every case, the market democratic program insists that interpretations of social justice that emphasize private economic liberties are by that fact morally superior to interpretations of social justice that do not. Any conception of liberal justice that diminishes the agency of individuals with respect to the deeply personal economic choices that structure their lives—whatever its other attractions—is defective from the moral point of view.

Later in this book I will provide a detailed example of how the market democratic research program might look when put into action. Indeed, I will offer a market democratic interpretation of the most prominent and sophisticated high liberal approach to social justice of them all: the approach that Rawls calls justice as fairness. But I will not merely provide a market democratic reading of Rawlsianism. I will argue that my market democratic interpretation of justice as fairness—what I call free market fairness—is morally superior to the social democratic interpretation of justice as fairness developed by Rawls himself.

Although I focus on Rawls, my aim is not to marry market democracy to the Rawlsian program. Far from it. I intend to market democratize the Rawlsian schema simply because, once adjusted to accommodate the importance of private economic liberty and the moral values that attend it, the Rawlsian schema leads to a conception of liberal justice that I myself find most attractive. High liberals fancy their view *Liberalismus sapiens sapiens* and consider traditional classical liberalism a *Cro-Magnon* precursor of their view. Extending the evolutionary metaphor, free market fairness is *Liberalismus sapiens superior*: high liberalism in genetically enhanced form.[18]

Not everyone drawn to the market democratic framework will accept my contention about the moral primacy of free market fairness.

Some will object that Rawls shaves the dice so strongly to the left that his framework cannot provide an ideologically neutral starting place. Others may object to the high degree of idealization of the Rawlsian approach, an approach that allows concerns of practical feasibility to become relevant only at late argumentative stages. Fair enough. Nonetheless, by showing how the leading left liberal theory of justice might be market democratized, I hope to embolden others who, like me, are dissatisfied with the moral status quo. I hope that people who share my twin attraction to economic liberty and to social justice might begin developing their own market democratic interpretations of social justice, and then stand up their own market-democratized conceptions of social justice as rivals to the social democratic views.

Institutions

To continue with our preliminary sketch of market democracy, let me say something about the institutional requirements of this hybrid approach. Following Avner Greif, we can think of an institutional regime as "a system of social factors that conjointly generate a regularity of behavior."[19] Institutions influence outcomes without determining them. I shall outline two regime types that satisfy the moral requirements of market democracy. To prepare the ground for our discussion of specific regime types, I begin by considering the institutional orientation of market democracy, contrasting it with the orientations of high liberalism, libertarianism, and (traditional) classical liberalism.

As we have seen, the institutional orientation of high liberalism is toward expansive governmental involvement in the economic life of the community. High liberals advocate powerful branches of government designed to correct market distributions and, over time, bring those distributions more into line with the requirements of social justice (on their preferred social democratic interpretation of those requirements). Believing that citizens have only attenuated liberty interests in the realm of private economic decision making, left liberals enthusiastically encourage the distributive branches of government to grow. With respect to the distributive requirements of justice, liberal government is like a fruit tree. Only with sufficiently broad and thick distributive branches will there be an adequate supply of fruit to be handed down to the needy citizens. By spreading these branches of government, high liberals seek to promote conditions in which citizens can seek to develop the moral capacities they have as responsible self-authors.

Libertarians and classical liberals, of course, are wary of adding all these branches to the liberal institutional tree. Following Hayek, classical liberals see social resources as growing from the ground up, a result of ambitions and efforts of citizens pursuing diverse life plans on the basis of information available only to themselves. Classical liberals might allow some of these branches. But they regard government planning in these areas as economically inefficient, so would accept such government programs only in heavily pruned form. Libertarians, for their part, might argue that the distributive branches of government favored by high liberals should be lopped off altogether. Only self-owning citizens, freely contracting with each other and devoting their own resources to whatever projects they deemed best, can create a society that is genuinely organic and true.

Institutionally, the market democratic approach is more like that of the classical liberals than that of the libertarians. However, market democracy does not advocate such institutions on grounds of efficiency, utility, or natural rights. Market democracy sees thick economic liberty as among the first-order requirements of democratic legitimacy. Citizens have liberty interests in making economic decisions, especially when those decisions intimately affect the development of their character and the shape of their lives. Fully specified accounts of market democracy would need to distinguish the *core* economic liberty interests of citizens from liberty interests that are more peripheral. Only with a fully specified account in hand could we determine exactly the market democratic attitude toward each of the various branches of government advocated by high liberals (regarding full employment, the price system, the distribution of property, and transfers of wealth and income in pursuit of social justice). The general account I have given so far, though, can take us a considerable way toward this goal.

Market democracy's commitment to thick economic liberty conditions many aspects of market democratic governance. Along with a right to occupational choice, for example, democratic legitimacy also requires that citizens be recognized as holding a powerful set of rights of working. Free citizens of a democratic society must be allowed to employ their own bodies and time in productive activities of their own choice and under conditions they as individuals deem appropriate and reasonable.[20] Along with the right to hold personal property, democracy also requires the recognition that citizens have rights to the private ownership of productive property. Rights of exclusion of that sort are needed for the independence of citizens, freeing them from reliance on the state regarding the provision of their most basic needs. Such rights also empower citizens as "consumers," that is, as adults who set long-term plans for themselves and then live and develop their own characters in light of those goals.

The many branches of government proposed by high liberals, where they are permitted at all, must not violate core economic liberties such as these. The range of self-authorship serves as our evaluative standard here. Each of these branches must do enough to allow citizens the chance to live as responsible self-authors, but without doing so much that citizens find the stories of their lives being written by others, however benevolent or well-meaning those others might be. The history of real democratic societies suggests that this second parameter—the one marking the place where governments infringe upon the economic liberties of citizens by doing too much—most zealously needs to be guarded.

As Freeman correctly notes, an implication of the claim that economic liberties should be recognized as basic rights is that "it limits considerably a liberal society's ability to regulate the uses of property, economic contracts, and business transactions and activities."[21] Equally important, however, an implication of the social democratic claim that economic liberties should *not* be treated as basic is that it considerably expands the economic decision-making power that is placed in the hands of democratically elected officials, simultaneously limiting the freedom of individuals to make choices about those economic aspects of their own lives. From a market democratic perspective, those latter points send up more important warning flares than Freeman's point.[22]

The distinctive tendencies of market democracy can be seen in the way it pursues aspects of governmental activity that are common to all regimes. Thus market democratic regimes may exercise police powers: controlling poisons and dangerous substances; providing genuinely public goods such as military defense and, perhaps, public roads and bridges. But the tendency of market democratic regimes is to look to market-based solutions before turning to simple regulatory ones.

Market democratic regimes (unlike strict libertarian ones) allow the state to create tax-funded safety nets for citizens in great need. Such regimes may even include such guarantees in their constitutional structure. Still, within market democracies the total income of individual citizens and families is mainly to be determined competitively via a price system. In pursuit of equal opportunity, market democracies would very likely include tax-based support for education. But unlike social democratic regimes, market democracies have a principled preference for vouchers and other private-public partnership systems over more uniform, state-run systems of schooling. In pursuit of equality of opportunity, market democracies include an antidiscrimination law. But here as elsewhere, governmental programs are always under pressure to minimize intrusions on the economic liberties of individual citizens, and also on the other rights of citizens. Indeed, as we will see below, market democracies see an antidiscrimination law as a way of enhancing core economic liberties of citizens. Speaking generally, market democracies think an antidiscrimination law should be applied aggressively when it comes to the hiring in the public sector, but less so in the nonpublic domains of economic life.

Market democracy affirms a principle of regulatory oversight. A well-functioning market society needs a strong government not only to define property rights and enforce contracts but also to monitor all sectors of the economy, including the financial industry, to prevent deception and fraud. Market democracies may also allow the state to have some responsibility for setting monetary policy. But here again market democratic regimes see government practices in that area as properly seeking mainly to protect and enhance the value of the market-generated property holdings of citizens. Legislative bodies may enact programs in pursuit of substantive equality with respect to all the rights of citizens—provided, of course, that whatever measures they propose respect the basic rights of citizens, considered as an integrated set. That said, the deep idea of market democracy is to reduce the range of economic activities in which the government in a liberal society would feel any *need* to take a direct and active role.

For example, many workers and employers object to the one-size-fits-all approach of regulations setting minimum wages, limiting working hours, establishing elaborate requirements regarding workplace sanitation, systems of occupational licensure, and so on. Such policies are usually associated with the progressive thinking of the early twentieth century. Many such regulations were first proposed during the era of industrial capitalism. In that era, many citizens saw such measures as vitally important parts of a decent society. Until 1937, the Supreme Court read the Fifth Amendment and the contract clause of the written US Constitution as securing strong rights of economic liberty.[23] To many, that traditional reading of the Constitution tied the hands of well-meaning legislators seeking to limit the number of working hours imposed on vulnerable workers. Within the system of industrial capitalism, workers at the bottom of the economic order, after all, are vulnerable to being exploited by their employers. Decisions individual workers might make to work in certain conditions, at certain wages and for certain hours, might not really be free if, as a matter of practical fact, the only option those citizens had was starvation (or a life of petty crime). Decency required a measure of economic paternalism.

Market democracy is open to allowing legislative bodies to have some ability to regulate work hours/wages/conditions—at least in extreme cases. Workplace conditions that patently threaten the health or safety of workers (or other citizens) can properly be regulated— either under the government's normal police power or as a requirement that the state protect other basic (noneconomic) rights of citizens. But the underlying logic of market democracy runs in the opposite direction from that of social democracy on regulatory issues such as these.

Market democracy sees economic growth as an antidote to the problem of worker vulnerability in postindustrial societies. The relation of workers to employers is dramatically different within the personalized economy than it was during the early stages of industrial capitalism. In the face of an employment offer, or a proposed change in workplace conditions, citizens within a fast-growing market democracy have enhanced power as individuals to bargain for better conditions, or even to walk away. Growth has changed the premises upon which the "economic paternalism" of the early social democratic theorists was based.

The issue of growth provides a marker of the alternative orientation offered by market democracy. Historically, social democrats have been ambivalent (or even skeptical) about economic growth. In the mid-1800s, Mill advocated the ideal of the stationary-state economy. In 1930 Keynes argued that once a certain amount of growth had been achieved, the "economic problem" would have been solved and we should adjust our morals and our political institutions accordingly.[24] Writing in the early 1970s, Rawls also expressed his openness toward regime types that provided slow or no growth. By contrast, market democratic regime types are enthusiastically progrowth. They do not look forward to the earliest day at which the attention of citizens can be reformed and turned away from problems of economic production. Instead, they seek to create social conditions in which economic creativity can be unleashed in the world without any predetermined limit or cap.

Environmental issues sometimes loom behind these disputes about the moral value of growth. Some left liberals view natural resources in essentialist and zero-sum terms. On this approach, the world is said to "contain" a certain quantity of natural resources such that the use of resources by some leaves a diminished store of resources for others. By contrast, market democracy tends to see resources in context-dependent ways. Whether a country should be counted as having many "natural resources" depends on the cultural context. Cultures with easy access to sperm whales were once considered to be richer in natural energy resources than those with petroleum (or uranium) deposits. Further, market democracy emphasizes that property rights typically *increase* social wealth rather than making less wealth available for others. Even with population questions, market democracy offers a different view from the social democratic paradigm. It is fundamental to market democracy to see people not only as consumers of goods but also as producers and innovators. Of course, market democracy advocates economic growth only within the boundaries of long-term environmental sustainability. But here again advocates of market democracy see the facts differently than do advocates of the social democratic no-growth regime types. They see capitalism and environmentalism as standing in a potentially positive relationship to each other.[25]

Market democracy also sees taxation in a different light. Market democracy does not view the tax system as a means for "spreading around the wealth." Speaking generally, it does not view the extraction of wealth from any part of the population with the aim of lessening inequality as a requirement of justice as fairness. The central purpose of taxes is simply to raise revenue for necessary government functions rather than to correct distributions of wealth in accordance with some external standard of justice (say, by leveling down the holdings of the wealthy).[26] In principle, if tax revenues could be raked up off the ground like leaves instead of being extracted from people, market democracy would prefer that method. Of course, market democracy allows that the tax system can be used to ensure that the market functions more efficiently and justly, as when taxes are imposed to internalize externalities (for example, in cases of industrial pollution). Generally, though, market democracy sees the core purpose of the tax system to be that of raising revenues to support governmental programs needed to give substantive value to citizens' rights and liberties (including, as we shall see, to their economic freedoms). Market democracy relies primarily on organic, bottom-up systems—most notably, people's creative uses of their economic liberties. Rather than a fruit-bearing tree, they see government as a framework designed to allow all classes of citizens to benefit from the talents of their fellow citizens.

Market democracies allow taxation for a variety of important purposes, including military defense. But they allow that power only in a tightly constrained way. James Madison proposed that the US Constitution include a provision that would forbid the government from taking on any debt for wartime purposes—believing that politicians should be able to go to war only if they could make the case to the current generation of citizens to pay for that war themselves. Madison's proposal accords with the institutional spirit of market democracy. Market democracy would provide only a limited budget for military matters and a small budget, if any, for foreign aid. This does not mean that market democratic interpretations of social justice generate no duties of international aid: they may very well include such provisions. But market democratic regimes, as is their wont, seek to satisfy these requirements by market-based methods: by advocating free trade zones, for example, and defending the economic liberties of migrant workers. On the international level, to invoke a libertarian epigram, market democratic regimes advocate free trade, free migration, and peace.

In all these ways, market democracy calls for a government of strictly limited economic powers. Market democracy rejects the contention of the early twentieth-century Progressives that the best way for a liberal state to respect its citizens is by systematically insulating them from individual economic decision making. From the perspective of market democracy, the institutions of European social democracy are a gilded cage. Henrik Ibsen memorably described how patriarchal marriage arrangements, while seeming to minister to the interests of women, actually were oppressive.[27] For liberals, what is centrally objectionable about patriarchy is that it inhibits the ability of individual women responsibly to construct lives of their own. Feminist writers of the nineteenth century, such as Angela Grimke and Voltairine de Cleyre, consistently connected the cause of feminism with the ideal of private economic liberty. Patriarchy stunts the capacity women have for responsible self-authorship, especially in the area of economic decision making.[28] Market democracy picks up this feminist insight and applies it against social democracy.

Like a patriarchal marriage, a social democratic society may look benign from the outside and may even offer material advantages from the inside. But liberal justice requires that we put political autonomy first. A reciprocity-based conception of social justice requires that we reject the temptation to trade off the political autonomy of individual citizens for other goods and values—however attractive or pleasant those other values might seem.[29] Liberal justice requires that we ask of any regime: does this regime create the social conditions in which all citizens, viewed as individuals, can exercise and develop the moral powers they have as citizens: the capacity for responsible self-authorship, and the capacity to also respect the self-authoring capacity of their fellow citizens? Justice as fairness, especially through its first principle, requires that the liberal state, in its social-justice-inspired desire to care for its citizens, not step into a patriarchal relationship toward them. In the conditions of affluence that characterize the personalized economy, market democracy may satisfy this standard better than social democracy.

Along with recommending branches of government, high liberals also typically describe a range of institutional regime types—however hypothetical—that might satisfy (their preferred interpretation of) social justice. Rawls's two favored regimes, property-owning democracy and liberal democratic socialism, are both examples of what I am calling social democratic regime types. While providing constitutional protection to widely defined sets of civil and political liberty, such regimes provide little protection to private economic liberty.

Instead, in their various ways, social democratic regime types concentrate economic decision-making power in the hands of deliberative political bodies. Unhindered by strong economic rights held by citizens, those bodies are empowered to enact policies and programs in direct and self-conscious pursuit of the requirements of justice as fairness.

Consider *property-owning democracy*. This quasi-capitalistic political form recognizes some limited rights to the private ownership of productive capital.[30] For example, along with providing a host of state-based service programs, property-owning democracy seeks to equalize property holdings and skill endowments between each generation. It empowers political bodies to enact systems of steeply progressive taxes on gifts and inheritances, and to create and administer a variety of investment programs for the middle class. Fair equality of opportunity is further pursued by an extensive system of state-run schools and, perhaps, by a system of nationalized health care. Property rights are defined primarily by legislatures in pursuit of these goals rather than being constitutionally entrenched and protected by courts as rights held by citizens. Whereas welfare-state capitalism relies upon ongoing transfer programs to redistribute wealth on an annual (or monthly) basis, property-owning democracy aims to equalize property holding between generations. Intergenerational tax transfer programs, along with heavy regulation of the workplace, are perhaps the prime strategies by which property-owning democracies seek to satisfy the difference principle and provide citizens with the fair value of their political liberties. Property-owning democracies also seek to provide citizens with the fair value of the political liberties by nationalizing the funding of political parties. For example, those regimes would strictly limit, or simply forbid, campaign contributions from private individuals or groups. Instead, the state would allocate funds to the political parties out of its tax revenues. Within property-owning democracies, the state would also allocate money to support political speech—perhaps by supplementing, or perhaps simply by replacing, nonpublic media groups.

Rawls provides few details about the regime type he calls *liberal (democratic) socialism*. However, he does claim that democratic socialism realizes justice as fairness. Generally, democratic socialism carries to an extreme the social democratic strategy of social construction. That strategy, as we have seen, is one of removing power from private hands and placing that power in the hands of collective, democratic organs—all while carefully affirming the civil and political freedoms of individual citizens, of course. Under liberal socialism, economic liberties are defined so that all productive capital is collectively owned. Private ownership of productive property is forbidden, or tolerated only in special cases. Worker-managed firms compete with one another within a kind of market socialist economy.[31] Liberal socialism affirms the ideal of the democratic workplace. Decisions about the compensation and benefit packages of workers, as well as investment decisions bearing on the future of the firm, are to be made democratically by the workers. The "economic liberties of socialism" are collective, democratically enacted powers. They are not liberties that protect independent economic decision making by individual citizens.

These are highly idealized political forms. In practice, such regimes would be feasible only in extremely rare cultural and economic conditions—if in any at all. Still it is useful to have these idealized descriptions before us. They provide points of orientation, normative "stars" off which advocates of social democracy can take bearings as they evaluate the actual social orders around them. A fully developed market democratic paradigm would also have need for such idealized types, orienting "stars" of its own, and for similar reasons. What might those different stars look like? What navigational paths might they open for people committed to steering their societies in the direction of liberal justice, even if that means running against the academic headwinds of the day?

High liberals typically distinguish a range of social democratic institutional regime types that might realize justice as fairness: welfare state capitalism and property-owning democracy and liberal socialism, for example. We might think of these regime types as lying on a continuum, with welfare state capitalism allowing the most room for the interplay of free markets, and liberal socialism holding the far "left" end of direct political control of economic affairs. The question of which of these candidate regime types most fully realizes the requirements of liberal justice presumably will depend upon sociological background conditions, such as the stage of economic development of the particular society. In a similar fashion we can distinguish a range of market democratic regime types that might realize justice as fairness (on a market democratic interpretation yet to be offered). Allow me to describe two such regime types. Let's begin with a regime type I call *democratic laissez-faire*.

Democratic laissez-faire is the most thoroughly capitalistic market democratic regime type. Institutionally, this regime type resembles the political structures advocated by libertarians such as Murray Rothbard. Like all market democratic regime types, democratic laissez-faire affirms a wide range of private economic liberties as among the basic liberties of citizens. Its constitution (whether written or unwritten) protects the economic liberties of citizens, along with their civil and political liberties, as basic rights. Laissez-faire capitalism seeks the most completely privatized scheme of education that is possible. To encourage innovation and enhance parental choice, such regimes would allow the state to impose few if any curricular requirements on educational institutions. Such regulations would be limited mainly to the prevention of false advertising, fraud, and protection against clear dangers to public health. Some variants of democratic laissez-faire might permit the liberal state to levy taxes to support a schooling program for children of the most needy. But such state support for education would be seen as a kind of last resort when the rising affluence of the society does not allow every child the chance for a decent education.

Democratic laissez-faire would take a minimalist, "safety-net" approach to other social service concerns as well. Some variants might empower the state to tax people to support health services for the truly poor, or to assist the jobless, and so on. Regarding health care, such regimes might adopt some version of a "defined contribution" plan—whereby the government provides a predefined amount of money to needy citizens that they could use to purchase insurance on an open (read: lightly regulated) market. Regime types of this sort might take a similarly minimalist approach to the legal requirements of equal opportunity. They would apply an antidiscrimination law to hiring by state agencies. But such regimes would tend not to police the policies of private firms, relying instead on market pressures to seek out and reward people in appropriate ways. If democratic socialism represents the height of skepticism about market mechanisms (and of optimism about political decision making) in pursuit of liberal justice, democratic laissez-faire marks the high point of optimism about market mechanisms (and skepticism about political decision making) in that regard.

A second market democratic regime type is what I call *democratic limited government*. Also enthusiastically capitalistic, this regime type allows a greater degree of direct government intervention in economic affairs. Institutionally, democratic limited government resembles the policies advocated by classical liberals such as F. A. Hayek and Milton Friedman. Legally, it bears some similarity to the constitutionalism of the United States prior to the revolution in jurisprudence that accompanied the New Deal.

Like all market democratic regime types, democratic limited government affirms a wide range of private economic liberties as among the basic liberties of all citizens. Regarding education, democratic limited government emphasizes diversity, experimentation, and parental/familial choice. Unlike democratic laissez faire, however, this regime type accepts that substantial and ongoing state funding may be necessary to make those educational choices real. There is a continuum by which democratic limited government might allow tax-funded support for education: from a tax credit for tuition payments, to a safety-net voucher program, to a universal voucher program. Democratic limited government may allow the state to impose some accreditation requirements on schools, and may make room for curricular requirements (for example, in the area of civic education).

Regarding the requirements of formal equality of opportunity, democratic limited government applies an antidiscrimination law more widely than democratic laissez-faire. This regime type would allow such laws to scrutinize hiring decisions by business, for example, and in the real estate and banking sectors. While such laws might be said to restrict the economic liberties of some (say, the freedom of bankers to make loans according to whatever criteria they choose), democratic limited government sees such laws as protecting more core economic liberties (such as the liberty of people to pursue a profession, start a business, or purchase homes).[32] Regarding the provision of social services, democratic limited government shares the preference of democratic laissez-fair for private market-based approaches. The constitution of democratic limited government regimes may include a safety net in the form of a minimum income. Such regimes might also allow the state to provide needy citizens with predefined grants to be spent on health insurance (this against the background of a genuinely competitive market for such products). Instead of the range of state-based social services provided by social democracies, these regimes might even adopt plans such as the one proposed recently by Charles Murray. On Murray's plan, the state would pay an income to every citizen *instead of* constructing an elaborate public system for poor relief.[33] Regarding monetary policy, democratic limited government is typically committed to some fairly hard form of currency, and perhaps to a policy of expanding the money supply at a slow, fixed rate.

Like the regime types of social democracy—liberal socialism, for example, and property-owning democracy—democratic laissez-faire and democratic limited government are idealized types. They are not complete descriptions of any recommended political regime. Any society that sought to emulate these forms would need to fill in many important details. The normative analysis of these regime types that we conduct in later chapters similarly will require that we develop this preliminary account. Still, like the sketch of social democratic regimes that high liberals such as Rawls provide, it will be useful to have this sketch of democratic regime types before us. For now, this sketch will serve as a kind of mental marker for the institutions of market democracy.

The Challenges to Market Democracy

The market democratic research program is likely to face objections from both the left and from the right. Traditional thinkers from both sides may be skeptical of market democracy's ambition to combine economic freedom and social justice. High liberals, for example, may be skeptical of the depth of market democracy's commitment to social justice. Market democracy's affirmation of a thick conception of economic liberty, in their view, *rules out* a commitment to social justice. After all, respect for the private economic rights of citizens would significantly curtail the power of the state to enact the regulatory and redistributive programs long associated with left liberalism. Without such regulations and programs, small numbers of people might establish themselves as private economic czars, leaving many citizens destitute and politically disempowered. Under these conditions, many free and equal citizens would be unable to achieve economic independence and so be unable to pursue a wide range of reasonable life plans.[34] Unlike the institutions favored by high liberals, the institutional forms of market democracy *allow* significant violations of liberal justice. This is a powerful and familiar worry about enthusiastically capitalistic social ideals. Call this the challenge from the left.

Libertarians and traditional classical liberals also will likely object to market democracy, but for very different reasons. While perhaps applauding market democracy's defense of thick economic liberty, these thinkers will object to market democracy's commitment to social justice. Social justice requires that the talents and abilities of some be unjustly harnessed for the benefit of others. Further, the pursuit of social justice is incompatible with the ideal of society as a spontaneous order of free citizens. Even if it could be shown that market democratic regime types can realize the requirements of social justice (say, as a matter of ideal theoretic analysis), these thinkers will want to know why they should care about social justice in the first place. Call this the challenge from the right.

The rest of this book elucidates the market democratic framework by taking up these challenges. Before we begin, however, there is a problem that must be faced. Debates between advocates of economic liberty and advocates of social justice often slip between different levels of argumentation. As with many debates on political topics, objections based on purely moral grounds are routinely blended with more practical objections of feasibility. Sometimes this is done strategically, as when partisans evaluate their own preferred institutions solely in terms of the good those institutions intend to achieve but evaluate rival institutions by pointing to the practical difficulties those regimes face. To avoid such difficulties, I distinguish three levels of political argumentation (there may well be others, but they do not concern us here). I call these three levels *political philosophy*, *political theory*, and *public policy*.

By *political philosophy*, I mean a level of purely moral discourse about political questions. This is the level at which one focuses narrowly on the task of *identifying* the morally appropriate standard for the evaluation of a society's basic institutions. The task of political philosophy is to move from some very general ideas about the moral nature of persons and society to a determinate set of principles of justice. That set of principles may admit of more than one (just) interpretation. In that case, part of the task of political philosophy is to identify that range of just interpretations. Political philosophy also includes the project of identifying a range of institutional regime types that strive to bring about and sustain the social conditions in which those principles of justice could be satisfied.

Political philosophy identifies conceptions of justice and sets of regime types that realize the conditions set out in those principles. The conclusions reached at the level of political philosophy need not be completely permanent or timeless. Developments in human genetic engineering, or other very radical changes in technology for example, might someday require a rethinking of even the very general moral ideas upon which conclusions reached on this level are based. But political philosophy reaches out in the direction of the permanent and the timeless. Findings here represent our best philosophical attempt to identify the standards and institutional regimes of justice.

By *political theory*, I mean not a level of moral identification but one of regime *advocacy*. This is the level of argument at which one says which broad type of regime one thinks is most likely to most completely satisfy the moral standard identified at the level of political philosophy. One makes this determination in light of one's evaluation of the economic, social, and historical conditions of some society (or set of societies) viewed in a long-term or epochal way. Political theory begins by attending to the principles of justice and the range of morally permissible candidate regimes as identified at the level of political philosophy. Then, in light of a broad-gauged evaluation of social conditions, one advocates some particular candidate regime type as being most likely to actually satisfy the (broad-gauged) requirements of justice. At the level of political theory, feasibility concerns are increasingly brought in, but still only in a very general way. When we advocate one or another type of political regime— say, liberal (democratic) socialism or democratic laissez-faire capitalism—as the appropriate goal for some particular society, or set of societies—say, for the United States of America, or for the set of Western liberal constitutional democracies—we are operating at the level of what I call political theory.

Note that this distinction between political philosophy and political theory allows for the carving out of a third level of political argument, a level we might call public policy. *Public policy* is the level at which, within the regime type adopted at the level of political theory, and guided by the moral principles identified at the level of political philosophy, one decides which particular laws, regulations, and public initiatives one ought to pursue. Political philosophy is the level of identification. Political theory is the level of advocacy. Public policy, we might say, is the level of *campaign*. Public policy, to be done responsibly, requires that one make recommendations (or offer normative evaluations) of near-term political questions. In doing this, one is guided by the norms identified at the level of political philosophy, but one also must consider the full range of feasibility constraints described, say, in the literatures of economics, sociology, history, institutional theory, and more. Public policy, as I mean that term, is the argumentative level at which we might offer normative evaluations of recent political trends within actual societies. Compared to political philosophy, public policy is an enormously complex, multidisciplinary task.[35]

To fully exposit market democracy and explain its relevance to any actual liberal society or set of societies, we would need to work across all three of these argumentative levels. Only then might we hope to be in position to discharge the responsibility that many people think makes normative political thinking fully worth doing in the first place: the responsibility of giving normative guidance to citizens in real societies who seek to navigate their societies into the safe harbor of justice. This would be a complex, multidisciplinary undertaking. I have neither the space nor the competence to discharge that responsibility in this book.

Further, as I have emphasized, I see market democracy as a research framework. My contention is that the central moral claim of market democracy—that thick economic liberties are among the basic rights of liberal citizens—might be grafted onto any of a range of prominent "left liberal" accounts of social justice. From there, detailed market democratic interpretations of those theories of social justice might be developed and then stood up as moral rivals to the social democratic interpretations with which we are all so familiar. Or so I contend.

A complication here is that prominent accounts of social justice such as the ones I have mentioned—Rawlsian, luck egalitarian, capabilities-based, for example—have typically been worked out at a variety of levels of political argumentation: political philosophy, political theory, public policy or, often, unsettled mixtures of these three. Indeed, even people working in the same school sometimes disagree about which level of argumentation is the most compelling or appropriate one upon which to exposit their view. Anyone wishing to work within the market democratic paradigm must keep this complication constantly in mind. If we are to track the best work that has been done by high liberals in developing their theories of distributive justice, we must be prepared to move with them to whatever level of argumentation is required in order to make the market democratic challenge stick.

To make market democracy attractive, we next address objections from traditional classical liberals on the one side and from traditional high liberals on the other. In particular, we need to show traditional left liberals that they can maintain a commitment to social justice even while coming to accept the moral importance of thick economic liberty. Caring about the poor, and insisting that social institutions be arranged so as to maximally benefit them, is compatible with defending the private economic freedoms of one's fellow citizens. Just as important, we need to show people already committed to private economic liberty that they have no reason to fear or object to the imperatives of distributive justice. In the next chapter, I take up that latter task, seeking to make social justice attractive to classical liberals. I then turn to the high liberals, beginning with a theory of social justice that many of them already find attractive, and then proposing a market democratic interpretation of that theory I hope many of them will recognize as morally more attractive still.

CHAPTER 5

Social Justicitis

The Distributional Adequacy Condition

Opposition to social justice is a fixed premise of the classical liberal and libertarian traditions. This arc of opposition runs from Hume, to Hayek, to Nozick and beyond. In Hume's classic statement: "Render possessions ever so equal, men's different degrees of art, care, or industry will immediately break that equality. Or if you check these virtues, you reduce society to the most extreme indigence; and instead of preventing want and beggar in a few, render it unavoidable to the whole community."[1] Hayek argues that "justice" applies only to the products of deliberate human will. A free society is a spontaneous order rather than a made thing: distributions emerge as a product of human action but not of human design. Within the context of a market society, Hayek says, the phrase *social justice* "does not belong to the category of error but to that of nonsense, like the term 'a moral stone.' "[2] Nozick advocates "historical" principles of justice and rejects Rawls's theory of justice for being "patterned." Goods come into the world morally attached to producers. Attempts to impose patterns violate liberty. Indeed, Nozick rejects the whole "redistributive" approach to justice: "There is no more a distributing or distribution of shares than there is a distributing of mates in a society in which persons choose whom they shall marry."[3]

Orthodox libertarians stand on solid ground when they reject social justice. If the foundational principles of libertarianism (self-ownership, say, or some principle of natural liberty) generate unassailable rights to property, then taxation of that property in pursuit of the distributional requirements of social justice is unjust. Indeed, the very positing of distributional patterns as requirements of justice is a moral error.[4] Libertarians may reluctantly accept talk about distributive justice in a derivative sense: whatever distributions emerge from market-based procedures might be called "distributively just."[5] Further, as Loren Lomasky notes, libertarians might allow informal uses of the term to refer not to what people are obligated to do politically, but to what it might be good or praiseworthy for them to do. But in no case can social justice play the role of a final, process-independent standard of evaluation that might justify the coercive use of state power toward some distributive goal. As Lomasky puts it, "ideals of 'distributive justice' have no political standing."[6]

As noted earlier, traditional forms of classical liberalism have often been presented with less philosophical consistency than have recent expositions of libertarianism.[7] As a result, the logical disposition of classical liberalism toward social justice is also less clear. Unlike the deductive chains that bind libertarians to a rejection of distributive justice, the chain connecting classical liberals to that conclusion has a number of weak and uncertain links. When they object to social justice, classical liberals often slip between different argumentative levels—sometimes basing their objections on practical worries about the pursuit of distributive ideals by direct governmental programs, and other times seeming to base their objections on purely moral grounds. Still, classical liberals have been among the most strident opponents of social justice.

Traditional classical liberals and libertarians oppose social justice so strongly that their reaction seems almost biological. From the market democratic perspective, many defenders of private economic liberty suffer from a malady that I shall call *social justicitis*. *Social justicitis*, as I use that term, refers to a strongly negative, even *allergic*, reaction to the ideal of social or distributive justice.[8] For libertarians, given the foundationalist biology of their view, arguments on behalf of social justice may be as threatening as a bee sting is to some people: a direct and mortal threat to the heart of their system. However, the anatomy of classical liberalism is more complex.

Within systems of classical liberal thought, social justicitis typically begins as an adverse reaction to talk about social justice at the level of immediate political practice that I call public policy. This is no surprise; within actual political campaigns, demands for social justice have long served as attacks upon private economic freedom. After securing a foothold in the realm of public policy, however, the malady quickly infects the whole classical liberal scheme. It spreads next to the level of regime advocacy that I call political theory, and unless it is arrested there, it soon masquerades as a reason for classical liberals to reject the ideal of social justice at the identificatory level of political philosophy.

There is a difference between the strains of social justicitis afflicting libertarians and classical liberals. This difference is important to the development of market democracy, as we shall see later in this chapter when I argue that classical liberals, at least, should embrace the idea of social justice. First, though, I would like to address libertarians and classical liberals as a group. By doing so, I hope to soften up the opposition to social justice within both camps. Few classical liberal or libertarians have adopted "Social Justice!" as a slogan, or rallied beneath banners emblazoned with its distributional demands. Yet the idea of social justice, or something very like it, has long played a quiet role in defenses of classical liberalism and libertarianism alike.

Most all prominent classical liberals and libertarians share a curious feature: while rejecting the idea of distributive justice, they defend their preferred institutional forms by predicting that these institutions will produce distributional patterns that benefit the poor. Free market thinkers typically leave unclear what role they see these expressions of concern playing within their arguments. Most often we find these distributional concerns peeking out from the interstices of their official (property-rights affirming) arguments. In making these predictions, however, many classical liberals imply that they accept a further normative idea. That idea, rough and inchoate, is that a system of social and economic institutions is rightly applauded only if that system works to the benefit of the least well-off members of society. A system that does *not* work to the benefit of the working poor is defective from a moral point of view.

Of course, one can express a concern about the shares held by the poor without committing oneself to a full-blown theory of fair shares. It is one thing to claim that some set of institutions benefits the least well-off and applaud that (alleged) fact about those institutions. It is a different thing to say that such institutions are to be applauded because they are intended to benefit the least well-off. And it would be different yet again to assert that institutions are to be applauded only if they are designed to benefit the least well-off for the sake of the least well-off.

There are ways to explain away these expressions of concern. On traditional consequentialist defenses of classical liberalism, for example, economic productivity might well be said to require social stability.

If a predictable effect of the operation of the system of natural liberty is that the poor will be benefited, this may head off social unrest and other threats to productive stability. The positive distributional effects of capitalism on the poor might be applauded simply on those grounds.

These expressions of concern for the poor might also be explained away by libertarians. The justification for the system of economic freedom rests atop the principle of self-ownership. Will this system tend to be beneficial to the poorest class? Most advocates of the system of natural liberty say it will. But they tend to mention this prediction merely as a happy aside. The claim that economic freedoms predictably benefit the poor is merely a buttressing argument. A system that benefits the poor is not something we are required to secure for people as self-owners.

Still, for reasons that remain undertheorized, I believe that many thinkers in the free market tradition rely on the claim that the program of economic freedom and limited government benefits the poor. They need this claim to do some additional, independent justificatory work in support of their ideal of limited government. By considering the patterns of predictive claims classical liberals and libertarians make, we find clues about moral commitments that float in the background of their official argumentative positions. Whatever their official positions, thinkers in the free market tradition often employ predictions about the beneficial effects of capitalism as though they were something very like a necessary condition for defending classical liberalism at all.

Many classical liberal and libertarian thinkers implicitly accept some version of what I call *the distributional adequacy condition*. According to this condition, a defense of any version of liberalism is adequate only if it includes the claim that the institutions being endorsed are deemed likely to bring about some desired distribution of material and social goods. That desired distributional standard might be expressed in *egalitarian* terms: the distribution must be expected to satisfy some criterion about the relative holdings of citizens, where some equalizing of those shares is taken to be desirable. Alternatively, that standard might be expressed in *sufficientarian* terms: the distribution must work out in such a way that every citizen (or class of citizens) holds some target bundle of real goods, regardless of how the size of that bundle compares to those held

by others. Some authors appear to endorse a distributional requirement in *maximizing* terms: a market-based set of institutions is recommended because, compared to alternative sets of institutions,
market-based institutions are expected to produce the largest real
bundle of goods for the poor over time. Or, slightly differently, the
institutions of laissez-faire are recommended because they maximize
the expected utility of all citizens. Other times, these distributional
concerns are expressed in capabilities-based terms: free market institutions are recommended because they are expected to bring about
conditions in which citizens can develop their (diverse) functional
capabilities. Many times, classical liberals appear to endorse a distributional adequacy condition that blends more than one of these
distributional ideals. Speaking generally, though, many classical liberals and libertarians do endorse something like the distributional
adequacy condition: a set of political and economic institutions, in
order to be fully justified, must be expected to work to the benefit of the least well-off. And classical liberals and libertarians do
this even while loudly claiming to reject any ideal of distributive
or social justice.

This chapter begins by tracing a line of concern for the poor that we
find running though the classical liberal and libertarian traditions.
Part of my goal here is simply to gather normative materials that we
might use in later chapters to indicate how the market democratic
affirmation of thick economic liberty might be made compatible with
a wide variety of approaches to distributive justice. By showing the
diversity of the distributional concerns that appear across the free
market tradition, I hope to make plausible my suggestion that market
democracy is above all else a general research program: it is not wed-
ded to any particular account of democratic justice. Market democracy's foundational commitment to thick economic liberty allows it
to remain eligible (and, I hope, attractive) to a wide range of distributional suitors. Let's begin.

Hit Parade: Property and the Poor

According to John Locke, the great end of government is the securing
of people's right to property. Locke says that the state's protection
of property rights encourages the productive possibilities of human

creativity, since "labor puts the difference of value on every thing." Locke believed that inequalities in material holdings could be justified by the different degrees of industry of self-owning persons. But from the earliest stages of his argument, Locke expresses concerns for the material well-being of all citizens—the most fortunate and the least fortunate alike. Locke says that an effect of the operation of his property-protecting political scheme is that under it, even the poorest will do well. Thus "a day labourer in England," Locke tells us, "feeds, lodges and is clad" better than a king in America—that is, a (naturally bountiful) place where this system is not fully in place.[9]

But this is proto-Rawls. The "day labourer" in seventeenth-century England was indeed "the representative member of the least well-off class." Locke is taking care to point out that even the least well-off wage laborers will fare better in this system than in other systems. After all, what if the class of day laborers were *not* made better off under Locke's preferred scheme? What if they grew steadily and precipitously worse off? Would Locke just say: Too bad? Natural rights carry foundationalist justification, so are issues of material well-being thus mere sidebar niceties? In a world where the facts on the ground were such that gains to the wealthy came only with losses to the poor, it seems doubtful that Locke would expect his argument about the importance of property rights to convince anybody. A system that predictably produced such effects could not plausibly be said to make good on Locke's ideal that people be treated as free and equal children of God. Nor would such a system be likely to win people's consent.

Locke's sense of the importance of a positive material outcome for the poor explains his need to carve out moral permissions in the cases where the expectation of well-being is not realized. Thus Locke writes, "common Charity teaches, that those should be most taken care of by the Law, who are least capable of taking care for themselves."[10] Locke returns to this theme in an often-quoted line from the *First Treatise*: "As Justice gives every Man a Title to the Product of his honest industry and the Fair acquisitions of his Ancestors . . . so Charity gives every Man a Title to so much out of another's Plenty, as will keep him from Extream want, where he has no means to subsist otherwise."[11] Locke takes pains to point out that the political system he recommends can be expected to work to the benefit of the working poor.

Bernard Mandeville is best known for his disquieting suggestion that even the most vicious forms of vice and greed could result in positive cooperative outcomes, if only those vices would be properly channeled. In his early satirical poem, "The Grumbling Hive" (1705)—which would later provide the core for *The Fable of the Bees*—Mandeville suggested that private vices could lead to pubic benefits, at least when vice is by justice "lopt and bound." Yet Mandeville took pains to point out that the commercial system he favored worked to the material benefit of the least fortunate. More, Mandeville claims that his preferred market-based institutions maximized the benefits to the least well-off working class. Mandeville wrote: "THUS Vice nurs'd Ingenuity, / Which join'd with Time and Industry, / Had carry'd Life's Conveniencies, / It's real Pleasures, Comforts, Ease, / To such a Height, the very Poor / Liv'd better than the Rich before, / And nothing could be added more."[12] Compared to other possible systems, Mandeville claims, market society *maximizes* the benefits to the least well-off class.

Adam Smith's concern for the laboring poor was central to his attack on mercantilism. Under mercantilism, the politically powerful were able to craft highly specific rules and regulations that enabled them to maintain or even extend their advantaged positions.[13] In this way the mercantilist system exploited the poor and fixed people in their classes. As Smith put it, "It is the industry which is carried on for the benefit of the rich and the powerful, that is principally encouraged by our mercantile system. That which is carried on for the benefit of the poor and indigent, is too often, either neglected, or oppressed."[14] By contrast, Smith argued, the open market system of natural liberty benefited the least well-off and allowed for more social mobility. Indeed, Smith was so concerned to demonstrate the positive effects of commercial freedom on the poor that contemporary critics such as Robert Malthus criticized him for not differentiating between the wealth of nations and "the health and happiness of the lower orders of society."[15] Smith cares *too much* for the working poor.

It is possible to read Smith as expressing a concern for the material well-being of the poor out of simple prudential grounds. After all, as Smith notes, "Servants, labourers and workman of different kinds, make up the greater part of every great political society."[16] Perhaps Smith mentions the positive material effects of his system on the poor simply to demonstrate that no great problems of social unrest need be worried about from that direction. But Smith's writings often suggest that he devotes so much attention to the question of how the system of natural liberty will affect people's material holdings for moral reasons of reciprocity. Society is a cooperative venture. The wealth enjoyed by any individual is in part made possible by the actions of all the others. This gives every citizen a moral claim to consideration when questions of material distribution arise. As Smith puts it: "It is but equity, besides, that those who feed, cloath and lodge the whole body of the people, should have such share of the produce of their own labor as to be themselves tolerably well fed, cloathed and lodged."[17] This may not quite reach the ideal expressed by the early Rawls of citizens' being committed to "share in one another's fate," but a moralized idea of reciprocity is working in the background in Smith's arguments.[18]

We find concern about patterns of material outcomes in the work of the American founders, such as James Madison. Americans typically see a concern for the material well-being of the poor as a recent development in American history. On this view, founders such as Madison had a quaint but simple faith in property rights as bulwarks against tyranny. The naive and unscientific application of the Lockean ideas of the founders, however, rendered America an increasingly class-riven and undemocratic society—an error of navigation that was at last identified by Progressive thinkers and then acted upon by FDR's New Dealers and later progressives (now with a small "P"). But Madison's views were more Lockean, and in that sense more materially egalitarian, than this story suggests.

Madison is sometimes accused of acquiescing to a rigid form of material inegalitarianism. In his early writings, Madison apparently accepts the idea that there will always be two great classes in America, one wealthy and one poor. Madison's acquiescence to class-based inequality is often said to be revealed most clearly in his account of how liberal property rights can be reinforcing of democracy. By accepting secure, government enforcement of property rights, Madison argued, the poor can reassure the wealthy that the core of their wealth will not be confiscated through majoritarian measures. The wealthy, with their elite status thus secured, will be more likely to participate in popular government of the sort demanded by the less well-off—rather than using their economic power to subvert democratic self-government. With members of the wealthy class participating in democratic processes, the poor in turn have reason to participate as well—rather than breaking off into open class warfare. Secure rights to property are thus justified in terms of their tendency to support democratic self-governance, an argument run against a background acceptance of a society divided into classes.

Significantly, however, Madison defends the economic liberties laid out in the US Constitution in terms of the benefits of those liberties to the least well-off members of society. Madison thought the Constitution, with its system of dual and divided sovereignty and thick economic liberty protected by the state constitutions, would make possible a strongly commercial society. Commercial society, unlike a mercantilist one, would encourage a great dispersion of property ownership across the entire population. So Madison defended strong rights to private productive property not only because of the ameliorative effects of rights with respect to class-based threats to democratic processes.[19] Just as important, Madison defended property rights in terms of the direct material benefits of such rights to all members of society, rich and poor alike. As Stephen Holmes says, on Madison's view, property rights "are productive not merely protective; they contribute to overall prosperity, enhancing the well-being of *the poorest members of the community*; with economic growth, the proportion of property owners in the population will increase."[20]

Madison's argument about the productive, material egalitarian effects of property rights is no mere aside or throwaway. Taken by itself, Madison's argument that property rights bring opposed class interests into democratic equipoise would make little sense. Democracy assumes equal moral standing of participants. The great language of the founding documents all advert to that deep ideal. This is why Madison *combines* the productive with the protective justifications for property rights the way he does—rather than simply setting forth the protective, class-balancing considerations. Madison sees himself as working out the political and institutional implications of the grand phrases of equality that framed the Declaration and the Constitution.

For Madison, it was obvious that a concern for political equality within the classical liberal tradition required a concern for the material holdings of all members of society. Indeed, Madison noted with approval the widespread sentiment that American institutions favored the poor classes of citizens. Thus: "It has been said that America is a country for the poor, not the rich. There would be more correctness in saying it is the country for both, where the latter have a relish for free government; but, proportionally, more for the former than the latter."[21] Madison defends the American system on the grounds that it is designed to be *especially* advantageous to the poor.

If classical liberal luminaries such as Locke, Mandeville, Smith, and Madison accept something like a distributional adequacy condition, why do classical liberals get such a bad rap with respect to their concern for the poor? It is probably Herbert Spencer's fault. Spencer speaks with contempt of louts who hang about tavern doors, who fight with and seek to cheat one another, refuse to take work of any kind, instead stealing the wages of their own wives for drink. Regarding such people, Spencer asks: "Is it natural that happiness should be the lot of such? Or is it natural that they should bring unhappiness on themselves and those connected with them? Is it not manifest that there must exist in our midst an immense amount of misery which is a normal result of misconduct, and ought not be dissociated from it?"[22]

It is true that Spencer thinks that in every type of society there would be dishonest, violent people who refuse to work or care even for themselves. When dealing with such people, Spencer thought there could be no social remedy but prison, or slow dissolute death. But on this point Spencer's position is much like that of mainstream high liberals—even if Spencer's language is more colorful. Rawls, for example, accepts that even a "well-ordered" liberal democratic society will include people he calls "politically unreasonable." Among the politically unreasonable, presumably, will be people we might call "economically unreasonable." Such people make economic demands on their fellow citizens, the force of which they would refuse to recognize if made by their fellow citizens against them. Thus high liberals typically deny that surfers (or other less romantic, chronically nonproductive people—say, adult, full-time surfers of the World Wide Web) have a right to be clothed, housed, provided boards (or bandwidth), and fed. Surfers who make such demands, like Spencer's tavern louts, effectively deny the equality of their fellow citizens. They seek to use the state to harness the talents and efforts of their fellow citizens for their own ends, while refusing to allow their own talents to be made use of in any socially meaning-ful way.[23]

Like Locke, Spencer acknowledges that there would be different degrees of industry and talent among the ranks of normal industri-ous people, and that material inequality would be a natural result. Intriguingly, though, Spencer is sensitive to the modern liberal dis-tinction between hardships that result from people's choices and hardships that result from bad luck. He writes: "Accidents will still supply victims on whom generosity may be legitimately expended. Men thrown upon their backs by unforeseen events, men who have failed for want of knowledge inaccessible to them, men ruined by the dishonesty of others, and men in whom hope long delayed has made the heart sick, may with advantage to all parties be assisted."[24] It is not always clear what role Spencer sees for the state in such cases, and it would be prochronistic to label Spencer a "luck egalitarian." Still, Spencer is clearly concerned about the distribution of goods that would likely emerge under the free market institutions he endorses.

Despite his reputation for disregarding the poor, Spencer does not justify the classical liberal society in terms of benefits to the suppos-edly deserving wealthy. Instead, Spencer advocates liberal institu-tions in terms of the material benefits he predicts that system will provide to *all* the members of the society—at least all those who were nonviolent and willing to work. In a fascinating exchange with the socialist H. M. Hyndman, for example, Spencer says the system of individual economic freedom is justified because of its benefits to the poorest workers. Regarding Hyndman, Spencer writes: "Many things he reprobates I reprobate just as much; but I dissent from his remedy."[25] Concerning the obligations of society to the least well-off members of the working class, Spencer agrees with the broad aims of the socialists. His difference with them is primarily about means, not ends.[26] Spencer too endorses something like a distributional ade-quacy condition.

The list goes on. During the Progressive era, Ludwig von Mises complained that advocates of the New Liberalism "arrogate to them-selves the exclusive right to call their own program the program of welfare." Von Mises calls this "a cheap logical trick." Just because classical liberals do not rely upon direct, state-based programs and agencies to secure the material well-being of citizens, this does not mean that classical liberals are any less concerned for the poor.[27] In defending his preferred regime of thick economic liberty and strictly limited governmental power, Von Mises writes: "Any increase in total capital raises the income of capitalists and landowners absolutely and that of workers both absolutely and relatively. . . . The interests of entrepreneurs can never diverge from those of the consumers."[28] If capitalism benefits the poor not just in real terms but also relative to the wealthy, then capitalism is *especially* beneficial to the poor.

Von Mises is often read as advocating an uncompromising system of individual economic liberty on the basis of a consequentialist claim that such a system maximizes overall productivity. However, notice what Von Mises does *not* say here. He does not say: "Classical liberal institutions generate the greatest aggregate wealth and so, even though such institutions predictably deposit 20 percent of the population in a position of hereditary class inferiority, this is OK." Instead, Von Mises thinks capitalist institutions are justified, at least in part, because he believes the likely outcome of voluntary exchanges under those institutions will be materially beneficial for all citizens. Inequalities are justified, Von Mises seems to be saying, because they work to the benefit of the least well-off members of society (that is, the workers are benefited relatively as well as absolutely). Of course, this is an empirical claim: it might turn out to be true; it might turn out to be false. But to understand the nature of the moral case Von Mises makes for the regime of wide economic liberty, we must consider that he makes that claim. Von Mises accepts some version of the distributional adequacy condition. Indeed, Von Mises is explicit about the justificatory role he sees this playing in this argument. Thus: "In seeking to demonstrate the social function and necessity of private ownership of the means of production and of the concomitant inequality in the distribution of income and wealth, we are at the same time providing proof of the *moral justification* for private property and for the capitalist social order based upon it."[29]

Von Mises emphasizes that humans must always cooperate within the framework of societal bonds. "Social man as differentiated from autarkic man must necessarily modify his original biological indifference to the well-being of people beyond his own family. He must adjust his conduct to the requirements of social cooperation and look upon his fellow men's success as an indispensable condition of his own."[30] In commercial society, no person is an isolated atom. Commercial competition is merely one form of social cooperation. Society, according to Von Mises, is a cooperative venture for mutual gain.

Ayn Rand famously defends a doctrine of egoism. Egoism, as Rand uses that term, is a claim about the grounds of concern rather than a claim about its scope. Rand's ethical egoism is the claim that reasons for actions should be grounded in the self-interest of the agent. Rand understands an agent's self-interest widely, so that her brand of egoism does not rule out a strong concern for one's friends, nor even an attitude of general benevolence to all humankind.[31] (This is why heroes of her novels are depicted as capable of forming intense friendships.) Nonetheless, Rand's egoism serves as a foundation for her defense of a libertarianism that starkly rejects all ideas of distributive justice. How interesting therefore that Rand thought it necessary to pen the following lines: "The skyline of New York is a monument of a splendor that no pyramids or palaces will ever equal or approach. But America's skyscrapers were not built by public funds or for a public purpose: they were built by the energy, initiative and wealth of private individuals for personal profit. And, instead of impoverishing the people, these skyscrapers, as they rose higher and higher, kept raising the people's standard of living— *including the inhabitants of the slums*, who lead a life of luxury compared to the life of an ancient Egyptian slave or of a modern Soviet Socialist worker."[32]

Rand's concern for the material well-being of her least well-off fellow citizens is not merely a concern that such citizens be better off than Egyptian slaves (or modern socialists). Rand takes pains to point out that capitalism is a positive benefit to all who are willing to engage in productive work: "Capitalism, by its nature, entails a constant process of motion, growth and progress. It creates the optimum social conditions for man to respond to the challenges of nature in such a way as best to further his life. *It operates to the benefit of all those who choose to be active in the productive process, whatever their level of ability.*"[33]

In *Atlas Shrugged*, the most productive and innovative members of society, tired of being accused of exploiting others, go on strike. The American economy collapses. Rand's message is that the less talented need the more talented more than the more talented need the less talented. There is no concern for the poor shown in that message. But notice that, as Rand takes pains to show, the strikers only *hasten* an inevitable collapse. In *Atlas Shrugged*, socialist economies have been collapsing long before the book's hero, John Galt, calls a strike. And Rand goes out of her way to show that the people who suffer the most from these collapses are not her heroes (they find ways to make do in any situation), or the well connected (they use their connections to exploit others), but the deserving but less talented members of society.

So, in *Atlas Shrugged*, the bad guys try to exploit Rand's heroes, but Rand makes clear that the innocent poor are the ones who suffer the most as a result. If Rand were utterly unconcerned for the poor, why would she take such great pains to make this point? Is it a mere *reductio ad absurdum*: "I couldn't care less if the poor starve but I know that you socialists do, so here you go?" I don't think so. Even avowedly egoistic defenses of libertarianism recognize the moral imperative that material benefits of social cooperation reach the least well-off class.[34]

For Hayek, recall, the deep justification of property-protecting institutions is that such institutions have the ability "to enhance the probability that the means needed for the purposes pursued by the different individuals would be available."[35] Hayek defends the version of liberalism he prefers because he thinks this system best assures that everyone will possess the material means and enjoy the opportunities that might make their formal rights and liberties valuable.[36] As with Von Mises, Hayek's defense of market-based institutions relies at least partially on an empirical claim. Hayek claims that, as a matter of fact, market-based institutions will have the effect of most greatly improving the chances of all citizens, included the poorest, to achieve their purposes. Whatever truth value one assigns to this empirical claim, it cannot be denied that this claim is central to the moral case for the Great Society that Hayek makes.[37] Hayek too accepts some version of the distributional adequacy condition.

Milton Friedman? Friedman notes that a capitalist society, where people are free to make payments according to product, will be marked by considerable material inequalities. The heart of Friedman's case for capitalism is his belief in the dignity of the individual, a dignity that we respect when we allow people to develop according to their own lights, subject only to the proviso that they not interfere with other free individuals when doing so. However, Friedman claims: "capitalism leads to less inequality than other systems."[38] He often returns to this theme, arguing that "a free society in fact tends toward greater material equality than any other yet tried." Yet Friedman hastens to add that while the liberal may "welcome" this fact, "he will regard this as a desirable by-product of a free society, not its major justification."[39] But what exactly makes this by-product "desirable" and in what sense is a liberal right to "welcome" it? Like many historical figures in the classical liberal tradition, Friedman feels the need to consider the (hoped-for) distributional consequences of his liberal view.

According to Murray Rothbard, "The advent of liberty will immeasurably benefit most Americans." Notice that Rothbard does not claim that a movement toward economic liberty will benefit *all* classes. Strong private economic liberties reduce the ability of politicians to manipulate the market. Such liberties thus force businesses to compete with one another to provide the best goods at the lowest prices to consumers, rather than competing with one another by manipulating the political process. So, while the defense of economic liberty will benefit most people, Rothbard says some will assuredly lose: "those who have been feeding at the public trough." He continues: "And these special interests and ruling elites will not surrender their ill-gotten gains so readily. They will fight like hell to keep it. Libertarianism is not a message of treacle and Camelot: it is a message of struggle."[40] Libertarianism is a struggle on behalf of the weak against the interests of insider elites.

Robert Nozick provides a broadly Kantian defense of libertarian rights. A political community that violates libertarian property rights thereby treats people as means rather than as self-originating sources of ends. But Nozick emphasizes the positive material effects that as a practical empirical matter he predicts will result from the protection of property rights. In the course of his discussion of the Lockean requirement that appropriations must leave "as much and a good" for others—a requirement that Nozick himself amends to say that appropriations must not worsen the condition of others— Nozick enthusiastically describes these hoped-for effects:

> It increases the social product by putting means of production in the hands of those who can use them most efficiently (profitably); experimentation is encouraged, because with separate persons controlling resources, there is no one person or small

group whom someone with a new idea must convince to try it out; private property enables people to decide on the pattern and type of risks they wish to bear, leading to specialized types of risk bearing; private property protects future persons by leading some to hold back resources from current consumption for future markets; it provides alternative sources of employment for unpopular persons who don't have to convince any one person or small group to hire them, and so on.[41]

Eric Mack advocates natural rights to property on the basis of what he calls the "self-ownership principle" (or "SOP"). However, Mack puts an interesting twist on this familiar libertarian idea. Describing the attitude of the advocate of SOP, Mack writes: "'I am a friend of markets,' he says, 'partially because I expect markets to work as well as friends of markets expect them to. . . . [But] If markets do fail conspicuously vis-à-vis a given individual in ways that *worsen her position by blocking her from bringing her self-owned powers to bear in the world* that person will have a just complaint under the SOP.'" Mack appears to accept a distributive standard, though one aimed at the negative goal of avoiding situations where the opportunity to develop human capacities is worsened. Indeed, Mack might even be read as affirming the idea, familiar from the high liberal tradition, that the function of the state is to secure conditions necessary to the development and exercise of the moral powers people have as citizens. By emphasizing the importance of "self-owned powers," Mack certainly *tempts* that interpretation.[42]

Richard Epstein makes a concern for the least well-off the centerpiece of his moral argument in favor of classical liberalism over Progressive versions of social democracy (and over property-absolutist versions of libertarianism). Why does Epstein advocate the classical liberal system of thick-but-not-absolute economic freedom? Ultimately, Epstein does so because he believes this latter system will be more robustly positive-sum than any alternative system. "The private voluntary contracts that may result [under classical liberal institutions] are positive-sum games for the parties to them, and whatever harm ordinary contracts of sale and hire wreak upon competitors (and it is real harm, no doubt) is more than offset by the gains to the parties and to consumers. We are all systematically better off, therefore, in a regime in which all can enter and exit markets at will than in a social situation in which one person armed with the monopoly power of government, can license or proscribe the actions of others."[43] According to Epstein: "Competition enhances social welfare." Thus: "For that social reason, and not for any fascination with the 'possessive individualism' that the Progressives denounced, the [system of competition] should be favored and protected while the [system of aggression] is deplored and restricted."[44]

It is not only academics (and novelists) who affirm the distributional adequacy condition. Politicians who staunchly defend property rights often affirm some version of this condition too. Ronald Reagan was famously critical of socialism abroad and of the welfare state at home. Yet Reagan distinguished the aims of those programs, which he claimed to share, from the programs themselves. In a speech given in 1966, Reagan said: "The Great Society grows greater every day—greater in cost, greater in inefficiency and greater in waste. Now *this is not to quarrel with its humanitarian goals* or deny that it can achieve those goals. But, I do deny that it offers the only—or even the best—method of achieving those goals." A better way to fight poverty, Reagan said, was through traditional American ideals of capitalism and enterprise. "Have we in America forgotten our own accomplishments? For 200 years we've been fighting the most successful war on poverty the world has ever seen."[45] Human needs are best met through the actions of ordinary people seeking to make their mark in the world, not by creating new branches of government.[46]

Toward the end of his political career, Reagan gave a speech offering an alternative to Roosevelt's famous "second bill of rights" speech. In that speech, Reagan proposed a renewed commitment to what he called "America's Economic Bill of Rights."[47] Rejecting libertarian absolutism, Reagan noted that the American founders saw economic liberties as being on a moral par with the other traditional rights: "as sacred and sacrosanct as the political freedoms of speech, press, religion, and assembly." Reagan described four economic freedoms: freedom to work, freedom to enjoy the fruits of one's own labor, freedom to own and control property, and freedom to participate in a free market. These rights allow for regulation and taxation of various kinds, but Reagan warned that beyond a certain level taxation and regulation could reduce a people to servitude. Economic freedoms, Reagan argued, "are what links life inseparably to liberty, what enables an individual to control his own destiny, what makes self-government and personal independence part of the American experience."

Naturally, left liberals may be skeptical of some of these expressions of concern for the poor, especially when mouthed by politicians. But I do not call attention to these passages in the hope of convincing people on the left of the hidden humanitarian agenda of the political right. Rather, my aim is to encourage classical liberals and libertarians to reflect upon the pervasiveness of these expressions of concern about distributive outcomes on the part of philosophers (and, perhaps, politicians) whose work they admire.

As we have seen, different thinkers in the classical liberal school regard different patterns of material holdings as meriting applause. What's significant is that thinkers in the classical liberal tradition are nearly unanimous in affirming some version or other of what I am calling the distributional adequacy condition. From their many different perspectives, classical liberals and libertarians converge on the idea that the defense of market society is strengthened by assertions that the institutions of this society are advantageous to the poor.[48]

Classical liberals rarely (if ever) use the language of social justice in describing the distributive benefits of market society. Many were writing before social justice had emerged as a concept, so I am not claiming that these thinkers did affirm social justice (secretly, say). Some of them who were aware of social justice, Milton Friedman for example, explicitly deny that their concerns for the working poor are based on any commitment to that ideal.[49] So when I describe these thinkers as affirming a distributional adequacy condition, we should keep in mind that adequacy conditions come in different strengths. For some, the claim that free market institutions benefit the poor may serve as a necessary condition of those institutions being normatively justified; for others, their benefiting the poor may simply be a condition those institutions must meet if they are to be more fully attractive. Showing that classical liberals *care about* the material holdings of poor citizens (or at least, showing that many of them *claim* to care about that) is different from showing that they think all citizens are *owed* that concern as a matter of social justice. Still, most every journey begins with a first step.

Market democracy applauds these defenders of thick economic liberty. In their various ways, most all these classical liberal and libertarian thinkers recognize a commitment to consider the distributions of shares that they anticipate their preferred political regime would generate across all classes of citizens. In doing so, from a market democratic perspective, these classical liberal and libertarian thinkers come very close to an attractive idea that lies near the very heart of social justice. This is the idea that institutional regimes should be evaluated in terms of the benefits they provide to all citizens subject to them. In particular, institutional regimes should be evaluated in terms of how those systems are expected to affect the interests of the working poor.

Market democracy urges libertarians and classical liberals to embrace this idea. Material benefits that are said to accrue to the poor by the platform of thick economic liberty are not merely buttressing attractions of that system. Nor should those (hoped-for) benefits be boasted about merely for their tendency to support economic productivity or some other aggregative good. Instead, classical liberals should advocate the system of economic liberty *because* that system advances the interests of all citizens, and most notably the interests of the poor. Classical liberals should affirm the condition of material adequacy, that is, as an expression of their commitment to reciprocity. When a set of institutions works to the benefit of the least well-off members of society there is a specific reason that that set of institutions is to be applauded: it is to be applauded for respecting citizens as free and equal self-governing agents, with citizens of every class shown the same moral respect. Classical liberals should be concerned about how the system of thick economic liberty and limited government affects disadvantaged citizens because they should insist that the distribution of goods and opportunities be fair.

As we saw earlier, libertarians and traditional classical liberals tend to reject social justice for different reasons. While libertarians typically reject social justice on deductive grounds: the redistributive requirement of social justice violates the rights of self-owners. The objections put forth by classical liberals tend to be more oblique and varied. Perhaps the most powerful classical liberal critique is that social justice, as a concept, is incompatible with the ideal of a society of free individuals. Put another way, the pursuit of social justice corrodes the spontaneous order upon which a free society depends. Hayek presents the most prominent critique of this sort. He rejects social justice in sharp, uncompromising terms. And yet here, as so often in Hayek's work, there is surprising nuance and subtlety.

Indeed, Hayek's famous defense of spontaneous order illuminates a path toward market democracy.

Hayek's Critique

Through his theory of spontaneous order, Hayek offers the most sustained and prominent classical liberal argument against social justice. Hayek's critique rests on the claim that only products of deliberate human design can be just or unjust. Intriguingly, though, spontaneous social orders of the sort that classical liberals advocate are *themselves* products of deliberate human design. This opens an important pharmaceutical opportunity. Hayek's theory of spontaneous order offers an over-the-counter cure for *social justicitis*. Hayek's theory of spontaneous order offers the beginnings of a distinctively classical liberal conception of social justice: Benadryl for free-marketeers.

Hayek runs his critique of social justice across all three of the argumentative levels we distinguished in the previous chapter. Sometimes Hayek focuses on what he sees as the pernicious tendencies of talk about "social justice" at the level of public policy. In the context of the political debates of his day, Hayek notes that appeals to social justice are enormously effective. "Almost every claim for government action on behalf of particular groups is advanced in its name, and if it can be made to appear that a certain measure is demanded by 'social justice,' opposition to it will rapidly weaken." When invoked in public debates about whether or not to create some new governmental social service program, Hayek complains that the invocations of social justice have an "open sesame" effect.[50]

Other times, though, Hayek runs his critique at a more foundational level. For example, Hayek argues that the term "social justice" is "empty" and lacks "any meaning whatever"—at least within the context of a society affirming traditional liberal values.[51] He compares a belief in social justice to a belief in witches or ghosts.[52] Because of its effectiveness as a cloak for coercion, Hayek asserts, "the prevailing belief in 'social justice' is at present probably the gravest threat to most other values of a free civilization."[53] To talk of justice in terms of social justice is "an abuse of the word."[54] According to Hayek, "the term is intellectually disreputable, the mark of demagogy or cheap journalism which responsible thinkers ought to be ashamed to use because, once its vacuity is recognized, its use is dishonest."[55]

To give the concept of social justice any meaning within a free society one would have to completely transform the social order. To make sense of "social justice," Hayek tells us, we would be required "to treat society not as a spontaneous order of free men but as an organization whose members are all made to serve a single hierarchy of ends."[56] To achieve this transition, central values that formerly governed that society—most notably the value of personal freedom—would have to be sacrificed. Instead of laws taking the form of impersonal rules equally applicable to all, laws would increasingly need to take the form of specific commands issued by authorities on the basis of information only they could be in position to hold. The very form of social order found with the Great Society is therefore incompatible with social justice as a concept. To accept the standard of social justice requires the rejection of the Great Society and its transition into a regime of a very different type. Distributional justice is not the realization of the liberal promise of equal freedom: it is the betrayal of that promise. Let's look more closely at this argument.

Hayek's critique of social justice is based on his idea of order. For Hayek, an *order* is: "a state of affairs in which a multiplicity of elements of various kinds are so related to each other that we may learn from our acquaintance with some spatial or temporal part of the whole to form correct explanations concerning the rest, or at least expectations that have some chance of proving correct."[57] To unpack this idea, let's consider three (admittedly homey) examples: a grouping of sugar crystals, a Lego model, and the collection of items distributed across the floor of a messy child's room.

Consider first a grouping of sugar crystals, say, a cluster of rock candy on a string. Rock candy forms as a result of the molecular properties of sugar (sucrose) and water. When sugar is dissolved in warm water, the lattice bonds of the sugar crystals are broken. The sugar molecules bond to the molecules of water, creating a solution. When the solution is cooled, the solubility of the water decreases and the solution becomes supersaturated. If the cooling is continued, and a host is introduced—say, a stick or a string—the sugar molecules begin to recrystallize on the surface of the host. As the process continues, the lattice bonds of the sugar molecules continue to reform, creating larger and more complex crystals.[58]

Contrast the string of rock candy with another complex structure, say, a Lego model of the Death Star. The Death Star is one of the most complicated of all the models made by Lego Group. The large box contains 3,449 small plastic pieces and an instructional booklet with many painstaking pages of step-by-step construction instructions. The rules are highly specific and a person, or team of persons, must carry out each step precisely as specified. Each instructional step requires that every previous step be completed precisely in accord with the overall plan.

The Lego model of the Death Star and the string of rock candy are both complex organizational structures. Yet each is a product of an importantly different type of organizational process. The bringing together of the Lego parts into the form of the completed Death Star requires the constant application of goal-directed reason on the part of some organizing agent or team of agents (in this case, an agent that is external to the model being constructed). It is that agent's commitment to the end specified in the instructions, and the agent's skill in interpreting and carrying out those instructions, that determines how closely the resulting assemblage of plastic pieces will resemble the picture on the box.

By contrast, the molecular units that are to compose the rock candy crystals are not moved by any unified intentional agent—whether internal or external—according to some overall plan. The crystals are built as a result of the way the particular units react to one another. Those reactions, in turn, are governed only by general rules of molecular motion. No one can know in advance what precise shape the rock candy will take. Unlike the principles governing the construction of the Lego model, the principles governing the construction of the crystals are endogenous or intrinsic. A rock candy crystal is a self-organizing or spontaneous system. The model is *made*; the crystals *grow*.

Of course, not every collection of parts counts as an order in the systems theory sense. Consider our third example, the items on the floor of a child's room. There may be a great variety of things strewn across the surface of the floor: a pajama top, a wet towel, a stuffed toy eel, and a homework assignment (due tomorrow). These items are not fixed in any set places in relation to each other. While the items may often be in motion, there are no rules governing the changes that occur among them. When crossing the room, the boy may kick the eel so that it now rests atop the wet towel. In picking up his pajama top, he may inadvertently nudge the homework assignment so it now rests completely under the bed.

If we knew the exact location of one of the items on the floor (for example, if we knew that the wet towel is now precisely in the middle of the floor), this information would not help us in predicting the locations of the other items around it. Even if we had general knowledge of the causes of change on the child's floor (that the child often walks between his bed and his bulletin board) and were given further pieces of locational information (the pajama top is now adjacent to the damp towel) this would not help us chart the overall pattern, the direction or rate of change, of the items on the floor with respect to the others. These items can meaningfully be picked out as a group—"differentiated," as the political geographers might say. We can distinguish this grouping from other groupings—the collection of items next door on the floor of the boy's (equally) messy sister, for example. But this property does not make the collection of items on the child's floor an order in Hayek's sense. The units of this grouping are not related to one another according to any system of organizing principles, whether intrinsic or extrinsic. This grouping is not an order, whether made or grown, in the system's theory sense. Its existence is merely definitional.

Hayek's critique of distributive justice relies upon a similar set of distinctions applied to human groupings. As mentioned in chapter 1, Hayek distinguishes two great types of social order, and a form of rule or law correspondent to each. To demarcate the two types of social order, recall, Hayek uses the classical Greek terms *cosmos* and *taxis*.[59] He invokes two further Greek terms, *nomos* and *thesis*, to distinguish a type of rule appropriate to the construction of each type of social order.

An "order," in the systems-theory sense that concerns us, is a grouping so arranged that we can use our knowledge of some parts to form correct predictions about the grouping's other parts. Not all human groupings count as orders in this sense.[60] But many human groupings do. Indeed, it is the possibility of orderliness in social life that makes purposive action possible. To satisfy even the simplest of ambitions, humans must consider the nature of the rules that govern and coordinate the behavior of the people in the various social groupings in which they take part. It is our ability to learn which rules are likely to effectively govern the likely actions and reactions of other parts of the system, and to combine our understanding of the operative rules with particular pieces of information held by each of us, that makes even the simplest forms of intentional action possible in the world.

Hayek uses the term *cosmos* to describe a spontaneous order, the social analogue of our collection of rock candy crystals. On the social level, a cosmos is a type of human order that forms or comes to exist independently of any act of human will directed toward that end. Because it was not constructed according to the dictates of any unified will, there exists no single end or purpose the system as a whole must serve.[61]

The form of rule that is distinctive to *cosmoic* structures—a type of rule that Hayek calls *nomos*—reflects this openness about ends. By *nomos*, Hayek means "a universal rule of just conduct applying to an unknown number of future instances and equally to all persons in the objective circumstances described by the rule, irrespective of the effects which observance of the rule will produce in a particular situation." Hayek continues, "Such rules demarcate protected individual domains by enabling each person or organized group to know which means they may employ in the pursuit of their purposes, and thus to prevent conflict between the actions of the different persons. Such rules are generally described as 'abstract' and are independent of individual ends."[62] Nonetheless, the regularities of behavior that characterize the elements of a *cosmos* may make that type of order extremely useful for the diverse purposes of its members. In social settings, *nomoi* function like the rules of molecular chemistry in the case of rock candy.

By contrast, Hayek uses the term *taxis* to describe a made order, the societal analogue of our Lego model. By *taxis*, Hayek means a group of humans brought together into an organizational structure with the aim of realizing some unified, identifiable goal. Hayek calls the distinctive form of rule distinctive to *taxitic* structures a *thesis:* "any rule which is applicable only to particular people or in the service of the ends of rulers." Theses may be general to various degrees and will normally be general enough to refer to a multiplicity of particular instances. As a logical matter, the difference between *nomos* and *thesis* is necessarily one of degree rather than kind. But the distinctive tendency of *theses* is to shade imperceptibly from rules in the usual sense into particular commands.[63]

Within a *taxis*, the knowledge and purposes of the organizer determine the particular shape of the order at any given time. Members of a *taxis* are put in their places and assigned their distinctive tasks in light of the end being pursued by the grouping as a whole.[64] In this sense, a body of *theses* is more like the rulebook in our Lego box, and less like the laws of molecular chemistry.[65]

What type of order is most appropriate for people who affirm the liberal ideals of free and equal citizenship? It would be difficult for those ideals to be realized within nonordered social conditions—the analogue of the items on the floor of the child's room. The literature on "failed states," perhaps, could be read as providing examples of social worlds that fail to count as *orders* in the systems-theory sense. Such worlds lack the predictability of rule-governed societies, whether *taxitic* or *cosmoic*. Investments, whether of capital, time, or even of attention, become problematic in such conditions. Without orderliness, human reason has trouble getting traction in the world. Social change becomes a product of drift and happenstance rather than public reason or, say, mutually advantageous exchange.

For Hayek, the greatest example we have of *cosmos* is liberalism, especially as interpreted within the English and Scottish tradition. In Adam Ferguson's famous phrase: "Many human institutions are the product of human action, but not of human design." The great examples of *taxitic* social order are provided by the socialist states of the twentieth century. Hayek thinks that his arguments against socialism, though, also push against a social democratic interpretation of liberalism, precisely because those institutional regimes have as their goal the pursuit of social justice.

First, a *cosmos* typically can make effective use of more information than can a *taxis*. To pursue a goal by means of a *taxis* organization, the only information that can be utilized in the rational structuring of the relations of its members is information that can be gathered, organized, and acted upon by the directing agency.[66] This directing agency plays a role within the organizing structure of a *taxis* much like that played by a set of fuses (or, in the case of state socialism, perhaps, of a central fuse) within the electrical system of a house. Whatever the other advantages of such organizational systems, the unit-capacity of those organizing elements places a limit on how much information can rationally be put to use within the organization. "The knowledge that can be utilized in such an organization will . . . always be more limited than in a spontaneous order where all the knowledge possessed by the elements can be taken into account in forming the order without this knowledge being first transmitted to a central organizer."[67]

This does not mean that a *cosmos* order will always be more effective than a *taxis*. As Hayek says elsewhere, "It is probably true that, at any given moment, a unified organization designed by the best experts that authority can select will be the most efficient that can be created." But Hayek warns that such a form of organization will not likely remain efficient for long, especially if that initial design is made the starting point for all future evaluations of how the goods might best be provided, and if those initially put in charge are allowed to be the main judges of what changes might be necessary.[68]

Taxitic structures operate under a complexity constraint that is typically more restrictive than that within *cosmoi*. A *cosmos* has no such limiting element. (To adopt the terms of Michael Polanyi, the decision-making structure within a *cosmos* is "poly-centric" rather than "mono-centric."[69]) This information consideration may itself help us determine whether it is best to understand modern society as a whole as a *cosmos* or *taxis*. When we consider a comprehensive system such as a society—a system whose features dramatically influence the life chances of its members—the most important determinant, however, is moral. This moral determinant is derived from the factor that generates that complexity constraint. In deciding whether it is appropriate to treat some society as a *taxis* or as a *cosmos*, we must ask whether it is appropriate to treat all the members of that grouping as though they all shared a single, predetermined goal, a goal that could be in principle knowable in advance of actions undertaken by any of them. We ask, that is, whether it would be appropriate for those people to live their lives within a system of rules that takes the form of particular commands.

In place of the idea of a unified goal or end, Hayek says, thinkers in the liberal tradition treat liberty as the highest value. For Mill, liberty involves people pursuing their own good in their own way. Similarly, Hayek defines freedom as using one's own information in pursuit of one's own ends. The idea that human beings should be allowed to direct their own lives is reflected in the form that rules take within liberal societies. Rather than understanding laws as particular commands issued from authorities in light of their best determination of what immediately needs to be done in order to advance the society toward its given social end, liberals see rules as general multipurpose tools. While a fierce critic of utilitarianism, Hayek's approach remains broadly consequentialist. Rules with an appropriately general form facilitate the creation of an order in which individuals may coordinate their activities. By such coordination, Hayek contended, each might increase the likelihood that his own purposes and ends might be realized.[70]

Hayek writes, "To judge actions by rule, not by particular results, is the step which made the Great Society possible. It is the device man has tumbled upon to overcome the ignorance of every individual of most of the particular facts which must determine the concrete order of a Great Society."[71] This approach to law, because it is impersonal and general, enables each person to act on the basis of information that is often available only to that individual. For this reason the form of social order that values freedom thus turns out to bring about a greater satisfaction of human aims than any deliberate human organization could hope to achieve.

When Hayek says that this system was "tumbled upon," he means that these were discovered through the experiences of countless human encounters rather than being created through some deliberate process. The rules that make up the liberal system did not spring forth ready-made from the mind of any philosopher or from the deliberations of any legislative body, the way the booklet of directions in a Lego box might have been created. Instead, the rules emerged through a process that Hayek describes in evolutionary terms. Hayek says, "The rules of conduct which prevail in the Great Society are . . . not designed to produce particular foreseen benefits for particular people, but are multipurpose instruments developed as adaptations to certain kinds of environment because they help to deal with certain kinds of situations."[72] Hayek likens *cosmoic* rules to a pocketknife. A person setting out on a walking tour may take along the pocketknife not for a particular known anticipated use but because past experience has shown the general value of having a knife along. So too, Hayek explains, "the rules of conduct developed by a group are not means for known particular purposes but adaptations to kinds of situations which past experience has shown to recur in the kind of world we live in."[73]

Because these rules come down to us by an evolutionary process of selection, we often may not be able fully to understand or explain why these rules function well toward the realization of human purposes. These rules come down to us because the group that had them prevailed, but sometimes even the reason why the group originally adopted them and the reason they in fact prevailed may be quite different. "And although we can endeavor to find out what function a particular rule performs within a given system of rules, and to judge how well it has performed that function, and may well as a result try to improve it, we can do so only against the background of the whole system of other rules which together determine the order of action in that society."

Appeals to "social justice" threaten to destroy the fruit of this evolutionary process. State socialism represents the constructivist approach to social rule making in its extreme form. But Hayek sees the European branch of liberalism favored by social democrats as also founded on a commitment to constructivist, rather than evolutionary, forms of rationality. Social justice is a quintessential product of constructivist rationality.

Justice, Hayek claims, applies only to situations that are the product of someone's will. To make sense of the concept of social or distributive justice, the rules governing the Great Society would need to be changed so that resulting distributions could be thought of as being the result of someone's will. A demand for social justice is a demand that the form of social order be changed from a *cosmos* into a *taxis*. The processes of social growth and change in that order would need to be altered so that the society would be less like a growing crystal and more like a model undergoing situation-specific assembly. This change can be effected only by a change in the character of the rules governing the society.[74] General, multipurpose rules need to be replaced by more finely tailored directives. In Hayek's terminology, *nomoi* must be replaced by *theses*. At the level of institutions, this is analogous to a regime in which citizens pursing social construction in light of their constitutional protections becomes replaced by a regime in which citizens pursue social construction by voting for, and following, ever more finely tailored legislative directives.[75]

Hayek thinks liberal democratic states are particularly vulnerable to attacks on freedom via demands for "social justice" at the immediate level of public policy. After all, the appeal to social justice is an appeal to inject human intentionality directly into parts of the social world that stand visibly in need of improvement. It is an appeal for *somebody* to do *something*. However, Hayek says the doctrine of social justice threatens to destroy the very basis of morality itself: gradually at first, but then ever more completely, it replaces the ideal of freedom of personal decision with the habit of dependence upon other people's power.[76] Echoing concerns expressed by David Hume, Hayek writes, "like most attempts to pursue an unattainable goal, the striving for it will produce highly undesirable consequences, and in particular lead to the destruction of the indispensable environment in which the traditional moral values alone can flourish, namely personal freedom."[77]

The pursuit of any distributive ideal runs into a knowledge problem. There are no rules of just individual conduct upon which individuals in a market order might act that might bring about such a (putatively desired) distribution, and thus no way for any of the members of society to know what actions they ought to perform to realize the desired distribution.[78] The only way a society could achieve social justice, therefore, would be for the members of that society to submit to a governmental apparatus that would specifically direct the actions of each so that the desired distribution could be realized and maintained. That apparatus would have to be especially intrusive in the economic dimensions of citizen's lives. In issuing directives to correct for inequalities that would arise between individuals or different classes of individuals, one would have to abandon the ideal of treating all citizens according to the same rules. More important, such a program would substitute a principle of collective decision making for the principle of individuals ordering their own values on the basis of information known only to themselves. This would be to abandon the ideal of personal freedom, which Hayek sees as the very root of liberal morality.

Benadryl for Free-Marketeers

So Hayek rejects the idea of social justice in an uncompromising way. He allows for a social safety net but carefully distinguishes that from any requirement of social justice.[79] Within the liberal world of the Great Society, there is not even conceptual space for the idea of social justice: the phrase *social justice* "does not belong to the category of error but to that of nonsense, like the term 'a moral stone.'"[80] This, or something like it, is what I take to be the standard interpretation of Hayek's attitude toward social justice. The conduct of individuals as they exercise their economic liberties in the marketplace may be just or unjust. But it would be meaningless to describe the distributional patterns that result from market transactions as just or unjust. There is abundant textual support for this interpretation. As Hayek says, justice "clearly has no application to the manner in which the impersonal process of the market allocates command over goods and services to particular people: this can be neither just nor unjust, because the results are not intended or foreseen, and depend on a multitude of circumstances not known in their entirety to anyone."[81]

However, Hayek is a thinker of complexity and nuance. Without denying the force of the consensus interpretation, it is worth attending to some discordant notes within Hayek's writings. These notes open the possibility for a significantly different interpretation about the implications of Hayek's theory of spontaneous order with respect to distributional ideals.[82] Most interesting to us, some of these notes form a pattern, even a leitmotif. When we pick up that tune, we find that Hayek's theory of spontaneous order—despite his protests—positively rests upon some (conceptually prior) distributional standard, a standard like the one an account of social justice typically provides.

First, against the consensus interpretation, Hayek sometimes affirms the cogency of social justice, at least as a logical concept. For example, he tells us that "the benefits and burdens . . . apportioned by the market would in many cases have to be regarded as very unjust if [they occurred as] a result of deliberate allocations to particular persons."[83] Of course, as Hayek emphasizes, in a free society such distributional patterns are not the result of deliberate design, and thus he says the concept *justice* cannot be applied to their evaluation. But what evaluative standard is Hayek invoking when he says that some market distributions, if they had been intended, would be unjust? Hayek's view, it turns out, is not that society-wide distributional patternings are themselves inappropriate objects for evaluation by standards of justice. It is the application of that standard to patternings *that lack intentionality* that he deems inappropriate. So Hayek's argument against social justice rests on his point that, in free societies, intentionality does not seep throughout the system, rather than on the claim that there is no logical space for talk about the justice of distributions of goods across a society.[84]

However, all political orders are the product of human intentionality. To see why, consider our paradigm of spontaneous order, the crystals of rock candy on a string. As the solution cools, crystal facets begin to form according the general rules of molecular chemistry. The particular forms those crystal structures will take are beyond the predictive power of even the most sophisticated scientist. The crystals grow according to their own internal principles; no one controls or intends the precise outcome of that process of growth. And yet at a more general level, human intentionality and conscious design pervade the entire process. After all, some one or some group had to decide to create the conditions in which the candy crystals could spontaneously form. Someone had to mix up and heat the solution of sugar and water. Someone had to cut the piece of string to some desired length, weight one end, attach the other end to a pencil or other support, and then dip the weighted end of the string in. The makers of rock candy are in this way very like the designers of a constitution to govern a liberal society. Even without being able (or seeking) to control the details of the order that will emerge, both sets of orders require a maker, and that maker's intentionality pervades the order that results.

According to Hayek, the rules of just individual conduct that most effectively govern a liberal social order are rules we discover, rather than rules we attempt to create. But this jurisprudential theory—even for those who accept it—does not eliminate the role of intentionality in the formation of social orders. After all, we also discover rather than create the molecular rules governing candy crystal formation. Such discoveries do not eliminate the human intentional element in the case of candy making. On the contrary, it is our discovery of such rules (or our "construction" of them) that gives intentionality its traction in the world.[85]

Experience and observation have taught candy makers that different rates of cooling, and different volumetric ratios of sucrose to water, will tend to produce crystals of different shapes and sizes. Makers of candy know that sugar crystals produced in a spotlessly clean container will tend to be larger than those produced in less clean containers, since in the clean container the molecules reform intensively on the string rather than being dissipated on other microscopic features of the environment. Sophisticated candy makers have learned that by introducing seed crystals to the string they can produce dramatically larger crystals: seed crystals encourage the lattice bonds of the sugar molecules to reform themselves more intensively on the site of preexisting crystals, whatever their size.

It is knowledge of molecular rules that makes human intentionality effective, given some norm that allows us to identify good candy making from bad. This does not require that people micromanage the system in hope of achieving any particular arrangement of molecules. Candy-making standards are formulated in general terms. Candy makers know that large crystals are desirable no matter the particular arrangement of the facets thereon. When they evaluate rival candy-making systems, they prefer those that produce crystals of that sort.

With sugar crystal orders, so too with human social orders: once basic laws are discovered, we employ intentionality to tweak the system to our purposes. In the domain of political institutions, those purposes are defined ultimately by our theory of justice.

Hayek, following Smith, often compares the order of the Great Society to a complex game. But as Hayek notes, we must always seek to control unwanted outcomes "by improving the rules of the game."[86] In Hayek's view, people have consented to retain and agreed to enforce the rules of just individual conduct associated with classical liberalism because they have discovered that following such rules best improves the chances of all to have their wants and needs satisfied. This system has this effect, according to Hayek, because it provides the procedure that makes it most likely that the information dispersed across a society can be harnessed to the benefit of all.

A cost of adopting the classical liberal system, as Hayek emphasizes, is that all particular individuals and groups within the system incur the risk of unmerited failures and disappointments. That cost can never be eliminated, though Hayek emphasizes the importance of our using our reason to minimize such disappointments. "It is a procedure which of course has never been 'designed' *but which we have gradually learned to improve* after we discovered how it increased the efficiency of men in the groups who had evolved it."[87] Whether our aim is to produce larger candy crystals or conditions more favorable to the ideal of greater freedom for all, the designers of orders cannot evade the responsibilities that come with the discovery of their capacity to use their reason to bend spontaneous processes toward human purposes.

Hayek sometimes writes as though the distinction between *cosmos* and *taxis* is an existential distinction. A social order either *is* a *taxis* or it *is* a *cosmos*. Since a *cosmos* has no purpose while a *taxis* has a particular purpose, a social order either has a particular purpose or it has no purpose. On this existential reading, the distinction between *cosmos* and *taxis* is absolute, and there can be no shading or overlap between these two social forms.[88] The consensus reading of Hayek, which sees him as rejecting social justice as a concept, typically rests on some version of this idea.

There is another reading of this distinction, however, that fits better with the deep architecture of systems theory. On this reading, the distinction between *cosmos* and *taxis* is not so much a distinction between kinds of social order, but a distinction between two *strategies* for social construction. Cosmos and taxis represent two different ways of seeking to give traction to normative reasoning in the social world. Viewed this way, Hayek's distinction between *cosmos* and *taxis* should be understood as a contribution to debates among liberals at the level of regime-type advocacy, rather than at the level where liberals identify their deepest normative ideals.

Hayek's neglected essay, "The Confusion of Language in Political Thought," begins with Hayek's familiar description of a *cosmos* as a self-regulating system. The order within such a system results endogenously from the regularities of the behavior of its elements. Those within a *taxis*, by contrast, are imposed by an external, exogenous agency. Regarding that purposive agent, Hayek tells us: "Such an external factor may induce the formation of a spontaneous order also by imposing upon the elements such regularities in their responses to the facts of their environment that a spontaneous order will form itself."[89] Hayek then describes this as an "indirect method" of securing a social order, and he ascribes to it all the moral and informational advantages of *cosmoic* as opposed to *taxitic* social structurings. Crucially, Hayek emphasizes the importance of distinguishing between the spontaneity of the order and the spontaneity of the forms of behavior of the elements within such an order. "A spontaneous order may rest in part on regularities which are not spontaneous but imposed." Hayek concludes, "For policy purposes, there results thus the alternative whether it is preferable to secure the formation of an order by a strategy of indirect approach, or by directly assigning a place for each element and describing its function in detail."[90]

This distinction between "direct" and "indirect" strategies admits many divisions of degree. For example, Hayek believes that a legal order restricted to expositing and enforcing rules of just individual conduct will encourage the formation of a complex social order. By making use of local knowledge, such an order will tend to maximize the freedoms of all citizens (that is, will provide all citizens with their best chance at realizing their goals and ambitions). In some exceptional areas though—such as schooling—Hayek believes that more direct methods will be required to realize this goal of equal freedom for all. In advocating public funding of education, for example, Hayek is advocating *taxis*-style rules by which social resources would be collected and directed to the particular purpose of providing the means for equal schooling for all. Even in such cases, though, there are less direct and more direct methods available. While advocating that the government guarantee that these means be made available for schooling, Hayek expresses his "grave doubts whether we ought to allow government to administer them"—preferring, it seems, some more competitive scheme involving educational vouchers.[91] This accords with the central classical liberal idea that the social rules should encourage the creation of diverse goods (including diverse forms of education) to suit the diverse interests, characters, and values of free citizens. Hayek's master maxim of feasibility seems to be that for both moral and informational reasons designers of legal orders for liberal societies should typically prefer the least direct (or most indirect) methods of realizing their social goals. This maxim guides Hayek to advocate the institutional regime of commercial society at the level of what I call political theory. And it would guide him also when considering various specific public policy options that might be proposed within that type of regime.[92]

On the reading I am proposing, Hayek's rejection of social justice turns out to be primarily an expression of skepticism of the direct, *taxitic* approach to social construction on grounds of feasibility. At the level of political theory, and especially at the level of public policy, Hayek presents his theory of information as giving us reason to be wary of *taxitic* strategies of social construction.[93] But Hayek's famous critique of social justice gives us no reason to object to social justice at the identificatory level of political philosophy.[94] His idea of spontaneous order makes conceptual space for "constructivist" norms to evaluate both the product and the processes of spontaneous orders.

When considering any social system as a whole, *cosmos* and purpose, far from being opposites or antagonists, go together. In the social setting, spontaneous orders seem positively to require such normative evaluations: evaluations, that is, in terms of social justice.

This reading of Hayek makes ready sense of some passages that have long perplexed Hayek scholars (scholars in the traditional "Hayek-rejects-social-justice" school).[95] In the preface to *The Mirage of Social Justice*, Hayek notes that while he was completing his book an important, and seemingly rival, approach to liberal justice had appeared in Rawls's *Theory of Justice*. Hayek tells his readers that he decided not to include an extended discussion of Rawls's theory because, despite what he expects to be the first impression of many readers, the differences between his general conception of liberal justice and that of Rawls are "more verbal than substantive." According to Hayek, he and Rawls "agree on what is to me the essential point."[96] How can this be?

Jeremy Waldron claims that Hayek mistakes a superficial point of agreement between himself and Rawls about justice for a deeper form of agreement.[97] As Waldron notes, Rawls thinks the problem of justice must be approached with a holistic emphasis on institutional structures rather than with an eye on distributive questions taken in isolation. To elucidate this point, Waldron invites us to imagine an occasion in which the economic institutions of some society happened to yield a particular distribution, D1, that is inferior in terms of the difference principle to another particular distribution, D2. Does liberal justice require that we immediately reallocate the wealth so as to achieve D2 (say, by a special tax on the rich)? As Waldron observes, Rawls and Hayek agree that justice, in itself, generates no such requirement. So in this sense they are on common ground. Yet looking deeper, Waldron says Rawls's and Hayek's *reasons* for that conclusion reveal that they hold fundamentally different understandings of the nature of liberal justice.

The reason Rawls does not see justice as generating imperatives regarding the correcting of particular (unjust) distributions springs from his conception of justice as having a holistic application. Confronted with a society characterized by unjust distributional pattern D1, Rawls does not immediately see justice as requiring corrective measures. There may be many considerations, including the requirements of stability and of publicity, that might count against such corrective measures. Yet on Rawls's understanding of the nature of justice, the observation of any particular instance of injustice *would* lead Rawls to ask more general questions about the society. For example, Rawls thinks our commitment to justice would require that we ask how that unjust distribution arose, and then to consider whether the basic structure of the society might be adjusted to make it less likely that similarly unjust distributions arise in the future.

However, according to Waldron, Hayek's reasoning here is quite different. Like Rawls, Hayek denies that liberal justice requires immediate correctives to D1. But this is *not* because Hayek, like Rawls, takes a holistic approach to justice that emphasizes structures and general institutional forms. Rather, Hayek rejects distributive correctives to D1 because Hayek rejects the idea that liberal justice applies to distributive questions on any level, whether regarding particular distributions or social structures taken as integrated wholes. Adopting the consensus reading, Waldron makes this point by quoting Hayek: "justice is not concerned with those unintended consequences of a spontaneous order [such as a market] which have not been deliberately brought about by anybody."[98] The differences between Rawls's and Hayek's understanding of liberal justice are thus substantive indeed.

I suspect that things are more complicated here than Waldron perceives. As we have seen, Hayek—and in this quite unlike Rawls—sometimes asserts that the concept *justice* can be applied only to human actions. His more careful formulations, however, reveal a more nuanced view: "To apply the term 'just' to circumstances other than human actions *or the rules governing them* is a category mistake."[99] If "justice" can be applied not only to actions but also to rules governing those actions, presumably that term can be applied to whole systems of rules—systems such as that given by a constitutional order, whether written or unwritten. This is precisely Hayek's view: "there unquestionably also exists a genuine problem of justice in connection with the deliberate design of political institutions, the problem to which Professor John Rawls has recently devoted an important book."[100] Justice can sensibly be applied to the rules governing a society's basic social and economic institutions. This can be accomplished through an evaluation of the general tendency of the effects of those rules on the social order and the people within it.[101]

At the level of moral identification, Hayek objects to the term "social justice" only when it is used to evaluate particular distributions of goods that happen to emerge within a market society. In rejecting that sense of social justice, Hayek's position is very like that of Rawls. Indeed, Hayek approvingly quotes an early essay of Rawls's on this point. Hayek writes: "the task of selecting specific systems or distributions of desired things as just must be [as Rawls says] 'abandoned as mistaken in principle, and it is in any case not capable of a definite answer.'"[102] So, for Hayek as for Rawls, particular distributions of goods that happen to emerge in a society governed by liberal principles cannot in themselves be described as just or unjust. The justness of a society can be tested only by considering the general distributional tendencies of the social order that emerges within that system of rules.[103]

Hayek affirms that there is a genuine problem of justice in connection with the deliberate design of political institutions. To solve that problem of justice, intriguingly, Hayek developed a decision mechanism that is very like the device that Rawls, decades later, would call the original position. A good society, according to Hayek, is one in which the chance of any person achieving their desired aims is as great as possible. Hayek interprets this to mean that if we were selecting among a range of candidate social systems, the most just system would be the one we would choose to live in if we were deprived of personal information that might taint our choice from the perspective of objective fairness. In one formulation of this idea, Hayek says: "we should regard as the most desirable order of society one which we would choose if we knew that our initial position in it would be determined purely by chance (such as the fact of our being born into a particular family)."[104] Yet Hayek worries that even this test might allow the fact of differing natural skills and talents to influence the fairness of the selection. After all, "the attraction such chance would possess for any particular adult individual would probably be dependent on the particular skills, capacities and tastes he has already acquitted." So Hayek thinks fairness requires that we thicken the information filter on this choice scenario. He does this by suggesting that we should ask which systems would be chosen, not simply by individuals who do not know the place they would occupy, but by representative heads of families reasoning under that same informational constraint.[105]

Rawls, like Hayek, denies that liberal justice properly generates correctional imperatives with respect to particular distributional patterns that emerge as a product of (free) social activity. But Hayek, like Rawls, believes that liberal justice may properly be applied holistically when we evaluate deliberately designed institutions—such as those institutions that support the development of market-based society. In pointing out these very substantial points of agreement between Hayek and Rawls, however, I am not suggesting that remaining disagreements between them about the *particular requirements* of liberal justice are merely verbal. Famously, Hayek never provides a theory of social justice. And, as we will see later, the interpretation of liberal justice that Rawls affirmed (especially toward the end of his career) includes many features to which we can confidently predict Hayek would vociferously object.

Nonetheless, the general point remains. A commitment to the ideal of a free society as spontaneous order is compatible with the affirmation of some external standard of holistic evaluation, including a standard that expresses distributional concerns. Indeed, against the consensus reading, I would even go further in emphasizing the role of social-justice-like concerns within the Hayekian view. Social justice, we might say, gives the Great Society its point. It provides the evaluative standard that allows us to know when the equal freedom promised by liberalism is in danger of being lost and explains to us why that threat is something worth fighting back against. Indeed, for Hayek, we might say, the phrase "The Great Society without social justice" belongs not to the category of error but to that of nonsense. That phrase would make about as much sense as "naturally occurring rock candy on a string."

Hayek does not like the term "social justice." As a matter of practical political experience, Hayek sees calls for social justice as having led to the erosion of personal freedom and to the rise of deadening bureaucracies (not to mention the bundling up of people into the dangerous militarist collectives of "nations"). True to the deep biology of his theory of spontaneous order, Hayek affirms not merely the conceptual coherence of evaluating a liberal society in terms of what Rawls and others refer to as social justice. He also affirms the *moral necessity* of a society's basic institutions passing muster by social and distributive standards.

After all, it is a liberal theory of (social) justice that tells us why we should affirm the ideal of thick economic liberty, and the other general rules of just individual conduct on which Hayek says the preservation of an economically free society depends. Such a theory also tells us which *taxitic* deviations from the model—such as a tax-funded safety net, or special funding for schooling—can be pursued without conflict to our commitment to the ideal of freedom, and which deviations cannot.[106] Whether orthodox libertarians might affirm a similar conception of spontaneous order is a question I leave for others. But classical liberals who follow Hayek can affirm a conception of spontaneous order that makes room for social justice. Recently, leading classical liberals have begun to do exactly that.

CHAPTER 6

Two Concepts of Fairness

Warming up to Market Democracy

Political philosophy is witnessing the emergence of a new form of classical liberalism. For decades left liberal scholars wishing to introduce their students to market-friendly versions of liberal justice could responsibly discharge that duty by teaching a unit on Nozick (or some other prominent post-Rawlsian libertarian). Things have changed. These days, cutting-edge work by market enthusiasts is more likely to come from classical liberals than from libertarians. Indeed, among philosophers, the days of orthodox libertarianism seem numbered. One reason is that philosophical defenses of private economic liberty increasingly make room for moral ideals long associated exclusively with the left, such as the ideal of social justice. Strict libertarianism is biologically averse to such ideals. But classical liberalism, with its longer and more explicit history of concern for the working poor, is congenitally open-minded about distributive questions.

Brink Lindsay and Will Wilkinson, at the time scholars at the Cato Institute, recently created a stir by advocating a fusion of libertarian and left liberal ideas: what they call "liberaltarianism." In a widely read essay, Lindsay describes liberaltarianism as a pragmatic alliance, offered at the level of political discourse that we call "public policy." Lindsay's paper focuses on specific policy issues upon which he believes a political coalition of libertarians and left liberals might be built up. However, Lindsey, like Wilkinson, hopes that "liberaltarianism" might be developed at the deeper argumentative levels that I call political theory (the realm of regime advocacy, recall) and possibly even at the level of political philosophy (the realm of identification). At the close of his article, Lindsay writes: "If a new kind of fusionism is to have any chance for success, it must aim beyond the specifics of particular, present-day controversies. It must be based on a real intellectual movement, with intellectual coherence. A movement that, at the philosophical level, seeks some kind of reconciliation between Hayek and Rawls."[1]

In another popular harbinger of change, Charles Murray, a social scientist and policy analyst at American Enterprise Institute, recently surprised many old-school libertarians by advocating a version of the guaranteed minimum income scheme. The idea of a guaranteed minimum income has recently gained currency with thinkers on the left, who view it as a supplement to existing social democratic programs. By contrast, Murray proposes that the American welfare state be replaced by a direct $10,000 per year income to be paid from a flat tax on incomes.[2] Murray thinks people should be given "seed" money, unconditionally and repeatedly (say, via direct monthly deposits to peoples' checking accounts), all funded by tax revenues. Many people will initially waste those funds. Still, Murray hopes such a system would draw people into the community of economically responsible citizens, people who believe that the American dream applies even to them.

Murray hastens to reassure his readers that he still considers himself a libertarian as a matter of principle.[3] The libertarian solution to poverty and inequality, as Murray says, would be to eliminate transfer taxes and programs completely and let the free market determine allocations. "Leave the wealth where it originates, and watch how its many uses, individual and collaborative, enable civil society to meet the needs that government cannot." Murray says: "If I could wave a magic wand, that would be my solution." The problem, Murray tells us, is that there is no political support for the libertarian solution. Thus he describes his proposal of a guaranteed income as a kind of second best.[4]

We can see the distributional adequacy condition at work in Murray's description of the social effects he expects from libertarianism. What's most interesting about Murray's position, however, is that the rationale he actually gives in support of the guaranteed minimum income scheme is not libertarian. Nor, despite his official pronouncements, does Murray advocate this scheme simply as a matter of political compromise. Instead, Murray advocates a guaranteed minimum income on the basis of the same moral reasons that left liberals use to argue for social justice.

Thus, immediately after conceding the political impracticality of libertarianism, Murray tells us "there is another sticking point for many people with which I am sympathetic: People are unequal in the abilities that lead to economic success in life." In Murray's view, inequalities in wealth that result from people's choices are nonproblematic: responsibility for our choices is an essential part of a free life. If one person freely chooses a life of productivity and another freely chooses a life of sloth, no one can object to the differences in wealth that result. However, echoing the high liberals, Murray notes that "inequality of wealth that is grounded in unequal abilities is different."

Most often, the distribution of natural talents—looks, brains, charm, even industriousness—cuts several ways, so that advantages someone enjoys in one area are balanced by disadvantages in others. But some part of the population, through no choice of their own, predictably ends up being disadvantaged on a number of these dimensions all at once. From this, Murray concludes: "When a society tries to redistribute the goods of life to compensate the most unlucky, its heart is in the right place, however badly the thing has worked out in practice."[5] Murray's objection to left liberalism is primarily an objection to the practical failures of its distributive schemes rather than to the moral rationale for fair distribution. Distribution of goods in society, Murray seems to be saying, should reflect choices people make rather than features about them that result from brute luck. Rather than hewing to orthodox libertarianism, Murray shares concerns with luck egalitarians: just institutions should seek to be choice sensitive and luck insensitive.[6]

While classical liberals are warming to the idea of social justice, many of them remain ambivalent in their embrace. James Buchanan and Richard Epstein argue that anyone who accepts Rawls's original position as an appropriate device for identifying political norms should reach classical liberal conclusions. But neither Buchanan nor Epstein accepts that Rawlsian device. Loren Lomasky posits a twin world containing a Twin Harvard in which a Twin Rawls uses Rawlsian premises to reach libertarian conclusions. But Lomasky's Twin Harvard also contains a Twin Nozick who argues his way from self-ownership to Rawlsian high liberalism.[7] Daniel Shapiro argues that the best way to achieve social justice is by adopting free market capitalism. But Shapiro emphasizes that his own first commitment is to free market capitalism not social justice.[8]

More dramatically, a group of philosophers, many of them associated with the University of Arizona, have begun crafting new forms of classical liberalism, a distinguishing feature of which is an affirmation of left liberal ideals.[9] Against the moral status quo, recall, market democracy questions the idea that the best moral defenses of private economic liberty need to be naturalistic or ends-directed in the ways long assumed by libertarians and classical liberals. Simultaneously, market democracy questions the assumption that the "public reasons" form of political justification long associated with the political left must turn one inevitably toward the support of left liberal political institutions. Instead, the market democratic paradigm sees the ideal of democratic citizenship as leading to a hybrid account of liberalism, one that combines a commitment to private economic liberty with a commitment to a theory of distributive justice. Leading figures in this Arizona School have begun putting meat on these market democratic bones.

In a striking development, Gerald Gaus has broken with traditional classical liberal and libertarian forms of justification. Rather than beginning with an ideal of self-ownership, natural rights, or some conception of consequentialism, Gaus joins the left liberal mainstream in asserting that liberal politics should be based on a conception of persons as free and equal moral agents. He calls this general approach "justificatory liberalism." As Gaus notes, the most prominent formulation of justificatory liberalism comes from Rawls, who uses that approach to defend an expansive understanding of the liberal state. This has led many to assume that the justificatory or, as I prefer, the "deliberative" approach to liberalism leads inevitably toward left liberal political positions. Gaus insists, however, that Rawls's particular formulation of justificatory liberalism is merely one among many possible variants. Gaus revives and remakes a tradition of public reasoning found in Locke, Rousseau, Kant, and even in the new liberal British Hegelians such as Bernard Bosanquet and T. H. Green. Gaus claims that justificatory liberalism, properly understood, leads to classical liberal political institutions.[10]

Gaus's theory of justificatory liberalism is philosophically rich. Indeed, Gaus's theory may be the most important account of public reason since that of Rawls. Since justificatory liberalism does not require literal consent, every account of public reason includes some form of idealization. But, Gaus notes, there are many rival ways to formulate the requirements of public reason. Compared to Rawls's theory, Gausian public reason attends more closely to the diversity of moral and empirical beliefs actually held by the citizenry for whom coercive principles are being designed, even while avoiding populism.[11] Respect for persons requires that coercion be conclusively justifiable to the reason of all citizens, and there is a strong presumption against coercing others. Gaus applies this public reason test to laws (not just constitutional essentials). As a result, the proper test for a law's validity is difficult to meet.

Gaus's theory of justificatory liberalism inclines toward classical liberal political conclusions. Marshaling empirical evidence, Gaus argues that "there has never been a political order characterized by deep respect for personal freedom that was not based on a market order with widespread private ownership in the means of production."[12] Contra Rawls, extensive private ownership of productive property and protection of a wide range of other private economic liberties are requirements for the protection of civil liberties that all liberals hold dear. Significantly, "once an extensive system of private ownership has been justified, redistributive proposals are manifestly coercive."[13] Within the constraints of Gausian justification, many redistributive proposals could not meet the test of public justifiability. While ruling out the aggressively redistributive regimes favored by high liberals, Gaus does not see his conception of justificatory liberalism as leading to a strict libertarian ideal. Nonetheless, the requirements of public justification, and liberalism's principled aversion to coercion, leads to the more moderate positions affirmed by many classical liberals. As Gaus puts it, "justificatory liberalism tilts towards classical liberal positions."[14]

While Gaus's work brings classical liberalism close to market democracy, Gaus does not go all in. Market democracy, recall, affirms a thick conception of economic liberty as a first-order requirement of some broader conception of social justice, a conception that includes distributive imperatives relevant to the goods and opportunities held by members of all social classes. Gaus comes close to this conclusion: "some rights of private property and some redistributive (i.e., welfare) rights are, I think, elements of a publicly justified conception of justice."[15] Gaus's theory appears to justify a social safety net, and possibly more. Nonetheless, Gaus tells us that the justificatory case for property rights "defeats the claim that justificatory liberalism necessarily endorses a strongly egalitarian theory of justice."[16]

Within Gaus's conception of justificatory liberalism, "principles of social justice [are] not stable under full justification."[17]

As we noted, once a thick conception of private economic liberties achieves justification within a market democratic framework, *redistributive* proposals will indeed face high justificatory hurdles. However, affirming government branches designed to redistribute property is quite different from affirming the idea that the basic political and economic institutions of society, viewed holistically, must be arranged to satisfy some distributive criterion (for example, one that attends to the concerns of citizens from all the classes of actual societies about the fairness of the distribution of social goods and opportunities that results from their cooperative activities). It would be interesting to see whether, within the Gausian conception of public reason, full justification could be achieved with respect to any system *without* the inclusion of a holistic principle of social justice of that sort. However that may be, Gaus's pathbreaking work on public reason brings classical liberals to the *very brink* of market democracy.

Others in this movement have focused less on the justificatory aspects of this new form of classical liberalism and more on its substantive moral commitments. For example, Jason Brennan says that Rawls's enthusiasm for ideal theory generates a paradox. Using many of Rawls's own economic premises, Brennan suggests that market based societies are more likely to achieve social justice than Rawls's preferred regimes (such as liberal socialism, especially in its no-growth formulations).[18] But ideal theory leads Rawls to identify those market-based societies as unjust. Rawlsians are thus forced to choose between success and a symbolic concern for success. For Brennan, however, this is not a mere *reductio ad absurdum*. Brennan's worries about ideal theory spring from a concern about how best to exposit (and realize) values he shares with high liberals. Thus, "modern egalitarian liberals often correctly identify the test of a flourishing society: the end or minimizing of domination, poverty, and medical want, and the spread of education, opportunity, peace, and full political autonomy."[19]

David Schmidtz is among the most prominent contemporary defenders of limited government and thick economic liberty. In work done with Jason Brennan, however, Schmidtz has dismayed orthodox libertarians by affirming an ideal of positive liberty.[20] Schmidtz and Brennan seek to explode what they see as a long-standing myth about liberty. According to this myth, there are two forms of liberty, positive and negative. Negative liberty concerns the absence of constraints. According to the myth, negative liberty is the liberty of classical liberals and libertarians. Rights to private property, for example, are paradigm protectors of negative liberty. Property owners have freedom of property if others are forbidden to interfere with their uses of that property (as when, say, they exchange their property for property held by others). By contrast, positive freedom involves not merely the absence of constraints, but the effective or "real" ability to pursue projects and goals. Positive liberty is the liberty of the critics of classical liberalism: Marxists, socialists and left liberals. These critics see negative liberty as connected to purely formal conceptions of equality and, for that reason, as being morally impoverished. What does it matter to say that everyone is "free" to have tea at the Ritz, for example, if they have no money in their pockets?

Schmidtz and Brennan suggest that the myth that one must choose one liberty or the other has been perpetuated because both sides share an assumption: liberty, whether understood positively or negatively, is something government must directly protect. "Both sides agree that government has the job of promoting liberty (whatever liberty turns out to be), and both sides agree that the government should support it in a direct manner."[21] For people on the right, government supports liberty directly by protecting the negative rights and liberties of citizens (rights to private property prominent among them). For people on the left, government supports liberty directly by enacting an array of social service programs (welfare rights, for example).

Schmidtz and Brennan reject this assumption about the role of government. Challenging libertarian orthodoxy, Schmidtz and Brennan affirm the importance of positive liberty. Indeed, they agree with left liberals that positive liberty may even be the most important form of liberty: it is the form of liberty that explains why our formal freedoms are valuable in the first place.[22] However, putting a new wrinkle into this old debate, Schmidtz and Brennan continue to affirm the importance of negative liberties, most notably in the economic realm. Market institutions are justified in part because they have a history of actually producing positive liberty, not by official guarantees but indirectly.[23] So Schmidtz and Brennan argue that both negative and positive liberty are important. But against the libertarian tradition, they insist that negative liberty's importance resides in large part in its ability to promote positive liberty. By directly supporting negative liberties (such as robust rights of private ownership), governments indirectly support positive liberty. Economic liberties promote the spontaneous development of unimaginably complex webs of cooperation. Those webs bring people into contact with one another peacefully, creating the supply of goods and opportunities people need if their formal freedoms are to become real.

In his independent scholarly work, Schmidtz routinely blends traditional classical liberal values, such as the ideal of desert, with recognizably high liberal values, such as the ideal of reciprocity.[24] Schmidtz is a pluralist about justice, arguing that justice is a concept comprised of irreducibly diverse elements.[25] "What I really favor," Schmidtz says at one point, "is whatever helps people to pursue their projects in peaceful and productive ways."[26] While skeptical of Rawls's ambition to produce an account of justice with "completeness," Schmidtz affirms core ideas within justice as fairness. Central among these is the idea that social institutions must benefit all classes of contributors, including the worst off. Schmidtz writes: "Rawls's most central, most luminously undeniable point is that a free society is not a zero-sum game. It is a mutually advantageous cooperative venture."[27] In Schmidtz's view, one of the principle ways of deciding among competing conceptions of justice, as well as competing conceptions of social morality more broadly, is by asking how those conceptions would facilitate people living well, in conditions of peace, prosperity, and opportunity.[28] Schmidtz calls justice as fairness "a vision with grandeur" and urges readers to focus positively on the insights in the Rawlsian account.[29]

Schmidtz's work on desert has a special place in the emerging school of new classical liberalism.[30] Philosophers sometimes argue that since people do not deserve their genetic and familial advantages, they cannot claim to deserve the social goods they acquire by exercising them. Even the ability to make a strong effort can be eliminated as a "desert basis" in this way. Within political philosophy, arguments against desert often serve an ideological function: they clear the moral ground so that arguments in favor of distributive justice may be launched. Arguments in favor of desert, by contrast, seek to invest the moral ground, typically with property claims. Such claims, if they can be defended, prevent or hinder the launch of distributive justice arguments by entangling them in a thicket of desert-based flora.

Schmidtz's approach is refreshingly different. First, Schmidtz widens the field of discussion about desert by defending a counterintuitive claim: "We sometimes deserve X on the basis of what we do after receiving X."[31] On being offered a tenure track job at a research university, for example, a young scholar may vow to work especially hard to deserve it. When President Obama was awarded the Nobel Peace Prize upon the birth of his presidency, many of his supporters expressed their hope that he would go on to conduct American foreign policy so as to deserve that honor. Examining the many ways people use the concept of desert as they get about their daily lives (and evaluate the performances of others), Schmidtz teases out neglected dimensions of desert. "Compensatory" models of desert concern how we evaluate deservingness based on things people did before they receive rewards. By contrast, "promissory" models, such as those just described, concern the way we evaluate people's deservingness after they receive opportunities: such forms of desert are "forward-looking."[32]

In a break with tradition, Schmidtz defends desert in a manner that far from entangling arguments for social justice strengthens and improves them. As we saw earlier, Margaret Holmgren thinks justice requires that individuals be secured the most fundamental benefits in life (compatible with like benefits for others). According to Holmgren, "The opportunity to progress by our own efforts is a fundamental interest."[33] Schmidtz agrees and also approvingly quotes Richard Miller: "Most people (including most of the worst off) want to use what resources they have actively, to get ahead on their own steam, and this reflects a proper valuing of human capacities."[34] If philosophers wanted a sure-fire way to set back the interests of the working poor, Schmidtz observes, they would be hard pressed to find a better method than to convince such people that whatever they have accomplished or whatever they might aspire to accomplish in their lives, they personally deserve no praise for it.

According to Schmidtz, Rawls's difference principle, which requires that we prefer institutions that work to the advantage of the poor, does not compete with desert but instead can support the idea that people deserve a chance. The difference principle can do this if Holmgren is correct that people have a fundamental interest in having the chance to prosper by their own merit. As Schmidtz puts it: "the difference principle supports principles of desert if it is historically true that the least advantaged tend to flourish within, and only within, systems in which honest hard work is respected and rewarded."[35] Personal desert and distributive justice can work together.

To appreciate the force of this point, we need to look closely at the machinery of the difference principle. As Philippe van Parijs has noted, one of the most vexing interpretive problems about Rawls's difference principle concerns the correct way to describe the "distribuendum"—that is, the good that the difference principle directs us to maximize. That good (or, more precisely, that complex index of social primary goods—see below) is intended to secure for people the "social bases of self-respect": roughly, (1) a confidence in one's own self-worth, and (2) a sense that one is properly esteemed by others.

We will take up these issues for ourselves in a moment. For now, notice how suggestive Schmidtz's argument for desert is here. If Schmidtz and Holmgren are right, then among the goods that the difference principle directs us to maximize are material goods that people knowingly come by through their own efforts and by their own merit. Holdings that one deserves, and that are publicly recognized as being deserved (say, by a culture that praises hard work), look like particularly powerful social bases of self-respect. Thus, in Schmidtz's hands, pro-desert arguments need not entangle the "distributive justice rocket." Instead, Schmidtz shows defenders of distributive justice how to bring desert aboard. By doing so, we find that the rocket becomes able to orbit more closely to the concern that inspires the firing of the rocket in the first place: the concern to secure a social world in which every citizen can feel self-respect for whatever role each plays in the cooperative venture that is social life. As Schmidtz says: "society is not a zero-sum . . . game, but a cooperative venture in which the pie's size is variable. Almost all people can have a better life than they could have had on their own, and the reason is simple: Other people's talents make all of us better off."[36] People are right to esteem one another for the contributions they make based on their special talents. Merit and desert are not competitors to social justice, but vital components thereof.

I see market democracy as an explication and extension of this intellectual movement. According to market democracy, society is not something private, the mere sum of whatever contracts individuals might enter into with one another for their self-interested reasons. Nor is society an economic efficiency machine designed for no higher moral purpose than increasing aggregate wealth. Rather, society, in its moral essence, is a public thing. A society is a cooperative venture for mutual gain between citizens concerned to honor the freedom and equality of one another across generations. The institutions of a society committed to respecting citizens in this sense must seek above all to create conditions in which individuals can develop and exercise the moral capacities they have as citizens. Chief among these is the capacity for responsible self-authorship and the capacity to honor their fellow citizens as persons who have the capacity to be responsible self-authors. To create those conditions, citizens must respect the core liberty-interests of their fellow citizens, including the interest their fellow citizens have in making life-defining economic decisions in light of their own character, values, and dreams. The institutions of a free society must be justifiable to all classes of citizens, including the most poor. This requires that the basic political and economic structures be designed so as to ensure that all groups benefit.

No classical liberal has ever accepted this complete cluster of moral ideas. Market democracy suggests that it is time they did. Market democracy affirms a thick conception of economic freedom as a requirement of social justice. It is this twin commitment that makes a view market democratic in my sense.

Applying the Theory

As I have stated, I think of market democracy as a research program rather than as any one particular view. As a research program, a great variety of different liberal views might be developed within a broadly market democratic framework. For example, while affirming a thick conception of private economic liberties as basic rights, market democracy leaves room for disagreement about the precise content of those basic economic liberties. Similarly, while all liberals assign special weight to basic rights when they conflict with other social values, market democracy allows for a range of reasonable disagreement about just how strictly the priority given to basic rights should be understood.

Market democracy breaks with traditional classical liberal and libertarian traditions in founding politics on a deliberative ideal of democratic citizenship. However, as even our brief account of Gaus's work makes plain, market democracy makes room for a variety of rival conceptions of the nature of public reason. It thus also makes room for rival accounts of the justificatory conditions that must be satisfied if a society is to be just and legitimate. Closely related, arguments that seek to combine economic liberty and social justice might be presented at a variety of argumentative levels. Some defenses, worked out primarily at the level I call political theory, might be closely concerned with empirical claims about how rival institutions are likely to function in practice. Other such arguments, worked at the level I call political philosophy, might abstract further away from such practical questions and focus more on the quality of the regime's moral intentions (with questions about the practical likelihood of such regime's actually realizing its intentions being bracketed to some significant degree).

More dramatically, I believe it might be possible to adjust and develop *whole schools* of left liberal social justice in a market democratic direction. The institutional proposals of policy analyst Charles Murray, as we have seen, appear to be motivated not merely by concerns of practical expediency but by a deeper commitment to some version or other of "luck egalitarianism" (admittedly, only very roughly described in Murray's work). It would be interesting to see how a political philosopher who shared Murray's sense of the moral importance of private economic freedom *and* Murray's intuition that in some sense morally just distributions are ones that emerge more from people's choices than from brute luck might work up a full theory from those ideas. Or, to take a very different approach, it would be interesting to see what some market democratic version of the "capabilities approach" might look like. Margaret Holmgren says that people have a fundamental interest in advancing through their own efforts. This claim about the moral importance of personal economic autonomy likely would ring true for many of the women in developing countries to whom leading capabilities theorists such as Martha Nussbaum devote much attention. Could such an interest be built up in such a way that gained it a central place on the list of the basic human capabilities? How might the inclusion of such a capabilities interest affect the wider distributive aspects of the capabilities approach?

Even the "liberal republican" approach defended by Philip Pettit might be market democratizable. Nondomination has traditionally been worked out by "free labor" advocates in ways that run strongly toward democratic control of the workplace. But a bedrock concern for freedom and nondomination might equally well be used to justify a regime of private economic liberty. The call of republicans to "maximize freedom" does not constitute a theory of liberal justice: republicans focus on freedom, not fairness. But republicans such as Pettit see their concern to secure social conditions of nondomination as yielding redistributive principles, such as guaranteed minimum income. But if such a guaranteed income scheme were paired with a host of other service programs, as typically has been the case on social democratic interpretations, might a case be made that such programs dominate the choices of individuals? If so, the republican commitment to nondomination may require respect for a wide range of private economic liberties.

However that may be, the central challenge for market democracy would be the same across all these schools. How, within the distinctive parameters and values of that particular school, might a case be made for the moral importance of private economic liberty? If such a case can be made, might that help us to begin thinking in new ways about the distributive requirements distinctive to that school? Without seeking to answer these questions, I invite others to begin considering them.

To demonstrate the power of the market democratic approach, I would now like to select a single school of left liberal social justice and show in detail how that school might be "market democratized." The school I select is that headed by John Rawls. In particular, I wish to offer a market democratic interpretation of the view that Rawls calls justice as fairness. I wish to demonstrate how one can affirm a thick conception of economic liberty while simultaneously being committed to the various distributive requirements of a Rawlsian fairness-based conception of justice.

I select justice as fairness for a variety of reasons. First, and most obviously, Rawls's theory is the most widely known and highly regarded left liberal theory of justice. Rawls's theory is also the most fully developed such theory. Because it has been elaborated so extensively, it can help us identify a great range of issues that would require a response (perhaps in the form of an alternative moral requirement) from a market democratic perspective. Justice as fairness thus sets out an unusually large number of discrete normative challenges that any market democratic interpretation must meet, one by one.

Further, I choose justice as fairness because it may seem to pose a particularly hard case for market democracy. Rawls runs his institutional arguments primarily at the level of what he calls "ideal theory." On this, the level that I call "political philosophy," institutional regimes are evaluated primarily by the quality of their moral intentions rather than on more practical grounds such as the likelihood of their actually working well in practice. This looks like an uphill battle for market democracy. Capitalist institutions are traditionally defended on practical grounds, with advocates of socialism viewed as more idealistic (even if, regrettably, socialism faces problems of feasibility in the real world). A shadow from this falls across our evaluations of liberal regimes, with the regimes furthest to the left being the most idealistic even if, regrettably, not the most feasible. By following Rawls up into the realm of ideal theory, I will be required to sort out and focus narrowly on the case for market democracy that can be made on *moral* grounds rather than practical ones. By accepting the challenge of comparing market democratic regimes with the left liberal ones at the level of ideal theory, I intend to "visit left liberals where they live."

Most important, I choose justice as fairness simply because, once it has been adjusted and corrected according to market democratic principles, it is the conception of liberal justice I find most compelling. This does not mean that I agree with Rawls's interpretation of justice as fairness: far from it. But when I think about the conception of market democracy that most closely reflects my own political convictions, it is a market-democratized version of justice as fairness that becomes most vivid to me.

Rawls's focus on fairness and the position of the least well-off, his idea of citizens with moral powers, his claim that "first principle" concerns about rights are properly accorded some strong priority over "second principle" considerations of distribution, his conviction that there is a realm of political argumentation that is properly conducted at a very high level of abstraction from concerns about feasibility ("ideal theory"), all these ideas are appealing to me. Of course, Rawls's failure to appreciate the moral importance of private economic liberty is the most significant defect in his own interpretation of justice. But that moral defect of Rawls's own interpretation generates moral shortcomings in other parts of his interpretation of justice as fairness too, most notably a failure to appreciate the importance and power of spontaneous forms of order. By market democratizing Rawls's theory, I hope to show what justice as fairness might look like when corrected of its left liberal biases and defects. I shall call this view *free market fairness*.

In presenting free market fairness, I do not mean to close off other ways of "marketizing" the Rawlsian view (there are many market democratic pathways that might be cut within the Rawlsian woods, I am sure). Along with working out the details of free market fairness, I shall also defend this interpretation as the *morally best* interpretation of liberal justice. Again, I do not mean to close off or discourage inquiries in any of the other directions (or on any of the other levels of political argumentation) that I have mentioned. In particular, I welcome fellow classical liberal travelers to defend versions of market democracy on the more practical, less idealized grounds that I, in choosing to follow Rawls into the realm of ideal theory, must soon leave behind. Likewise, I welcome fellow travelers to develop their own capabilities-based, luck egalitarian, or perhaps even "liberal republican" versions of market democracy. Without rival market democratic accounts of social justice standing before us, it will be difficult to assess my claim that of all the conceptions of liberal justice, the interpretation I call free market fairness is normatively superior. If alternative classical liberal interpretations of social justice should arise, I would welcome the chance to turn to them and compare their moral attractions to that of my own preferred fairness-based market democratic view.

For now, though, as a consequence of the ideological conformity of our profession, the main adversaries of my market democratic conception of liberal justice all stand together on the political left. So when I say that free market fairness is the morally most attractive account of social justice, I actually mean something (somewhat) more modest: compared to the familiar left liberal interpretations of justice as fairness, my market democratic interpretation is morally best. In particular, I hope to show that free market fairness is more morally ambitious, and by the very fact, more morally attractive than Rawls's social democratic interpretation of that view.

The Argument Ipse Dixit

I begin by setting out a definition of justice as fairness, purposefully given in generic terms. According to justice as fairness, liberal justice can be formulated into two lexically ordered principles. The first principle specifies a set of basic rights and liberties held equally by all citizens. Among these basic liberties, the political liberties—and those liberties alone—are to be given some special protection.[37] The second principle indicates how social and economic goods must be distributed. Regarding equality of opportunity, justice as fairness affirms the traditional liberal idea that positions must be formally open to all. Additionally though, justice as fairness requires that inequalities in opportunities must be arranged so that they satisfy some substantive criterion of fair equality of opportunity. Finally, justice as fairness affirms the difference principle: inequalities are justified only if they maximally benefit the working poor.[38] (Justice as fairness also includes a principle of just savings, and can be extended with respect to issues of environmental justice and duties of international aid, though I shall touch on those issues only toward the end our discussion.)

Scholars long steeped in Rawls will notice that even this generic definition has a "social democratic" flavor and hue. For example, Rawls's canonical formulation of the first principle makes no *definitional* mention of the requirement that the political liberties be accorded special attention. "First: each person is to have an equal right to the most extensive scheme of equal basic liberties compatible with a similar scheme of liberties for others."[39] Rawls's subsequent claim that the political liberties, and those liberties alone, require special protection could easily be read as an accretion to justice as fairness that is peculiar to Rawls himself, rather than a settled feature of the general view that must be accepted and accounted for by anyone attempting to work out a market democratic alternative reading. So too, Rawls's canonical formulation of the second principle makes no *definitional* mention of the requirement that institutions should be designed to maximize the advantages of the least well-off: "Second: social and economic inequalities are to be arranged so that they are both a) reasonably expected to be to everyone's advantage and b) attached to positions and offices open to all."[40] Again, accepting the stipulation that such goods must be maximized makes things harder for market democracy. Nor does the canonical formulation make any *definitional* requirement that opportunities be distributed in a way that is fair.

This is not a book about Rawls, so I will not rehearse the various arguments that Rawls and his followers offer in support of each of those ideas. Instead, allow me simply to say that personally I find the arguments the Rawlsians give for elucidating the requirements of justice as fairness in those ways to be, on balance, convincing. So I accept these requirements as parts of the definition of justice as fairness. This means I accept the challenge of showing how a regime that affirms a thick conception of private economic liberty might satisfy all the requirements of justice as fairness so conceived.

Viewed from afar, our general definition of justice as fairness may seem to set out reasonably clear requirements. However, as we bend closer, we see that our general definition of justice as fairness is thick with ambiguities. Our general definition contains many component parts, each of which might be filled out in a variety of ways. Anyone seeking to specify the requirements of each component immediately encounters hard choices and, sometimes, discovers tensions between (and within) the components. We have already considered one of these difficulties at length: if some set of liberties is to be given foundational protection as "basic liberties," how are we to decide which economic liberties are "basic" and which are not? But our generic definition of justice as fairness presents us with other interpretive challenges. For example, if the political liberties require some sort of special protection, what exactly is that protection? If citizens are to enjoy equality of opportunity in a way that is "fair," what exactly does fairness require in that realm? The difference principle, let's say, requires that we maximize benefits to the least well-off. But how exactly are we to decide what counts as a "benefit," and by what metric are we to determine when such benefits are maximized?

One response to these interpretive problems is purely exegetical. Confronted with the many ambiguities within the general definition of justice as fairness, we might simply study Rawls's texts and adopt whatever specification of each component he provides. But such an approach would be unsatisfying in a number of ways. Most trivially, Rawls's views about the best interpretation of justice as fairness change through time. Sometimes these changes are unidirectional, and Rawls's later texts make quite clear what interpretation he ultimately affirms.[41] But other times—as with the fair value of the political liberties requirement, various aspects of the difference principle, and even the priority relations of some of his main subprinciples—Rawls's final texts are far less determinate.[42] With many of the definitional components of justice as fairness, Rawls provides significantly different formulations at different places. Not all those formulations seem to square equally well with Rawls's announced moral commitments.[43]

A more important problem with the exegetical approach is that here, as elsewhere in philosophy, arguments ipse dixit ("because he said it") are of limited interest.[44] At the extreme, the exegetical approach treats justice as fairness as a plot in the archaeology of ideas, rather than as a living, growing research paradigm.[45] Rawls is one of the most creative and profound thinkers in the liberal tradition. We honor Rawls when we think of him as humbly inviting future scholars to think along with him within the general normative framework he devises, rather than as a Moses-like figure who before his death handed down a set of finished rules to his chosen people. The same is true of Hayek and his framework.

In this spirit, I propose that we treat justice as fairness, like Hayek's theory of spontaneous order, as a living research program. The general definition of justice as fairness laid out above leaves room for a significant (but bounded) range of disagreement about the requirements of liberal justice. These ambiguities and tensions are fundamental features of justice as fairness. They spring from the complex nature of the bedrock liberal idea that citizens are free and equal moral beings.

The ambiguities and tensions within justice as fairness open up a possibility that must honestly be faced: people who are committed to the idea that citizens should be treated as free and equal self-governing agents may reasonably resolve the tensions and ambiguities within justice as fairness in different ways. In particular, as there is a social democratic interpretive tradition of justice as fairness, our generic definition makes space for the development of a market democratic one as well: notably, the view I call free market fairness.

The prominence of the social democratic tradition—and the historical fact that this was the approach taken by Rawls—cannot secure the supremacy of that interpretive path. Instead, in the end the choice between market democratic and social democratic interpretations of justice as fairness must be made on *moral* terms. No matter how great the weight and inertia of the moral status quo, in philosophy the best argument wins.

Over the next two chapters, I lay out the moral case for free market fairness. To prepare the ground, I shall now mark a main point of difference between this approach and the more familiar social democratic one. This is a difference between interpretations of justice as fairness that emphasize the *status* of liberal citizens and interpretations that emphasize their *agency*.

Justice as Fairness: Status or Agency?

Consider the first principle of justice as fairness. This principle states that each person has an equal claim to a fully adequate scheme of equal basic rights and liberties. The rights and liberties of this scheme are to be given a high degree of protection. For example, they may be entrenched constitutionally as basic rights of individuals and associations. As we have seen, however, there are different ways to specify the rights and liberties on the list, especially with respect to the economic liberties. Market democrats and social democrats, while equally committed to justice as fairness and all its surrounding ideas, enumerate the economic liberties that are to be protected by the first principle in their own distinctive ways.

Following Mill, thinkers in the high liberal tradition see the value of economic liberty in instrumental terms. As Keynes put this idea: "The strenuous purposeful money-makers may carry all of us along with them into the lap of economic abundance. But it will be those people, who can keep alive and cultivate into a fuller perfection, the art of life itself and do not sell themselves for the means of life, who will be able to enjoy the abundance when it comes." When the day of prosperity arrives, the ambitions that might lead to still further economic growth should be classified as "morbid psychoses."[46] According to Rawls, "What men want is meaningful work in free association with others. . . . To achieve this state of things great wealth is not necessary. In fact, beyond some point it is more likely to be a positive hindrance, a meaningless distraction at best if not a temptation to indulgence and emptiness."[47]

It is easy to imagine economic and cultural conditions in which a thick conception of economic liberty might not be valuable to citizens. For example, strong individual freedoms of economic contract might not be valuable during a stage of capitalism within which a large population of unskilled wage laborers is threatened by domination by a small class of avaricious capitalists. Or, as a matter of economic principle, or of science fiction imagination, we might posit a future world in which wealth had exhausted the creative capacity of mankind such that economic striving would be pointless (and for that reason, perhaps, deemed psychotic).[48] However, the disputes we are considering about the appropriate way to specify the content of the first principle, and the other components of justice as fairness, does not turn on historical, sociological, or futuristic contingencies of that sort. The dispute about whether the basic economic liberties should be interpreted thickly or thinly must be considered in a more idealized way.

The generic formulation of justice we are discussing belongs to what Rawls calls the "special conception of justice." This conception, unlike the "general conception," is understood to apply only in social conditions favorable to the attainment of social justice.[49] So when high liberals argue for a thin reading of the economic liberties in the first principle, this cannot be a recommendation based ultimately on localized empirical observations (nor can it be one based on science fictive imaginings about the plausibility of "infinite" economic growth). Instead, high liberals must defend their platform of economic exceptionalism on straightforwardly *moral* grounds. They must take a position about what formulation of the basic economic liberties most appropriately tracks the interests citizens have when they find themselves living in economic and historical conditions favorable to the achievement of justice. They must say that within the social conditions that might most fully stimulate citizens to develop their moral powers, and most effectively expand their evaluative horizons, those "purposeful" and "strenuous" projects protected by the thick conception of economic liberty will require no basic protection.

And this is indeed the moral position that high liberals take. They are skeptical that independent economic activity would be a highly valued part of a just society. What people really desire and need, in addition to "meaningful work in free association with others," is leisure: freedom from want, freedom from hunger, and freedom from care. When a society reaches the point of affluence that makes the achievement of justice possible, people should turn away from private economic activities and toward the real (and thus primarily noneconomic) business of living. Keynes writes: "Thus for the first time since his creation man will be faced with his real, his permanent problem—how to use his freedom from pressing economic cares, how to occupy the leisure, which science and compound interest have won for him, to live wisely and agreeably and well."[50] That is the traditional high liberal vision of a society in which citizens are experiencing the blessings of liberal justice.

Free market fairness offers a different view. First, simply as an empirical matter, notice that—against the predictions of Mill and Keynes—the experience of rising affluence has not blunted the desire for economic growth among citizens of Britain and America. Quite the contrary. Affluence seems to have unlocked unexpected human creative energies—energies the expression of which have upended the expectations of early critics of capitalism. On the consumer side, prosperity has done more than make bread and butter cheaper. It has also brought an abundance of cultural goods and other opportunities for personal growth within the reach of ordinary people. People's appetite for such goods shows no sign of letting up.

At least as important, rising affluence has wrought changes in the personal experience of productive activity—not just for elites but for ever-wider swaths of working people as well. In conditions of affluence, many people experience work not simply as a meaningless chore—an hourly affront to their self-respect, or an experience they endure only because they must. Rather, for many people, commercial activity in a competitive marketplace is a deeply meaningful aspect of their lives. People express themselves, they grow up and become who they are, in part because of their experiences as independent participants in the cooperative venture that is economic life. For many people, the pursuit of a career is intimately entwined with the role of provider for children, aging parents, and spouses. People who work hard to improve the prospects of their loved ones are esteemed for their efforts, and rightly so. The essential dignity of these economic activities probably obtains at every stage of economic development. But this aspect of independent economic activity is vivid in conditions of affluence. For many citizens at least, the personal value of independent economic activity is sustained or even increased as their societies grow wealthy.

Free market fairness draws moral lessons from the observation of these empirical trends. With prosperity, the exercise of thick private economic liberty is for many citizens an essential condition of responsible self-authorship. Some of the things citizens need to become responsible self-authors can only be found in independent economic activity: confronting challenges, overcoming obstacles, making one's way in life to support oneself and those one loves. On the market democratic vision, the economy of a well-ordered liberal society would be dynamic and growing, not static or stationary. What Keynes calls the "economic problem" is not a problem to be solved and put aside—as though that problem, and that problem alone, were for liberals a mere "prejustice" problem. In terms of its role in allowing the development of the moral powers of self-authorship, market democracy sees the "economic problem" as having some of the same features as the "religious problem," the "associative problem," or any of the other "problems" that require people to make choices and perform action in pursuit of a life plan. These problems provide the stuff of life. By confronting these challenges, citizens exercise and develop the moral capacities distinctive to them as responsible self-authors.

Amartya Sen distinguishes two ways of thinking about outcomes. On what Sen calls the "culmination" approach, one focuses narrowly on the state of affairs that is realized: for example, the members of a family have food and housing. By contrast, on Sen's preferred "comprehensive" approach, the description of the outcome is enriched to include the processes and agencies that produced it.[51] Those agencies are aspects of whatever state of affairs is produced, and any account that omits them is impoverished. As Sen puts it: "A full characterization of realizations should have room to include the exact processes through which the eventual states of affairs emerge."[52] Sen's idea of "culmination outcomes" helps illuminate the importance of economic liberty to market democracy.

According to free market fairness, the economic problem is a problem to be *lived*. For many people, independent economic activity is an essential, ongoing part of a well-lived life. This is why market democracy sees private economic liberty as a requirement of political autonomy. For many productive citizens, it is not enough merely to know that the ones they love live well. It is also important to such people that they be the visible *cause* of that state of affairs. Causal relationships of this sort can be among the most intimate and personal forms of human bonding. A society that deprives its citizens of that experience might have certain attractions. But a society that deadens those connections of loving dependency would be "drained of life" in some important way.

For all these reasons, free market fairness has a different vision of a well-ordered society in which citizens, as free, equal, and independent authors of their own lives, enjoy the blessings of liberal justice. It is this difference in vision that allows the first principle guarantee of economic liberty to be interpreted in different ways from the social democratic and market democratic perspectives.

To gain a clearer picture of this dispute, consider another major component of justice as fairness: the difference principle. The difference principle requires that social and economic inequalities be arranged so that they are "to the greatest benefit of the least advantaged."[53] But what should be counted as a "benefit" to the least advantaged? Market democracy and high liberal social democracy share a foundational commitment to respect persons as free and equal citizens. So they can agree on a general answer to this question. The "benefits" described by the difference principle consist in the bundle of goods and values citizens need if they are to develop their two moral powers: the capacity for responsible self-authorship, and the capacity to honor their fellow citizens as responsible self-authors too. However, as they begin refining their account of the goods and values needed for that purpose, we find that market democracy and social democracy assess the weights of these "social primary goods" in different ways. To see the shape of this divergence, we need to wade a little way into the ocean of Rawlsiana surrounding the difference principle (henceforth DP).

Like all the main components of justice as fairness, the DP is a requirement of institutions. The DP requires that institutions be arranged so that any inequalities in socially desirable goods generated by those institutions maximally benefit the least well-off class of citizens. A set of social arrangements that does not work to the advantage of every individual member may still be just. What the DP rules out, though, are systems that disadvantage whole classes of citizens (for example, hereditary classes, whether defined racially or in terms of their role in the economy). The particular "least well-off" class to which Rawls says the DP applies is that of "ordinarily productive" citizens. In requiring that institutions must maximally benefit the least well-off, the DP requires that those institutions must benefit the class of people who work at the lowest end of the pay scale.[54]

The goods referred to by the DP are a subset of what Rawls calls "primary goods." While primary goods are goods that every rational person can be assumed to want, the difference principle concerns only those primary goods that "persons need in their status as free and equal citizens."[55] Under the "general conception" of justice, the DP serves as a conception of justice: it governs the distribution of all social values—rights, liberties, opportunities, wealth, and more.[56] Under the happier conditions of the "special conception," however, it becomes possible to assign strict priority to the equal distribution of the basic liberties of the first principle. Thus the first principle of justice rather than the DP now governs the distribution of basic rights and liberties. The scope of the DP is further narrowed by the priority that can now be given to the fair value of opportunities guarantee (as set out in the first part of the second principle). Thus, under the special conception, the DP concerns the distribution not of all goods and values but only of social goods whose distribution is not governed by the prior principles. It is the poor's share of *those goods* that the difference principle says must be maximized. Call these goods and values "difference principle specific goods" or, for short, "DP goods." But, then, what are the DP goods?

The ultimate concern of the DP is the way institutions distribute the social bases of self-respect. This is the complex bundle of goods that society owes its citizens if it is to respect their freedom, equality, and dignity. The DP goods make people's formal rights and freedoms personally valuable to them. But what exactly are these "social bases" on which the self-respect of citizens depends?

Self-respect is an elusive, quasi-psychological notion. Unsurprisingly, a great range of political goods might be claimed to be "social bases" of self-respect.[57] Multiculturalists argue that a secure cultural context of choice is a primary good—a precondition for the exercise of autonomy on which liberal self-respect depends. Feminists claim that women can only achieve equal dignity and self-respect in a community free of certain kinds of erotic literature and imagery. Citizens of faith sometimes say that their self-respect depends upon the public affirmation of divinity, consistent with separation of church and state. Socialists assert that wage and salaried labor is intrinsically demeaning of human dignity: self-respect requires the public ownership of the means of production.

The diversity of these claims helps make clear why Rawls generally uses income and wealth as a shorthand when applying the DP.[58] Somewhat more precisely, we can think of the DP goods as a consumption bundle with three main elements: income and wealth, powers and positions of responsibility, and social bases of self-respect.[59]

The difference principle directs us to choose institutional arrangements that maximize the bundle of DP goods enjoyed by the least well-off class. When we seek to apply this test, though, we face a difficulty. First, the directive to maximize this bundle of DP goods requires that each component good be measurable in itself. We must be able to measure each item on the list of DP goods so that we can detect when more or less of each is being delivered. More daunting, the test requires that we be able to quantify across the whole set of values. The test assumes that some *overall* index could be conceived, since the test requires that we make judgments about which candidate institutional systems do a better job maximizing the whole set of DP goods—"wealth and income" *and* "powers and positions of responsibility" *and* "the social bases of self-respect."

The difference principle here presents us with a profound interpretive problem. Ideally, the difference principle would direct us to prefer whatever set of institutional arrangements sought to maximize the bundle of DP goods by maximizing the poor's share of every item in the bundle. However, because of the very nature of the DP goods, this is not possible. Some of the DP goods are rivalrous, such that a choice to increase shares on one dimension of the bundle requires that we accept diminished shares on another.

Rawls thinks these difficulties can be overcome; at least, Rawls thinks we can roughly measure this set of goods in a way that enables us to make broad choices among rival regime types. When making these difficult judgments, we are to rely on rational prudence to help us discern which candidate regime types maximize the true interests of the least well-off in their role as free and equal self-governing agents.[60]

However, what is rational prudence? And whose conception of rational prudence are we to employ? Appeals to formulaic notions such as "what persons need in their role as free and equal citizens" or what they need if they are "to develop and exercise the moral powers they have as citizens" are of little help. After all, market democracy and social democracy wholeheartedly agree on those goals. What's in dispute is how best to interpret what a commitment to those values requires. High liberal social democracy offers us one interpretation. Market democracy offers us another.

As commentators such Jason Brennan and Sam Freeman have noted, there is something peculiar about Rawls's skepticism about capitalism, given his commitment to the difference principle.[61] After all, well-functioning capitalistic markets can be expected to produce greater wealth than the more socialistic regimes types that Rawls advocates (especially on the no- or slow-growth formulations of those regime types).[62] This increase in wealth may be materially beneficial to the poor—whether we assume with classical liberals that growth "touches" the poor, or with leftists such as Dworkin that programs of the welfare state can effectively benefit them. Capitalist economies better satisfy the difference principle by virtue of producing greater wealth over time.[63] Call this the greater wealth thesis.

Free market fairness and the more familiar social democratic interpretations of justice as fairness begin to diverge here. Regarding the exegetical quandary about how to reconcile Rawls's skepticism about capitalism and his commitment to the difference principle, Freeman writes: "The answer to this puzzle must be that Rawls's difference principle is the ultimate standard for distributing not only income and wealth, but also the social primary goods Rawls calls 'powers and positions of responsibility.'" Freeman's explanation continues: "By 'powers' he means legal and other institutional powers of various kinds, primarily those powers required to make economic decisions of various kinds, including powers of control over productive resources."[64] Rawls, like Mill, forsakes the greater wealth made available by enthusiastically capitalist regimes in preference for the slower-growing economies of worker-owned cooperatives or of property-owning democracy because of the superior workplace experience offered by those latter regimes. Socialistic or property-owning democratic economies may reduce the share of wealth in the consumption bundle of DP goods available to the least fortunate. But such economics better satisfy the difference principle by increasing the power of citizens to make economic decisions and by enhancing their power in the workplace. Call this the greater workplace power thesis.

To understand free market fairness, however, we need to take Freeman's argument a step further. On Freeman's analysis, the market democratic approach views wealth as more important to the self-respect of citizens; the social democratic one views power in the workplace (and the ability to make economic decisions generally) as more important. A problem with this analysis, however, is that increases in social wealth *themselves* enhance the power of workers. In affluent societies, even ordinary citizens can purchase stocks and bonds: in the era of the personalized economy, workers literally come to own the means of production.[65] More important, in affluent societies workers have more bargaining power than in poor ones. With a range of attractive job alternatives, workers can command higher salaries or leave their jobs in search of workplace experiences they find more attractive or fulfilling.

So the distinction between the greater wealth thesis and the greater workplace power thesis is porous. To demarcate the market democratic and social democratic interpretations of the difference principle, and so to explain Rawls's preference for worker-controlled schemes, we need to refine our thesis about the nature and importance of workplace power. What social democrats distinctively value cannot merely be that workers enjoy "powers required to make economic decisions, including powers of control over those resources." Market democracy values that too. Indeed, from a market democratic perspective, one of the greatest benefits of affluence is that it creates exciting new opportunities for workers—entrepreneurs, wage laborers, piecework subcontractors, and sundry others. So it turns out that what high liberals such as Rawls value in the workplace is not merely that citizens have greater power, but that their greater power takes a particular form: workers must have *democratic* powers to make economic decisions, including *democratic* powers of control over productive resources.[66] Powers of personal independence are not enough. Instead, each worker must have standing as a member with a vote. Liberal democratic socialism and property-owning democracy better satisfy the difference principle by democratizing the workplace. Call this the democratic workplace thesis.[67]

Market democracy and high liberal social democracy agree that workers should enjoy power in their places of work. So the real debate between them cannot be one between the greater wealth thesis and the greater workplace power thesis. The real debate is between the greater wealth thesis and the democratic workplace thesis. How should we decide which interpretation of the difference principle to prefer?

Recall that we are still working here within the special conception of justice. The debate between market democracy and social democracy about how best to interpret the difference principle is taking place under the assumption that citizens are already enjoying the benefits of fair equality of opportunity and all the elements on the first principle list of basic rights and liberties—including the political liberties. We are asking, *on the assumption that all of those other requirements are being met*, what is the best way to characterize the goods citizens need to further their goals and develop their capacities as responsible self-authors?

Recall also that some of the main goods in the DP index are partially (or strongly) rivalrous. The DP directs us to maximize benefits to the least well-off. We cannot simply say, yes, let's maximize their wealth by adopting enthusiastically capitalist economic structures and let's maximize their political standing in the workplace by adopting liberal (democratic) socialism. Nor can workers in stationary-state economies annually vote to give themselves the increasingly higher wages the workers in growing capitalist economies might over time come to enjoy. Here, as elsewhere in justice as fairness, we sometimes must face hard choices. For this reason, different interpretive schools, each equally committed to a democratic ideal of fairness, may reasonably disagree about how best to assign an overall weighting to the index of DP goods. In response to this interpretive dilemma, social democracy employs one form of rational prudence; market democracy, another.

As we have noted, Rawls is skeptical about the value of wealth, seeing it as a distraction or even a hindrance to the practice of liberal citizenship properly understood.[68] Indeed, Rawls suggests that parties in the original position might opt for a conception of justice that provides not a maximum minimum of wealth but rather a "satisfactory minimum." In Rawls's view, "There may be, on reflection, little reason for trying to do better."[69] On this approach, once some target level of wealth has been achieved, further increases in the income of the least well-off working citizens is less important than providing them with further assurances of their standing as political equals. One accomplishes this by seeking a more complete realization of people's status-equality throughout the various domains of people's daily lives, and within the workplace in particular. Eschewing economic growth, social democracy seeks instead to instill in the citizenry a sense of democratic solidarity.

Again, free market fairness offers an alternative perspective. The institutions of market democratic regime types are arranged so that the creative commercial capacities of citizens may be exercised freely, without any predetermined limit or cap. In part this reflects the market democratic contention that the personal exercise of wide economic freedom is an essential aspect of liberal self-authorship. Additionally, though, market democracy attends to the socialist concern that the worth of people's liberties is connected to their control of material resources. If liberal citizens lack personal control of material resources, that socialist critique goes, their rights and liberties may be of little value. Market democracy affirms this socialist insight and extends it. As people gain wealth, their formal freedoms become more valuable to them. As societies grow more affluent, more citizens have opportunities to travel the world, develop themselves intellectually or culturally, benefit from medical advances, enjoy new technologies, start business ventures, return to school or try new occupations, create organizations of various kinds, and, if they choose, walk into the Ritz and order tea. When considering the complex list of DP goods, free market fairness sees increases in income as holding out the promise of increasing the worth of the freedoms enjoyed by all citizens. Increases in prosperity increase the value of liberty. This is true of wealthy citizens. It is true of the working poor as well. In many ways, wealth fuels the experience of freedom itself.

What's more, free market fairness, like other market democratic approaches, is skeptical that what people really want is "meaningful work in free association with each other," at least if that turns out to mean the (literal) politicization of their workplaces. Market democracy sees that view as anachronistic: it springs from a well-meaning but outmoded conception of the nature of work in capital-ist economies. The well-paid workers we are assuming within the special conception already enjoy substantial power in their places of work—though that power comes in the form of personal inde-pendence rather than in the form of a vote or a voice in a committee meeting. The personal experience of affluence gives each a measure of power and independence when facing life's diverse challenges and opportunities. If offered the chance to have their wages lowered and their opportunities to participate in workplace committee meet-ings increased, market democracy is skeptical that many ordinary citizens would (or should) accept. After all, a reduction in wages amounts to a reduction in people's effective power to use their rights in pursuit of projects that are central to their lives.[70]

I invite readers, whatever their profession, to ask whether they would forego greater wealth for greater political control of their workplaces. For many professors, a general reduction in social wealth would mean not only lower salaries but also fewer opportu-nities to attend scholarly conferences, less research support, fewer scholarships for graduate students, more time spent grading student papers, diminished access to the work of others, slower comput-ers, and so on. Personally, I would not accept such sacrifices for the opportunity to have longer and more frequent department meetings. Of course, professors work within the special cartelized conditions created by the institution of tenure. My point is more general: profes-sors are not the only people who value their work, who find rhythms and comforts in their workdays, and would hear the clang of a bell calling them to a workplace committee meeting as an *infringement* on their independence rather than as an enlargement of it.

So, unlike social democratic interpretations of justice as fairness, free market fairness interprets the difference principle as requiring that we increase the income of the least well-off.[71] In affirming this interpretation, free market fairness does not suggest that citizens should *trade off* their rights and liberties for increases in personal income and wealth. Again, the market democratic claim about the importance of wealth is made entirely within the context of the "spe-cial conception" of justice. Thus free market fairness assigns special weighting to the wealth of the least well-off only in the context of a situation within which those citizens are already enjoying all the rights and liberties set out in the first principle, and within which all the requirements of fair equality of opportunity are being fully satisfied. Even within that highly specialized context, free market fairness does not claim that *only* increases in wealth are beneficial to people in their roles as liberal citizens. Rather, it recognizes all the items in the list of DP goods as being important to people as citizens. When offering an interpretation of what it means to maximize that complex index, however, market democratic approaches see increases in wealth and income as among the most important benefits that social institutions might provide to the working poor. For example, market democracy posits that individuals should be empowered to make their own decisions about how much time and attention to devote to the pursuit of wealth and how much to leisure activities. They think people should be empowered to make those decisions, even if this incurs some costs in terms of social solidarity. When forced to make hard choices between rival regime types, therefore, free market fairness directs us to prefer enthusiastically capitalistic regimes that embrace economic growth as a positive ideal.

Market democracy and high liberal social democracy interpret the requirements of fairness in different ways. As we have seen, the social democratic interpretation of the first principle affirms only a thin conception of economic liberty; the market democratic interpretation affirms a thick one. Regarding the difference principle, the social democratic interpretation seeks to maximize the experience of democratic equality in the workplace; free market fairness seeks instead to maximize the personal wealth of the poor. In a later chapter, we will fill out the requirements of free market fairness, sharpening the distinction between it and the social democratic interpretations. That discussion will focus on the different interpretations that might be given to the requirements of fair equality of opportunity, and on the different ways by which special weight might be assigned to the political liberties. For now, let me summarize our discussion by saying something general about why market democracy and social democracy take such different approaches to the requirements of political fairness.

We began this section by noting that the tensions and ambiguities within justice as fairness arise from the complex nature of a fundamental liberal commitment. That commitment is to respect citizens as beings who are both equal and free. The divergence between the market democratic and social democratic interpretations of justice as fairness reflects a tension within that complex value. That divergence, however, is not simply about which of these two values should be given precedence when they conflict—with market democracy advocating freedom, for example, and social democracy plunking down for equality. The dispute is more a matter of two different ways of understanding how those values relate to each other.[72] Within the context of an affirmation of justice as fairness, liberals see freedom and equality not as freestanding rivals but instead as tightly conjoined values that only make sense when operating together. As often has been noted, liberals do not see freedom and equality as alternatives or rivals to each other. Instead, liberals see "freedom" and "equality" as tightly conjoined modifiers of each other. One term specifies what it is that liberals value and the other specifies how it is that liberals value it.[73] One way to think of this difference would be to say that market democracy and social democracy take subtly different views about the best way to understand the *direction* of that modification. Social democracy, we might say, interprets fairness as calling on us to prefer institutions that respect citizens as *freely equal*. Market democracy, by contrast, emphasizes the requirement that we seek institutions that treat citizens as *equally free*.

Here is another way to think of this difference. Because it emphasizes the importance of treating citizens as equally free, market democracy gives special attention to the importance of *agency*, to what citizens *choose to do* as responsible independent agents. On this view, self-respect comes primarily from seeing oneself as a central *cause* of the particular life one is living. When market democracy measures the material welfare of citizens, it tends to think in absolutist terms. It thinks it is important that each controls as large a bundle of material and social resources as possible, so that each can exercise his/her rights and liberties effectively over the widest possible range of activities and endeavors that each can conceive. Market democracy thinks it is important to maximize the holdings of the least well-off citizens—even when doing so requires substantial departures from the ideal of material egalitarianism. (With respect to the difference principle, at least, market democracy is an unambiguously prioritarian view.[74]) Market democracy views the well-ordered society of liberal citizens as essentially dynamic. A well-ordered market democratic society is one in which all citizens are experiencing a distinctively liberal form of growth and development. The capacity of citizens to develop the moral powers they have as citizens is paralleled by the capacity of the society as a whole for growth and development. There is no natural limit to either.[75]

If the market democratic interpretations of fairness emphasize doing, the high liberal social democratic ones are concerned more with *being*. Such interpretations emphasize the *relational status* of citizens. In particular, social democracy emphasizes the importance of each citizen being recognized as an equal political participant in the shared life of the community. Self-respect comes primarily from being recognized by others in a certain way. While recognizing that citizens have lives of their own to lead, social democracy gives special weight to the ideal of solidarity. If market democracy is unambiguously prioritarian, social democracy has thicker egalitarian strands running through its concern for citizens. Indeed, the egalitarian impulse is so entwined with social democracy that some thinkers have argued that justice as fairness, properly understood, should be read as a *thoroughly* egalitarian view.[76] If liberalism is founded on an ideal of citizens who freely choose to be equal, for example, citizens could be expected to labor simply for the greater benefit of their fellow citizens.[77]

However that may be, the social democratic interpretation emphasizes the importance of each citizen being recognized as an equal participant in the collective decision-making procedures that abound within his/her ideal community. By contrast, basic rights and liberties in place, a marketized interpretation such as free market fairness seeks to maximize the material wealth personally controlled by the least fortunate. In doing so, market democracy hopes to provide such people with the largest possible share of fuel to power them as they pursue their diverse and precious plans of life.

I have argued that people attracted to the classical liberal ideal of private economic liberty and government of strictly limited power should get over their strong negative reaction to the ideal of social justice. Much work remains before we complete our account of free market fairness. But I have begun that account by showing how market democracy might interpret two main requirements of that doctrine—the content of the first principle and the requirements of the difference principle—in distinctively market-friendly ways. In a well-ordered liberal society erected along market democratic lines, citizens enjoy constitutional protection for a wide range of the private economic liberties associated with capitalism. But they do not use those liberties to exploit the less advantaged classes of citizens. Instead, the effect of the operation of the market democratic system is that the share of wealth enjoyed by the poor is maximized. To paraphrase Mandeville, under the institutions of limited government favored by market democracy, *the poor live better than the rich before, and nothing could be added more.*

At this point, however, an objection of a different sort must be faced. It is all very well to say that market democratic regimes *might* work to the material benefit of the least well-off. So too enthusiastically capitalistic societies *might* be exemplars of reciprocity and mutual respect, rather than sites of exploitation and social distrust. However, as a matter of practical feasibility, the institutions of market democracy are *highly unlikely* to come anywhere close to achieving those great goods. Even people who find market democracy attractive in theory have to admit that such regimes are unlikely to work well in practice. Worse, even if a society organized along market democratic lines should happen to prove beneficial to the poor (say, by satisfying a material prioritarian conception of distributive justice such as the one just sketched), that social form would still be morally objectionable. After all, left liberal regimes add a thick array of government branches designed to ensure that the requirements of distributive justice be met. By contrast, the market democratic affirmation of private economic liberty requires that any such government branches have strictly limited reach (where they are allowed at all). For all the good intentions they announce, therefore, market democratic regimes provide no institutional *guarantees* that wealth will in fact come into the hands of the poor, much less that the other requirements of social justice be met. In this sense, market democratic regimes allow for outcomes that are unjust when measured against the very distributive principles that I say they ought to affirm. I have mentioned this type of objection before. It is what I call the objection from the left.

This objection brings us to another feature of the Rawlsian model I find attractive. At the argumentative level of identification that I call political philosophy, Rawls thinks the morally most appropriate lens through which to evaluate political and economic institutions is what he calls ideal theory. In the next chapter, I explain and defend the Rawlsian conception of ideal theory. To begin, though, we should notice a certain irony in the objection to market democracy I just mentioned—the objection, that is, that even if market democratic institutional forms appear attractive in theory, they are unlikely to deliver the goods in practice and so are defective for that reason. The irony, of course, is that this form of this objection typically comes not from people on the left objecting to the starry-eyed idealism of capitalists. Rather, objections about feasibility typically come from people on the right who worry about what they see as the dangerous idealism of leftists. (Hayek, for example, criticizes socialists for disrupting the spontaneous order in reckless pursuit of the "chimera" of social justice.) To defend Rawls's general view of ideal theory, I begin by explaining why this type of objection has little force when applied against the idealism of left liberalism. I then turn to show why such arguments are equally ineffective when trained against the idealism of free market fairness.

CHAPTER 7

Feasibility, Normativity, and Institutional Guarantees

The Twilight of Left Liberalism?

The publication of *A Theory of Justice* began a multidecade run of enthusiasm among political philosophers for left liberal and social democratic institutional ideals. Rawls and his many talented followers confidently assured us that a moral commitment to social justice required a political commitment to extending and thickening the branches of government. Philosophers converged in defense of left liberal institutional forms—the welfare state or more social-democratic ideals such as property-owning democracy or liberal democratic socialism. Hegel would have smiled. For as the academic consensus tightened in favor of left liberalism, the political consensus about such institutions began to waver within actual liberal societies.

Early utilitarians such as Jeremy Bentham and James Mill were optimistic that scientific methods would soon render the social world subject to conscious control.[1] Through the middle years of the twentieth century, it was still plausible for politicians to express optimism about the direct-governmentalist approach. Franklin Roosevelt's pronouncement about the arrival of "competent administration" is emblematic. But citizens are now much more aware of practical obstacles that hinder the realization of Progressive dreams.

First, when social service programs are enacted in real liberal societies, those programs often turn out to be far more expensive than expected. In England, for example, the combined costs of welfare have increased eightfold in real terms since 1948, greatly outstripping the rise in national income. In the United States, after Medicare was enacted in 1965, the combined cost of Medicare, Medicaid, and Social Security was 2.5 percent of the GDP. By 2001, costs of those programs had more than tripled to 7.9 percent of the GDP.[2] The American Social Security program has been sustained by running directly on tax revenues and borrowing rather than on compounded interest income from the contributions of workers. Still, by the government's own projections, the social security system will soon be insolvent (unless the program's benefits are significantly scaled back, or taxes on workers still further increased).[3]

The problem of government debt is widespread. According to the Congressional Budget Office, America's public debt reached $7.6 trillion in 2009. That is 53 percent of the GDP, and economists predict that figure will soon pass 60 percent of the GDP.[4] Economists debate exactly what slice of that debt is connected to military ventures and other government activities, but all agree that social service programs are a significant and growing component.

State-based social service and insurance schemes generate unexpected moral costs as well.[5] If benefits are set low, the programs do not provide people with the material assistance they need to enable them to ride out tough times with dignity. If the benefits are set high enough to provide meaningful assistance, however, those programs generate perverse incentives that undermine the dignity of citizens in other ways. The idea of "poverty traps" was pioneered by scholars on the right: programs intended to lift people out of poverty sometimes create perverse incentives that keep people poor. But welfare experts on the left now widely acknowledge these problems as well.[6]

Sometimes the moral and economic costs of left liberal programs converge. Consider the case of public sector unions. In the United States, union membership in the private sector has decreased dramatically: falling from roughly one in five during the 1970s to less than one in thirteen in 2010. Union membership in the public sector, by contrast, has risen steadily. For a variety of reasons, public sector unions have successfully negotiated increasingly generous packages of pay and benefits for their members. According to some measures, a tipping point has been reached at which public employees on average enjoy job security and compensation packages superior to those of workers in the private sector. Along with exacerbating the problem of debt mentioned above, this creates tensions between members of the public and the private working classes.[7]

Left liberal regimes face other feasibility challenges. States with large public service sectors typically assume a broadly positive correlation between tax rates and tax revenues. However, as real marginal tax rates rise in liberal states, people's behavior changes. Wealthy people, sometimes including the politicians who write the tax laws, exploit loopholes in the tax code to avoid paying any significant tax.[8] Inflation and other factors lead to an ever-widening base of citizens subject to high taxes. When considering whether to take on extra projects, or deciding how soon to return to work from parenting, even middle-class people learn to calculate in the tax penalties that would be triggered by their decisions to work. As tax rates rise, noncompliance rises as well. (In the United States, the Internal Revenue Service recently estimated that the "tax gap"—the difference between taxes owed and taxes actually paid—is a robust 16 percent.[9]) Again, the idea that steeply progressive taxes may reach a point of diminishing returns was originally associated with politicians on the right.[10] However, as tax rates rose in the decades after World War II, prominent politicians on the left also accepted this idea.[11]

Economists continue to debate the relationship of tax rates (and tax type) to tax revenues, just as public policy analysts debate the effectiveness of rival schemes for delivering social services. In sketching these feasibility concerns I do not mean to be offering an all-things-considered empirical evaluation of left liberal or social democratic policies.[12] In some countries, traditional social democratic policies may continue to be pursued with a fair measure of enthusiasm and success. But within most western liberal democracies, large percentages of the population now look at those ideals with suspicion. This is particularly true of the United States. Within just fifty years, American citizens went from hearing one Democratic president tell them that the "era of competent administration has arrived" to hearing another promise that "the era of big government is over."[13]

Public choice economics illuminates the sources of this new pessimism about government. People on the left sometimes suggest that the problems of government inefficiency and corruption stem mainly from the fact that citizens hold unequal shares of wealth. If wealth could be made more equal, they suggest, many of these problems would be diminished or resolved. However, public choice economists suggest that the real problem is not so much unequal shares of wealth or power but rather a more intractable fact: so long as a wide range of economic questions are allowed onto the legislative agenda, the importance of those questions will differ to parties in ways that do not track inequalities in wealth or power. It is not the fact of differential wealth but the fact of differential interests that generates these problems of "government failure."[14]

Consider the phenomenon of concentrated benefits and dispersed costs. According to Mancur Olson, any proposed change within a system of social rules typically affects the interests of certain groups of citizens more than it affects the interests of citizens in the majority. Because small groups face low organization costs, this asymmetry distorts the outcomes of collective decision making. Philosophers sometimes worry that in democracies the majority (or the wealthy) can exploit the minority. In practice, the opposite often occurs. As Olson puts it: "There is a systematic tendency for exploitation of the great by the small!"[15] The phenomenon generates special problems for social systems that place substantial economic power in the hands of elected officials.

One of the most prominent of these problems is "rent seeking."[16] We can think of rent seeking as the spending of real resources with no improvement but rather a loss to production, with the objective of gaining wealth, power, or other advantages for oneself. Rent seeking is socially destructive but difficult to prevent. To take a classic example: a tariff on imported light bulbs may reduce consumer choice and be economically costly. The cost of the tariff to each citizen may be only a few extra cents per year. But that tariff might be worth millions of dollars to the small group of domestic light bulb producers. Since the domestic light bulb manufacturers are a small group, their organizational costs are low. The very fact that tariff rules are on the legislative agenda creates incentives for actors to bypass the economic market and seek instead to reap profits via the political system. Indeed, it may be rational for light bulb manufacturers to make political expenditures right up to the monetary value of the tariff to their own companies. The internal dynamics of collective decision procedures tend to favor the passage of many such measures, even when their overall social effect is negative.

We might hope other politicians would step in to prevent proposals with negative social costs from being enacted. However, things rarely work that way. After all, those other politicians also need to have special pieces of legislation passed, and they therefore need to rely on the support of fellow politicians to see those measures through. This process of "log rolling" is a regular part of political activity.

Because of the phenomenon of dispersed costs and concentrated benefits, there are systematic pressures toward waste, inefficiency, and corruption within legislative processes. The more economic power a society places in the hands of elected officials, the greater the pressures toward "political capture" and social waste.

As a purely practical matter, it is not obvious that an informed citizenry can be relied upon to prevent these forms of behavior. Every citizen knows that the chance of his one vote determining the outcome of a regional or national election is vanishingly low. Gathering detailed information about candidates is costly. From the perspective of each individual, therefore, it may be rational to remain ignorant about political matters.[17] Worse, since individual voters know their vote will not decide the election, they may cast their votes expressively, voting in ways that simply make them feel better ideologically. Many people have prejudices that are economically ill informed. For example, some evidence suggests that people are emotionally disposed to give greater weight to the protection of existing jobs than to policies that would create more jobs in the near future. If individual voters vote on their irrational biases, democracies will produce irrational policies.[18] Democratic decision procedures, on this view, may have an internal tendency to produce economically counterproductive policies. The structure of democratic decision procedures makes the policies systematically more likely to reflect the emotional, ill-considered attitudes of citizens rather than the more considered, deliberative assessments of which they might be capable.[19]

Recent work in social psychology deepens these worries. The ideal of democratic decision making posits diverse but deliberative political bodies reasoning with one another to enlarge their common viewpoint. Studies conducted by Diana Mutz, however, have brought us a new understanding of just how far actual societies are from achieving this ideal. People tend to deliberate only with people who share their own political convictions. As Mutz puts it: "Most people want to get along with others; they would prefer consensus to political disagreement. But given diverse viewpoints, they maximize their chances of achieving 'community' by gravitating toward like-minded others."[20] According to Mutz, there is a basic tension between the deliberative and the participatory aspirations of democracy. Deliberative democracy may sound wonderful in theory. As a practical matter, however, a polity can achieve its deliberative aspirations or it can achieve its participatory ones. Human psychology makes it unlikely that a polity could achieve both.

The psychological stresses within democracies identified by Mutz are amplified by the rise of identity politics. As issues of cultural identity become increasingly important to people, citizens may become less interested in problems of material distribution. For many citizens, political recognition may become more important than distributive justice—at least as distributive justice is traditionally conceived. Further, social democratic regimes typically aspire to universalized systems of care as an expression of the equal concern and respect owed each citizen. But cultures are worldviews. As such, cultures often carry with them distinctive ways of understanding all the components of life—birth, parenting, health, religion, education, work, saving, recreation, parental care, personal aging, and death. The drive toward uniform standards runs against this headwind. Even social democratic enthusiasts such as John Roemer admit that leftist political programs are most feasible in small countries that are "linguistically, ethnically, racially and religiously homogeneous."[21] Social service states are increasingly beset by demands from a culturally diverse citizenry to make vital life decisions in ways that reflect and honor their distinctive cultural values.

Globalization also creates special dilemmas for the political pursuit of social justice. Let's define globalization as the permeability of political borders to movements of people, ideas, goods, and capital. Globalization may increase the economic insecurity of citizens and so lead to the demand for stronger social safety nets. However, globalization forces political leaders to make hard choices between economic growth and policies of ever-raising taxes to maintain those social service programs. (It also leads to calls for tight restrictions on immigration in order to protect generous social service programs.) A country that embarks on a policy of high taxation faces the very real threat of capital flight. Political leaders can maintain their control over the economic life of their societies by closing down their borders—and enduring the economic consequences. If they want their economies to grow, however, they may need to enact more market-friendly reforms. Even if globalization is compatible with democracy, it seems corrosive of many welfare-statist and social democratic institutional ideals.

The combined effects of globalization and multiculturalism are so profound that some have wondered whether these developments pose challenges not merely to social democratic institutional forms but also to the ideal of social justice. Extending an idea of Hume's, David Miller formulates what he calls "the circumstances of social justice." As Miller says, "the concept of social justice apparently presupposes a relatively homogeneous political community whose directing agency, the state, has the capacity to shape its major institutions—and thus the final distribution of social resources—in the way the principles embedded in the concept prescribe." As Miller notes, some scholars worry that the rise of multiculturalism and globalization signal that we have moved beyond the circumstances in which "social justice" is relevant as a normative standard. Even staunch advocates of social democratic institutions have begun asking whether the travails of social democracies at the end of the twentieth century signal an end to the era of social justice.[22]

The closing decades of the twentieth century were marked by a growing awareness on the part of the general populace of the practical obstacles left liberal institutions face in their pursuit of social justice. But what about the *philosophers*? Should concerns about practical feasibility affect the way philosophers understand the moral requirements of liberal justice? If ordinary people in some countries stubbornly resist left liberal political reforms, should this affect the moral confidence that high liberal philosophers have in their view? Can problems of feasibility erode the foundations of normativity?

Realistic Utopianism

Philosophy, famously, is the love of wisdom. Political philosophy, by extension, might be expected to denote a love of wisdom about political topics. Traditionally, wisdom about politics has been understood to require a great breadth of understanding. Anyone hoping to give advice, or offer evaluations, about how people ought to live together politically would need a nuanced understanding of many facets of the human social condition: history, religion, economics, sociology, institutional theory, social psychology, moral philosophy, and more. One would need this breadth of understanding because recommendations about politics are ordinarily understood to be recommendations for people in our world, a world in which reality rarely conforms precisely to theory on any single disciplinary dimension. Political wisdom might seem to require that when we think about how our world ought to be ordered institutionally, we think about the practical consequences of our institutional recommendations. This would require that political philosophers attend not only to how things might possibly turn out. It would require that they think about how things are likely to turn out as well.

For example, in considering how our society ought to be organized institutionally, we cannot assume that people will always comply with the rules and the norms that guided the writing of those rules. It would be foolish to recommend a particular set of political institutions if our recommendation is based on the expectation that the individuals who take up the positions in those institutions will always behave precisely as we think they ought. Much experience suggests, and a growing body of theoretical literature confirms, that political institutions often generate perverse incentives—incentives that, unfortunately, lead people to act against the very norms theoretically attached to the roles the political institutions set out. Similarly, just because a regulation or law is intended to have some particular effect on society, we cannot assume that the regulation will produce the desired effect—or that in producing a desired effect it will not also produce a variety of unwanted effects as well.

So too, from a different ideological perspective, we cannot assume that markets will always work perfectly so that, for example, exchanges will be positive sum for all participants, or that the principle of comparative advantage will produce immediate benefits to all. Again experience suggests, and theory confirms, that in the real world markets rarely work that way. The character and behavior of particular actors along with informational constraints (or advantages) they experience, hidden costs or benefits from transactions (what economists call "externalities"), the prevalence (or absence) of commonly held resources, the stages of technological and social development, the specific rules governing any property rights regime, as well as the macrocharacteristics of the particular stage of technological and social development, always influence how close or far actual markets will be from realizing the expectations charted in our theoretical ideals.[23]

In light of these real-world deviations from our theoretical ideals, we can construct explanatory theories about why people, governments, and markets do not function in ways that correspond to our theoretical ideals. We can then build those theories of "failure" into our original theory, making our theoretical models ever more sophisticated and predictively powerful. But even then the complexity of social life gives political reality an uncertainty or, if you like, a stubbornness that renders our best explanatory theories mere approximations of the way things really are in any actual society at any given moment. In advocating any given institutional regime type over any other, wisdom requires that we not merely consider how things might go if conditions turn out to be favorable on all these dimensions. We must also consider how things are likely to go, given the stubbornness and complexity of human social life. When it comes to political topics, wisdom lies primarily in the skill of negotiating the boundary between theoretical ideals and practical realities.

The most striking characteristic of academic theorizing in the wake of Rawls has been the willingness of liberal theorists to separate the professional discipline of political philosophy from the more civic ideal of political wisdom. Contemporary high liberals seek to separate out and focus intensively upon a single dimension of political evaluation: the moral dimension. On this approach, the first task of political philosophy is not to provide guidance for political action or reform. Rather, that task of political philosophy is simply to identify principles of justice and a range of institutional regime types that might realize those principles.[24]

How are we to go about this task of political identification? Rawls's answer may surprise us. For while Rawls's topic is political, his approach to that topic is purely normative—or at least, it is as purely normative as he thinks the topic of politics allows. Rawls therefore invokes a series of modeling assumptions. These assumptions require that we abstract away from many of the most stubborn facts about political life. To identify principles of justice, for example, we are to assume that our principles are to govern a society with a more or less fixed membership. So instead of trying to figure out what justice might require in a society with soft borders, with goods, capital, and people freely crossing in and out, we invoke the simplifying assumption that the society's borders are closed.

Similarly, when conducting this identificatory task, we assume that the principles of justice, whatever they might turn out to be, will win the full motivational compliance of all citizens. In evaluating a candidate set of principles of justice, therefore, we run the evaluation by considering what social world those principles would tend to produce if everyone was willing to follow the rules correctly. Additionally, rather than thinking of society as riven by implacable differences of culture, race, religion, and class the way many societies are, the philosophical project of identification asks us to assume that the society is characterized by a more gentle "reasonable value pluralism." When identifying principles of justice, we put aside the voluminous empirical literatures that explain why some political systems face greater compliance problems than others.

The first identificatory task of normative political philosophy concerns principles. For high liberals, as for market democracy, this involves identifying a set of principles of justice that expresses our commitment to treat citizens as free and equal self-governing agents. The second identificatory task concerns institutions. When we turn to this second identificatory project, we seek to identify institutional regime types that "realize" the principles of justice. This process requires that we evaluate social systems in ways that are even more idealized. At the level of "ideal theory," we are to discover which regime types would be just by imagining that the institutions of each regime function well according to that regime's announced intentions and ideals.[25] Whether the regime type is a high liberal form of liberal socialism or some market democratic version of laissez-faire capitalism, we are to imagine that the distinctive maladies that other nonphilosophical disciplines tell us plague such systems have been cured. Thus citizens and elected officials alike always behave as justice requires them to behave. Economic planners have all the information they need so that every regulation and law produces its desired effects and no unintended ones. Labor markets, if the candidate regime includes them, perform as efficiently as envisaged in their textbook ideals. Political bureaucracies function without friction, waste, or avarice.[26] When asking whether any given regime type "realizes" liberal justice, we are to imagine that the sun that shines on it is warm; the rains that fall, gentle.

Many theorists, including some leading advocates of left liberalism, react in a guarded way to the idealization and abstraction that characterize recent liberal thought. Bruce Ackerman and Anne Alstott worry about "a certain utopianism that presently afflicts much liberal theorizing."[27] Amartya Sen argues that theories of justice should be developed in ways that help us better judge how to reduce injustice and to advance justice, "rather than aiming only at the characterization of the perfectly just society—an exercise that is such a dominant feature of so many theories of justice today."[28] According to Sen, a theory of justice is "a guide to reasoned choice of politics, strategies, or institutions." To develop such a theory, "the identification of fully just social arrangements is neither necessary nor sufficient."[29] David Miller argues that the primary task of political philosophy is to propose principles that citizens can act upon. Miller therefore advocates what he calls "political philosophy for Earthlings—political philosophy that is sensitive not only [to] general facts about the human condition but also to facts of a more specific kind, facts about particular societies."[30] Idealization moves political philosophy away from political reality, and this worries some left liberals.[31]

Other theorists, typically from positions still further to the left, have criticized high liberal thought for being *insufficiently* idealistic. G. A. Cohen argues that Rawls is not, properly speaking, developing a theory of justice. This is because Rawls's account of justice accepts too many facts about the world as *given*. In Cohen's view, justice, properly understood, is a fact-independent normative standard. The problem of identifying the just society is disconnected from questions about what societies are like now or about the way in which people typically act. Rawls's difference principle, for example, takes as granted the fact that people often act on self-interested reasons. In Cohen's view, this renders it a "rule of regulation" rather than a "principle of justice."[32] Justice demands that citizens possess a more altruistic motivational set than the Rawlsian person.[33] According to Cohen, Rawls argues at a level that sets the normative bar too low. It is institutional theorizing, not truly moral theorizing. As a result, as Sharon Krause puts it, Cohen "sees moral desirability as being fully independent of questions about practical feasibility."[34]

Classical liberals tend to have the opposite reaction. They think high liberals, and Rawls in particular, are too *little* concerned with the way things are likely to go. Perhaps this is because proponents of economic liberty sense that they are on strongest ground in their disputes with high liberals when discussions focus on practical questions about what actually works in the world, rather than on the questions of moral intention that dominate at the level of ideal theory. Not all recent thinkers in the classical liberal tradition object to idealization in political thought. Some libertarians, such Nozick, are quite comfortable deriving political ideals from "first principles." But many theorists in the classical liberal tradition do worry about issues of practical feasibility. They argue that concerns about practical feasibility should be built into the normative foundations of political views. If a political ideal is unlikely to work in practice, they say, it is defective as an ideal.

Advocates of thick economic liberty especially object to the way ideal theoretic analysis focuses narrowly on the quality of intentions. Sometimes we see this skepticism directed against the idealization high liberals employ when they go about the first task of political philosophy, the task of identifying the requirements of justice. David Schmidtz offers a powerful formulation of this skepticism. Schmidtz writes: "The compliance problem is not the second step. It is not something to be set aside as a task for so-called nonideal theory, as if the degree of compliance were an exogenous variable that could be dealt with separately. The compliance problem is an integral part of the first step. When one chooses a set of rules, one gets a particular compliance problem and a particular pattern of compliance along with it. Therefore, we cannot begin to know whether instituting a given set of rules will be to our mutual advantage unless we know how bad its associated compliance problem will be."[35] A robust concern for feasibility issues must inform our search for principles of justice.

Similar concerns have been raised about the idealization Rawls employs when evaluating candidate types of institutional regimes. Loren Lomasky suggests that feasibility concerns should be brought into the original position. Because that device is meant to model the idea of fairness, Lomasky suggests that it might be used to select institutional regimes as well. While the parties work behind a veil of ignorance that prevents them from knowing the particulars of their own social station, they are allowed knowledge of general sociological and economic facts. But what are those facts? Lomasky suggests that if parties are allowed access to the main findings of economic science of the past century, they will reject all versions of socialism. Further, in light of the findings of public choice economists, the parties will be skeptical of any regime that makes property insecure by placing great economic decision-making power on the legislative agenda—no matter how noble the objectives assigned to that legislature might be. Instead, Lomasky says, the parties will wisely prefer regimes that "erect constraints on the ability of political actors to redefine property rights in the service of some ostensible ideal."[36] The project of identifying institutions that would be fair, Lomasky suggests, is entwined with practical concerns about feasibility.

Jason Brennan, as we have seen, argues that ideal theory generates a paradox for high liberalism. Implicitly accepting the market democratic contention that the difference principle is best interpreted in material prioritarian terms, Brennan says that the expanding economies of enthusiastically capitalistic regimes will better satisfy that principle than the slow-growing social democratic ideals such as property-owning democracy. But Rawls's focus on the quality of intentions leads him to prefer those social democratic regime types. Brennan says, "Living by the difference principle via Rawls' favored institutions, e.g., is a way of enshrining concern for the poor, but it is not a way of helping them." Thus high liberals face a choice between actual success and symbolic concern for success.[37] A practical concern for the poor would lead us to the former. But a commitment to ideal theory directs high liberals toward the latter.[38]

We noted that Gerald Gaus has developed a novel approach to public reason.[39] Yet rejecting the Rawlsian notion of ideal theory, Gaus thinks political orders should be evaluated in large measure in terms of how well they are likely to perform in practice.[40] According to Gaus, Rawls's enthusiasm for ideal theory leads him to bizarre conclusions: for example, arguing "that market socialism, which has only been institutionalized by General Tito's repressive Yugoslav state, is within the class of acceptable regimes partly because it *protects* political liberties, whereas a welfare state such as the United Kingdom, which probably protects political rights as well as any regime in history, is unjust because it fails to protect the fair value of political rights." It is this "cavalier disregard for political reality" that has led so many left liberals to understate the importance of private property.[41]

I share the conviction of many classical liberals that market-based regime types look best when conversations turn to practical questions about how institutions function in the world.[42] I also share the conviction of Schmidtz, Lomasky, Brennan, and Gaus that questions about feasibility must be assigned some important role within the normative enterprise. The question is: Where within the normative enterprise do questions of feasibility belong, and where within that enterprise do such questions not belong? Again, I think of market democracy as a capacious research program. People who affirm the core market democratic idea—wide private economic liberty is compatible with social justice—are free to take very different views on the methodological question of how near to the facts, or how high above them, arguments about liberal justice should fly. So the Rawlsian methodology is merely one among many that might be adopted in defense of market democracy. Allow me to explain why I am attracted to the Rawlsian method.

David Estlund offers a striking defense of the methodological idealism that characterizes recent thinking in the high liberal tradition.[43] Normative theory is about how people should act. Therefore, Estlund explains, when identifying normative ideals it is appropriate to put aside questions of how we think people will act. A normative political theory would be utopian in the wrong sense if it required people to do impossible things. Yet a theory would be excessively realistic if it allowed practical concerns about how people are likely to act to drag down the normative bar.

Expanding upon Rawls's idea of "realistic utopianism," Estlund argues that the proper domain of normative thinking about politics lies between what he calls "complacent realism" and "moral utopianism."[44] A view is complacently realistic if it asks too little of people or institutions from a moral perspective. Estlund quotes from Rousseau's introduction to *Émile*: " 'Propose what can be done,' they never stop telling me. It is as if I were told, 'Propose doing what is done.' "[45] Such views concede too much to the way things happen to be. They are insufficiently aspirational. On the other hand, moral views can also go wrong by asking too much. A view is morally utopian if it makes demands that people or institutions could not possibly satisfy. Such views falsely impose their demands, since people are not morally failing if they fall short of standards they could not possibly live up to.[46]

Estlund therefore directs our attention to what he calls "the noncomplacent, non-utopian range of normative political theories."[47] Provocatively, Estlund thinks this range includes even theories he characterizes as examples of "hopeless realism." These are political theories that people could possibly live up to, and yet the probability of their actually doing so is very low and may even be zero. Estlund vigorously defends such hopelessly realistic political theories. According to Estlund, "The fact that people will not live up to [such theories] even though they could is a defect of the people, not of the theory."[48] This is a strong formulation of the Rawlsian thesis, and whether Rawls himself would accept it is a question I shall not consider. For us, the important idea to take from Estlund and Rawls is this: the project of identifying normative political principles is the project of determining how things *should* turn out. To allow that project to be constrained by worries about how things actually will turn out would be to fall victim to what Estlund calls "utopophobia."

The identificatory project of political philosophy is strongly normative. It directs us to transform existing institutions so that they become more like some institutional ideals and less like others. Political philosophy becomes directly action guiding, however, only when combined with empirical information. Estlund compares the identificatory project of political philosophy to the project of identifying an ideal place for a picnic.[49] Even if we could identify the position and character of an ideal picnic spot, it does not immediately follow that we should take hold of our baskets and hike straight toward it. There may be dangerous pits or bogs in the way, such that some more circuitous route would, as a practical matter, make us more likely actually to get there someday. Or there may be other spots, nearer and easier to get to, that—while lacking in some respects—might nonetheless be acceptable "second bests," at least for the time being. In deciding how to act, we need to consider empirical facts about the lay of the land. But without the institutional ideals identified by philosophy, we would have trouble knowing which institutional ideals are worth working toward.

Most Rawlsians would agree with Estlund's argument against utopophobia. There is an aspect of normative thinking about politics that, while recognizing the boundaries of the possible, properly asks us to abstract away from questions about how things are likely to turn out.[50] Political philosophy is like a citadel. It offers us a high place from which we can see. So long as our immediate interest is in identifying the requirements of justice, then high up in that citadel is where we want to be. It is from there that Rawls claims that his preferred left liberal regime types—property-owning democracy and liberal socialism—"realize" the requirements of social justice.

From this secure citadel of ideal theory, all the feasibility challenges confronting social democratic and welfare statist institutional forms can be answered, or at least put safely in their place. From the perspective of ideal theory, the merely practical problems that have led to so many frustrated dreams within actual liberal democracies are, in fact, merely practical problems. The high liberal assertion that the institutions of social democracy "realize" the values of liberal social justice is unsullied by the disappointments of government programs of the late twentieth century. Do people in liberal states facing steeply progressive taxes on their estates seek out loopholes to avoid paying those taxes? That has no bearing on the question of whether such people should pay those taxes. Do means-tested programs inadvertently create poverty traps that induce people to stay on the dole rather than take low-paying entry-level employment? From the perspective of political philosophy, this too is a defect of the people not the theory. After all, those people could do the right thing. They could seek and take work as soon as they are able—no matter how high the effective marginal tax rate on their decision to do so. The mere fact that many people in those positions do not, and likely will not, seek work has no bearing on the philosophical assertion that they should do so. Do public sector workers lobby for benefits packages so generous that they make the costs of service programs unsustainable? Again, so long as it is possible for people to do otherwise, these are defects of the people and the institutions— not of the theory.

Philosophy allows us to make a similar reply to the public choice economists who have described the systematic obstacles that are endemic to social democracy as a political form. Does the left liberal strategy of placing economic power in the hands of elected officials generate incentives that encourage socially destructive rent-seeking and log-rolling behavior? Do individual citizens vote on expressive grounds rather than on the basis of serious, dispassionate evaluation of candidate platforms? Again, it is our philosophical norms that allow us to recognize these behaviors as defective in the first place. Theories explaining the likelihood that people will behave in these ways cannot be allowed to reach up and pull down the normative bar. After all, that bar simply identifies what people in those positions should do, and what they could do, under favorable (though still possible) social conditions.

In principle, even challenges to social democracy that result from tectonic changes in the macroconditions of political life could be philosophically set aside in this way. Does rising multiculturalism make some modern societies so divided that political consensus on uniform social service programs is impossible? Does increasing globalization create a situation in which badly needed capital investments flee from states that seek to maintain large tax-fueled social service sectors? No problem. From the perspective of ideal theory, such states of affairs constitute no threat to the normative claim that social democratic institutional forms "realize" justice as fairness (on a social democratic interpretation of that standard). No one ever promised that the great good of social justice must actually be attainable in every imaginable historic, cultural, and economic epoch. Perhaps the high liberal conception of social justice is not achievable in an era of increasing multiculturalism and globalization. This might be a disappointing fact about our world. But it would not count as any criticism of the claim that the institutional forms of social democracy should be identified as "realizing" the values of liberal justice. To defend that claim, one need merely insist that under some maximally favorable (but still possible) set of historical, cultural, economic conditions, those institutions might conceivably create a social order in which all people could experience the good of liberal justice.

For all these reasons, Rawlsians insist that obstacles of feasibility cannot be allowed to drag down the normative bar the position of which we identify through the use of political philosophy. In politics, the normative is appropriately constrained by the sociologically possible, not the probabilistically likely. This is the sense in which the identificatory project of political philosophy correctly claims to be insulated from practical empirical observations about the social conditions in particular societies.

Utopophobia is an unjustified fear of idealized political discourse. In the face of utopophobia, thinkers in the high liberal tradition encourage their fellow philosophers to climb the tower of ideal theory confidently. Estlund, as we have seen, exhorts philosophers to defend the autonomy of the project of normative identification against all comers from the disciplines of the merely actual.

As I have indicated, I share Rawls's general view about the point, and proper method, of political philosophy. While agreeing with these high liberals about the dangers of utopophobia, however, I would add a word of a caution against yet another danger of political thinking, a danger that I call *philosophilia*. If philosophy is the love of wisdom, philosophilia is the love of philosophy, with or without wisdom. In the realm of politics, philosophilia is an attraction to idealized forms of political discourse that is so ardent that one comes to believe that ideal theory is the whole of political theory, such that a people come to believe that philosophical progress can be made by immersing oneself solely in the mainstream philosophical literature.

Like every grand passion, philosophilia carries a distinctive set of dangers.[51] In particular, philosophilia may blow smoke in our eyes when we contemplate the disparities between certain normative axioms that dominate academic thinking and the practical experiences of citizens within the liberal societies of our day. In this way, philosophilia may cause us to miss opportunities for intellectual growth, leaving us blinking in a kind of conservative moral stupor. If leading thinkers in some generation before us have labored to demonstrate that some progressive institutional regime of their day might, as a matter of ideal theory level analysis, satisfy the requirements of liberal justice, people attracted to that normative paradigm might fall into the complacent view that their task henceforth is merely to sit up in the citadel and defend that inherited ideological view (for example, by simply extending that same paradigm to new issue areas, or tinkering with its institutional requirements). In this way, the high liberal paradigm becomes ever safer from practical disappointments. Rising objections from ordinary people to that erstwhile "progressive" ideology might be taken merely as a reason to climb higher in the philosophical citadel, safely out of reach. This passion for idealization can make philosophers impervious to moral learning. Their methodological impulse is to climb up and away from the experiences of ordinary citizens, rather than to come down and listen closely to them.

When it comes to the evaluation of the moral significance of economic liberty, philosophilia tempts contemporary political philosophers to continue thinking the comfortable, rather than thinking the unthinkable. Philosophilia helps explain why the professional philosophical community has been so slow to take seriously the sentiments of middle-class people that their private economic liberties matter more rather than less to them as their societies grow wealthier. It is philosophilia, or something like it, that leads otherwise astute thinkers such as Thomas Nagel to treat the settled convictions of ordinary working people that they have some sort of de facto claim on the wages they earn as meriting no more professional attention than the objectively false beliefs such people have in response to complex problems in probability theory. Unwittingly, philosophers begin to treat the Political Problem like the Birthday Problem: a domain of inquiry in which their claim to authority is absolute.

By contrast, free market fairness is built from a constant awareness of the dangers of philosophilia. This approach does not allow the beliefs of ordinary people to *define* the nature of liberal justice. Still, it looks to the beliefs of such people as a source of insights that might enrich and freshen our philosophical discussions of that difficult question. If utopophobia is Charybdis, philosophilia is Scylla. Free market fairness is alert to both dangers and seeks to chart a course of its own between the two.

Idealization provides a degree of insulation to the social democratic institutions of market democracy against the feasibility objections from the right. By the same token, idealization insulates market democratic regime types from such objections from the left. But what *degree* of insulation against feasibility objections does ideal theory provide? To find out, we need to examine the test of ideal theory.

Aims and Guarantees

Liberal justice directs us toward institutions designed to enable citizens to develop their moral powers of responsible self-authorship. Market democratic regimes such as democratic limited government and democratic laissez-faire are designed with this goal in mind. The defining institutional feature of market democratic regimes is that they enshrine a wide range of private economic freedoms as basic constitutional rights. It is this platform of thick economic liberty that most clearly sheers off market democracy from liberal social democracy as a rival democratic form.

The emphasis free market fairness puts on private economic liberty generates a sphere of protection around the choices individual citizens seek to make regarding their economic affairs, affairs that are basic to their developing and carrying out of a plan of life that is their own. However, those constitutionally protected spheres significantly limit the scope of regulatory and legislative activity in economic affairs. Market democratic regime types make little room for the legislative programs by which social democratic regimes typically pursue social justice: aggressively redistributive taxation, state-based social service programs, extensive public regulation of the workplace, and such.

The crucial question thus becomes: if market democratic regimes treat economic liberty as constitutionally basic, can they realize all the requirements of justice as fairness? On the free market fairness interpretation of those requirements, for example, this would involve claiming that enthusiastically capitalistic regime types should be philosophically identified as providing the greatest possible share of wealth and income to the least well-off (thereby satisfying market democracy's material prioritarian interpretation of the difference principle).

High liberals typically employ a two-part test to determine how well any proposed regime type fares by the standard of justice as fairness. To "realize" justice as fairness, a regime type must (1) aim at justice as fairness and (2) include institutional arrangements intended to satisfy the principles of justice.[52] This analysis takes place at the level of ideal theory. Ideal theory is a technique that allows us to pick out and focus on moral considerations. Its does this by emphasizing questions of intentionality rather than of practical feasibility. When engaged in ideal theoretic analysis, we are to set aside concerns of feasibility that plague actual political societies. We imagine each candidate regime's institutions as they might function within favorable historical and cultural conditions.

It is easy to see why a regime must aim at justice as fairness if it is to be identified as realizing justice as fairness from the perspective of ideal theory. After all, ideal theory emphasizes the quality of moral intentions. When we ask whether a regime type aims at some standard of social justice, or rejects that standard of social justice, we are evaluating the quality of intentions in a particularly clear and direct way. What's more, this first prong of the ideal theoretic test helps satisfy the condition of publicity. According to the liberal principle of legitimacy, the use of political power is legitimate only if the citizens can accept the reasons on which the use of that power is based. The requirement of aiming effectively ensures that regime types make public the reasons or aims to which their particular set of institutions are in service. In this way the publicity requirement helps regimes satisfy the principle of legitimacy.

The second prong of the ideal theoretic test requires that along with aiming at justice as fairness, a regime type must also contain institutional arrangements of an appropriate sort. This requirement may seem puzzling because ideal theory directs us to focus our attention on normative issues of intentionality. It might seem that within ideal theory the mere fact of "aiming" does all the identificatory work. Perhaps any regime type can "realize" liberal justice simply by aiming at it: aiming to achieve some conception of social justice is a sufficient condition for "realizing" that conception. When exposed to feasibility concerns, the "R-value" of the insulation provided by idealization is 100 percent.[53]

However, while ideal theory does seek to focus our attention on the quality of intentions, it also seeks to do this in a way that avoids the dangers of utopianism. The second prong of the ideal theoretic test serves this function. This prong requires that the candidate social systems include arrangements that pursue justice in a realistic way. This requirement of realism is not one that concerns mere degrees of probability. As we have seen, in political philosophy, as in moral philosophy, one can correctly identify a moral standard even if the probability of that standard's being satisfied is extremely low (or even, as Estlund insists, zero). Rather, the requirement of realism in the second prong of our ideal theoretic test is one that concerns something more like *possibility*. This second prong requires that candidate regime types include institutional arrangements that could *possibly* bring the social relations of a given society into line with the requirements of justice as fairness. Ought implies can. By requiring that a regime type that aims at justice as fairness also includes institutional arrangements that could possibly bring about justice as fairness, this condition is satisfied. But "possibility" is an ambiguous standard. So how useful is this broad-gauged empirical test?

We can imagine cases in which this test of institutional possibility would be easy to apply. Imagine, for example, a regime type that— while officially aiming at justice as fairness—included institutional arrangements that directly contradicted that standard. To make this vivid, imagine a (fanciful) regime type called Liberal Command Theocracy. Liberal Command Theocracy aims at justice as fairness and thus affirms a general right of religious freedom as among the basic rights of liberal citizenship. The first principle of this regime type's constitution, however, declares that it is a command theocracy. As such, the governing powers have the authority to impose the religion of their choice on the citizenry, in clear violation of the liberal rights of religious freedom. The arrangements of Liberal Command Theocracy could *not possibly* satisfy justice as fairness in the obvious sense that those arrangements contradict that standard. Liberal Command Theocracy demonstrates one way a regime type might fail the institutional prong of our ideal theoretic test.[54]

Other forms of failure are equally easy to detect. For example, a candidate regime type might pursue justice as fairness by institutional arrangements that, while not contradicting that standard, have no causal connection whatsoever toward the attainment of the state of affairs the standard of justice requires. To make this vivid, imagine a (significantly more) fanciful regime type that I will call Liberal ChickenWingdom. Liberal ChickenWingdom aims at justice as fairness. But, imagine, the only institutional arrangement by which Liberal ChickenWingdom seeks to achieve justice as fairness is a law requiring that a chicken wing be buried in the garden behind the White House on the full moon.[55] While logically compatible with the achievement of justice as fairness, the institutional arrangements of Liberal ChickenWingdom can claim no causal link of any kind toward the satisfaction of the requirements of justice as fairness. These ways of failing the institutional prong of our ideal theoretic test are easy to detect.[56]

With other cases we also may feel confident in our application of the requirement of institutional possibility, even though it becomes more difficult to specify the sociological facts on which our confidence relies. Consider an imaginary regime type called Direct Democratic Liberalism (DDL). DDL aims at justice as fairness (say, on some social democratic interpretation of that standard). Further, DDL relies heavily on legislative processes in its attempt to satisfy all the requirements of that standard. For these reasons, DDL might be thought of as a (justice-realizing) form of social democracy. True to its name, however, DDL is a peculiarly *direct* democratic form of liberalism. The constitution of DDL (whether written or unwritten) sets out no rights or liberties. Indeed, DDL makes no place for judicial review of any kind. Instead, every political decision within this imaginary regime type is to be made by a simple majority vote among the entire populace (say, in real time by hand-held electronic devices). Fortunately, the citizenry that is governed by DDL institutions all affirm justice as fairness. So, the outcome of every vote can reliably be expected to respect the basic rights of citizens and all the other requirements of justice as fairness (again, on some preferred social-democratic interpretation).

Philosophers might reasonably disagree about whether DDL violates (or realizes) justice as fairness. On the Rawlsian approach to ideal theory, I expect DDL would be said to violate it. Even if we accept that DDL aims at justice as fairness (on its own preferred interpretation), the claim that its institutional arrangements might bring about justice as fairness seems not merely unlikely but, perhaps, impossible (at least in the context of any reasonably sized, reasonably diverse, liberal society). The problem is not merely a technological one concerning, say, the availability of the aforementioned hand-held vote-computation devices. Imagine that suitable devices exist. Still, imagining the citizens of DDL consistently voting to protect the rights of individuals, say, across generations and in the face of the value pluralisms that predictably emerge in societies as a consequence of those very rights, would seem to require that we suspend even the most general laws of political sociology. From the Rawlsian perspective of ideal theory, the problem is not merely that it may, as a practical matter, be very difficult to achieve (and maintain) social justice though the institutions of DDL. The problem is deeper than that. In a way that is hard to define with precision, it is *utterly unrealistic* to seek to achieve justice as fairness through the institutions of DDL. For a candidate regime to realize justice as fairness, it must include arrangements that seek justice in a way that is compatible with the general laws of political sociology. The mere fact that some proposed regime type aims at one's preferred conception of justice cannot be enough to qualify that regime type as passing this (admittedly ambiguous) test of sociological realism.

For similar reasons, of course, market democratic regime types such as democratic limited government do not automatically "realize" the requirements of free market fairness simply by announcing that they aim at doing so. Imagine a classical liberal view I shall call Rawlsian Property Absolutism (RPA). RPA, let us imagine, aims at some market democratic interpretation of justice as fairness. The institutional arrangement by which RPA pursues justice as fairness, however, is a constitution consisting of a single line: "Every citizen has an absolute right to private property and economic contract that the state shall do nothing to restrict, limit, or regulate in any way." Fortunately, however, the citizens living under RPA all affirm justice as fairness. So, we are to imagine, individuals there always use their absolute property rights in ways that satisfy the requirements of that normative standard. Property owners in RPA voluntarily provide whatever resources their fellow citizens need to practice their religions and to express their opinions freely. Citizens always refrain from entering into economic contracts by which some alienate their basic rights to others. To ensure that market democracy's material prioritarian interpretation of the difference principle is satisfied, merchants sell consumer items at discounted prices to the less advantaged citizens, and so forth.

As with Direct Democratic Liberalism, it seems plausible to say that Rawlsian Property Absolutism fails the ideal theoretic test of sociological realism. Perhaps its is logically (or physically) possible for a society governed by RPA to achieve justice as fairness. But RPA asks us to imagine people and institutions performing in ways that are incompatible with the most general laws of political sociology (psychology, economics, and social theory, for example).[57] When a real society in which RPA is instantiated fails to live up to justice as fairness, it would be a mistake to say that this is a defect of the people. The defect is in the institutional arrangements of the RPA regime type. RPA's "market democratic" strategy for pursing justice as fairness, like DDL's "social democratic" one, is sociologically unrealistic.

These cases are fanciful. But even in more realistic cases, the institutional prong of our ideal theoretic test may prove difficult to apply. Feasibility and possibility are easily separable as conceptual categories. But the precise point of demarcation between the two is often difficult to mark when we examine the complex strategies social systems employ in pursuit of normative goals. At the level of ideal theory, the boundary between feasibility and possibility sometimes blurs.

Consider an example drawn directly from the Rawlsian literature. In a well-known critique, Jon Elster objects to property-owning democracy—one of Rawls's preferred regime types. The steeply progressive inheritance taxes of property-owning democracy are meant to encourage wealthy people to make many small gifts, thus dispersing their wealth. However, Elster claims that the more likely effect of these measures will be that wealthy people will spend more of their wealth on luxuries for themselves and their loved ones. Call this the "consume-now" objection. Elster presents this as an objection to property-owning democracy that is based on the evaluative standard of feasibility.

Immediately after laying out the consume-now objection, Elster offers what he presents as a different kind of point. Even if the inheritance tax proposal could be implemented successfully—in the sense of inducing wealthy people to make many small gifts of their estates—Elster says the tax arrangements of property-owning democracy would not produce the distribution of property hoped for by high liberals. High liberals advocate steeply progressive taxes because they see justice as fairness as requiring that the ownership of property be widely dispersed. However, Elster claims, under this scheme, the wealthy are allowed to choose the particular people who get shares of their wealth. Many people, and perhaps whole classes of people, would be left out. Elster concludes, "I do not know which set of economic and psychological assumptions are needed to guarantee that everyone would be chosen by someone, except that they are almost certainly going to be implausibly stringent."[58] Call this the "wrong-distribution" objection.

What is the status of Elster's wrong-distribution objection? It might simply be an amplified feasibility concern. That is, while the consume-now objection states that the tax arrangements of property-owning democracy are unlikely to bring about justice as fairness, the wrong-distribution objection states that those arrangements are *very* unlikely to produce that desired effect. To fail the second prong of our ideal theoretic test, however, this type of objection would not be strong enough. To fail the test, the wrong-distribution objection would need to be an objection not of feasibility but of possibility. To show that property-owning democracy fails to realize justice as fairness, one would need to show that—because of the wrong-distribution objection, or for some other reason—the institutions of property-owning democracy could not possibly bring about the desired state of affairs.

As a purely exegetical matter, I believe that Elster's argument leaves the status of his wrong-distribution objection unclear. It could be read as an objection of feasibility, or as one of possibility. The second prong of the ideal theoretic test contains an ambiguity regarding the boundary between the merely unlikely and the positively impossible. This is an important point. It draws our attention to another danger of philosophilia: people may employ the test of sociological realism in ways that are constrained by merely *inherited* assumptions about sociological realism. In this way, people's ideological biases will influence their findings at the ideal theoretic level. People may judge the pursuit of a social goal by their own ideologically preferred institutions as challenging, but deem the pursuit of that goal via an ideological approach they dislike as impossible. People with the opposite ideological orientation may draw the opposite conclusion—and sometimes for equally biased reasons. We shall return to this problem before the end of this book. For now, it is enough simply to note that the ideal theoretic test exposes philosophers to these dangers.

Rawls is confident that the institutional arrangements of property-owning democracy satisfy the ideal theoretic test. Property-owning democracy realizes justice as fairness (on Rawls's social democratic interpretation of that standard). Perhaps Rawls thinks this because he imagines the details of the steeply progressive inheritance tax scheme of property-owning democracy differently than those of the scheme Elster critiques. More likely, I suspect, is that Rawls would interpret objections of the sort Elster raises as mere worries about practical feasibility. The point of ideal theory is to help philosophers with their task of normative identification. Along with identifying principles of justice that express our commitment to treating people as free and equal citizens, that task also involves the project of identifying social systems that might realize those principles. Rawls insists that philosophers should not allow worries about practical feasibility to lower their standards as they go about that identificatory task.

The ambiguity between feasibility and possibility noted, we can now tighten our ideal theoretic parameters, or at least we can be more precise about the limitations we face when seeking to tighten them within a broadly Rawlsian scheme. For a candidate regime to realize justice as fairness, let's say that the regime must include arrangements that seek justice *in a way that is compatible with the gen-*

eral laws of political sociology.[59] In evaluating any candidate regime type, we are to imagine that type of regime as it might operate under the most favorable—but still possible—set of historical, cultural, and economic conditions. In this, the philosophical project of normative identification reaches out toward evaluations that are timeless (or at least close to timeless). Even if the chance of some regime type actually securing justice for our society right now—given all the particularities of our society—is low, still philosophy should help us identify the full range of societal types that might possibly secure justice as fairness at some later time under more favorable conditions. Ideal theory is a citadel, a high place from which to see, in this sense.

Tickets to the citadel of ideal theory are not handed out for free, however. Methodological idealization obtains its power by gaining distance from the merely actual. Admission to the tower of identificatory idealization must be paid for in the coin of political relevance. Correctly identifying a range of regime types that might ideally "realize" liberal justice might in itself tell us absolutely nothing about which of those candidate regimes the citizens in any actual liberal society ought to work toward at any given time. Further, even if we could somehow know which regime to work toward, ideal theory would not obviously give us any way of knowing what the best institutional path to the instantiation of that just regime might be. Starting from a situation of identifiable injustice, there may be many partially just, and even some less just, forms that might best lead any given society to the moral promised land.

But then what of the other objection to market democracy I mentioned, the objection that market democratic regimes *allow* outcomes that violate justice as fairness? One of the central attractions of left liberal regime types, presumably, is that those regimes set out a host of "institutional guarantees" with respect to the requirements of justice as fairness (on social democratic interpretations of that standard, say). But providing a guarantee in the form of a government program is not the same as delivering the good in question. Indeed, if we consider the way real societies function, official guarantees in the form of government-run programs sometimes may make the delivery of the good *less* likely than it might otherwise be. As Schmidtz explains, the issuing of government guarantees regarding social goods not only collectivizes but also *externalizes* responsibility for the provision of those goods. This is why such guarantees sometimes exacerbate problems they were intended to alleviate: "If we wanted to guarantee that the poor would be left behind, here would be the way to do it: teach them that their welfare is someone else's responsibility."[60]

We must be cautious, then, when evaluating regime types according to what social outcomes they are said to "allow." Capitalist regimes, for example, are routinely criticized from a social democratic perspective for "allowing" a morally arbitrary distribution of goods across society. If this is meant as a criticism of the *moral ambitions* expressed within traditional classical liberal or libertarian defenses of capitalist institutions, then we can make ready sense of that charge. Classical liberals often suggest that market distributions define justice. They therefore reject external standards of evaluation such as those provided by justice as fairness. But such a charge immediately becomes ambiguous if leveled at versions of classical liberalism that have been reformed along market democratic lines.

Market democracy, after all, shares the same general moral ambitions as traditional high liberalism. Market democracy "allows" only distributions that satisfy an externally generated distributional norm, just as high liberals do (even though, again, each group interprets that distributional standard in its distinctive way). As a practical matter of *institutional functioning*, market democratic regime types "allow" for morally arbitrary distributions only in the same sense that social democratic ones do. As a practical matter, every regime type can fail to achieve its stated ideals and ambitions. In that sense, every regime "allows" distributions that fall short of its moral ambitions. So on both levels—that of moral ambition and that of institutional functioning—market democratic regime types and social democratic ones are on all fours with respect to what each "allows." Morally, both categories of regime type affirm justice as fairness and so disallow distributions that are arbitrary from that moral standard. Practically speaking, however, no regime can provide a fail-safe guarantee that its preferred institutional strategy will deliver desired goods. Insofar as either regime strategy might fail, both regime types do as a practical matter "allow" for distributions that are arbitrary from the moral point of view.

Ideal theory does not permit us to take the formal institutional guarantees of candidate regime types at face value. From the perspective of ideal theory, the institutional characteristic of "guaranteeing" is much like the aspirational characteristic of "aiming" at justice as fairness. The mere act of guaranteeing, like that of aiming, is not enough to *realize* justice as fairness. For a regime type to be identified as one that realizes justice as fairness, the institutional strategy by which that regime type pursues justice as fairness must be deemed realistic from the perspective of commonsense political sociology, regardless of whether the strategy of pursuit takes the form of some official state-backed "guarantee."

Of course, if some existing society adopts a just candidate regime type in pursuit of justice (i.e., a regime type that "realizes" justice as fairness at the identificatory level of ideal theory), that society's actual *achievement* of justice as fairness is another matter altogether. Indeed, the chance of any existing society achieving justice as fairness by means of any of the (identifiably just) candidate regime types may be vanishingly small, or even zero.

Two points should now be clear. First, if a regime type pursues justice as fairness by an institutional strategy that is utterly unrealistic in light of the general facts of political sociology, that regime type is unjust no matter how many official "guarantees" it includes. Second, and as a corollary, if some regime type pursues justice as fairness by a strategy that is within the boundaries of the sociologically realistic, that regime type is just. And it must be recognized as just no matter how *few* "guarantees" it includes.

But then what of market democracy? What if we hold market democratic regime types to the same standards of moral aspiration and sociological realism that high liberals employ when evaluating social democratic regimes?[61] As a matter of ideal theoretic analysis, can market democratic regimes satisfy the distributional requirements of free market fairness? In the next chapter, we find out.

CHAPTER 8
Free Market Fairness

The Difference Principle

The familiar "social democratic" interpretation of justice as fairness makes room for only a thin and attenuated conception of private economic liberty. By contrast, I defend a "market democratic" interpretation of justice as fairness that I call free market fairness. Free market fairness affirms a thick conception of economic liberty, seeing economic freedom as on a par with the other basic liberal freedoms. In this chapter I complete our sketch of free market fairness by focusing on institutions. What institutional framework might support a society that is both distributively fair and economically free?

To understand justice as fairness, on any interpretation, we must keep in mind that all the parts are meant to work together to define an overall standard of evaluation. Nonetheless, for ease of exposition, we will take up the component requirements one at a time. We shall move in ascending order of priority: difference principle (DP), fair equality of opportunity (FEO), fair value of political liberties, and the rest of the first principle guarantee of basic liberties. We shall then briefly evaluate market democracy in light of some secondary considerations of justice: the just savings principle, environmental justice, and duties of international aid.

Each section considers three questions. First, how does free market fairness interpret the component of justice as fairness in question and how does that interpretation compare to Rawls's social democratic interpretation? Second, given the standards of ideal theory, on what grounds might the institutional arrangements of social democratic regime types be claimed to satisfy the requirements of that component, on the social democratic interpretation? Third, by those same ideal theoretic standards, do the institutional arrangements of market democratic regime types satisfy the requirement in question, as interpreted by free market fairness?

The technical literature on justice as fairness is vast. Since the publication of *A Theory of Justice*, each component requirement, as well as the priority relations between them, has been dissected and elaborately analyzed by a whole generation of talented philosophers. Much if not all of that literature has been developed within what I am calling the social democratic interpretative tradition. In the face of this mass of technical literature, I cannot hope to provide a final formulation of an alternative, market democratic interpretation, such as the view I call free market fairness. Instead I confine myself to two simpler tasks. I introduced my free market fairness interpretation by talking about market democracy's distinctive approach to the basic economic liberties and to the difference principle. First, I shall attempt to fill out that sketch by saying more about the difference principle and then describing in general terms the distinctive approach free market fairness takes toward the other main component requirements of justice as fairness. As before, my idea is merely to introduce an alternative market democratic interpretation of justice as fairness.

Second, while completing my introductory sketch of free market fairness, I hope to make plausible a significant, albeit broad-gauged, empirical claim. That claim is this: as a matter of ideal theoretic analysis, if one accepts that the preferred institutional arrangements of social democracy—whether property-owning democracy, the welfare state, or liberal democratic socialism—should be recognized as providing a plausible (nonutopian) approach to "realizing" justice as fairness (on the social democratic interpretation of that standard), then one should also accept that the institutional arrangements of market democracy—the regime types I call democratic limited government or democratic laissez-faire—provide a plausible approach to justice as fairness as well (as interpreted by free market fairness). In this sense, market democratic regimes not only aim at justice as fairness; they also include institutional arrangements that are realistically designed to pursue that aim. Thus market democratic regime types "realize" justice as fairness. Evaluated from the perspective of ideal theory, this means that the institutions of market democracy are on all fours with those of social democracy. If social democratic institutional forms constitute "realistic utopias," then so do market democratic ones.

The significance of this point cannot be overstated. For if the preferred institutional arrangements of market democracy can match those of social democracy in terms of their capacity to "realize" justice as fairness, then left liberal concerns about the feasibility of market-based approaches to achieving social justice can be taken off the philosophical table. That accomplished, we see that market democracy poses not merely an institutional challenge to the social democratic tradition but a *moral* one.

Market democracy invites anyone attracted to justice as fairness to consider this question: which interpretation of justice as fairness, free market fairness or Rawls's social democratic one, most fully honors our commitment to treat citizens as free and equal self-governing moral agents? When this question is put directly before us, I believe that free market fairness steps forward as the morally superior view.

To begin, let's return to our discussion of the difference principle. The DP, recall, is a principle of reciprocity. We can understand it as generating two requirements, one weaker and one stronger. First, the DP says that a system of institutions that generates gains to the wealthy is permissible only if that system generates gains for the poor as well. Second, and more strongly, the DP requires that we maximize the gains to the least well-off. When considering candidate systems, therefore, the DP requires that we choose the system that brings about the greatest benefits to the lowest paid workers.[1] Keep in mind that the DP is designed to work in conjunction with the other components of justice as fairness (and, as we shall soon see, with the FEO in particular). Nonetheless, it is important to note that the DP, taken alone, imposes no ceiling on the degree of inequality that might characterize a just institutional regime.[2] Liberal citizens can live with self-respect even in conditions of unequal wealth.[3]

Market democracy affirms this general formulation of the difference principle. However, as we have seen, there are many ambiguities in this general formulation. Among the most important of these is the nature of the distribuendum—that is, DP-goods the experience of which is to be maximized. The nature of this distribuendum might be interpreted in a great variety of ways. When applying rational prudence to assess the weight of the complex index of DP-goods, social democracy and market democracy proceed in subtly different ways. While affirming the importance of wealth and income, social democracy tends to give special weight to the experience of democratic control of the workplace (and of economic assets generally), even if this requires some reduction in wealth. By contrast, free market fairness unambiguously seeks to maximize the personal wealth of the least well-off (within all the constraints of the special conception, as described above). Let's agree that free market fairness and the social democratic approach demarcate a range of reasonable readings of the distribuendum the worth of which to the least well-off is to be maximized. Let's now look at the institutions by which regime types from each school seek to realize the difference principle, on the interpretation of that component favored by each.

By what institutional arrangements do social democratic regime types seek to satisfy the DP? First, such regimes might provide a constitutional guarantee of a basic income to people in hardship.[4] This safety net might be expected to benefit the working poor—for example, by supporting the temporarily unemployed, or by providing some peace of mind to workers whose own jobs are insecure. The constitutionally mandated social safety net is merely a piecemeal measure, however. In keeping with the ideal of procedural justice, social democratic regime types take a thoroughgoing institutional approach to maximizing the position of the least well-off members of society. As we have seen, property-owning democracy and liberal socialist regime types include a whole host of direct governmental arrangements designed to equalize property holdings and educational achievement levels *between* generations of people. These include positive programs such as wide public support for education, cultural experiences, job training, health care, and more. Such regimes will also have branches of government empowered to pursue macroeconomic objectives, such as the pursuit of full employment.

Social democrats advocate such programs, presumably, because they worry market society will tend to produce a hierarchy of fixed social classes that will persist through the generations unless corrected by special government measures. While welfare state capitalist regime types rely mainly on steeply progressive taxes on income and savings to fund these programs, Rawls's preferred social democratic regime types employ more thoroughgoing measures as well: steeply progressive taxes on inheritances and gifts in the case of property-owning democracy, or the full public ownership of productive property in the case of liberal democratic socialism. In their attempt to satisfy the DP, these social democratic regimes rely on branches of government to sustain employment, adjust the money supply, set interest rates, regulate resource use, monitor the terms of competition between firms, maintain a competitive price system, and so on.[5] Under liberal democratic socialism, workers have direct standing as voters concerning the condition of their workplace and the direction of their firms. It is through various combinations of these measures that social democratic regime types seek to benefit the working poor. In measuring that bundle of benefits, as we have seen, social democracy tends to think that absolute levels of income are less important to the self-respect of those citizens than are various goods and positions that encourage the experience of solidarity.

What of market democratic regime types? By what institutional arrangements do such regimes seek to satisfy the DP? Like social democratic regimes, market democratic regimes can include a constitutional guarantee of a basic income or safety net. (This is a significant point of difference between market democracy and the strict libertarian interpretation of classical liberalism, recall.) Also like social democratic regimes, market democratic regimes take a thoroughly institutional approach to social justice. The DP is not viewed as a principle of redress, or of "redistributive" justice. Instead, that principle is something that guides market democracy when it comes to the choice of the social system considered as a whole. Unsurprisingly, however, the institutional approach market democracy takes to improve the condition of the least well-off is markedly different from that of social democracy.

Market democratic regimes seek to improve the condition of the least well-off by a strategy of wide private economic liberty, limited government, rapid economic growth, and by guarding the space within which a vibrant civil society might develop and grow. A strong and active government is vital to a well-functioning market democracy. Along with securing the civil and political liberties of citizens, market democratic regime types rely upon the state to refine and protect property rights, provide for the common defense, and provide for a small number of genuinely public goods. In their various ways, market democratic regime types seek to create an environment in which human industry, creativity, and ambition can be unleashed in a way that is maximally beneficial to all.

Classical liberal regimes are sometimes criticized for advocating a "trickle down" approach to economic affairs: markets are advocated primarily because they benefit the wealthy (or because they tend to promote aggregate wealth) and unconsumed social product is then allowed to percolate down to the less advantaged.[6] On that approach, markets are accepted as the moral standard for determining which distributions are just.

Free market fairness rejects the trickle down approach, just as it rejects the suggestion that market distributions define social justice. Instead, free market fairness takes a thoroughly democratic approach to economic questions. Its preferred regime types constitutionally protect a wide range of private commercial economic liberties. They do this as an interpretation of the requirement that the liberal state must respect every citizen as a free, equal, and independent member of society. Free market fairness further sees economic liberties as integrally linked to the socially constructive processes on which satisfaction of the wider, more substantive requirements of justice as fairness relies. On this approach, nonbasic economic liberties should be tailored and regulated in ways that promote an expanding economy.

What system offers the maximum benefits to the least well-off class of workers over time? Free market fairness insists that the system that most benefits the poor is the one that best encourages the production of goods, opportunities, and experiences that those citizens find valuable. According to free market fairness, the public affirmation of a system of commercial exchange that aims at raising the income of the least well-off is a profoundly democratic expression of reciprocity.

Social democracy and market democracy, as we have seen, interpret the difference principle in subtly different ways. When we consider the institutional strategy by which proponents of each seek to realize that requirement, though, the difference between these two approaches becomes stark. Social democratic regime types, we might say, take a *direct* approach to the satisfaction of the difference principle. Such regimes seek to improve the condition of the least well-off by erecting an array of state-based service programs and by strictly limiting the range of socially constructive questions that may be answered by way of competitive market mechanisms. Social democratic regime types set about the task of regulating the distribution of wealth and opportunities (whether within or between generations) by an elaborate system of government branches and an aggressive system of redistributive taxation.

By contrast, market democratic regime types employ an *indirect* strategy of social construction. Market democracies seek to maximize the position of the least well-off by creating the conditions for a robustly growing commercial society. Social democracies take a skeptical, even begrudging attitude toward commercial society. As Ronald Dworkin puts it, left liberals are at most "reluctant capitalists."[7] They allow issues to be addressed by competitive market mechanisms only in cases where, by their own economic lights, they see no viable state-based alternative. Market democracies, by contrast, positively embrace the idea of commercial society. They seek constantly to expand the range of social goals that might be pursued via mechanisms of competitive market exchange.

Let's take a closer look at this market democratic strategy. Along with protecting basic rights and liberties, a central role of the state is to create and maintain a system of incentives by which the industry and creativity of individual citizens can be harnessed toward social outcomes that are materially beneficial to all—and to the least well-off in particular. Market democracies are skeptical of collective decision-making procedures and the coercion that attends it. Instead, the market democratic idea is to allow social construction to be pursued in diverse and noncoercive ways whenever possible. Free market fairness emphasizes the importance of the personal control of material resources for this reason. We might say that social democratic regime types de-commodify society in the hope of politicizing it; market democracies seek to de-politicize social life by commodifying it. The state creates a framework that supports the growth of a complex spontaneous order: a *cosmos*, in Hayek's terms. That spontaneous order is at once an expression of freedom and a strategy by which market democratic regimes realize the distributional requirements of free market fairness.

This market democratic strategy does not assume that citizens are utility-maximizers—beings motivated to action only by carrots of material self-interest. But nor does market democracy claim to have any privileged understanding of what "men want"—whether that might be "meaningful work in free association with one another" or any other perfectionist value. Instead, market democracy thinks of citizens as free, independent, and self-governing agents. These citizens are taken to have the capacity to develop themselves as responsible self-authors, to determine *for themselves* what it is they want. And market democracy sees them as being committed to respecting that same capacity for self-authorship in all their fellow citizens. These citizens advocate market-based social structures for these reasons.

What should we think of the indirect strategy by which market democratic regimes pursue their distributional goals? To demonstrate that market democracies fail to realize the DP at the level of ideal theory, it would not be enough to assert that market democratic arrangements would be *unlikely* to satisfy the DP in any particular actual society in which those arrangements might be adopted. There is no economic or sociological law that can assure us that the adoption of market democratic institutions will ineluctably work to the material benefit of the least well-off working members of society, regardless of its particular historical, sociological, and technological condition. (Far less is there any law assuring that the adoption of those institutions must inevitably maximize the benefits to the poorest workers compared to the adoption of any other candidate system.) But so too, of course, there is no law that assures us that the adoption of social democratic institutional arrangements by any particular actual society must ineluctably yield a maximization of that bundle of social primary goods (even on their preferred interpretation of measurement).

As a practical matter, the *achievement* of social justice in any actual society is a difficult and, perhaps forever elusive, goal. And this is true for any interpretation of justice as fairness within our reasonable range. A candidate regime type that aims to realize justice as fairness fails to realize justice as fairness only if it pursues justice by an institutional strategy that clearly violates some widely recognized law of economics or political sociology. Is there any widely held law of economics or sociology that market democratic regimes violate in their pursuit of the DP?

One might claim that as a matter of economic law, any market-based system that permits material inequalities between citizens will be disadvantageous to the less well-off citizens—not just from the perspective of some vague value such as "solidarity" but from the perspective of people's real levels of income and wealth. If this were true, then market democracy would violate a law of political sociology. Market democratic regime types would violate the difference principle, even on the free market fairness interpretation of it (an interpretation, recall, which requires that the poor have personal control of the largest possible amount of real wealth).

Is there a reason to think that material inequalities are harmful to the holdings of the least well-off? One way to work out such a claim might be in terms of the idea of a fixed total social product. If the total social product is fixed, then distributions of the social product are zero-sum. Increases in the shares held by the wealthy require subtractions from the shares of the poor. One consequence of this (putative) law would be that any deviation from strict economic equality necessarily sets back the interests of some class of workers. Some Marxist theories take this form. Wage-labor economies generate material gains for owners of productive capital *at the direct economic expense* of the working class. Gains to the rich make the poor poorer. According to this objection, the institutional arrangements of market democracy *cannot possibly* work to the material benefit of the worst-off class of workers. Even as a matter of ideal theory analysis, market democratic regimes violate the DP.

However, few economists today accept the economic theory on which this objection is based.[8] No widely held economic law suggests that a program of strict economic equality benefits the poor. Similarly, there is no economic consensus on the Marxian idea that wage-labor economies work to the material disadvantage of working people. Social democrats who work within a broadly Rawlsian framework, in any case, would have little use for such economic hypotheses. Rawls allows for material inequalities among citizens at least in part because he thinks the incentive structures surrounding such inequalities might, in view of general economic laws, work to the advantage of the least well-off. The DP itself is predicated on the economic plausibility of this idea.

Jason Brennan suggests a thought experiment. Brennan invites us to compare two imaginary societies, ParetoSuperiorLand and FairnessLand. ParetoSuperiorLand is an enthusiastically capitalist society. It is divided into three roughly equal-sized classes, with an initial income distribution of 10, 20, and 40 economic units. FairnessLand, by contrast, is a property-owning democracy. When they adopt those institutions, the DP is satisfied by a distribution of 15, 19, and 24—an initial distribution, notice, in which the least well-off class is granted to be significantly better off than that in ParetoSuperiorLand.

TABLE 3

	ParetoSuperiorLand			FairnessLand		
	Poor	Middle	Rich	Poor	Middle	Rich
2000	10	20	40	15	19	24
2001	10.4	20.8	41.6	15.3	19.4	24.5
2002	10.8	21.6	43.2	15.6	19.8	25.0
2025	26.7	53.3	106.6	24.6	31.2	39.4
2050	71.1	142.1	284.3	40.4	51.2	64.6
2100	505.1	1010.1	2020.2	108.7	137.7	173.9

Over time, however, the relative position of the least well-off of classes in the two societies is reversed. The constitutional protection ParetoSuperiorLand accords to economic liberty encourages an efficient and growing economy. By contrast, the institutions of a property-owning democracy seek to maintain the 15-19-24 pattern by a strategy of pervasive government interference with the market's spontaneous allocation of resources, thus retarding growth. Brennan comments: "Such interference entails interrupting the information, incentive, and learning structure of the market, thus disrupting the operation of the equilibrium principles that generate efficiency and growth." Brennan charts the effects of these different strategies in Table 3. Assuming even a very small difference in the growth rates of real income for each of the classes—4 percent in ParetoSuperiorLand, 2 percent in FairnessLand—the relative position of the least well-off classes is soon dramatically altered (because the DP itself imposed no ceiling on inequality, notice that this result holds even when incomes grow at differential rates). After just twenty-five years, the income of the least well-off class of workers in ParetoSuperiorLand has caught up and passed that of the least well-off in FairnessLand. After one hundred years, the poorest in ParetoSuperiorLand are *far* wealthier than those in FairnessLand.

Brennan uses this example to show how regime types such as FairnessLand that "aim" at the DP may fail to achieve it (compared to regimes such as ParetoSuperiorLand that do not aim at it). Since only regime types that aim at DP "realize" justice as fairness, Brennan says this generates the paradoxical result that Rawls must recommend systems that cannot actually achieve the DP.[9]

Market democracy puts a twist on Brennan's analysis, for market democracy denies that regimes such as property-owning democracy or liberal democratic socialism have any exclusive claim to the mantle "FairnessLand." If Brennan's ParetoSuperiorLand has been constructed with the aim of maximizing the material shares of the least well-off over time, along with satisfying all the other requirements of justice as fairness, then ParetoSuperiorLand is FairnessLand as well.

Market democracies affirm a thick conception of economic liberty as a requirement of democratic legitimacy. Wide liberties of working and of private ownership are affirmed as requirements of citizens exercising and developing their evaluative horizons. When those liberties are curtailed, the ability of citizens to exercise and develop their moral powers is thereby stunted. But this market democratic emphasis on economic liberty also supports an institutional environment that under reasonably favorable conditions is conducive to robust economic growth. Rather than seeing the disadvantaged as passive beings requiring aid, the market democratic approach seeks to make such people *partners* in the solution to the problem of poverty. Market democratic regimes pursue a high-growth policy that seeks to maximize the wealth personally controlled by representative members of the least well-off class of wage laborers. If we consider the DP in isolation, therefore, market democratic regime types can make a strong claim to realize that requirement of social justice.

In explaining how market democratic regime types realize the DP, we do not need to deny that certain social democratic regime types might satisfy that requirement as well—on their preferred social democratic interpretation of that standard. For example, Rawls appears to think the difference principle requires that workers gain democratic control of their workplaces, even if this reduces their real wealth. As we have seen, free market fairness is skeptical of this idea. Rawls also seems to think that the question of which particular social democratic regime type—property-owning democracy or liberal socialism—will offer the fullest realization of justice may vary depending on cultural factors. As a moral matter, free market fairness flatly rejects that idea: liberal citizens have a basic right to private economic freedom, so regimes such as liberal socialism that deny that right are unjust. Nonetheless, focusing strictly here on the difference principle, we might extend the principle of ideal theoretic charity to include market democratic regime types along with the social democratic ones.[10] If liberal socialism and property-owning democracy should be recognized as candidates for realizing the DP on the social democratic interpretation of that standard, then democratic laissez-faire and democratic limited government should also be recognized as realizing the DP on the interpretation preferred by free market fairness.

However, we further note that market democracy stakes out a moral claim about the most appropriate way to interpret the requirements of the DP. Against the social democratic interpretation, market democracy asserts that—the other requirements of liberal justice in place—the best way to respect the freedom and equality of the least well-off citizens is to maximize their personal wealth and income (compared to other candidate regimes). Insofar as the regime types favored by social democracy do not seek to maximize the wealth of the poor, market democracy sees those regime types as defective from the perspective of justice as fairness. That such regimes also violate basic economic rights makes this a double-barreled moral charge.

Fair Equality of Opportunity

The next major component of justice as fairness concerns equality of opportunity. Justice as fairness, generically conceived, affirms the ideal of formal equality. But it supplements this traditional liberal commitment with the more demanding ideal of *fair equality*. The requirements of fair equality of opportunity (FEO) are developed from the idea of society as a fair system of cooperation over time. Within such a system, citizens are committed to respecting the dignity and autonomy of one another, even in the face of the many differences of talent and ambition that inevitably exist among them. They are committed, that is, to fairness.

Rawls suggests a number of slightly different interpretations of the principle of equal opportunity that he thinks might most appropriately characterize a society where citizens share that commitment. On his dominant "democratic interpretation," the idea of equal opportunity is entwined with the difference principle. Because literal equality of opportunity is neither possible nor desirable, FEO requires that social institutions be arranged so that inequalities of opportunity work to improve the opportunities of the worst-off class. Further, of rival systems that satisfy this requirement, we are to prefer the system that might most improve the opportunities of that disadvantaged class. According to fair equality of opportunity, therefore, "an inequality of opportunity must enhance the opportunities of those with the lesser opportunity."[11]

Like the difference principle, the fair equality of opportunity principle seeks to express a simple and attractive idea. Differences of talent, station, and ambition are ineliminable facts of the human experience: they are the stuff of life. But this does not mean that less advantaged citizens are destined to look upon the natural advantages of others with suspicion or envy. Instead, social institutions, while respecting the independence of each, should be arranged so that the citizens can look upon the talents of their fellow citizens as in some sense a common bounty. According to justice as fairness, inequalities of opportunity are acceptable so long as those inequalities improve the opportunities of the least fortunate. Within justice as fairness, this principle is urged not to rectify inequalities in people's natural or social starting places—as a way of compensating the unlucky. Rather, this principle flows from the ambition to create and preserve a constitutional framework within which people can engage with one another as free and equal citizens.

As with the difference principle, however, the market democratic and social democratic approaches allow us to choose between two quite different interpretations of the FEO. After all, what should be counted as an "improvement in opportunity?" Social democracy understands the essence of citizenship in a way that stresses the importance of status. It therefore interprets the ideal of "opportunity" differently than market democracy, with its emphasis on agency. This difference emerges most clearly when we consider the institutional strategy associated with these two rival liberal ideals.

Let's begin with the social democratic approach to liberalism. By what institutional strategy do social democratic regime types seek to realize fair equality of opportunity? Rawls does not provide a comprehensive list, but he emphasizes three institutional "arrangements" needed for FEO. First, FEO requires a system of taxation or of property ownership that could break up large concentrations of wealth. Again, the worry seems to be that commercial societies tend to create familial dynasties that will endure across generations unless broken up by the state. Property-owning democratic regime types seek to avoid this by imposing steeply progressive taxes on transfers of wealth between generations.[12] Liberal socialist regime types might proceed even more directly by nationalizing industry and/or creating a system of "market socialism."

Second, FEO requires strong public funding for schooling in the hope of thereby delivering equal educational opportunities for all. Under liberal socialism, the state runs all the schools for the benefit of the society. A similar approach would likely be taken by property-owning democracy. Rawls sometimes suggests that within property-owning democracy the delivery of equal educational opportunity might be accomplished by a system of private schools funded by a voucher scheme.[13] However, property-owning democracy, if it is to function well, requires far more than literacy, numeracy, and a basic awareness of the rights and liberties of citizens. It also requires a citizenry that is strongly committed to its many state-based programs and policies. It requires a citizenry that can be relied upon to head these calls to civic duty even when they are in tension with calls of loyalty to family, religion, and friends. This robust set of civic virtues must be inculcated uniformly in all citizens from youth. The logic of social construction within social democratic regime types runs strongly in the direction of universal, state-based schooling.[14]

Third, the ability of citizens to make the most of opportunities is significantly affected by their health. Social democrats worry that even a genuinely open and competitive market for health care services would fail to provide adequate health care for all. For this reason, Rawls says that FEO requires a government guarantee of basic health care. Social democratic regimes might accomplish this through a fully socialized system of medical care. Under property-owning democracy, this requirement might be satisfied through a network of health programs financed by the worker-owned cooperatives (subject to regulation to ensure their uniformity, etc.).[15] Either way, social democratic regime types require that state agencies provide high quality, affordable health care to all.

From the perspective of ideal theory, what should we think of the social democratic approach to the FEO requirement? Is the institutional strategy by which social democratic regime types pursue FEO sociologically realistic?

FEO requires that we seek an institutional framework within which inequalities in opportunities work to enhance the opportunities available to the least fortunate. Considered by itself, the first element of the social democratic strategy—that of "breaking up" concentrations of wealth—may seem unlikely to help with this. Rather than improving the opportunities of the least advantaged citizens, the taxation policies of social democracies seem directed more at "leveling down" the opportunities of the advantaged ones. If such policies slow economic growth, they actually reduce the opportunities of the least advantaged (compared to alternative systems). But, of course, the steeply progressive taxes of social democratic regime types are meant to work *in conjunction with* the array of positive social service programs such regimes provide. In an effort to improve the opportunities of the least well-off, the social democratic idea is to empower democratically elected officials actively to manage economic distributions. They are to extract wealth from the advantaged and use that wealth to create social service programs that will be advantageous to all citizens, especially the worst off. By guaranteeing every child a good education and high quality health care, social democratic regime types thus meet the requirements of FEO.

In the real world, of course, there is a yawning gap between *intending* to provide a good and *actually* providing that good. In particular, government-based "guarantees" for the delivery of some desired good—say, quality education for all—by no means ensure that those goods will actually be delivered. The theory of government failure developed during the late twentieth century disabused us of that illusion, just as the theory of market failure disabused the more Pollyanna-ish advocates of laissez-faire in the late nineteenth. Still, the fact that the state-centric delivery mechanisms of social democracy face daunting obstacles of feasibility is not a defeater at the level of ideal theory. Ideal analysis requires that we imagine regime types working well in light of their announced aims and intentions. We consider them operating under maximally favorable—but still possible—historic, economic, and cultural conditions. Viewed that way, the principle of ideal theoretic charity requires that we grant that the social democratic strategy for achieving FEO falls within the boundaries of the sociologically realistic. Social democratic regime types "realize" the FEO requirement of justice as fairness.

What of market democracy? By what institutional arrangements do market democratic regime types seek to satisfy the FEO requirement? And how should we evaluate those arrangements from the perspective of ideal theory?

Like the social democratic interpretations of justice as fairness, free market fairness begins by affirming the traditional liberal ideal of formal equality of opportunity. Of course, different market democratic regime types may pursue this requirement in different ways. The regime type I call democratic limited government, for example, might view the liberal commitment to formal equal opportunity as requiring laws protecting against discrimination in the workplace, in lending, or in housing. Because of the constitutional weight given to freedom of contract, any such regulations would have to pass a high degree of judicial scrutiny. The limitations such regulations impose on the right of contract could only be justified out of a concern to better protect the whole scheme of basic liberties, taken as an integrated set. Still, democratic limited government regime types might at least make room for such regulations. The regime type I call democratic laissez-faire, by contrast, relies more purely on the market in pursuit of the good of formal equality of opportunity. Under that regime type, business owners have wide freedom to hire and promote workers by whatever criteria they choose—even when such decisions may reasonably be said to be based on race, gender, religious beliefs, sexual orientation, or aesthetic judgments about a person's "looks."[16] As a matter of ordinary justice, though, free market fairness affirms that the legal system of a free society can neither impose legal disabilities nor confer advantages on the basis of ascriptive, status-based characteristics.[17]

Free market fairness also accepts the idea that education and health profoundly influence people's opportunities.[18] For this reason, all market democratic regime types insist that every citizen, regardless of birth status or economic class, is owed high quality health care and education as a matter of justice. If a regime type is to satisfy the FEO requirement, it must include arrangements intended to provide citizens with those goods. Not surprisingly, however, market democratic regimes and social democratic ones try to reach this goal by different paths.

Social democratic regime types do not protect capitalist economic freedoms as basic constitutional rights. As a result, they empower legislative bodies to create and administer monopolies (or heavily regulated quasi-monopolies) in pursuit of socially desirable goods. The constitutional design of market democratic regime types, by contrast, encourages market-based forms of social construction. The market democratic emphasis on capitalistic economic liberties effectively limits the reach of legislative and administrative bureaucracies with respect to distributive issues. Market democratic regimes thus emphasize market mechanisms in pursuit of a superior system of education and health care for all. Instead of collectivizing decisions, the market democratic strategy is to create systems with the maximum number of decision points. By increasing choice and empowering people to make use of local information available only to them, such regimes aim to encourage innovation and improve performance on the part of the providers. By emphasizing individual choice making, such regimes encourage attitudes of personal awareness and responsibility on the part of ordinary citizens. By unleashing these forces, market democratic regimes hope to create a system that steadily drives up the quality of schooling and health care available to all.

Speaking generally, market democratic regimes prefer private over public forms of education, a preference that becomes ever stronger at higher levels of education. Such regime types seek to empower families to decide individually how much to spend on education and which type of school each of their children will attend (if they attend a school at all). By empowering families, market democratic regimes create an environment that encourages educational entrepreneurs to create novel and diverse forms of schooling. The government might play some oversight role in licensing schools and requiring that broad-gauged achievement standards be met. For example, the state might require that the education of every child, whatever particular form that education might take, provide that child with literacy and numeracy skills, along with an understanding of their rights and duties as citizens.[19] But generally, the thrust of schooling within market democratic societies is toward a system of polycentric competition among providers and empowered decision making by families. The market democratic approach celebrates the diversity of human personalities, learning styles, and intelligences. It seeks to create a framework within which a network of schools is free to develop in a way that reflects and celebrates all those aspects of diversity too. Technological innovations have the potential to bring down the cost of education, while allowing it to be provided from more decentralized sources.[20] Such developments are highly compatible with the market democratic approach to schooling.

Democratic limited government regimes would emphasize public support of education by way of vouchers. On one such model, made famous by Milton Freidman, educational vouchers might be given directly to each family, who could then spend that voucher at a school of their choice.[21] Other limited government models—further "left" on the market democratic spectrum—might allow the families to choose from a variety of government-run schools in some territorial district (with the voucher then going to the chosen school).[22] The other pole of market democratic thinking with respect to educational provision would be occupied by various democratic laissez-faire regime types. Rather than providing public funding for education in the form of vouchers, such regimes might give tax breaks for money spent on education, or provide tax incentives to education providers. At the extreme, some democratic laissez-faire regimes might make no provision for public funding of education whatsoever, relying on the capitalist price system—and a vibrant civil society against the background of a growing economy—to provide high quality educational opportunities to all.

The market democratic approach to health care follows a similar pattern. Most generally, market democratic regimes prefer private, competitive systems for the delivery of health care services rather than state-based, monopolistic ones. By creating a system that enhances the choosing power of individual citizens, market democracy's hope to create competition among service providers and thus drive up the quality of health care available to all. Under democratic laissez-faire, this might be accomplished by creating a largely private but open market in health care, perhaps supplemented with a health care safety net for those in extreme need. Such a system should be designed to keep health care costs transparent, so that consumers might make rational choices about their spending in this area.

Democratic limited government regimes might include more collective plans for the provision of health care. For example, they might offer tax incentives to encourage citizens to purchase health insurance, preferably from competing private firms but possibly from firms that receive some public funding as well.[23]

Of course, none of these market democratic strategies can *guarantee* the delivery of the high quality health care and education for all required by free market fairness. But the "guarantees" of the state-based programs of social democratic regimes are no better in this regard. We must be aware of our own biases when evaluating these rival strategies. Some people, as a practical empirical matter, are skeptical of market-based approaches to social construction and optimistic about state-based approaches. Such people will believe that social democratic regime types are *much more likely* to deliver high quality health care and education to all than are market democratic ones. (Such people might be especially skeptical of laissez-faire versions of market democracy.) Other people, as a practical empirical matter, are skeptical of state-based approaches to social construction and optimistic about market-based ones. Such people will think that market democratic regimes are *much more likely* actually to deliver quality education and health care than social democratic ones. (Such people might be especially skeptical of socialist versions of social democracy.)

What should we make of these empirical disputes? From the perspective of ideal theory, they are merely reasonable differences of opinion about practical likelihoods. These differences spring from people's different evaluations of an enormously complex set of historical, psychological, institutional, and economic facts.[24] If the choice between the market democratic and social democratic approaches did turn on empirical questions such as those, advocates of market-based approaches should have no particular reason to fear the outcome. Fortunately though, ideal theory allows us to focus on a different and far simpler set of questions. We peel away those empirical complexities in order to isolate and focus upon a single normative problem. Does a regime type aim at securing elements of justice as fairness through a set of institutional arrangements that are sociologically realistic? Insofar as it does, that regime type must be identified as realizing justice from the perspective of ideal theory.

To this point, our discussion of fair equal opportunity has focused on "demand side" issues of the FEO requirement. Following the preferred analysis of advocates of social democracy, we have focused on the provision of education and health care, goods citizens need if they are to be in position to take advantage of the opportunities their society has to offer. To a point, this approach makes sense. After all, if people are uneducated and unhealthy, they will be unable to secure many of the desirable positions that are (formally) open to them in their society. From our discussion so far, market democratic regimes look like good candidates for realizing the requirements of fair equality of opportunity. At least, viewed from an ideal theoretic perspective, market democratic regime types fare no worse than social democratic ones regarding that requirement.

However, as emphasized by free market fairness, FEO requires that we evaluate rival regime types not simply on their ability to deliver particular *goods*, however vital those goods might be. FEO requires that we evaluate candidate regimes on their ability to deliver the morally requisite *opportunities*. The quality of opportunities available to people is always a function of two properties: (1) the abilities of the people and (2) the quality of the positions on offer. In measuring the quality of opportunities delivered by any candidate regime type, that second property is at least as important as the first. After all, education and health are only useful toward winning desirable positions if there are desirable positions on offer in the first place. But as we have noted, market democracy and social democracy interpret the idea of "desirable positions" in their own distinctive ways.

According to free market fairness, the aim of a liberal society is not simply to create a situation in which people compete on an even footing with others. Rather, the aim is to create a social world in which the moral powers of all citizens can be best stimulated and developed. A society reaching for that high goal requires a basic structure of a very special sort. The basic structure must be capable of generating a range of social positions that might give full play to the creative capacities of citizens living within a system of free institutions. When we consider these "supply side" issues, the differences between the social democratic and the market democratic approach to FEO become clearer still.

As we saw in our discussion of the difference principle, social democratic regime types do not place a high value on the personal exercise of economic liberty. From Mill's idea of the "stationary state economy," to Rawls's openness to no-growth versions of property-owning democracy and liberal socialism, social democracies promote the creation of positions the satisfactions of which are largely cashed out in deliberative, democratic terms. The worker-controlled firms of liberal socialism, for example, may eschew economic innovation and growth even as ideals. For people who value participating in collective decision making in the workplace (and whose dignity is enhanced by their knowledge that everyone else in their society is required to work under those same terms), social democracies will produce an abundance of desirable positions.

Market democratic regimes, by contrast, emphasize the importance of economic liberty. The division of labor is embraced within such societies. Under the favorable conditions we are to imagine during ideal analysis, market democratic regimes actively generate a wide range of attractive workplace experiences to the citizenry. By protecting the basic economic liberties of citizens, and by adopting policy measures aimed at fostering economic growth, market democracies encourage the continual unleashing of human creativity in the production of goods that one's fellow citizens find valuable. Workers within market democracies are free to create or to join cooperatively owned and managed firms, and some no doubt will be attracted to workplaces of that sort. But within the highly competitive and entrepreneurial economic environment of market democracies, there may well be proportionally fewer positions that offer people the daily experience of collective decision making about the managerial and investment issues facing their place of work. Still, compared to social democratic regime types, market democratic regimes aim to generate a far more rich, diverse, and demanding range of positions. Within such societies, *individual opportunity* is the very blood of economic life.

Market democratic regimes embrace the ideal of economic growth over time. As we saw when considering the difference principle, market democracies thereby seek to maximize the wealth and income of the least well-off over time. The aspirations of market democracies to increasing wealth is paralleled by the greater aspirations of such regimes to offer their citizens a more diverse and desirable range of employment opportunities—as required by free market fairness. Whether we consider factors on the demand side—such as their arrangement for the provision of quality medical care and schooling—or if we consider factors on the supply side—such as arrangements for the creation of diverse and desirable positions—market democratic regime types can make a strong claim to maximize the opportunities of the worst-off class of citizens over time. As a matter of ideal theory analysis, therefore, the claim of market democratic regime types to satisfy the fair equality of opportunity requirement is at least as strong as the claims made by social democratic regime types.

Political Liberty

The third major component of justice as fairness concerns the special place of the political liberties. The political liberties, recall, are among the basic liberties guaranteed by the first principle of justice as fairness. The political liberties include rights to vote and to participate in political campaigns, to speak (or protest) at political assemblies, and to seek and hold office. While our generic definition of justice as fairness seeks to ensure that citizens experience their other basic liberties at their fair value, we are also reading it to require that the political liberties be given some special weight.

To understand the special status accorded to the political liberties, let's take a moment to review the rationale for the fair value of the other basic liberties. Justice as fairness seeks to carve out a stable space between two extreme interpretations of the equal liberties requirement. One of those interpretations, widely associated with traditional versions of classical liberalism, says that the equal liberties should be guaranteed in a purely *formal* way. But that interpretation ignores the way unchosen aspects of social life—such as one's family of birth, or one's genetic endowments—affect the life prospects of citizens, thus threatening their status as free and equal participants in a shared social venture. The other extreme interpretation is associated with socialist thinkers, or with political radicals such as Babuef. Rejecting the ideal of mere formal equality, proponents of this view insist that all the basic liberties must be guaranteed in a way that ensures their *equal worth* to every citizen, regardless of the particular interests or choices of those citizens. Even if it were practicable, however, it would require that the state provide dramatically unequal resources to citizens, since some would choose to exercise their liberties on projects that require far greater resources than the projects chosen by others.

Justice as fairness seeks an intermediate path. As expressed by the difference principle, justice as fairness requires that social institutions be arranged so that citizens can experience all their basic liberties *fairly*. Against a background guarantee of formal political equality for all, justice as fairness allows different people to experience the worth of their various liberties at varying levels, so long as these differences are advantageous to the worst-off citizens.

However, justice as fairness sees the political liberties as being unlike all the other basic liberties in this regard. The political liberties have a special status. Let's say that the worth of a liberty to people increases if they can more fully express themselves or make their mark in the world in the domain of that liberty. Regarding many of the basic liberties—freedom of speech, or movement, or association, or of religious practice, for example—the worth of those liberties may vary from person to person depending both on which particular projects they choose and the degree of skill and industry they bring to their pursuit of those projects. Regarding most liberties, such variations do not threaten the status of citizens as free and equal social cooperators.

The political liberties, though, seem different. An enhancement of the worth of political liberty of one citizen may diminish the worth of political liberty to others. For example, imagine that the political connections of some group allows it to control the shaping of some legislative proposal. That group's expression of its will in the political domain comes at the direct expense of rival groups who preferred that the legislation be crafted in a different way. The space of political life, compared to that of artistic or religious or associational life, seems more strictly limited. The domain of political liberty, unlike that of religious or associational liberty, has zero-sum characteristics. Further, because political decisions trigger the coercive apparatus of the state, those decisions affect the life prospects of citizens in a uniquely profound and inescapable way. Inequalities in political power expose some citizens to domination by others. Inequalities in the worth of citizens' political liberties pose a particularly immediate threat to the status of citizens as free and equal cooperators.

For these reasons, justice as fairness, on our generic definition still, treats the political liberties in a special way. According to our generic statement of that standard, the political liberties—but none of the other basic liberties—must be guaranteed at something like their fair value.[25] However, here, as elsewhere, market democracy and social democracy interpret the requirements of "fairness" in their own distinctive ways.

Social democracy recognizes that every citizen has a life of her own to live. Yet social democracy, when balancing its diverse commitments, gives special attention to the *status* of citizens as political equals. For this reason, social democrats tend to interpret the fair value guarantee in terms of the quality of the experience citizens have as participants in political decision making. This social democratic tendency is reflected in Rawls's formulation of the fair value requirement: the worth of political liberties "must be approximately, or at least sufficiently equal, in the sense that everyone has a fair opportunity to hold political office and to influence the outcome of political decisions."

Free market fairness shares the social democratic idea that the status of citizens as political equals be fully respected. Yet taking a market democratic approach, free market fairness is less impressed by the symbolic importance of this ideal. Free market fairness tends to see the importance of political processes as reducible to questions about how well rules and regulations enable citizens to conceive of and carry out their distinctive life plans. This reflects the special attention that market democracy gives to the *agency* of liberal citizens. For this reason, free market fairness reads the "fair value" guarantee as requiring a system that protects every citizen from domination in the formulation of the rules and policies that are to govern cooperative life. Social democracy and market democracy affirm very different institutions in pursuit of political fairness.

Consider, first, social democracy. By what institutional arrangements do social democratic regimes seek to ensure that the equal political liberties be enjoyed by citizens in a way that is fair? The worth of the political liberties is particularly sensitive to inequalities of wealth and income. Social democrats and market democrats both affirm this important idea. After all, in a society with significant inequalities of wealth, the political system is liable to be turned into a battlefield, with groups mobilizing to use the power of the state to advance the interests of their group over those of other groups and of their fellow citizens generally.

Social democracies seek to address this problem head on. To satisfy the fair value of political liberty requirement, for example, such regimes seek systems designed to produce a pattern in which productive property is widely owned. Equating ownership of property with political power, they rely on self-conscious political mechanisms to produce this dispersal of power. All the main features of property-owning democracy—the steeply progressive system of taxation, the array of middle-class investment devices, and the expansive public support for schooling—are intended to work toward this goal. If inequalities in wealth and power threaten the fair operation of the political system, then the political system should be used to reduce those threatening inequalities.

Additionally, social democracy sees the fair value of political liberties requirement as calling for a variety of campaign finance reform measures. These measures are advocated in order to limit the damage to democratic processes that might be caused by any remaining inequalities in wealth and power within the society. Rawls, for example, says that the fair value of political liberties requires public financing to encourage free political speech. This would require the imposition of strict limits on private contributions to political parties (or possibly banning such contributions altogether).[26] By empowering state agencies to control the financing of political speech, social democratic regimes seek to ensure that all citizens will be able to experience political participation in a way that is fair.

From the social democratic perspective at least, the fair value of political liberties requirement generates demanding material egalitarian requirements. Rawls says that the first principle itself requires that "property and wealth must be kept widely distributed."[27] Indeed, some defenders of social democracy have seen the fair value guarantee of the first principle as so demanding that the difference principle may even be rendered redundant: if a society satisfies the first requirement, it has more than satisfied the second one.[28]

As always, there can be no guarantee that the institutional arrangements of social democratic regime types—their tax programs and publicly funded election schemes—will bring about the conditions of fair political equality. But the principle of ideal theoretic charity suggests that we should accept the social democratic strategy as sociologically realistic (i.e., as nonutopian). From the perspective of ideal theory, the institutional arrangements of social democratic regime types should be recognized as realizing the fair value of political liberties requirement.

What of free market fairness? Free market fairness sees the personal exercise of economic liberty as a necessary condition of citizens developing their moral capacities of self-authorship. From the market democratic perspective, however, inequalities of wealth are seen as a predictable consequence of the exercise of human reason within free institutions—much like different degrees of religious devotion, or of educational accomplishment. Free market fairness thus accepts large inequalities in the material holdings of liberal citizens (so long as the real material share of the poor is maximized, etc.).

As we have seen, by accepting material inequalities, market democratic regimes affirm a progrowth environment by which they seek to improve the prospects of the least well-off citizens, both in terms of the material holdings of such citizens and in terms of the quality of opportunities available to them. This very strength of market democratic regimes with respect to the "second principle" requirements may seem to be a weakness when it comes to the "first principle" requirement of fair political equality. After all, as social democrats emphasize, the worth of political liberties seems to be particularly sensitive to inequalities in wealth and influence. However, the question of what degree of material equality is needed to satisfy the fair political equality requirement is not one that can be answered a priori. On the contrary: the strength of those material egalitarian requirements is strongly dependent upon the regime type in question.

As we have seen, social democratic regime types seek to protect people from political domination by equalizing people's material holdings. They seek to do this by placing great economic decision-making power in the hands of elected officials (or directly in the hands of democratic bodies, in the case of workers' cooperatives). In this way, social democracies take a legislative approach to the problem of fair political equality. But this very approach exposes individual citizens to dangers of domination. For example, where exactly will rates and brackets be set for those various middle-class savings incentives? How, exactly, is the inheritance tax to be written? Will it exempt family farms? If so, will any other family businesses also be exempted? Which ones? Within the universal scheme of medical care, what categories of surgical procedure, and what classes of prescription medication, will be covered—and at which rates, and for patients with which health profiles? What percentage of tax revenues will go toward the concerns of the elderly and what percentage to the concerns of the young (such as education)? If national artistic, cultural, and scientific foundations are to be run by governmental appointees, who will those appointees be? Who will determine the grant-making priorities of such foundations from one administration to the next? If workplace rules are to be agreed upon collectively, what precisely will those rules be and how will they affect workers whose preferences diverge from those of the majority?

Small variations in the ways these economic questions end up being answered will have very great consequences for the actual life prospects of the citizenry. Those same small variations, however, sometimes also have very great consequences for powerful businesses and special interest groups (including, notably, politicians seeking reelection). The social democratic strategy for realizing fair political equality generates a feedback problem. The more significant the economic issues that such regimes place on the legislative agenda, the more significant the exposure of their citizens to the danger of political domination.[29] To prevent this domination, social democratic regimes seek to equalize wealth by placing further economic issues on the legislative agenda, thus further exposing their citizens to the danger of political domination.

Free market fairness takes a different approach to fair political equality. Instead of focusing on legislative programs, it directs regimes to protect citizens from the dangers of political domination by addressing the fair value of the political liberties requirement at the *constitutional* level. Free market fairness affirms a thick conception of private economic liberties as basic rights. As a result, market democratic regimes restrict the range of economic issues that are allowed onto the political agenda. In this way the constitutional structure of market democracies limits the ability of any group of citizens to dominate any other. The equal political freedom of citizens is secured not by (ongoing) attempts to equalize the holdings of citizens. Instead, free market fairness seeks to secure the ideal of equal political freedom up front, as a matter of constitutional right.

The difference between the market democratic and the social democratic approaches is vivid in the area of campaign finance reform. Justice requires that every regime includes arrangements that eliminate or minimize the corrupting influence of money in politics. One of the central findings of public choice economists is that there is a strong link between the amount of money attracted to political processes and the economic value of the issues under political discussion. The market democratic approach to secure the integrity of the political process is different and more thoroughgoing than the social democratic one. Rather than seeking to equalize political influence by constructing elaborate programs that seek to equalize wealth across society, market democracies secure political integrity by reducing incentives to corruption and domination in the first place. Free market fairness, we might say, seeks to secure the fair value of political liberty *ex ante*. Social democratic interpretations, by contrast, pursue that value *ex post*.

The free market fairness approach to fair political equality generates a number of desirable social effects. The most obvious of these effects, perhaps, concern economic growth. Within market democracies, economic energies and resources are channeled into productive competition with rival firms to produce socially valuable goods, rather than allowing those energies to be dissipated and corrupted in political contests. Equally important, perhaps, is the way this approach to fair political equality seeks to affect the character of political deliberation. Even while limiting the legislative purview, there will still be many important issues on the legislative agendas of market democracies. Within limited government regimes, for example, specific tax and education policies must be set. So too, market democratic regimes may often need to make decisions about environmental protection, workplace safety, the regulation of dangerous drugs and chemicals, defense spending, national indebtedness, and so on. But within market democracies, the quality of political discussion on all these issues is improved: discussion of these issues will be more responsible because economic trade-offs are kept visible.[30]

There is no guarantee that any particular society that adopts market democratic institutions will achieve the ideal of political nondomination. The market democratic strategy of securing fair political equality primarily as a matter of constitutional design might, as a matter of actual practice, go wrong in a variety of ways. For example, judges might adjudicate disputes in ways that systematically favor some classes of citizens over others. Even if market democracies allow only a narrower range of economic issues on the legislative agenda, special interest groups in those societies still might be motivated to "capture" political favors in a way that is unfair to their less well-connected fellow citizens. But, so too, the social democratic strategy of legislatively directed wealth redistribution and campaign finance control might, as a matter of practice, go awry at least as badly. If the social democratic strategy is deemed sociologically realistic, then the market democratic one must be deemed realistic as well. As a matter of ideal level analysis, therefore, market democratic regime types realize the fair value of political liberty requirement.

Generational, Environmental, and International Justice

This has been a rough sketch of the free market fairness interpretation of the main requirements of justice as fairness, and of the institutional strategies that market democratic regime types adopt to satisfy those requirements. To fully exposit market democracy, we would need to fill in many details that I have here merely touched upon. There are also a number of other dimensions of liberal justice that a complete account of free market fairness would need to address. Allow me to set out some simple markers indicating how market democratic regimes seek to satisfy some further requirements of liberal justice.

Let's begin with the problem of generational—or, as some prefer, intergenerational—justice. Every generation benefits from the contributions previous generations made to the general stock of cultural, technological, and financial capital. Because we experience life in sequential generations, it is impossible for any given generation to reciprocate the members of previous generations for those benefits. Instead, the most we can do is recognize our obligation to extend similar benefits to members of future generations. Thus, formulated generally, the principle of just savings requires that every generation save and invest for future generations whatever portion of their wealth it would be rational for them to have wanted the previous generation of citizens to save and invest for them.[31]

Because of the different attitudes they take toward the question of economic growth, this principle may generate different demands for market democratic and social democratic regime types. Social democratic regimes affirm ideals of slow or zero economic growth. Speaking roughly, therefore, the principle of just savings requires that social democracies include institutional arrangements that might save enough so that the standard of living of the previous generation might be *maintained*. Market democratic regime types affirm the ideal of positive growth. The principle of just savings requires that market democratic regimes include savings arrangements that might allow the standard of living of every generation to be *improved* over that of the previous generation. In this sense, free market fairness might interpret the requirements of the just savings principle as more demanding than social democratic interpretations of that principle.

Not surprisingly, social democratic and market democratic regimes seek to satisfy the requirements of just savings by very different institutional strategies. Social democratic regime types, as is their wont, seek to satisfy the just savings requirement by a variety of legislative measures and policies specifically directed at the goal of social saving. The steeply progressive inheritance taxes of property-owning democracy, for example, might be expected to generate a pool of resources that each group of legislators will hold in reserve and, perhaps, allow to grow by the accrual of interest. Legislators will raise funds for any new social programs they might enact, or for any increases to benefits of existing programs they might approve, by raising taxes rather than by dipping into this pool of government savings. In this way, each generation of legislators will inherit the savings made by previous generations of legislators.

Market democracies take a different approach. As a matter of constitutional design, such regimes are wary of the tendency of elected officials not merely to fail to save but also, worse, to overspend. So market democracies see the principle of just savings as generating a requirement of fiscal responsibility as a prerequisite of the formal requirements of the just savings principle itself. To meet those responsibilities, market democratic regimes are more likely than social democratic ones to include measures designed to address this danger of overspending. For example, such regime types might include constitutional measures that forbid governmental borrowing from future generations, such as James Madison's proposal mentioned earlier. Market democratic regimes are also vigilant against "indirect" forms of government borrowing, most notably by way of inflationary increases in the money supply. They typically bind themselves to a monetary mast of a fixed, gradual rate of money supply growth, or even to a metal standard.[32]

Generally, though, market democracies seek to satisfy the requirements of the just savings principle not by the actions of collective political bodies but by actions of individuals and family units. Market democracy's emphasis on property rights encourages savings and investment across the whole of the private sector (rather than in some governmental savings account). These savings keep resources in the private sector, allowing for the creation of jobs and increases in productivity that potentially benefit citizens of every class. Commercial societies empower people to dream that by working hard and saving responsibly, their children might enjoy a life that is materially richer than their own. Without ignoring people's ordinary sense of civic concern for all future citizens, market democracies tap the special concerns people feel for their children and grandchildren. In this way the market democratic approach to the principle of just savings seeks to work with the grain of human nature.

The difference between the market democratic and the social democratic strategies again is stark. The central taxation policy of property-owning democracy, recall, is one of steeply progressive taxes on the gifts or bequests that parents might make to their children and grandchildren. The progrowth taxation policies of market democratic regime types might well include some component that taxes intergenerational bequests. For example, such taxes might be enacted on the grounds they were a growth-friendly method of defraying the costs of government services. But unlike their role within social democratic ideals such as property-owning democracy, heavy taxes on family lines would not be a first point of emphasis. On the contrary, market democratic tax policies are designed to encourage the accumulation of personal wealth throughout all levels and dimensions of society, including along family lines. After all, as market democratic regimes emphasize, the savings parents make for their children are not antisocial or zero sum. Instead, citizens of market democracies see such savings and investments as contributions to a larger social pool of saving and investments. Through the operations of capital markets, those "private" savings provide growing benefits to all future generations.

Of course, there can be no guarantee that market democracies' decentralized, family-based, approach to savings would actually satisfy the requirements of the just savings principle. Perhaps some generations of people will decide not to save and pass on to their descendants as much as they might reasonably have expected their ancestors to have saved and passed onto them. However, as before, we must consider these worries through the lens of ideal theory. If the legislative approach of social democracy is deemed sociologically realistic when viewed through that lens, then the family-based strategy of market democracy is realistic too.[33] As a matter of ideal theory analysis, market democratic regime types satisfy the principle of just savings.

Environmental justice raises more complicated issues. The main problem is that our moral duties regarding the environment under justice as fairness have not yet been clearly worked out. Deep ecologists, many inspired by the work of Aldo Leopold, argue that nature has intrinsic value, so that some duties of environmental justice are duties to the environment.[34] How could such concerns be cashed out in terms of political fairness? One possible approach, discussed by Peter Wenz, might be to "thicken" the veil of ignorance in the original position to make it less anthropocentric. Parties might be modeled as being denied knowledge of what species they belonged to, so that the principles they select would include requirements of fairness to nonhuman beings. However, as Wentz notes, such an approach would face a variety of daunting obstacles, not the least of which would concern the rationality of nonhuman animals and the (apparent) exclusion of nonanimal kingdoms and landforms.[35]

A different approach might be to describe the requirements of environmental justice as obligations owed, not to nature itself, but to future generations of citizens. The principle of just savings might be extended to cover such concerns. How might such a principle be formulated? Just as there is an ambiguity about the nature of the "distribuendum" governed by the difference principle (concerning the nature of the good or goods to be distributed), so too we might exploit an ambiguity in the nature of what we might call the "savuendum" of the just savings principle (regarding the good that must be saved). Perhaps justice as fairness requires that members of each generation adopt institutions that would preserve the environment (including stocks of natural resources, however defined) in ways that it would have been rational for each generation to have wanted previous generations to have preserved it for them.[36]

There are difficulties with this approach as well. Some threats to the environment, such as anthropogenic climate change, are transnational or global in nature. Whether the original position can be adapted to address transnational issues is an open question. Further, a more complete principle of environmental justice would need to address the unequal distribution of burdens from environmental damage that may be experienced by members of the same generational cohort. Still, let's take the principle I just mentioned as a rough marker for a principle of environmental justice within justice as fairness: justice requires the members of each generation to protect the environment in ways they might wish members of previous generations to have protected it for them.

Free market fairness, let's say, affirms this principle. As with the principle of just savings, such a principle may seem especially daunting within the enthusiastically progrowth framework of market democracy. To see how market democratic regime types might satisfy the requirements of environmental justice, lets step back and consider how threats to the environment arise.

In Garret Hardin's classic formulation, a "tragedy of the commons" occurs when individuals and groups, seeking to maximize their own gains, consume natural resources and spread the burdens, or "tragedy," across a population. Hardin describes cattle grazing on an open plain: "Each man is locked into a system that compels him to increase his herd without limit—in a world that is limited." With free access to resources held in common, rivalries emerge that bring scarcity and "ruin" as humans compete for finite supplies.[37] Similarly, economic competition between firms can generate negative externalities, such as pollution of waterways or the air, as firms seek to minimize the costs of their productive activities. Along with the general threats just mentioned, economic competition encourages the development of worldwide commodity chains. Such chains allow polluters to escape accountability, increasing the threat to the environment as a whole.[38]

For all these reasons, left liberals tend to see private economic liberties as threatening to the environment. They take a regulatory approach to environmental protection, curtailing those economic liberties in order to achieve benchmarks of environmental health. Legislative bodies and administrative bodies, such as the Environmental Protection Agency in the United States, are given wide power to oversee the economy. All aspects of commercial activity—not just industrial firms but farms, schools, and residential home building, must pass precisely tailored tests of environmental sustainability and public stewardship. Markets threaten the environment; legislative bodies protect it.

Market democratic regime types also make room for some regulatory activity in response to the requirements of environmental justice. For example, the regime I call democratic limited government might allow zoning requirements of some kinds, for example, to distinguish zones of commercial and residential development. It might use the tax code to encourage private groups to purchase lands for preservation, or even allow tax revenues to be used to purchase land for national parks and the like.[39] Still, the fundamental orientation of market democratic regimes toward the problem of environmental sustainability is different from that of social democratic ones: market democracy sees private economic liberty as a protector of the environment.

As Garret Hardin noted, when a good yields itself to private ownership, the structure of the incentives can change in a way that makes the economic agents better stewards.[40] If a common field is privatized, the owner of the field has reason to protect that resource from the ruin of overgrazing. Economic liberties of private ownership can prevent the negative externalities from the use of a particular resource from being spread across society. David Schmidtz writes: "Private property is the preeminent vehicle for turning negative commons into positive-sum property regimes."[41] Ownership breeds responsibility. Market democracies therefore seek to thicken ownership, in part by expanding the range of things that are made subject to legal ownership by private individuals and groups. Property rights can be crafted and extended so as to make economic agents responsible not just for the quality of fields but also waterways and even the atmosphere.

Market democracy also attends to public choice concerns about the regulatory approach to environmental protection favored by social democracies. Information is costly not only in the private sector but in the political one as well. The regulatory approach rests ultimately on political processes that in turn rely upon blocks of voters. For reasons discussed earlier, such voters typically do not have the information they need to make rational decisions about the environment. Further, environmental damage typically occurs when people lack accountability. But this applies to political actors no less than to economic ones: the farmer is more accountable with respect to his field than is the politician in whose general jurisdiction that field lies. What's more, when political actors do not directly share the opportunity costs, such as higher energy prices, less technological innovation, or a weaker economy with less growth, overprotection can occur.[42]

By contrast, market democracy is optimistic about the capacity of markets to track subtle changes in people's concerns about environmental issues, and about the ability of markets to generate diverse avenues by which people can act on those concerns for themselves. At the turn of the twentieth century, for example, the global market for fair trade products was expanding at over 10 percent a year; that for organic products at 20 percent per year. These international movements are examples of the emergent, bottom-up approach to environmental sustainability favored by market democratic regimes. As with the other aspects of justice, there can be no guarantee that the property-rights-based approach of market democracies will satisfy the requirements of environmental justice. But here again, we are examining the institutions of market democracy at the level of ideal theory. If we grant that the institutional arrangements of social democratic regimes pass the ideal theoretic test of "realistic utopianism," we must recognize the arrangements of market democracies as passing that test too.

A complete liberal theory of justice also would include principles about the fairness of the distribution of global wealth, or at least about the duties that liberal societies owe to members of less fortunate societies.[43] In developing what he calls a "law of peoples," Rawls imagines a second original position in which representatives of states convene to work out principles to govern their relations and duties toward one another. Many high liberals have argued that the result of such a thought experiment would be a very demanding principle of global distributive justice, and perhaps even a kind of global difference principle.[44] While Rawls was skeptical of global principles of distributive justice, he did think that liberal justice should include what he calls "duties of assistance" owed by (well-functioning) liberal societies to less well-off peoples around the world.[45] While not technically a principle of global distribution, such a duty of assistance may generate stringent requirements. Beyond wealth and material aid, as Freeman notes, such a duty may require that liberal regimes adopt policies that benefit less wealthy nations in areas of "education, infrastructure, agriculture, technology, cultural development, etc."[46]

By what institutional arrangements might social democratic regime types seek to satisfy the requirements of international justice? Property-owning democracy and liberal socialism might seek to discharge their duties of developmental assistance with programs of foreign aid, perhaps in conjunction with a variety of governmental initiatives aimed at specific areas of developmental need (medical care, clean water programs, the construction of new schools, and the like). These international aid programs might be funded by domestic taxes. Alternatively, social democratic regime types might support proposals that development programs be funded by special taxes on international trade or, perhaps, a tax on international currency transactions such as that proposed by the American economist James Tobin.[47]

Free market fairness could also be developed so as to include principles of international justice, whether via some principle of global distributive justice or a Rawlsian duty of assistance. Not surprisingly, though, market democratic regime types would likely take a very different institutional approach to fulfilling the international duties that were generated by that (marketized) standard of fairness. First, and most obviously, market democracies advocate free and mutually beneficial trade between people regardless of their nationality. As emphasized previously, market democracy is promarket not probusiness. Because regimes such as democratic limited government and democratic laissez-faire affirm a wide range of private economic freedoms as constitutionally protected rights, those regimes limit the range of economic issues that are allowed onto the political agenda. Market democracies are highly skeptical of import tariffs, agricultural subsidies, and other forms of economic protectionism. Instead, market democracies aim continually to expose domestic firms to competition, both from fellow national and from international sources. By allowing entrepreneurs and firms from around the world free access to their domestic economies, market democracies allow such people to share in their wealth—including capital, organizational, technological, and cultural goods alike.[48]

Further, as mentioned previously, market democratic regime types advocate freer immigration policies than is typical of social democratic regime types, burdened as those latter regime types are by their costly public service sectors. Free market fairness sees wide freedom of economic contract as a basic right. As a consequence, market democracies might advocate a more free world market in labor. As a matter of moral justification, as well as of practical feasibility, there are a number of complicated issues here. For example, free market fairness might cash out these rights to cross-border mobility for economic purposes in terms of a liberty of citizens of market democracies to enter into economic contracts with whomever they choose. Or, on less nationalistic variants, free market fairness might affirm rights of worker mobility as universal human rights held by workers regardless of nationality.[49]

When combined with their commitment to free international trade, the generous immigration policies of market democracies may go a long way toward fulfilling the international duties of assistance (or of global distributive justice). The development economist Lant Pritchett marshals data from World Bank reports to estimate the economic effects of freer migration policies. According to Pritchett, if thirty affluent countries of the Organization for Economic Cooperation and Development loosened their immigration restrictions so as to allow just a 3 percent rise in their labor forces, citizens of poor countries would gain roughly $300 billion. This figure dwarfs the $70 billion that rich countries currently give to poor countries through traditional programs of "foreign aid." Intriguingly, Pritchett also calculates that wealthy nations would experience significant financial gains from polices allowing greater labor mobility, mainly through increases in returns to capital and reductions in the cost of labor.[50]

In practice, market democracy's programs of freer international migration and trade might turn out not to be helpful to people in poorer nations: perhaps such policies would turn out to worsen the condition of such people and benefit only the members of the already-wealthy countries. Or perhaps these policies would impose hardships on the lowest paid wage earners in the wealthy countries that would not immediately be overcome by the benefits of society-wide economic growth. But as a matter of historical fact, the top-down approach to development favored by social democratic regime types face feasibility problems that are at least as daunting.[51] From an ideal theoretic perspective, therefore, the institutions of market democratic regimes must be recognized as satisfying the duties of international aid.

A final important cluster of international issues concerns problems of militarism and peace. Considered in their idealized forms, social democratic regimes and market democratic ones may be equally committed to the ideal of international peace. It is worth noting, though, that market democracy is the heir to the particularly strong tradition of international noninterference, antimilitarism, and even pacifism. Hayek, for example, argues that one of the main threats to peace is the "artificially fostered economic solidarity of all the inhabitants of any one country." By treating the resources of different nations as the exclusive properties of those nations as wholes, those resources become causes of international friction and envy rather than goods that can be seen as being in any sense a common bounty. Policies of economic exclusion prepare the ground for war. To encourage peace, Hayek writes: "It is neither necessary nor desirable that national boundaries should mark sharp differences in standards of living, that membership of a national group should entitle to a share in a cake altogether different from that in which members of other groups share."[52] Indeed, like many classical liberals, Hayek expresses an openness to international institutions and even to supranational forms of governance—provided that the functions and powers of any such bodies be strictly limited by their respect for the private economic liberties of citizens.[53]

From George Washington's warning to avoid the dangers of exclusive economic and military pacts with other countries ("foreign entanglements"), to James Madison's proposal of a constitutional provision requiring political leaders wishing to go to war to raise funds from current taxes (rather than hiding the costs through borrowing), advocates of limited government have long been among the strongest critics of the politico-military establishments common within contemporary states.[54] Market democratic regimes have a constant theme of restricting the discretionary power of political leaders by limiting their economic power. This does not guarantee that market democracies will not develop vast military complexes. But the very idea of a large publically funded military-industrial complex runs against the grain of market democracy. To meet the requirements of international justice, the disposition of market democratic regimes can be captured in a simple phrase: free trade, free migration, and peace.

Free Market Fairness as a Moral Ideal

The distinctive characteristic of market democracy, in all its variations, is that it affirms a thick conception of private economic liberty while being committed to a distributive ideal of social justice. According to what I call the objection from the left, recall, these are incompatible commitments. If market democratic regimes constitutionally entrench a thick set of private economic liberties, this precludes those regimes from having the government programs and institutions required to bring the distribution of goods into line with the distributive requirements of justice. This makes the enthusiastically capitalistic regime forms of market democracy highly unlikely to operate in a way that benefits the poor. Even if market democratic regimes are defined as "aiming" at social justice, such regimes do not provide government programs that guarantee that justice will be achieved. Market democracies allow unjust distributions to arise and persist, and so are unjust for that reason.

I believe that this objection, or something like it, underlies the skepticism about capitalism felt by many people on the left. Presented as an objection to the view I call free market fairness, however, this objection is simply confused. Like the high liberal defenses of their preferred social democratic forms, my defense of market democratic regimes runs at the identificatory level that I call political philosophy. At that level, we do not identify abstract regime types as just or unjust by asking practical questions about *how likely* we think each of them might be to actually achieve justice if adopted, say, by some particular society in some particular set of historical and economic conditions. (Though, again, advocates of market-based regimes should have no qualms about meeting the social democrats on those more empirically grounded, feasibility-tracking terms.)

Instead, political philosophy is about *aspirational* standards. When working at that level of political argument, our task is to identify regime types that realize liberal justice as a matter of ideal theory. For a candidate regime type to achieve this, it must aim to satisfy that standard of justice by means of institutional arrangements that even if unlikely to fully achieve justice if adopted by any actual society are not utterly utopian with respect to that aspiration.

As a matter of ideal theoretic analysis, high liberals argue that a range of social democratic regime types—liberal (democratic) socialism, property-owning democracy, and perhaps some versions of the welfare state—realize the distributive requirements of liberal justice (on their own preferred interpretation of that distributive standard). When we evaluate the regime types of market democracy, we must apply this ideal theoretic test in an even-handed way. When we do this, as we have just seen, we find that a range of market democratic regime types—democratic limited government and democratic laissez-faire—also realize the distributive requirements of liberal justice (on market democracy's interpretation of that standard).

So the philosophical choice between social democratic institutional forms and market democratic ones is not a choice that can be made by empirical evaluations of practical feasibility. Nor even is it a choice that can be made by looking through the lens of ideal theory: as a matter of ideal theoretic analysis, market democratic regime types and social democratic ones both realize justice as fairness, on the particular interpretation of that standard favored by each. Property-owning democracy and democratic limited government; liberal (democratic) socialism and democratic laissez-faire: as a matter of ideal theoretic analysis, each qualifies as a "realistic utopia."

Thus, ultimately, the choice political philosophers must make between market democratic regime types and social democratic ones is not in any sense a practical one. That choice is instead strictly *moral*: which conception of fairness, the social democratic one or the free market one, offers us the more inspiring ideal?

John Rawls and other high liberals of the late twentieth century could discern only limited moral value in private economic liberty. Against libertarians and traditional classical liberals, these high liberals affirmed a robustly substantive conception of equality. This led high liberals to develop the ideal of social justice, which requires that we adopt institutions that benefit the least advantaged. When pressed to fill in the details of this requirement, however, high liberals tend to emphasize the importance of the *status* of citizens over that of their *agency*. When forced to choose between institutions designed to maximize the wealth of the least advantaged and institutions designed to reduce inequalities between them, high liberals tend to plunk down for the latter. Rawls's claim to know that what people really want is "meaningful work in free association with others" (rather than a higher material standard of living), and his preference for socialism over even the tepidly capitalistic institutions of the welfare state, are emblematic of this high liberal orientation.

Free market fairness pursues a different, and more lofty, moral ideal. Market democracy challenges the high liberal suggestion that we respect people as free and equal self-governing agents by restricting the range of choices they are allowed to make in the economic areas of their lives. Market democracy rejects economic paternalism, however well motivated it might originally have been. Instead, market democracy insists that economic activity and decision making are essential aspects of responsible self-authorship; protection of economic liberty is a requirement of democratic legitimacy itself. To create the conditions in which citizens with diverse plans and interests can jointly develop their capacities of self-authorship, market democracy insists that citizens must be accorded rights ensuring them a sphere of sovereignty regarding the economic questions of their lives, just as they are to be protected when confronting intellectual, associational, and religious questions.

Free market fairness also challenges the high liberal claim that the most appropriate way to "benefit" the least well-off is by redistributing wealth in pursuit of some material egalitarian standard (whether within generations or between them). Our market democratic approach interprets the requirements of fairness differently. The (fuller) scheme of basic rights and liberties in place, we benefit the least advantaged when we adopt institutions designed to maximize the real bundle of wealth and income that the least fortunate among us personally controls. The enthusiastically capitalistic regime types of market democracy are explicitly and unapologetically designed to pursue this goal.

By maximizing the wealth of the poor and broadening the range of basic rights and liberties enjoyed by all citizens, free market fairness pursues a uniquely ambitious conception of the moral requirements of democratic community. In this sense, the market-friendly regimes of market democracy are not merely *among* the regime types that philosophers must recognize as fair. Instead, these free market regimes are the fairest of them all. Evaluated by the quality of its moral intentions, market democracy is the most highly evolved form of liberalism.

Conclusion

For too long the conceptual landscape of liberal thought has lain in a deep freeze. On one side, we have the camp of the traditional libertarians and classical liberals. They affirm the importance of private economic liberty on grounds that require them to reject any notion of distributive justice. If rights are founded on a principle of self-ownership, for example, discussions about justice in the distribution of shares get cut off before they begin. On the other side, we have the camp of the traditional high liberals. They affirm accounts of social justice that force them to restrict the ability of individuals to engage in independent economic activity. If justice is centrally concerned with securing the equal political status of citizens, for example, this requires institutions with such expansive powers that the private economic liberties of citizens must be truncated and curtailed.

Property rights *or* distributive justice. Limited government *or* deliberative democracy. Free markets *or* fairness. One side or the other, everyone must choose.

On this bleak scene, I have pointed to a third possibility. For between these two camps, in the hazy distance, high upon a hill, there is a terrain of liberal theorizing that I call market democratic. Market democracy takes a fundamentally deliberative approach to the questions of political life. Rather than seeing society as something private, market democracy sees society as an essentially public thing: political and economic structures must be justifiable to the citizens who are to live within them, whatever their social class. Society, in its moral essence, is a cooperative venture between citizens committed to respecting one another as responsible self-authors. This democratic outlook leads market democracy to affirm a thick conception of economic liberty, with such liberties scoring fully on par with the other basic liberal rights and freedoms. That outlook also makes market democracy enthusiastic about the system of commercial liberty, looking to that system to maximize the wealth personally controlled by the least advantaged citizens. Social and economic institutions must be arranged that way, according to market democracy, as a requirement of liberal justice.

Market democracy combines ideas that have long seemed un-combinable: private economic liberty *and* social justice; spontane-ous order *and* democratic self-governance; free markets *and* fairness. Market democracy makes room for them all.

I have worked out and defended a particular market democratic view that I call free market fairness. Free market fairness offers a uniquely attractive way of combining a concern for economic liberty with a concern for social justice. Free market fairness, I believe, is a morally superior account of liberal justice.

My approach has been constructive rather than critical. Free market fairness leaves the moral foundations of the existing camps largely unmolested. For this reason, I anticipate that some old-schoolers from both sides—high liberal and libertarian—will simply hunker down, go about their business, rather than picking up and moving to the new building area I have surveyed.

This is fine with me. It is difficult to convince the already-committed to adopt a different view. With respect to such readers, my aim is modest: I hope merely to have shown that market democ-racy is a viable alternative to the traditional high liberal and libertar-ian views. I think of this book as directed above all to ideologically uncommitted readers, some of them people who, like me, have long felt the moral pull from both sides; others, intellectual adventurers who, let's imagine, are arriving on this scene for the very first time. I invite such people to look carefully at the full range of liberalism's ideological options, and to set their sights high.

Libertarians and classical liberals, to their great credit, have long defended the importance of individual liberty—including the freedom of individuals to make fundamental economic decisions according to their own values. However, they justify those economic freedoms in a way that makes them incapable of responding offi-cially to the great ills that sometimes befall persons, or whole classes of persons, through no fault of their own. To high liberals, orthodox libertarianism seems like a cold and heartless view. There is some-thing to this charge, I think.

High liberals, for their part, pioneered the idea of social or distrib-utive justice. Social institutions are just only if they work to create a social world in which all citizens benefit from the talents of each other, with no class of citizens exploited by others or through bad luck left behind. However, high liberals interpret this idea in a way that leads them to curtail basic liberal freedoms. To classical liberals and libertarians, there is something bullying (and morally condescending) in the forms of coercion that high liberals espouse. This worry too carries a sting.

Market democracy invites open-minded readers to consider a positive alternative to this familiar dichotomy. From the market democratic perspective, liberal justice involves not only the specification of a set of basic rights but includes distributive requirements as well. But where high liberals tend to adopt a social democratic interpretation of the distributive requirements of social justice, market democracy takes a different approach. In seeking to benefit the least well off, we must take care to do so in ways that respect the autonomy and dignity of those citizens. We do this when we adopt enthusiastically pro-growth institutions designed to increase the wealth those citizens personally control. According to free market fairness, my own preferred market democratic approach, a fair share is the largest possible bundle of real wealth that might be procured for (by!) the least fortunate, consistent with respecting the rights of other citizens.

The emphasis of free market fairness on personal wealth and income does not involve trading off rights and liberties for mere material goods. On the contrary, the wider array of rights and liberties affirmed by free market fairness in place, wealth is important because it increases the worth of the rights and liberties of the most poor. Economic growth and material wealth are not bad things. Nor are they things to be cast aside lightly (say, by those wishing to impose on others their own ideal of the "democratic workplace"). For people who are secure holders of liberal rights, wealth empowers them to become authors of lives truly their own. Free market fairness interprets the distributive requirements of social justice in ways that honor those citizens, whatever life script each chooses to compose.

Market democratic views such as free market fairness advance enthusiastically capitalistic policies under the banner of social justice. By doing so, market democracy highlights the moral attractions of the market-based approach to social order. In time, this might help make proposals for limited government become politically attractive too.

As I write these words, at the start of the second decade of the twenty-first century, liberal polities around the world are roiled with self-doubt and confusion. The crises facing liberal societies are not only fiscal or governmental, they are moral crises as well. Many ordinary people are uncertain what *moral principles* they ought to appeal to as they chart a way forward. This is particularly true within the United States. Indeed, ordinary citizens there seem to be caught in the grip of a dichotomy very like the one that has long fixed political philosophers in their stark and oppositional camps. On one side, we see a mass movement advancing an anti-tax, anti-entitlement platform that, in its extreme form, rejects the very idea of social justice. On the other, a movement that, in the name of social justice, rejects market society and perhaps even capitalism itself.

Economic freedom *or* social justice. Everyone has to choose. On the political level, as on the conceptual one, there exists no common ground. Thus the contestants enter battle knowing that, when the dust settles, one side will win and the other will lose.

The elites of high liberalism, despite themselves, have encouraged this dichotomous way of thinking. According to the reigning academic ideology, after all, there is only one institutional path towards social justice. To make market-based societies more just, these elites have instructed us for decades, the basic institutions of those societies must be made more social democratic. After all, according to the high liberal orthodoxy, a commitment to justice requires a diminishment of private economic liberty and a corresponding concentration of economic decision-making power in the hands of legislators and other government officials. A just society, on this vision, would be a place of *solidarity*. Citizens there would decide together how many hours anyone would be allowed to devote to work each week and at what wage, at what age they must retire, the sort of health and benefits package it would be appropriate for each of them to enjoy, the type of schooling their children would all receive, and much more. A commitment to social justice means submission to mutual economic rule. The alternative is libertarianism, a view high liberals decry as manifestly unjust (and possibly illiberal too).

The market democratic paradigm invites us to step free from this polarizing scheme. Free market fairness offers a syncretic and morally superior guide to political action. Free market fairness is a perfectly general view that might be taken up and considered by citizens of any liberal society anywhere. While offering a moral ideal that is general in this sense, free market fairness also offers a fresh interpretation of the constitutional order of the world's most prominent market-society, the United States of America.

From the high liberal perspective, as from the orthodox libertarian one, there is nothing exceptional, or particularly worth venerating, in the traditional moral and constitutional order of America. That order, as we have seen, sets out strong (but limited) private economic liberties and, in its doctrine of enumerated powers, greatly (but not absolutely) limits the discretionary power of the government in economic affairs. No wonder criticism of traditional American institutions and values has long been a staple of the high liberal camp. Those "first born children of the commercial age" have nothing to teach contemporary scholars about the meaning or requirements of social justice.

There is an alternative. Americans have long felt that there is something of vital moral importance about the distinctive values and institutions of their land. America, at its best, is not simply a place where economic winners and economic losers come to get sorted out. It is a land where citizens share a dream of real opportunity for all. America, in its ideal at least, is a land committed to the proposition that all people are by nature free and equal moral agents, each with lives of their own to lead. Such citizens properly demand institutions that allow the distinctive talents and ambitions of their fellow citizens to be given their fullest possible play, with citizens of every class the political equals of all others, and no class left behind.

Free market fairness gives philosophical structure to these inchoate but familiar ideas. A central thesis of this book is that a democratic commitment to social justice does not require a commitment to the institutions of left liberalism—whether the welfare state, liberal socialism, or some rights-protecting version of social democracy. The market democratic approach offers a more robust and morally ambitious account of the institutions we need if we sincerely wish to respect our fellow citizens as free and equal self-governing agents. Like the traditional American creed, free market fairness sees mutual respect as calling for institutions that honor people as central causes of their own lives. Free market fairness insists that an opportunity for a life of freedom and independence is owed, not just to the wealthy, but to citizens of every economic class: entry-level workers, single parents, members of the middle class, and trailer park residents, too. Respecting the full range of liberal rights is part of this, but it is not all. Public institutions must be designed to allow even the poorest citizens to accumulate and personally control the greatest possible bundle of wealth. The institutions of free market fairness are a framework for spontaneous order. As such, those institutions are designed to unleash the ambitions and creative capacities of responsible individuals as they go about their busy lives.

Free market fairness encourages citizens of every class to join in the enterprise of building a world that is ever better, ever richer, and ever fuller for all. Within that world, people share a commitment not so much to an ideal of solidarity but to one of *opportunity*. This emphasis on individual opportunity over group solidarity is not a rejection of social justice. It is an interpretation of that ideal's fulfillment. I call this intrepetation of liberal justice free market fairness. But I don't mind if others give it a less formal name. Call it: social justice, American style.

Notes

Introduction

1. "I, Pencil," *The Freeman*, December 1958. Emphasis in original.

2. Joyce Appleby, *Capitalism and a New Social Order: The Republican Vision of the 1790s*, 49.

3. Originally published in *This Week Magazine*. Later reprinted in *Reader's Digest*, October 1952, p. 10, and January 1954, p. 122, lacking these words: "I will never cower before any master nor bend to any threat" and "to stand erect, proud and unafraid." Source: *Dictionary of Quotations*, at http://www.bartleby.com/73/71.html.

4. According to one study, 64 percent of Ivy League professors identified themselves as "liberal" or "somewhat liberal." None identified as "conservative." Center for the Study of Popular Culture, "Professor Survey," December 31, 2002.

5. John Rawls, *A Theory of Justice* (Cambridge, MA: Harvard University Press, 1971) (henceforth: *TJ*), and the revised edition, John Rawls, *A Theory of Justice* (Cambridge, MA: Harvard University Press, 1999) (henceforth: rev.), *TJ*, 17/16 rev.

6. Murray Rothbard, *For a New Liberty: The Libertarian Manifesto*, rev. ed.

7. *TJ*, 102. This phrase was deleted from the revised edition. For an interesting discussion of this change, see Lomasky, "Libertarianism at Twin Harvard."

8. F. A. Hayek, *Law, Legislation and Liberty*, vol. 2, *The Mirage of Social Justice*, 68–69. (Henceforth: *Mirage*.)

9. John Rawls, *The Law of Peoples: With "The Idea of Public Reason Revisited,"* 1st ed., 49–50. (Henceforth: *LP*.)

10. Jan Narveson equates liberty with property and as a result says "[it] is plausible to construe all rights as property rights." Narveson, *The Libertarian Idea*, 66.

11. Larry Tempkin, "Egalitarianism Defended," 764–82.

12. Derek Parfit, "Equality and Priority."

13. The term was made famous by Brink Lindsay who, it is important to note, used it in the context of a proposal for a strategic political alliance: "Liberaltarianism."

14. "When philosophy paints its grey in grey, then has a shape of life grown old. By philosophy's grey in grey it cannot be rejuvenated but only understood. The owl of Minerva begins its flight only with the falling of dusk." G.W.F. Hegel, "Preface," in *Outlines of the Philosophy of Right*, 16.

15. Inflation-adjusted GDP per capita income rose from $5,557 in 1900 to $43,926 in 2007. Nominal wages rose from $140.00 in 1900 (where 1860 = 100) to $16,166.00 in 2007. Adjusted for inflation, this amounts to an increase of 4.5 times. (These data are from http://www.measuringworth.org/USwages/). I thank Mark Koyama, an economic historian in the Political Theory Project at Brown University, for discussing this data set with me.

16. Tim Montgomerie, "Tesco, Purveyors of Jobs, Cheap Food and Social Justice."

17. CBS News, "Death (Tax) Takes a Holiday: But Nearly Everyone Wants It Repealed," at http://www.cbsnews.com/stories/2001/03/14/politics/main278884.shtml, from March 14, 2001.

18. Jesse McKinley, "A Tax on Nips and Tucks Angers Patients, Surgeons," *New York Times*, November 30, 2009.

19. "Fanfare for the Common Man: Is Economic Populism on the Rise in the Democratic Party?" *The Economist*, November 23, 2006.

20. Thomas Spragens, *Getting the Left Right: The Transformation, Decline, and Reformation of American Liberalism*, 198.

21. Adam Swift, "Social Justice: Why Does It Matter What the People Think?"

22. Samuel Bowles and Herbert Gintis, "The Inheritance of Inequality," 3-30. See also Pew Trust, "Pew-Commissioned Poll Finds Americans Optimistic about Prospects for Economic Mobility Despite the Recession," March 12, 2009.

23. Isaiah Berlin, for example, uses the term "libertarian" to denote a wide range of views that insist on the protection of personal freedom, and so lists John Stuart Mill as an exemplar of libertarianism. Berlin, "Two Concepts of Liberty," 124.

24. I thank Jason Swadley for suggesting these terms.

25. Libertarian political philosophers include Robert Nozick, Eric Mack, and Jan Narveson. For an excellent survey of the varieties of libertarian thought, see Matt Zwolinski, "Libertarianism," at http://www.iep.utm.edu/libertar/.

26. Samuel Freeman, *Rawls*, 45.

Chapter 1: Classical Liberalism

1. The use of the term *liberal* in a political sense came later. Alan Wolfe dates the first use to 1810, by Spanish delegates in Cadiz seeking an end to feudal privileges. Wolfe, *The Future of Liberalism*, 18.

2. For the transformation of English feudalism from a Saxon to its later Norman manorial form, see Harold Berman, *Law and Revolution: The Formation of the Western Legal Tradition*, esp. 295–332. The classic account of feudalism as a social order is Marc Bloch, *Feudal Society*.

3. See Bernard Siegan, *Property Rights: From Magna Carta to the Fourteenth Amendment*, 5–60.

4. I am not claiming that the concept of "ownership" was present during this period in a full or mature sense. See T. M. Honoré, "Ownership," 109 (who cites Pollock and Maitland, *History of English Law before the Time of Edward I*, vol. 2, p. 4).

5. Arthur Hogue, *Origins of the Common Law*.

6. Primogeniture and entailment were devices that prevented the division of large estates. Primogeniture, for example, required that landed property be bequeathed to the firstborn son.

7. For an overview, see Richard Pipes, *Property and Freedom*, 121–51.

8. The classic statement in the English context is Sir Robert Filmer, *Patriarcha*.

9. On the stirrings of capitalist sentiments during this period, see Christopher Hill, *The Century of Revolution, 1603–1714*, 2nd ed.

10. Quoted in William Uzgalis, "John Locke," *The Stanford Encyclopedia of Philosophy*.

11. John Locke, *Two Treatises of Government*, see II.2, sect. 4. A helpful overview is Karen Vaughn, "John Locke's Theory of Property," 5–37. See also Ruth Grant, *John*

Locke's Liberalism; Michael Zuckert, *Launching Liberalism: On Lockean Political Philosophy*.

12. Significantly, Locke adds: "he who appropriates land to himself by his labour, does not lessen but increase the common stock of mankind." *Two Treatises of Government*, II.37. Much ink has been spilt trying to understand the nature of Locke's "Proviso." Three distinct non-Proviso readings have been developed by Jeremy Waldron ("Enough and as Good Left for Others," 319–28), David Schmidtz ("When Is Original Appropriation 'Required'?" 504–18), and John Tomasi ("The Key to Locke's Proviso," 447–54).

13. Locke writes: "it is plain, that Men have agreed to disproportionate and unequal Possession of the Earth, they having by a tacit and voluntary consent found out a way, how a man may fairly possess more land than he himself can use the product of, by receiving in exchange for the overplus, Gold and Silver, which may be hoarded up without injury to any one." *Two Treatises of Government*, II.50.

14. *Two Treatises of Government*, II.124. For Locke, property rights are "subject to the Government and Dominion of that Commonwealth," *Two Treatises of Government*, II.120. But government cannot take people's property arbitrarily: *Two Treatises of Government*, II.138, esp. II.139–40. The people unite in society "for the mutual Preservation of the Lives, Liberties and Estates, which I call by the general name, Property" (*Two Treatises of Government*, II.123).

15. David Hume, *A Treatise of Human Nature*, Book III.

16. Nathan Rosenberg and L. E. Birdzell Jr., *How the West Grew Rich: The Economic Transformation of the Industrial World*, 14.

17. Mark Koyama, "Evading the 'Taint of Usury.'" See also Koyama, "The Political Economy of Expulsion: The Regulation of Jewish Moneylending in Medieval England."

18. Adam Smith, *An Inquiry into the Nature and Causes of the Wealth of Nations*, 687–88.

19. Regarding individual conduct, Smith wrote, "Mere justice is, on most occasions, but a negative virtue, and only hinders us from hurting our neighbors . . . we may often fulfill all the rules of justice by sitting still and doing nothing" (D. D. Raphael and A. L. Macfie, eds., *The Theory of the Moral Sentiments*), II.ii.1.9, 82. Further: "In the race for wealth, and honours, and preferments, he may run as hard as he can, and strain every nerve and muscle, in order to outstrip his competitors. But if he should jostle, or throw down any of them, the indulgence of the spectators is entirely at an end. It is a violation of fair play, which they cannot admit of." II.ii.2.1, 83.

20. Quoted in Ian Simpson Ross, *The Life of Adam Smith*, 108.

21. Quoted in Joyce Appleby, *Capitalism and a New Social Order: The Republican Vision of the 1790s*, 26, who cites Smith, *The Wealth of Nations*, 22.

22. Appleby, *Capitalism and a New Social Order*, 33.

23. Adam Smith, *Lectures on Jurisprudence*, 341, quoted in Samuel Fleischacker, *A Short History of Distributive Justice*, 62.

24. Gertrude Himmelfarb suggests that Smith's focusing of attention on the hardships of the working poor is Smith's distinctive contribution, more important even than his account of free trade. See Samuel Fleischacker, *A Short History of Distributive Justice*, 64.

25. According to mercantilism, prosperous countries are those that export more than they import. To maintain a positive cash flow, mercantilism empowers favored state actors to devise specific tariffs and other restrictions on trade. For a discussion of the effects of mercantilism on the poor, see David Schmidtz and Jason Brennan, *A Brief History of Liberty*, 137–42.

26. Regarding the tax on luxury vehicles, Smith says his idea is that "the indolence and vanity of the rich [can be] made to contribute in a[n] . . . easy manner to the relief of the poor" (Fleischacker, *A Short History of Distributive Justice* 63, which cites Smith, *The Wealth of Nations*, edited by R. H. Campbell, A. S. Skinner, and W. B. Todd, 752).

27. Adam Smith, *Wealth of Nations* (henceforth: *WN*), I.viii.27, 91.

28. As Hume's colleague, Adam Ferguson, put it, social order and law could be "the result of human action, but not the execution of any human design." Ferguson, *An Essay on the History of Civil Society*, pt. 3.2.

29. T. S. Ashton, *The Industrial Revolution, 1760–1830*, 4. More generally, see Joel Mokyr, *The Enlightened Economy: An Economic History of Britain, 1700–1850*.

30. That slate is contoured by empirical "contingencies" that affect the particular shape of each society: the personality of leaders, the detailed character of the constitutional and institutional order, the population size and age, the social norms, the stage of economic development, the quality of climate and soil, the abundance of natural resources, the proximity of rival states, and more.

31. The historiography of the American founding has moved in a "multiple traditions" direction in recent years. See, for example, Alan Gibson, *Interpreting the Founding*, chap. 6.

32. Quoted in James W. Ely, *The Guardian of Every Other Right: A Constitutional History of Property Rights*, 43. More generally, see Gordon Wood, *The Radicalism of the American Revolution*.

33. On the contested meanings of liberty in this era, see François Furstenberg, *Beyond Freedom and Slavery: Autonomy, Virtue, and Resistance in Early American Political Discourse*.

34. On the emergence of a Jeffersonian conception of individual liberty, see Appleby, *Capitalism and a New Social Order*. The quotation from Samuel Latham Mitchell earlier in this paragraph is from ibid., 74. For a critique of Appleby, see John Ashworth, "The Jeffersonians," 425–35.

35. As John Trenchard wrote in 1721, "All Men are animated by the Passion of acquiring and defending Property, because Property is the best Support of that Independency, so passionately desired by all Men" (quoted in Ely, *The Guardian of Every Other Right*, 17).

36. I am grateful to Greg Weiner for discussion of these issues, especially with respect to Madison's views.

37. See Jennifer Nedelsky, *Private Property and the Limits of American Constitutionalism: The Madisonian Framework and its Legacy*.

38. For discussion, see Ely, *The Guardian of Every Other Right*, 54, from which the Madison quotation also is drawn.

39. Ely comments: "Madison's decision to place this language [securing property] next to criminal justice protections, such as the prohibitions against double jeopardy

and self-incrimination, underscores the close association of property rights with personal liberty," *The Guardian of Every Other Right*, 54.

40. In his essay "Property," for example, Madison argued that property was not secure "where arbitrary restrictions, exemptions, and monopolies deny to part of [the] citizens that free use of their faculties, and free choice of their occupations, which not only constitute their property in the general sense of the word; but are the means of acquiring property." Madison also spoke against unequal and arbitrary taxation, protesting against any system in which "arbitrary taxes invade the domestic sanctuaries of the rich, and excessive taxes grind the faces of the poor." Quoted in Ely, *The Guardian of Every Other Right*, 55–56.

41. Ibid., 54. The Seventh Amendment, which allows jury trials for common-law suits concerning property, is also significant here.

42. See William Novak, *The People's Welfare: Law and Regulation in Nineteenth-Century America*.

43. I am indebted to George Thomas for discussion about educational funding in the early republic.

44. "The Virginia Report," in Meyers, ed., *The Mind of the Founder*, esp. 258.

45. See Bernard Siegan, *Economic Liberties and the Constitution*, chaps. 3 and 4.

46. The phrase is from Meyers, *The Mind of the Founder*, xiii.

47. David Armitage, *The Declaration of Independence: A Global History*.

48. Gordon Wood, *Empire of Liberty*, 355.

49. Wood used this phrase in response to a question from the audience after a lecture on "Empire of Liberty" (John Carter Brown Library, Brown University, September 16, 2009).

50. Again, this is an idealized vision and the importance of slavery must be kept constantly in view. See Edmund Morgan, *American Slavery, American Freedom: The Ordeal of Colonial Virginia*.

51. According to Thomas Paine, "The cause of America is in great measure the cause of all mankind." *Common Sense*, introduction.

52. Alexis de Tocqueville writes: "although there are rich men, a class of rich does not exist at all, for these rich men have neither corporate spirit nor objects in common" because they "are constantly becoming poor or retiring from business." Tocqueville, *Democracy in America*, 557. Marx similarly refers to "the United States of North America, where, though classes already exist, they have not yet become fixed, but continually change and interchange their component elements in constant flux." Chapter 20: "How an Aristocracy May be Created by Industry," in *The Eighteenth Brumaire of Louis Bonaparte* (in Marx and Engels, *Collected Works*, vol. 11, 111). Both quotations are from Elster, "Comments on Krouse and McPherson," 148n10.

53. Von Mises, *Human Action*; Friedman, *Capitalism and Freedom*; Hayek, *The Constitution of Liberty*.

54. Hayek describes the "conditions of freedom" as: "a state in which individuals are allowed to use their own knowledge for their own purposes." *Law, Legislation, and Liberty*, vol. 2, 8.

55. Ibid., vol. 1, 125.

56. For example, Hayek sometimes says that judges must sometimes correct the evolved laws. But if they are to make such corrections, there must be some independent standard that can be used to evaluate judge-made law.

57. Hayek, *Law, Legislation, and Liberty,* vol. 2, 1. Hayek also speaks of the importance of securing "the conditions in which the individuals and smaller groups will have favorable opportunities of mutually providing for their respective needs," and of creating "conditions likely to improve the chances of all in the pursuit of their aims." Ibid., 2.

58. Hayek, "The Use of Knowledge in Society," 519.

59. Hayek, *The Constitution of Liberty,* 21. (Henceforth: *Constitution.*)

60. *Constitution,* 153–61.

61. Hayek, "The Use of Knowledge in Society," Internet edition, page 1.

62. Hayek, *Law, Legislation, and Liberty,* vol. 1, 107. See also 112 and, esp., 126.

63. "Classical liberalism rested on the belief that there existed discoverable principles of just conduct of universal applicability which could be recognized as just irrespective of the effects of their application on particular groups" (ibid., vol. 1, 141).

64. Ibid., vol. 1, 141. For similar claims about the incompatibility of formal equality and substantive equality, see *Law, Legislation, and Liberty,* vol. 2, 82 and 108, and *Constitution,* 231.

65. *Law, Legislation, and Liberty,* vol. 1, 142.

66. *Law, Legislation, and Liberty: Mirage,* on vouchers: 84; on orphanages: 87–88; on minimum income: 88. *Constitution,* 285–86; on education: *Constitution,* 325–40.

67. *Law, Legislation, and Liberty: Mirage,* 87. Hayek writes: "One may well feel attracted to a community in which there are no extreme contrasts between rich and poor and may welcome the fact that the general increase in wealth seems gradually to reduce those differences. I fully share these feelings and certainly regard the degree of social equality that the United States has achieved as wholly admirable" (*Constitution,* 77).

68. *Constitution,* 313–34.

69. *Constitution,* 224–25.

70. Hayek, *The Fatal Conceit: The Errors of Socialism.*

71. I thank Adam Tebble for several illuminating conversations on this topic.

72. Hayek, *Law, Legislation, and Liberty,* vol. 1, 141–42.

73. *Constitution,* 230. Also: "As in all other fields, the case for subsidization of higher education (and of research) must rest not on the benefit it confers on the recipient but on the resulting advantages for the community at large," 330.

74. James Nickel, "Economic Liberties," in *The Idea of a Political Liberalism: Essays on Rawls,* 155–76. My category of "economic liberties" includes a range of what Wesley Hohfeld calls rights-relations, in *Fundamental Legal Conceptions.* See also Lawrence Becker, *Property Rights: Philosophical Foundations,* 11–21.

75. A classic discussion is Anthony Honoré, "Ownership," in *Oxford Essays in Jurisprudence,* 107–47, at 108.

76. For a definition along these lines, see John Rawls, *Justice as Fairness: A Restatement,* 114. (Henceforth: *JF.*) We return to this issue below.

77. The capitalist conception of economic liberty makes space for socialist forms of workplace organization (for example, by empowering property owners to found co-

ops and other worker-controlled firms), whereas the socialist conception of "economic liberty" is more rigid. See Daniel Shapiro, "Why Rawlsian Liberals Should Support Free Market Capitalism" and "Liberalism, Basic Rights, and Free Exchange."

78. A superb discussion of these issues is Samuel Freeman, "Capitalism in the Classical Liberal and High Liberal Tradition."

Chapter 2: High Liberalism

1. Quoted in Fleischacker, *A Short History of Distributive Justice*, 77.

2. Quoted in ibid., 78.

3. "It has to be granted from the first that the more violent the passions, the more necessary are the Laws to contain them; but . . . it would still be worth enquiring whether these disorders did not arise together with the Laws themselves; for then, even if they could repress them, it is surely the very least to expect of them that they put a stop to an evil that would not exist without them." Jean-Jacques Rousseau, *Discourses and Other Early Political Writings*; Victor Gourevitch, ed., *Discourse on the Origin and Foundation of Inequality among Men, or Second Discourse, by Jean-Jacques Rousseau*, part 1, sect. 41, 155. (Hereafter: *Second Discourse*.)

4. *Second Discourse*, Part 2, sect. 58, 188.

5. Rousseau's importance does not lie merely in his suggestion that commercial society will be marked by material inequalities: all the early liberal thinkers were aware of that fact. What's significant about Rousseau is his claim that the social order, far from being "natural," is a social product all the way down. See Dennis Rasmussen, *The Problems and Promise of Commercial Society: Adam Smith's Response to Rousseau*.

6. Marx, *On the Jewish Question* (1844).

7. Marx, *The Communist Manifesto*.

8. Mill describes this as "a sphere of action in which society, as distinguished from the individual, has, if any, only an indirect interest; comprehending all that portion of a person's life and conduct which affects only himself, or if it also affects others, only with their free, voluntary, and undeceived consent and participation." Mill, *On Liberty*. Library of Economics and Liberty, at http://www.econlib.org/library/Mill/mlLbty1.html. Sect. I.12, as quoted in Swadley, "Economic Liberties and the High Liberal Tradition," 14.

9. Daniel Jacobson, "Mill on Liberty, Speech, and the Free Society," at 293–95.

10. Mill, *On Liberty*, p. 15, chap. 1, sect. 11.

11. Jacobson comments: "Since the life of a capitalist does not necessarily violate the rights of others, it constitutes a permissible way of life. While this means that capitalism cannot be prohibited, it does not follow that 'capitalist acts between consenting adults'—to borrow a phrase from Robert Nozick—are within the sphere of liberty" ("Mill on Liberty, Speech, and the Free Society," 295).

12. Mill, *Principles of Political Economy*, II.ii., sect. 4. (Hereafter: *PPE*.) The next sentence reads: "Like all other proprietary rights, and even in a greater degree than most, the power of bequest may be so exercised as to conflict with the permanent interests of the human race."

13. I take this quotation of Mill from Sam Freeman, who cites *PPE*, IV, 7, p. 758 ("Capitalism in the High Liberal Tradition," 54–80). This paragraph, and the one immediately above borrow from Freeman's fine discussion of Mill. Errors are my own.

14. I borrow this quotation from Jason Swadley, "Economic Liberty and the High Liberal Tradition" 16, who cites *PPE*, 755 (IV.6.7).

15. See *PPE*, 769–94, esp. at 775.

16. This phrase serves as the title of chapter 3, book 1 of *The Wealth of Nations*.

17. See Alfred Chandler, *The Visible Hand*. See also Joel Mokyr, *The Enlightened Economy*. A lively introduction to these issues is Rosenberg and Birdzell, *How the West Grew Rich: The Economic Transformation of the Industrial World*.

18. In 1931, James Truslow Adams, who coined the phrase "the American Dream," wrote: "The farmer of Jefferson's day was independent and could hold opinions equally so. Steadily we are tending toward becoming a nation of employees— whether a man get five dollars a day or a hundred thousand a year. The 'yes-men' are as new to our national life as to our vocabulary, but they are real. It is no longer merely the laborer or factory hand who is dependent on the whim of his employer, but men all the way up the economic and social scales" (*The Epic of America*, 409).

19. According to Hayek: "Coercion occurs when one man's actions are made to serve another man's will . . . for the other's purpose." Thus, "Even if the threat of starvation . . . impels me to accept a distasteful job at a very low wage . . . I am not coerced" (*Constitution*, 117, 121).

20. Monopoly is a board game published by Parker Brothers, a subsidiary of Hasbro.

21. I use the metaphor of the Monopoly board game to illustrate the modern liberal objection to the classical liberal conceptions of formal equality. I am not suggesting that social life shares the zero sum characteristics of Monopoly.

22. For a discussion of this ideological transition, see Michael Freeden, *The New Liberalism: A Ideology of Social Reform*.

23. It is difficult to overstate the importance of this claim to classical liberalism as it is traditionally conceived. Freeman writes: "The most enduring and (I believe) persuasive classical liberal justification of the economic liberties is cast in terms of the conditions required to establish and maintain economically efficient market allocations of resources and distributions of income and wealth." He continues, "It is also the primary feature of classical liberalism that distinguishes it from what I call the 'high liberal tradition.'" "Capitalism in the Classical Liberal and High Liberal Tradition."

24. According to Keynes: "The outstanding faults of the economic system in which we live are its failure to provide for full employment and its arbitrary and inequitable distribution of wealth and income." Keynes claims that "measures for the redistribution of incomes in a way likely to raise the propensity to consume may prove positively favourable to the growth of capital." John Maynard Keynes, "The General Theory of Employment, Interest and Money."

25. Quoted in Cass Sunstein, *The Second Bill of Rights: FDR's Unfinished Revolution and Why We Need It More Than Ever*. Taken from Roosevelt's address to the Commonwealth Club, San Francisco, California, September 23, 1932.

26. Indeed, according to Ely, "the contract clause figured in more Supreme Court decisions than any other section of the constitution during the nineteenth century," *The Guardian of Every Other Right*, 68.

27. Ibid., 82.

28. Quoted in ibid., 119, who cites *New State Ice Co. v. Liebman*, 285 U.S. 262, 311 (1932).

29. When the Court struck down his agricultural program, Roosevelt said: "Are we going to take the hands of the federal government completely off any effort to adjust the growing of national crops, and go right straight back to the old principle that every farmer is a lord of his own farm and can do anything he wants, raise anything, any old time, in any quantity, and sell anytime he wants?" FDR Press Conference, May 31, 1935. Listed under: National Recovery Act Supreme Court. Accessed at *http://newdeal.feri.org/court/fdr5_31_35.htm*.

30. The seminal legal text is footnote 4 of Justice Stone's opinion in *United States v. Carolene Products Co.*, 304 U.S. 144 (1938) (upheld prohibition on the interstate sale of "filled milk" on strength of legislative assertions about health hazards regarding such products). An important precursor is *Nebbia v. New York*, 291 U.S. 502 (1934) (upheld constitutionality of law fixing the price of milk).

31. For a critical discussion of this change, see Jonathan Macey, "Some Causes and Consequences of the Bifurcated Treatment of Economic Rights and 'Other' Rights under the United States Constitution," 141–70. The 1937 Supreme Court case of *West Coast Hotel v. Parish* (upholding constitutionality of Washington statute imposing a minimum wage for women) is pivotal. According to Ely: "The decision in *West Coast Hotel* marked the virtual end of economic due process as a constitutional norm. Since 1937 the Supreme Court has not overturned any economic or social legislation on due process grounds" (*The Guardian of Every Other Right*, 127). Macey comments: "Unlike previous opinions, which balanced any intrusion on individual economic liberty against the government's authority to impose health and safety regulation, *West Coast Hotel* declined to afford any weight to the economic liberty of the parties being resulted. Wholesale approval of every aspect of the New Deal followed shortly thereafter" ("Some Causes and Consequences of the Bifurcated Treatment of Economic Rights and 'Other' Rights under the United States Constitution," 153–54).

32. Article 1, Section 8 of the US Constitution gives Congress power "to regulate Commerce with foreign Nations, and among the several states."

33. Sunstein calls Roosevelt's address "the greatest speech of the twentieth century." *The Second Bill of Rights*, 10.

34. "We cannot be content, no matter how high [our] general standard of living may be, if some fraction of our people—whether it be one-third or one-fifth or one-tenth—is ill-fed, ill-clothed, ill-housed, and insecure." Sunstein provides the full text of the speech in Appendix I. All these quotations are from *The Second Bill of Rights*, 242–43.

35. In *Justice as Fairness: A Restatement*, Rawls admits: "there are indefinitely many considerations that may be appealed to in the original position and each alternative conception of justice is favored by some consideration and disfavored by others" (133–34).

36. Notice that the difference principle does not require that the least fortunate *be given* whatever share of resources would maximize their position. Instead, when comparing whole social systems, we are to rank them in light of that hoped-for effect.

37. In the Kurt Vonnegut story "Harrison Bergeron," a totalitarian state forces citizens literally and completely to "share one another's fate." Agents of the state attach weights to the bodies of the strong, ugly masks on the faces of the beautiful, and implant alarm bells in ear canals of the intelligent (to break their concentration). See *The Magazine of Fantasy and Science Fiction* (October 1961).

38. There are many variations here. Prominent formulations include Richard Arneson, "Equality and Equal Opportunity for Welfare," 77–93; and Ronald Dworkin, *Sovereign Virtue.*

39. The difference principle is not primarily a principle of redress: "It does not require society to try to even out handicaps as if all were expected to compete on a fair basis in the same race" (*TJ*/rev., 101). Instead, Rawls takes a holistic approach to justice: "The main problem of distributive justice is the choice of a social system" (*TJ*/rev., 274).

40. Adam Smith described people as simultaneously "self-interested" and "other regarding." Rousseau and Kant offered accounts of the moral powers of citizens. For an illuminating discussion of the idea of moral powers in Rousseau and Kant in relation to that of Rawls, see Thomas A. Spragens Jr., *Getting the Left Right*, 68–71.

41. John Roemer distinguishes the self-direction prized by liberals from the Marxist ideal of self-realization. Whereas the Marxist ideal of self-realization requires struggle and transformation in a particular direction, the liberal ideal emphasizes agency. For liberals, self-direction involves carrying out a plan of life that one affirms for oneself, whether this consists of enjoying fine meals or counting blades of grass. *A Future for Socialism*, 10–11.

42. For Rawls's summary of the moral powers, see Rawls, *Justice as Fairness: A Restatement*, 18. (Hereafter: *JF*.)

43. Some might argue that a society wishing to provide each citizen with the social bases of self-respect must distribute wealth evenly. Rawls, however, argues that reciprocity allows for citizens to live with self-respect even in conditions of unequal wealth (*JF*, 138).

44. Richard Arneson, "Luck Egalitarianism: An Interpretation and Defense," 1–20; Ronald Dworkin, *Sovereign Virtue* and "Equality, Luck, and Hierarchy," 190–98.

45. Amartya Sen, *Inequality Reexamined*; Martha Nussbaum, *Women and Human Development: The Capabilities Approach.*

46. Rawls lists the basic liberties in a variety of ways, sometimes including a narrow range of economic liberties and in other places omitting mention of the economic liberties altogether. For a sampling, see *TJ*/rev., 195; *JF*, 144, 177; *Political Liberalism*, 5, 290–91, 299 (henceforth: *PL*).

47. *PL*, 298.

48. *TJ*/rev., 54.

49. John Maynard Keynes, "Economic Possibilities for Our Grandchildren," 6.

50. Dworkin, 1978, 133; 1981, 313, 338—as cited in Kymlicka, *Contemporary Political Philosophy*, 86. Ronald Dworkin, *Justice for Hedgehogs.*

51. Mill, 1965, 953, cited in Kymlicka, *Contemporary Political Philosophy*, 88.

52. Quoted in Freeman, *Rawls*, 87, who cites Rawls, *The Law of Peoples: With "The Idea of Public Reason Revisited,"* 113–20. (Hereafter: *LP*.)

53. *TJ*/rev., 274.

54. For a helpful discussion of these ideas, see Freeman, *Rawls*, 442.

55. *TJ*/rev., 242–51. See also *PL* (introduction to the paperback edition), lvi–lvii.

56. *TJ*/rev., 135–49. See also *JF*, 138–39.

57. *JF*, 137. Similarly, see *LP*, 49–50; *TJ*/rev., 65–75 and 270–74; *PL*, lvi–lvii and 262–65, 286–88.

58. Nozick, *Anarchy, State and Utopia*.

59. Samuel Fleischacker, *A Short History of Distributive Justice*, 121. Similarly, Jeffrey Paul describes Nozickian libertarianism as the "recent successor of Lockean liberalism," in *Reading Nozick*, 4. Comparing the philosophical clarity of Nozick's conception of equality to that of Hayek, Chandran Kukathas notes "a certain looseness" on the part of Hayek, in *Hayek and Modern Liberalism*, 223. Hayek self-deprecatingly describes himself as a "muddle-headed thinker"—one who is better at considering political ideas broadly than with technical precision. See Hayek, "Two Types of Mind," in *The Trend of Economic Thinking*.

60. A point Tom Palmer rightly emphasizes. See Doherty, *Radicals for Capitalism: A Freewheeling History of the Modern American Libertarian Movement*, 484.

61. Hayek, *Constitution*, 248–49.

62. Milton Friedman appears to see the safety net as a requirement of beneficence. See Friedman and Friedman, *Free to Choose*, 110. More generally, see Milton Friedman, *Capitalism and Freedom*, 177–95.

63. Rothbard, *For a New Liberty: The Libertarian Manifesto*, 39.

64. I am using Nozick merely as an exemplar of libertarianism. There are many other philosophically important formulations of what I am calling libertarianism, though some blur into classical liberalism on the one side or into anarcho-capitalism on the other. Among the most important book-length studies are: David Friedman, *The Machinery of Freedom* (New York: Harper and Row, 1973); Murray Rothbard, *The Ethics of Liberty* (Atlantic Highlands, NJ: Humanities Press, 1982); Norman Barry, *On Classical Liberalism and Libertarianism* (London: Macmillan, 1986); Loren Lomasky *Persons, Rights and the Moral Community* (New York: Oxford University Press, 1987); Jan Narveson, *The Libertarian Idea* (Philadelphia: Temple University Press, 1988); Randy Barnett, *The Structure of Liberty: Justice and the Rule of Law* (Oxford: Oxford University Press, 1998); Christopher Morris, *An Essay on the Modern State* (Cambridge: Cambridge University Press, 1998); Tibor Machan, *Individuals and Their Rights* (La Salle, IL: Open Court, 1989). Influential essays include: Ayn Rand, "The Nature of Government," and "Man's Rights," in *The Virtue of Selfishness* (New York: Signet, 1963); Eric Mack, "Self-Ownership and the Right of Property," *The Monist* 73 (October 1990): 519–43; Roy Childs, "Objectivism and the State: An Open Letter to Ayn Rand," in *Liberty against Power: Essays by Roy Childs, Jr.*, ed. J. K. Taylor (San Francisco: Fox and Wilkes, 1994); John Hasnas, "Reflections on the Minimal State," *Politics, Philosophy, and Economics* 2, no. 1 (2003): 115–28; Eric Mack, "Self-Ownership, Marxism, and Egalitarianism: Part I: Challenges to Historical Entitlement," *Politics, Philosophy, and*

Economics 1, no. 1 (2002): 75–108; Tom G. Palmer, *Realizing Freedom: Libertarian Theory, History, and Practice* (Washington, DC: Cato Institute, 2009). A sophisticated overview of the literature is Matt Zwolinski, "Libertarianism," in *The Internet Encyclopedia of Philosophy*. Despite the differences between all these "libertarian" thinkers, I shall accept Freeman's general definition: "Libertarianism is a doctrine of self-ownership. Absolute rights of property and freedom of contract are its most fundamental liberties" (*Rawls*, 52).

65. According to Walter Block, a self-described anarcho-capitalist: "contract, predicated on private property, [can] reach to the furthest realms of human interaction, even to voluntary slave contracts." "Towards a Libertarian Theory of Inalienability," 39–85, at 46. By contrast, Hayek explicitly denies that the doctrine of freedom of constraints entails that all contracts are enforceable (*Constitution*, 243). Historically, liberal societies have refused to enforce "unconscionable" contracts. See Schmidtz and Brennan, *A Brief History of Liberty*, 43.

66. Mack, "Self-Ownership and the Right of Property," 519–43.

67. Rasmussen and Den Uyl, who develop a highly original Aristotelian account of libertarianism, emphasize that this policy makes room for charitable activity. *Norms of Liberty: A Perfectionist Basis for a Non-Perfectionist Politics*, 311.

68. Narveson, *The Libertarian Idea*, 66.

69. Gaus comments: "It is . . . unfortunate that so many have viewed Robert Nozick's somewhat doctrinaire defense of the 'night-watchman state' as definitive of the classical liberal tradition." In "Coercion, Ownership, and the Redistributive State: Justificatory Liberalism's Classical Tilt," 236n12.

70. Hayek's most important political work, *The Constitution of Liberty*, was originally published in 1960. Milton Friedman's *Capitalism and Freedom* appeared in 1962. Michael Oakeshott's "Rationalism in Politics" came out in 1962. Von Mises's *Human Action* (arguably the second most important classical liberal work of the twentieth century) was published in 1949, with a revised edition appearing in 1963. Was there ever a richer or livelier decade of classical liberal scholarship?

71. In the course of his critique of "pure libertarianism," Richard Epstein argues that "the [US] Constitution is unambiguously in the classical liberal camp." *How Progressives Rewrote the Constitution*, 16, see also 134–35.

72. Thomas Nagel, "Libertarianism without Foundations."

73. Freeman, "Illiberal Libertarians: Why Libertarianism Is Not a Liberal View," 105–51.

74. John Stuart Mill provided an early formulation of this high liberal position: "It is not freedom to be allowed to alienate [one's] freedom." Quoted by Stuart White, who dates the quotation to 1859 but does not provide original citation information. See White, "The Citizen's Stake and Paternalism," in Wright, ed., *Redesigning Distribution*.

75. Freeman, *Rawls*, 395.

76. *PL*, 262–65. See also *JF*, 83 and *LP*, 48.

77. Freeman, "Illiberal Libertarians," esp. on pages 147–51.

78. Vallentyne and Steiner, *Left-Libertarianism and Its Critics: The Contemporary Debate*; Michael Otsuka, "Self-Ownership and Equality: A Lockean Reconciliation."

79. I thank Jan Narveson for a series of e-mail messages sent over the summer of 2010 that deepened my understanding of the problems here.

80. Ryan made this remark to me during a conversation in Princeton in 1993.

81. David Schmidtz describes having dinner with Nozick in 1999 and asking him about the evolution of his political views. Here is Schmidtz's account: "Nozick thought that being a libertarian implied roughly that everything should be for sale, so long as the exchange was truly consensual. He changed his mind about the desirability of that when he realized that there is more than one way of counting as a free country. Not interfering with freedom is one thing. Beyond that, there is also the question of what a country stands for . . . Nozick gradually came to believe that, apart from the question of what our actions accomplish, there is the question of what our actions symbolize. *Even if it were clear that respecting your right to contract yourself into slavery would enhance your freedom, enforcing such a contract would not be a way of standing for freedom.* "Review of Debra Satz's, *What Things Should Not Be for Sale*" (emphasis mine). Schmidtz's account helps make sense of Nozick's cryptic remarks in *The Examined Life*, 286–87, which could be read as a repudiation of libertarianism, and in *Invariances: The Structure of the Objective World*, 263, 281, where Nozick appears to endorse a revised version of that view. In an interview with Julian Simon late in his life, Nozick insisted that he remained a libertarian. See Doherty, *Radicals for Capitalism*, 494.

82. Barbara Fried, "Left Libertarianism: A Review Essay," 66–92.

83. Kymlicka, *Contemporary Political Philosophy*, 160. For a similar claim, though one that carefully distinguishes classical liberalism from libertarianism, see Freeman, *Rawls*, 117–18.

84. Nagel, "Rawls and Liberalism," in Freeman, ed., *Cambridge Companion to Rawls*, 63.

85. Ibid., 66. Dworkin describes the classical liberal conception of formal equality (or, justice as equal opportunity) as not merely mistaken but "fraudulent"—quoted in Kymlicka, *Contemporary Political Philosophy*, 57. Cass Sunstein describes the theory of individualism that undergirds classical liberal interpretations of American law as "confused and pernicious" and as "incoherent, a tangle of confusions" (*The Second Bill of Rights*, 3).

86. While I adopt this use of the term "democracy," note that its appropriation by justificatory liberals is not unproblematic. In morally neutral terms, we might say that a society is democratic to the extent that fundamental political power is held equally by all members of that society. Democracy, on this view, concerns the way power is held rather than the way political institutions are justified. I thank Jason Brennan for discussion of these issues.

87. Freeman, "Capitalism in the Classical Liberal and High Liberal Traditions," 55.

88. See especially Robert Higgs, *Crisis and Leviathan: Critical Episodes in the Growth of American Government*.

Chapter 3: Thinking the Unthinkable

1. A generation earlier in Britain that phrase had been a rallying cry for dissident defenders of economic liberalism such as F. A. Hayek and Harry Seldon. See Richard

Cockett, *Thinking the Unthinkable: Think Tanks and the Economic Counter-Revolution in England, 1931–1983*.

2. See Douglass North and Robert Paul Thomas, *The Rise of the Western World: A New Economic History*, 1.

3. Keynes, "Economic Possibilities for Our Grandchildren," 1–2.

4. Quoted in Kling and Schulz, *From Poverty to Prosperity*, 58.

5. Erik Eckholm, "Prolonged Aid to Unemployed Is Running Out," *New York Times*, August 2, 2009. I am aware that readers from the left may see these softened effects as resulting primarily from generous governmental aid programs (made possible by growth), while readers from the right are more likely to see them as direct consequences of growth itself. That is fine with me. I use the examples to call the attention of all readers to the fact of growth.

6. Maddison, as calculated per note 15 of the introduction of this book.

7. McCloskey, "Growth, Quality, Happiness, and the Poor," 6.

8. Ibid., 11.

9. Quoted in ibid., 10–11.

10. McCloskey attributes the example of Carnegie to Otteson, *Actual Ethics*, 165.

11. McCloskey continues: "Like the realization in astronomy in the 1920s that most of the 'nebulae' detected by telescopes are in fact other galaxies unspeakably far from ours, the Great Fact of economic growth, discovered by historians and economists in the 1950s and elaborated since then, changes everything." McCloskey, "Growth, Quality, Happiness, and the Poor," 7. See also Angus Maddison, *Contours of the World Economy, 1–2030 AD*.

12. McCloskey, "Growth, Quality, Happiness, and the Poor," 26.

13. With rising affluence, people within many liberal societies increasingly spend "around" the state: religious parents homeschooling, growth of private medical care options, and much more. See Field, "What, Then, Was Unthinkable?" See also Rockwell, "The State Expands, and Weakens." "Let me present the following metaphor of how I imagine the relationship of the productive matrix of human voluntarism to exist alongside the leviathan state. Imagine a vigorous game of football with fast and effective players, cooperating with their teams and competing with the other team. . . . This mastodon is powerful and authoritative, more so than ever, but it can hardly move. It can bat its trunk at players that prove especially annoying, even impale them on its tusks, but it cannot finally stop the game from taking place. And the longer these players confront this strange obstacle, the better they become at working around it, and growing stronger and faster despite it." Found at http://www.lewrockwell.com/rockwell/empire-shrinks.html.

14. Field, "What, Then, Was Unthinkable?," 21.

15. Nagel, *The Myth of Ownership*. We examine Nagel's argument below.

16. Judt, "What Is Living and What Is Dead in Social Democracy," 1.

17. While politicians on the left often find reliable support among the wealthy and the poor, many have noted a growing weakening of support among the middle and working class. This was a much-discussed feature of President Obama's election victory in 2008. See Thomas Edsall, "Rich Dem, Poor Dem: Class War in Obamaland."

18. Graetz and Shapiro, *Death by a Thousand Cuts: The Fight over Taxing Inherited Wealth*, 120, 121.

19. Morrissey, "Proposed 'Botox Tax' Draws Wide Array of Opponents."

20. *The Atlantic*, "National Unemployment Rate Unchanged at 10.0% in December," at http://www.theatlantic.com/business/archive/2010/01/national-unemployment-rate-unchanged-at-100-in-december/33174/.

21. Citation to data mentioned by Graetz and Shapiro, *Death by a Thousand Cuts*, at 119.

22. Quoted in Spragens, *Getting the Left Right*, at 209. Graetz and Shapiro, *Death by a Thousand Cuts*. The quotations come from the authors' presentation of their findings at the Brookings Institution on March 24, 2005. According to a poll taken in 2005, 75 percent of Americans believe it is possible in America to start out poor, work hard, and become rich. This belief is particularly robust among working-class people. See David Leonhart, "A Closer Look at Income Mobility," Class Matters: Special Section, *New York Times*, May 14, 2005, at http://www.nytimes.com/2005/05/14/national/class/15MOBILIT-WEB.html.

23. Spragens, *Getting the Left Right*, 208. Spragens, himself a left liberal, argues that the fixation of recent left liberals on abstract ideas of social justice has cut liberalism off from its populist roots. I find this aspect of Spragens's lively and provocative book highly congenial to my project.

24. A classic of this genre is Karl Polanyi, *The Great Transformation: The Political and Economic Origins of Our Time*.

25. Daniel Bell brilliantly forecast many of these economic changes, even though Bell's vision of the moral implications of these changes was considerably less clear. *The Coming of Post-Industrial Society: A Venture in Social Forecasting*.

26. Kling and Schulz, *From Poverty to Prosperity*, 46–50.

27. Roberts, *The Modern Firm: Organizational Design for Performance and Growth*. I thank Lant Pritchett for bringing Robert's important work to my attention.

28. I am not saying that this is the only viable form of capitalism in a postindustrial era. Some see state capitalism as a potentially stable, long-term rival. See Bremmer, *The End of the Free Market: Who Wins the War between States and Corporations?*

29. Koch and Smith, *The Suicide of the West*, 106. Other dimensions of the personalized economy are discussed by Tyler Cowen, *Create Your Own Economy: The Path to Prosperity in a Disordered World*; Roger Bootle, *Money for Nothing: Real Wealth, Financial Fantasies, and the Economy of the Future*; and Diane Coyle, *The Weightless World: Strategies for Managing the Digital Economy*.

30. Field, "What, Then, Was Unthinkable?," 7.

31. For one exposition of the proof, see Samuel Goldberg, *Probability: An Introduction*. I thank David McIlroy for suggesting this example.

32. The example of Terry is based loosely on the experiences of a colleague of mine at Brown, who is an energetic campaigner for Democratic candidates. Amy's Pup-in-the-Tub is a pet grooming business in Warren, Rhode Island, located adjacent to the coffee house where much of this book was written, though again details are illustrative only.

33. I am indebted to Jason Brennan for discussion of these issues.

34. Freeman, "Illiberal Libertarians," 129–30.

35. "Our property is nothing but those goods, whose constant possession is establish'd by the laws of society; that is, by the laws of justice." David Hume, *A*

Treatise of Human Nature, 491. Milton Friedman says: "what constitutes property and what rights the ownership of property confers are complex social creations rather than self-evident-propositions." *Capitalism and Freedom*, 26.

36. Nagel and Murphy, *The Myth of Ownership: Taxes and Justice*, 8.

37. Ibid., 33.

38. I am not saying that this argument defeats all (or any) versions of libertarianism. For one thing, as Geoffrey Brennan points out, criminal prohibitions against murder are also socially elaborated notions, but this does not mean that murder lacks any character of wrongness in the state of nature. "The law might add moral authority to the norm against murder, but the moral authority of the norm against murder exists independently of the law that makes murder criminal. So the fact that private property is defined by law does not, of itself, determine whether property has independent moral authority." Brennan, "The Myth of Ownership: Liam Murphy and Thomas Nagel." See also Gerald Gaus's compact critique of the Murphy/Nagel thesis, in "Coercion, Ownership, and the Redistributive State: Justificatory Liberalism's Classical Liberal Tilt," 233–75, at 259.

39. Nagel and Murphy, *The Myth of Ownership*, 16–17.

40. Thomas Nagel, "What Is It Like to Be a Bat?"

41. *PL*, 338–39.

42. Ibid.

43. Ibid., 298.

44. For an alternative to the Rawlsian interpretation, see Gerald Gaus, *The Order of Public Reason*.

45. *JF*, 41.

46. Consider another example: imagine a society that tailored the right of religious freedom to allow the practice of any religion whatsoever—so long at such practice was conducted only in private homes.

47. *JF*, 46.

48. Jeremy Waldron's formulation of the principle of legitimacy captures this idea: "I shall argue that liberals are committed to a conception of freedom and respect for the capacities and the agency of individual men and women, and that these commitments generate a requirement that all aspects of the social should either be made acceptable or be capable of being made acceptable to every last individual." "Theoretical Foundations of Liberalism," 128.

49. I thank Jason Swadley, Zak Beauchamp, and Jason Brennan for discussion of these ideas.

50. *JF*, 46–47.

51. Nickel, "Economic Liberties," 156.

52. For example, I am a shareholder in a cooperatively owned ski area (Mad River Glen, in Fayston, Vermont). As a member of that co-op, I participate in deliberations about how we will manage our collectively owned property (such as our decision, enthusiastically ratified year after year, to ban snowboarders from our mountain).

53. Murray, *In Our Hands*, 82 (emphasis mine).

54. Murray, "The Happiness of the People," 7, 8–9.

55. Conversations with Charles Larmore sharpened my understanding of these issues, even though our convictions on these matters diverge.

56. Waldron, "Socioeconomic Rights and Theories of Justice" (working manuscript November 2010, electronic copy available at http/ssrn.com/abstract=1699898, p. 3). Most democratic theorists argue that private property is publically justifiable so long as welfare rights are also guaranteed (typically by the state). For a sophisticated discussion of this position, see Corey Brettschneider, *Democratic Rights: The Substance of Self-Government*, esp. 114–35.

57. *TJ/rev.*, 155–57 and 386–87.

58. I develop this idea in "Can Feminism Be Liberated from Governmentalism?," in *Toward a Humanist Justice: Essays in Honor of Susan Okin*.

59. Margaret Holmgren, "Justifying Desert Claims: Desert and Opportunity," 265–78. See also David Lewis Schaefer, *Illiberal Justice: John Rawls vs. the American Political Tradition*, 41.

60. *TJ/rev.*, 476, emphasis mine.

61. F. A. Hayek, "The Use of Knowledge in Society."

62. John Gray, *Post-Liberalism*, 314.

63. Friedman, *Capitalism and Freedom*, 15.

64. Drawing on the work of Henry Shue, Nickel calls arguments for economic liberty of this type "linkage arguments" (in "Economic Liberties," 157). For historical discussion, see Richard Pipes, *Property and Freedom*.

65. "Making Philosophy Matter to Politics," *New York Times*, December 2, 2002.

66. *TJ/rev.*, 86.

67. *TJ/rev.*, 274.

68. Krouse and McPherson, "A 'Mixed'-Property Regime: Equality and Liberty in a Market Economy," 103.

Chapter 4: Market Democracy

1. According to Freeman: "Rawls's conception of justice is *democratic* in that it provides for equal political rights and seeks to establish *equal opportunities* in educational and occupational choice" (*Rawls*, 44, all emphases in original; see also 216–67).

2. I owe this formulation to Jason Swadley.

3. For a helpful discussion of how the recognition of economic liberties as basic nonetheless allows for regulation of the scope of those liberties, see James Nickel "Economic Liberties," 170.

4. Freeman, *Rawls*, 57 (emphasis mine). Also, "*Unregulated* economic liberties then render practically impossible many persons' adequate development of their moral powers, and therewith freedom and equality and their having fair opportunities to pursue a reasonable conception of the good. This is the underlying message in Rawls's explicit rejection of basic economic liberties," 58 (emphasis mine).

5. Freeman writes: "Most people believe that it is more important that they be free to decide their religion, speak their minds, choose their own careers, and marry and befriend only people that they choose, than that they have the freedom to drive without safety belts and as fast as they please, use their property *without regulation*, or enter into just *any kind* of financial dealing that is beneficial to them" (Freeman,

Rawls, 45–46, emphasis added). But market democracy does not affirm economic freedoms in absolutist, unregulated forms, any more than the Rawlsian high liberals affirm freedoms of speech or religion in absolutist or "unregulated" forms.

6. Lionel Robbins, *The Theory of Economic Policy in English Classical Political Economy*.

7. Most notably, Charles A. Murray, *In Our Hands: A Plan to Replace the Welfare State*.

8. I am indebted to Jason Swadley for this term, and for several illuminating conversations about this topic.

9. Freeman, *Rawls*, 45.

10. The account of Kant's theory of property given in this paragraph, as well as the contrast between Kant and Locke developed in the next paragraph, is informed by research done for me over the summer of 2010 by Jason Swadley, as well as by an unpublished paper by Swadley titled "Economic Liberty and the High Liberal Tradition" (draft of August, 2010). I also rely on Arthur Ripstein's discussion of Kant's views in *Force and Freedom: Kant's Legal and Political Philosophy*. Applications of these ideas to market democracy are my own.

11. Freeman, "Illiberal Libertarians," 106. Note that in a departure from my usual terminological practice, I am here using the term "high liberal" to denote a method of justification rather than a set of substantive moral commitments. Classified in terms of his substantive moral commitments, Kant is a classical liberal (on which, see immediately below).

12. "*Freedom* (independence from being constrained by another's choice), insofar as it can coexist with the freedom of every other in accordance with a universal law, is the only original right belonging to every man by virtue of his humanity." Immanuel Kant, *Doctrine of Right*, 393.

13. Allen Wood writes: "Kant's political philosophy or theory of right, considered by itself, is merely a version of classical liberalism." Wood continues: "It is based on two familiar liberal tenets: (1) Competition is nature's means for the development of human faculties; and (2) The state's function is to regulate competition by protecting property and coercively enforcing formal principles of right" ("Kant and the Problem of Human Nature," 22 [quoted in Swadley, "Economic Liberties and the High Liberal Tradition," 5]).

14. In the opening lines of *Anarchy, State, and Utopia*, Nozick states: "Individuals have rights, and there are things that no other person or group may do to them (without violating their rights). So strong and far-reaching are these rights that they raise the question of what, if anything, the state and its officials may do" (ix).

15. David Hume, *A Treatise on Human Nature*, 490–93.

16. Kant, *Doctrine of Right*, 468 (quoted in Swadley, "Economic Liberties and the High Liberal Tradition," 12).

17. I owe this phrase to David Estlund.

18. In the X-Men comics series published by Marvel Comics, *Homo sapiens superior* are the evolutionary progeny of the species *Homo sapiens*.

19. Avner Greif, *Institutions and the Path to the Modern Economy: Lessons from Medieval Trade*, 30.

20. I am assuming here, as always, that these wider economic liberties are being exercised in ways compatible with other basic rights.

21. Freeman, *Rawls*, 58.

22. Hayek writes: "It is no slur on democracy, no ignoble distrust of its wisdom, to maintain that, once it embarks upon such a policy [say, of increasing taxes in support of distributive aims], it is bound to go much further than originally intended" (*Constitution*, 272).

23. The period of laissez-faire constitutionalism in the United States is usually said to have ended in the late 1930s. See Ely, *The Guardian of Every Other Right*, 119–34.

24. Keynes, "Economic Possibilities for Our Grandchildren."

25. Important work here includes: Terry Anderson and Donald Leal, *Free Market Environmentalism*; Julian Simon, "Population Growth, Natural Resources, and Future Generations"; and David Schmidtz, "The Institution of Property" and "When Preservationism Doesn't Preserve," in *Environmental Ethics: What Really Matters, What Really Works*, ed. David Schmidtz and Elizabeth Willott.

26. The contrast with Rawls is stark. Regarding the steeply progressive taxes of property owning democracy, Rawls says, "the purpose of these levies and regulations is not to raise revenue (release resources to government) but gradually and continually to correct the distribution of wealth." *TJ*/rev., 244.

27. Henrik Ibsen, *A Doll's House*.

28. See John Tomasi, "Can Feminism Be Liberated from Governmentalism?" Superb collections of original sources, with commentary, are Wendy McElroy, ed. *Freedom, Feminism, and the State: An Overview of Individualist Feminism*, and McElroy, ed. *Individualist Feminism of the Nineteenth Century: Collected Writings and Biographical Profiles*.

29. James Nickel, following Joseph Raz, writes: "The ideal of autonomy holds that adults of normal intelligence and capacities should not turn over or be forced to turn over the management of their lives to other parties—even if those parties could manage their lives better than they can. This ideal holds that people should be the authors of their own lives to a considerable degree" ("Economic Liberties," 161).

30. The term *property-owning democracy* has a complicated history. At the start of her third term as prime minister, Margaret Thatcher used the term to describe her Conservative Party's ideal of low taxation and social deregulation ("Thatcher: We Are Building a Property-Owning Democracy," *Time*, June 22, 1987). By contrast, Rawls takes the term "property-owning democracy" from the left-liberal ideal of James Meade (*Efficiency, Equality, and the Ownership of Property*), *TJ*/rev., 242. An influential discussion is Richard Krouse and Michael McPherson, "Capitalism, 'Property-Owning Democracy,' and the Welfare State," in *Democracy and the Welfare State*, ed. Amy Gutmann (Princeton, NJ: Princeton University Press, 1988), 79–105. On the choice between liberal democratic socialism and property-owning democracy, see *JF*, 138.

31. A seminal exposition of market socialism is Oskar Lange, *On the Economic Theory of Socialism*. In 1920, Ludwig von Mises argued that state socialist economies face an insurmountable calculation problem: without price signals, planners have no rational way of allocating the factors of production. (Ludwig von Mises, "Economic Calculation in the Socialist Commonwealth," Archiv für Sozialwissenschaften, vol. 47 [1920], translation published in Hayek, *Collectivist Economic Planning*.) Hayek argues that Lange's market socialism does not overcome the socialist calculation problem

("Two Pages of Fiction: The Impossibility of Socialist Calculation," in Nishiyama and Leube, eds., *The Essence of Hayek*). For a normative defense of market socialism, see David Miller, *Market, State, and Community: Theoretical Foundations of Market Socialism*.

32. Like democratic laissez-faire regimes, these limited government ones would generally oppose schemes of government licensure of professions as restrictions on economic liberty. In cases where such government licensure were allowed, though, democratic limited government would be likely to see an antidiscrimination law as applying with special force.

33. Murray, *In Our Hands*. Murray's proposal bears some resemblance to the minimum income scheme Milton Friedman proposed in *Capitalism and Freedom*, esp. 191–94. For a discussion of the philosophical issues, see Matt Zwolinski, "Classical Liberalism and the Basic Income."

34. Freeman, *Rawls*, 57.

35. See also Bruce Ackerman, "What Is Neutral about Neutrality?," 372–90 (esp. sect. "II. Possible Worlds"); G. A. Cohen, "Facts and Principles"; and David Miller, "Political Philosophy for Earthlings."

Chapter 5: Social Justicitis

1. Hume, *An Enquiry concerning the Principles of Morals*, sect. III, pt. ii, 155. For discussion, see Samuel Fleischacker, *A Short History of Distributive Justice*, 12.

2. Hayek, *Law, Legislation, and Liberty*, vol. 2, *The Mirage of Social Justice* (hereafter: *Mirage*), 78. For other formulations of Hayek's claim that "social justice" is logically incoherent, see *Mirage*, 62, 69, and 96.

3. Nozick, *Anarchy, State, and Utopia*, 149–50.

4. Eric Mack, "Distributionism versus Justice," *Ethics* 86, no. 2 (January 1976): 145–53.

5. "If the domain of 'justice' is coextensive with the rights that people have," Loren Lomasky states, "then any sets of property holdings that emerge from rightful activity are, by definition, (distributively) just." Sam Freeman attributes a similar position to Nozick (*Rawls*, 128, 142).

6. Lomasky, *Persons, Rights, and the Moral Community*, 125.

7. I am thinking in particular here of work by Nozick, Jan Narveson, Eric Mack, and, to the degree that he counts as a libertarian rather than a classical liberal, Loren Lomasky.

8. I am aware that in strict medical parlance, "justicitis" refers to a form of inflammation, rather than to an allergy proper. I use the term metaphorically (though I am heartened to learn from my friend, Dr. Jami Star, of quasi-allergenic forms of inflammation such as nasal congestivitis).

9. Locke, *Two Treatises of Government, Second Treatise*, II, sect. 41.

10. Locke, "Some Considerations of the Consequences of the Lowering of Interest and the Raising the Value of Money" (1691). At http://socserv.mcmaster.ca/econ/ugcm/3113/locke/consid.txt. I thank Dennis Rasmussen for bringing this passage to my attention.

11. Locke: "Charity gives every Man a Title to so much out of another's plenty, as will keep him from extreme want, where he has no means to subsist otherwise" (*Two Treatises of Government, First Treatise*, I.4. sect. 42).

12. Mandeville, "The Grumbling Hive" (1705), in *The Fable of the Bees*, 37.

13. The Statute of Apprentices, which limited the ability of workers to choose when and where to work, is one example of this. The Settlement Act, which limited the mobility of poor people, is another.

14. Smith, *Wealth of Nations* (hereafter: *WN*), IV.viii.4, 644; see also IV.viii.49, 660.

15. I am indebted to Dennis Rasmussen for discussion of these issues, and for this quotation from Malthus.

16. *WN* I.viii.36, 96.

17. Ibid.

18. After describing Smith's theory, Fleischacker comments: "Smith thus gives us essentially the same justification for inequalities that John Rawls was to propose two centuries later: they are acceptable if and only if the worst-off people under a system of inequality are better off than they would be under an egalitarian distribution of goods" (*Short History of Distributive Justice*, 39).

19. See John Tomasi, "Governance beyond the Nation State: James Madison on Foreign Policy and 'Universal Peace.'"

20. Stephen Holmes, *Passions and Constraint: On the Liberal Theory of Democracy*, 29–30, emphasis mine.

21. Madison to Francis Corbin, November 26, 1820. In Gaillard Hunt, ed., *The Writings of James Madison, Volume IX: 1819–1836*, 38–41 (quote is at 40–41). (This is from a facsimile via the Online Library of Liberty.) I thank Greg Weiner for this quotation and for improving my understanding of Madison's position on economic liberty.

22. Spencer, "The Coming Slavery," in *Man versus the State*, 32.

23. For an alternative view, see Philippe van Parijs, *Real Freedom for All: What (If Anything) Can Justify Capitalism?* (New York: Oxford University Press, 1995).

24. Spencer, *Social Statics*, 326.

25. Spencer, *Man versus the State*, 69–70.

26. Spencer stood against calls to nationalize the English economy, just as he stood against "Progressive liberal" attempts to regulate private labor agreements. In "The Coming Slavery," Spencer explicitly says that his main objection to socialism is founded on his concern for the workers, not the owners.

27. Von Mises, *Human Action*, 834.

28. Von Mises, *Liberalism: In the Classical Tradition*, 164–65. Conversation with George Reisman deepened my understanding of this passage from Von Mises, even though he does not fully share my reading of it.

29. Von Mises, *Liberalism: The Classical Tradition*, 33, emphasis mine.

30. Ibid., 14.

31. I thank Roderick Long for discussion of these features of Rand's egoism.

32. Rand, "Monument Builders," in *The Virtue of Selfishness: A New Concept of Egoism*.

33. Rand, "The Divine Right of Stagnation," in *The Virtue of Selfishness: A New Concept of Egoism* (emphasis mine).

34. I owe these ideas about *Atlas Shrugged*, and much of the wording in these two paragraphs about the novel, to Jason Brennan.

35. Hayek, *New Studies in Philosophy, Politics, Economics, and the History of Ideas*, 132–34.

36. Hayek says, "The proletariat which capitalism can be said to have 'created' was thus not a proportion of the population which would have existed without it and which it had degraded to a lower level; it was an additional population which was enabled to grow up by the new opportunities for employment which capitalism provided" ("History and Politics," in *Capitalism and the Historians*, 16).

37. As David Miller puts it (albeit with evident sarcasm): "if people believe Hayek, then even a coalition of the poor will eschew government redistribution in favor of the trickle-down effect of the free market" (*Principles of Social Justice*, 256).

38. Friedman, *Capitalism and Freedom*, 169.

39. Both quotations are from ibid., 195.

40. Quoted in Brian Doherty, *Radicals for Capitalism: A Freewheeling History of the Modern American Libertarian Movement*, 417.

41. Nozick, *Anarchy, State, and Utopia*, 177. For discussion of this point, see Matt Zwolinski "Libertarianism," *The Internet Encyclopedia of Philosophy*.

42. Eric Mack, "Self-Ownership, Marxism, and Egalitarianism: Part II: Challenges to the Self-Ownership Thesis," 237, emphasis mine.

43. Epstein, *How The Progressives Rewrote the Constitution*, 15.

44. Ibid., x–xi, 16. See also 74.

45. Reagan continues: "We built the West without waiting for an area redevelopment plan. San Francisco, destroyed by fire, was rebuilt by Californians who didn't wait for urban renewal. We have fought our wars with citizen-soldiers and dollar-a-year men." Terry Golway, *Ronald Reagan's America: His Voice, His Dreams, and His Vision of Tomorrow*, emphasis mine.

46. On democratic capitalism generally, see Michael Novak, *Three in One: Essays on Democratic Capitalism, 1976–2000*.

47. Ronald Reagan, "Remarks Announcing America's Economic Bill of Rights, July 3, 1987." Steven Calabresi, who was at the time a member of Reagan's White House staff working under Kenneth Cribb, contributed ideas to the speech. I thank Calabresi for bringing this speech to my attention.

48. Other advocates of thick economic liberty and limited government who might be added to this list include: Benjamin Tucker, Ezra Haywood, Lysander Spooner, Voltairine de Cleyre, Albert J. Nock, Frank Choderov, and contemporary libertarian scholars such as Kevin Carson, Gary Chartier, and Sheldon Richman. The Catholic free market tradition running from Lord Acton to Michael Novak offers another rich vein of resources.

49. Friedman, *Capitalism and Freedom*, 195.

50. *Mirage*, 65.

51. Ibid., 69 and 68, respectively. See also 96.

52. Ibid., 66.

53. "What we have to deal with in the case of 'social justice' is simply a quasi-religious superstition of the kind which we should respectfully leave in peace so long as it merely makes those happy who hold it, but which we must fight when it becomes the pretext of coercing other men. And the prevailing belief in 'social justice'

is at present probably the gravest threat to most other values of a free civilization." *Mirage*, 66–67.

54. Ibid., 62

55. Ibid., 97. "I believe that 'social justice' will ultimately be recognized as a will-o'-the-wisp which has lured men to abandon many of the values which in the past have inspired the development of civilization—an attempt to satisfy a craving inherited from the traditions of the small group but which is meaningless in the Great Society of free men." Ibid., 67.

56. Ibid., 75.

57. Hayek, *Law, Legislation, and Liberty, vol. 1, Rules and Order*, 36.

58. See International Gem Society website, at http://www.gemsociety.org/info/igem17.htm. Written by Don Clark, CSM President, and Jain and Jain, "Learning the Principles of Glass Science and Technology from Candy Making."

59. Hayek borrows the term "cosmos" from Joseph Schumpeter, *History of Economic Analysis*, e.g., 467; see Hayek, *New Studies in Philosophy, Politics, Economics and the History of Ideas*, 73. On systems theory generally, see Michael Polanyi, *The Logic of Liberty*, esp. the section titled "Two Kinds of Social Order," 190–202. Polanyi also mentions a crystal as an example of what he calls "a spontaneously attained order" (191).

60. As a definitional matter, for example, we could sensibly pick out the grouping of redheaded natives of Rhode Island who were born in January. But the members of the grouping—being of different ages, having different interests, skills, and educational backgrounds, living in different places—are not an order in the system's theory sense.

61. For a helpful discussion of the intellectual roots of this idea, see Ronald Hamowy, *The Scottish Enlightenment and the Theory of Spontaneous Order*.

62. Hayek, *New Studies in Philosophy, Politics, Economics and the History of Ideas*, 77. "A command regularly aims at a particular result or particular foreseen results, and together with the particular circumstances known to him who issues or receives the command will determine a particular action. By contrast, a rule refers to an unknown number of future instances and to the acts of an unknown number of persons, and merely states certain attributes which any such action ought to possess." *Mirage*, 14.

63. Hayek, *New Studies in Philosophy, Politics, Economics and the History of Ideas*, 77.

64. *Mirage*, 15.

65. These two general forms can function at various levels and as subsets of each other. A corporation may be described as a *taxis* operating within the *cosmos* of a competitive market order, for example. The distinction between cosmos and taxis blurs on other dimensions as well. Chandran Kukathas comments: "This distinction between exogenously and endogenously created structures is not always clear cut since many structures that are 'made' could not be 'made' unless particular substructures will form spontaneously. A digital watch cannot be made without relying on the spontaneous orders formed by liquid crystals when an electric charge is generated. Nevertheless, the distinction between the *processes* of order formation can be sustained." *Hayek and Modern Liberalism*, 87.

66. Hayek, "The Use of Knowledge in Society," 519–30.

67. Hayek, *New Studies in Philosophy, Politics, Economics and the History of Ideas*, 75.

68. *Constitution*, 250.

69. Polanyi, *The Logic of Liberty*, esp. 208–20.

70. John Gray characterizes Hayek as an indirect utilitarian (*Hayek on Liberty*, 59–61). Kukathas, more convincingly, argues that Hayek is best thought of as a type of consequentialist but not a utilitarian because Hayek's discovery-approach arguments "do not point to any end point to be achieved" (*Hayek and Modern Liberalism*, 196).

71. *Mirage*, 39.

72. Ibid., 4.

73. Ibid., 4–5.

74. Hayek writes: "while the deliberate uses of spontaneous ordering forces . . . thus considerably extends the range and complexity of actions which can be integrated into a single order, it also reduces the power that anyone can exercise over it without destroying the order" (*Mirage*, 75).

75. While traveling to a Federalist Society conference on Hayek's legal theory, I read an article about an experimental food stamp program being conducted in western Massachusetts. In a group of test communities, a 30 percent discount was being applied to food stamp purchases of selected fruits and vegetables in an effort to reduce the obesity of poor people. Whatever effects that particular program might turn out to have on the food stamp recipients in those communities when put into practice (whether in terms of their weight or their self-esteem), it is a striking example of a "taxitic" directive. Patrick G. Lee, "Food Stamp Discount for Buying Produce," *Boston Globe*, August 19, 2010, B1 Metro.

76. *Mirage*, 99.

77. Ibid., 67.

78. As Hayek puts it, "there are no principles of individual conduct which would produce a pattern of distribution which as such could be called just, and therefore also no possibility for the individual to know what he would have to do to secure a just remuneration of his fellows" (ibid., 83).

79. "It is essential that we become aware clearly of the line that separates a state of affairs in which the community accepts the duty of preventing destitution and of providing a minimum level of welfare from that in which it assumes the power to determine the 'just' position of everybody and allocates to each what it thinks he deserves" (*Constitution*, 252).

80. *Mirage*, 78. For other formulations of Hayek's claim that "social justice" is logically incoherent, see ibid., 62, 69, and 96.

81. Ibid., 70. Similarly, Michael Oakeshott criticizes Hayek for advocating "a plan to resist all planning" (*Rationalism in Politics and Other Essays*, 26).

82. Critical discussions I have found helpful include: Adam Tebble, *F. A. Hayek* (New York: Continuum International Publishing Group, 2010), esp. 63–72; Kukathas, *Hayek and Modern Liberalism*, 86–104; John Gray, *Hayek on Liberty*; Theodore Burczk, *Socialism after Hayek* (Ann Arbor: University of Michigan Press, 2006), esp. 54–57; Anna Galeotti, "Individualism, Social Rules, Tradition: The Case of Friedrich A. Hayek," 163–81, 168–70; João Carlos Espada, *Social Citizenship Rights: A Critique of F. A. Hayek and Raymond Plant*; and a lively collection of articles by David Johnston, Steven Lukes, and Edward Feser in *Critical Review* 11, no. 1 (1997).

83. *Mirage*, 64.

84. By contrast, Gerald Gaus defends what we might call a "pure-discovery" reading of Hayek: "Why All Welfare States (Including Laissez Faire Ones) Are Unreasonable," 3, 24, 28–29, 31. On that reading, it is difficult to make sense of Hayek's own claims about the affinity of his view of justice to that of Rawls (on which, see below).

85. The question of what role intentionality can have, of course, is crucial. Kukathas comments: "while Hayek has developed a theory of the spontaneous ordering forces of society, he has not come up with an explanation of the extent to which reason can criticize and try to alter the direction of social development" (*Hayek and Modern Liberalism*, 104).

86. *Mirage*, 99.

87. Ibid., 70–71, emphasis mine.

88. When Hayek describes the Great Society as a cosmos, on this reading, he means that form of social order that has no purpose, including that of a satisfying normative ideal that might be defined by a (distribution-sensitive) conception of social justice.

89. Hayek, *New Studies in Philosophy, Politics, Economics and the History of Ideas*, 74. I am indebted to Adam Tebble for first bringing this passage to my attention.

90. Ibid., 74–75. For an early formulation of this distinction between direct and indirect strategies of social construction, see Herbert Spencer, "The New Toryism," in *The Man versus the State*, esp. 14–15.

91. *Mirage*, 84.

92. Lomasky asks which strategy of social construction works better, markets or political processes: "the most important finding of the first century of post-Adam Smith economics is that the second strategy pays off better than the first. Indirection triumphs over direct pursuit of the desideratum. The most important finding of its second century may be that the aims of social justice also are better pursued by an indirect strategy." "Libertarianism at Twin Harvard," 192.

93. "The prime public concern must be directed not towards particular known needs but towards the conditions for the preservation of a spontaneous order which enables the individuals to provide for their needs in manners not known to authority." Thus: "The most important of the public goods for which government is required is thus not the direct satisfaction of any particular needs, but the securing of opportunities of mutually providing for their respective needs." *Mirage*, 2.

94. Michael Novak suggests another level at which Hayek might affirm the coherence of social justice: the level at which individuals work for the general good (in Hayek's case, as a public intellectual). Novak, "Hayek: Practitioner of Social Justice, 'Social Justice Properly Understood' Celebration of Friedrich Hayek's 100th Birthday," in *Three in One: Essays on Democratic Capitalism, 1976–2000*, 135.

95. David Miller says: "Hayek and other earlier critics of the idea [of social justice] believed that the pursuit of social justice was feasible but mistaken" (*Principles of Social Justice*, 256). See also Steven Lukes, "Social Justice: The Hayekian Challenge," 65–80; David Johnston, "Hayek's Attack on Social Justice."

96. *Mirage*, xiii. It should not be lost on readers that Hayek makes that statement in the preface of a book called *The Mirage of Social Justice* in reference to a book titled *A Theory of Justice*.

97. Waldron, "Socioeconomic Rights and Theories of Justice," 14–16. See also Arthur DiQuattro, "Rawls versus Hayek," 307–10.

98. Waldron "Socioeconomic Rights and Theories of Justice," 15, quoting Hayek, *Mirage*, 38 and 166n.

99. *Mirage*, 31.

100. Ibid., 100; DiQuattro, "Rawls versus Hayek," esp. 307–10.

101. Thus Hayek notes regarding the term "social justice" that "it is to the present day sometimes employed in learned discussions to evaluate the effects of the existing institutions of society." The footnote to that sentence cites Rawls's *TJ* as an example. For yet another approving reference to Rawls, see footnote 16 on *Mirage*, 74. Hayek there notes that for Rawls, as for thinkers in the classical liberal tradition, justice in a competitive system is to be found in the way that competition is carried on rather than in its particular results. Hayek appears to mean "in the way it is carried out" as evaluated by the general tendency of the effects of competitions carried out *under such rules and institutions*.

102. *Mirage*, 100, quoting Rawls, "Constitutional Liberty and the Concept of Justice," *NOMOS VI: Justice*, New York, 1963, p. 102. *Mirage*, n. 44, p. 183, bracketed material mine. The quotation from Rawls continues: "Rather, the principles of justice define the crucial constraints which institutions and joint activities must satisfy if persons engaging in them are to have no complaints against them. If these constraints are satisfied, the resulting distribution, whatever it is, may be accepted as just (or at least not unjust)."

103. A similar argument on behalf of "social justice" might be developed from within the work of Milton Friedman. Friedman emphasizes that rights of property are complex social creations. According to Friedman: "The ethical principle that would directly justify the distribution of income in a free market society is 'to each according to what he and the instruments he owns produces'" (*Capitalism and Freedom*, 162). However, as Sam Freeman has pointed out, "The implication [of these two propositions] is that we stand in need of some principle to specify the rules of property that underwrite the classical liberal precept: "To each according to what he and the instruments he owns produces" ("Capitalism in the Classical Liberal and High Liberal Tradition," 35). Until some such principle is elucidated, Freeman says the idea of ownership and property are mere "placeholders." From a market democratic perspective, it is a theory of social justice that provides that needed elucidation.

104. *Mirage*, 132. Hayek says he first came to appreciate this point in 1940, when he was living in London under the German bombing. Facing the real possibility of death, Hayek received offers from several neutral countries (among them the United States, Argentina, and Sweden) to place his young children with some unknown family with whom they would remain if he did not survive. "'This led me, as abstract speculation perhaps never could have done, to realize that where my children were concerned, rational preferences should be guided by considerations somewhat different than those that would determine a similar choice for myself' (a person with a known set of characteristics such as age, gender, professional accomplishments, tastes

and interests, and so forth)." *Mirage*, n. 25, p. 188. I thank Keith Hankins for calling my attention to this footnote.

105. As Hayek puts it: "the best society would be that in which we would prefer to place *our children* if we knew that their position in it would be determined by lot" (*Mirage*, 132, emphasis added). For Hayek, as for Rawls, the key point to keep in mind is that "a person in an established position inevitably takes a different attitude from that which ought to be taken in considering the general problem" (*Mirage*, n. 25, p. 188).

106. At one place, Hayek concedes that his strong aversion to social justice may well be "unduly allergic." *Mirage*, 97.

Chapter 6: Two Concepts of Fairness

1. Lindsey, "Liberaltarians" *The New Republic*, December 11, 2006, at http://www.tnr.com/article/politics/liberaltarians.

2. Murray, *In Our Hands*.

3. Murray refers readers to his *In Pursuit: Of Happiness and Good Government* (New York: Simon & Schuster, 1988) and *What It Means to Be a Libertarian* (New York: Broadway Books, 1997).

4. Murray, *In Our Hands*, 4.

5. Ibid., 5.

6. There are also luck egalitarian elements in Hayek, as when he suggests that the primary justification for public support of education is to "eliminate the effects of accident" (*Constitution*, 333).

7. Lomasky, "Libertarianism at Twin Harvard," 178–99.

8. Shapiro, "Why Rawlsian Liberals Should Support Free Market Capitalism," 58–85; "Liberalism, Basic Rights, and Free Exchange," 103–26; and *Is the Welfare State Justified?*

9. Gerald Gaus and David Schmidtz are professors in the Philosophy Department at the University of Arizona; Jason Brennan earned his PhD there; I completed a master's at Arizona before transferring to Oxford. In mentioning the connection of these scholars to Arizona, I am not suggesting that work on this new paradigm is only being done by Arizona philosophers. Nor, certainly, am I suggesting that every political philosopher at Arizona works from this orientation. Some of Arizona's most prominent political philosophers, notably Thomas Christiano, manifestly do not.

10. See especially Gaus, *The Order of Public Reason: A Theory of Freedom and Morality in a Diverse and Bounded World*.

11. Gaus, "Reasonable Pluralism and the Domain of the Political: How the Weaknesses of John Rawls's Political Liberalism Can Be Overcome by a Justificatory Liberalism," 229–58.

12. Gaus, "Coercion, Ownership, and the Redistributive State," 252.

13. Ibid., 259.

14. Gaus, *The Order of Public Reason*, 273.

15. Gaus, *Contemporary Theories of Liberalism: Public Reason as a Post-Enlightenment Project*, 214. See also Gaus, "Coercion, Ownership, and the Redistributive State," 237; and Gaus, *Social Philosophy*, chaps. 7–11.

16. Gaus, "Coercion, Ownership, and the Redistributive State," 237.

17. Gaus, *The Order of Public Reason: A Theory of Freedom and Morality in a Diverse and Bounded World*, 521, for discussion see 359–70. Like Hayek, Gaus appears to treat "social justice" as a concept that by definition calls for state-based redistributive measures.

18. Rawlsians might dispute this aspect of Brennan's argument, arguing that "benefits" to the poor must be measured not only in terms of wealth and income but also in terms of worker control of the workplace. I discuss this issue below.

19. Brennan, "Rawls' Paradox," 288. Intriguingly, Brennan writes: "Rawls' assumption that one can do ideal theory first, and then look at compliance issues and how institutions actually work second, may be what leads him to problems mentioned in this paper. Further empirical investigation may show us that the solution is to abandon some of Rawls' favored institutions *even if we should keep his theory of justice*" (298, emphasis mine).

20. Schmidtz and Brennan, *A Brief History of Liberty*. For a libertarian reaction, see Tom Palmer, "Liberty is Liberty," in *Cato Unbound*, at http://www.cato-unbound.org/2010/03/12/tom-g-palmer/liberty-is-liberty/.

21. Schmidtz and Brennan, "Conceptions of Freedom."

22. Kevin Vallier, who wrote his dissertation at Arizona under the supervision of Gaus, has described *The Order of Public Reason* as similarly being "rooted in positive liberty" (e-mail correspondence of March 2, 2011).

23. Schmidtz and Brennan, *A Brief History of Liberty*, esp. 120–68.

24. For example, Schmidtz affirms what might be called an egalitarian concern for self-esteem and so describes as "noble" a system of cooperation that enables all citizens to live as "contributors to a community of contributors." David Schmidtz and Robert Goodin, *Social Welfare and Individual Responsibility*, 3–96, at 94. For Schmidtz on desert, see especially "How to Deserve," reprinted in David Schmidtz, *Person, Polis, Planet: Essays in Applied Philosophy*, 93–116.

25. Schmidtz, *Elements of Justice*.

26. Schmidtz and Goodin, *Social Welfare and Individual Responsibility*, 95.

27. Schmidtz, *Elements of Justice*, 196.

28. Ibid., 9–12; Schmidtz, *Rational Choice and Moral Agency*, 155–211. Roughly speaking, Schmidtz's overall moral theory is a kind of sophisticated rule consequentialism. On Schmidtz's theory, what we call "social justice" doesn't occupy the status of what he would call a principle of justice. Instead, for Schmidtz, what we call "social justice" is part of a rule of recognition by which we discover what the norms of justice and social morality are. I thank Jason Brennan for discussion of these ideas.

29. "Accordingly, our task is not to dwell on details, but to reflect on the extent to which we share this grand vision: (a) liberty comes first, and (under normal circumstances) must not be sacrificed for anything; (b) we judge a society by asking whether it is good for all of us, whether it truly is a land of opportunity, and by looking at the quality of life obtained by its nonprivileged members; finally (c) we believe that this is what we would choose if we were choosing impartially" (Schmidtz, *Elements of Justice*, 195–96).

30. Earlier, I called this the Arizona School. Elsewhere, Jason Brennan calls it "neoclassical liberalism." John Tomasi and Jason Brennan, "Classical Liberalism," in *The*

Oxford Handbook of Political Philosophy, ed. David Estlund (New York: Oxford University Press, 2011.) In its "high" forms, it might be called market democracy, or even free market fairness.

31. Schmidtz, *Elements of Justice*, 41, see especially the discussion at 34–56.

32. Schmidtz writes: "We distinguish outcomes that owe something to a person's character from outcomes that do not. Desert makers, if there are any, are relations between outcomes and internal features of persons. We need not (and normally do not) assume anything about what caused those features" (Schmidtz, *Elements of Justice*, 36).

33. Ibid., 56, citing Holmgren, "Justifying Desert Claims: Desert and Opportunity," 274.

34. Schmidtz, *Elements of Justice*, 56.

35. Ibid., 57.

36. Schmidtz continues: "Talented bakers don't *capture* pie. They *make* it. The rest of us have more pie, not less, when talented people put their talent to work" (ibid., near 216).

37. Rawls, e.g., *PL*, 5.

38. "Social and economic inequalities are to be arranged so that they are both: (a) to the greatest benefit of the least advantaged, consistent with the just savings principle, and (b) attached to positions and offices open to all under conditions of fair equality of opportunity" (*TJ* 302/266 rev.).

39. *TJ*/rev., 53.

40. Ibid.

41. In response to criticisms by H.L.A. Hart, for example, Rawls famously revised his early formulation of the first principle of justice.

42. In his late work, Rawls openly records his own uncertainty about the correct way to specify the fair equality of opportunity principle, and even about the correct priority relation of that principle to other components of justice as fairness. "Some think that the lexical priority of fair equality of opportunity over the difference principle is too strong, and that either a weaker priority or a weaker form of the opportunity principle would be better, and indeed more in accord with fundamental ideas of justice as fairness itself. At present I do not know what is best here and simply register my uncertainty. How to specify and weight the opportunity principle is a matter of great difficulty and some such alternative may well be better" (*JF*, 163n44).

43. Philippe van Parijs writes: "the difference principle comes in many variants depending on choices made along many dimensions. Some of these choices are clearly, consistently, and rightly made by Rawls. In other important dimensions, his choices are not so clear, not so consistent, and/or not so clearly right. Depending on which choices are made, one will end up with hardly any just inequality or a tremendous amount." "Difference Principles," in *The Cambridge Companion to Rawls*, ed. Samuel Freeman, 233.

44. "He himself said it." This style of argument is an example of the informal fallacy known as *argumentum ad vercundiam*.

45. I owe the phrase "archaeology of ideas" to David Estlund, who I heard use it informally in a different context.

46. John Maynard Keynes, "Economic Possibilities for Our Grandchildren," (1930), 6.

47. *TJ*/rev., 257–58. Like many of his progressive forebears, Rawls here uses language from Marx, who distinguishes "estranged labor" from "creative production in free association with fellow producers" (see 75–77 of *The Marx-Engels Reader*, ed. Tucker). I thank Robert Taylor for calling my attention to this passage in Marx.

48. For a libertarian interpretation of a postscarcity world, see Cory Doctorow, *Down and Out in the Magic Kingdom*. In Doctorow's account, units of esteem from others (called "wuffies") take the place of money as scarce and highly desired goods.

49. For the distinction between the "special" and the "general" conceptions of justice, see Parijs, "Difference Principles," who cites *TJ*, 152/132 rev.; *TJ*, 62/54 rev.; *TJ*, 83/passage omitted 72 rev.

50. Keynes, "Economic Possibilities for Our Grandchildren," 6. Mill writes, "It is scarcely necessary to remark that a stationary condition of capital and population implies no stationary state of human improvement. There would be as much scope as ever for all kinds of mental culture, and moral and social progress, as much room for improving on the Art of Living and much likelihood of its being improved, when minds ceased to be engrossed by the art of getting on" (*Principles of Political Economy*, 129).

51. Amartya Sen, "Maximization and the Act of Choice."

52. Amartya Sen, *The Idea of Justice*, 22.

53. *TJ*, 83/72 rev.

54. See, e.g., *JF*, 179. Many criticize Rawls's interpretive decision to focus on "ordinarily productive" citizens, arguing, for example, that the disabled or unemployed should be considered within the purview of the DP test. For example, see Martha Nussbaum, *Frontiers of Justice: Disabilities, Nationality, Species Membership*, chaps. 1 and 4. For a Rawlsian response, see Samuel Freeman, "Frontiers of Justice: Contractarianism vs. the Capabilities Approach," *Texas Law Review* 85 (2006): 385–430.

55. *TJ*/rev., xiii. In particular, the DP goods are those *social and economic advantages* that are valuable to people as citizens. This is to mark Rawls's distinction between social primary goods—the distribution of which is a matter of justice—and what he calls natural primary goods—the distribution of which is neither just nor unjust (*TJ*, 62/54 rev.; *TJ*, 102/87 rev.).

56. *TJ*, 62/54 rev.

57. Freeman, for example, offers the following descriptions of the threats to self-respect of the sort that concern justice as fairness: threats to self-respect may cause people "to feel diminished," or to perceive themselves as "less than civic equals" of more advantaged others, or "to see themselves as failures" (*Rawls*, 131).

58. It is worth emphasizing: justice as fairness is not based ultimately on the promotion of the material welfare of citizens generally, or even that of the worst-off class. Instead, justice as fairness is based on an ideal of respect for the freedom, independence, and dignity of equal citizens. It remains an open question, however, what role the promotion of material welfare might play in service to that ideal. As market democracy emphasizes, we should not be biased against the possible importance of material wealth to people's self-respect.

59. In what Parijs describes as Rawls's "canonical" formulation, the list of DP goods consists in the following items: "income and wealth, powers and prerogatives of office and positions of responsibility, and the social bases of self-respect" (Parijs,

"Difference Principles," 211–12, citing *TJ*, 62/54 rev.; *TJ*, 93/80 rev.; *PL*, 181, etc.). However, the importance of some of these goods, such as wealth, seem reducible to that of others, such as income. More important, the distribution of some of these goods (or dimensions of them) would appear to be governed by lexically prior principles ("powers of office" by fair equality of opportunity, for example). In his later work Rawls explicitly adds leisure to the list of primary goods (*JF*, 179).

60. *TJ*, 94/80 rev.; for a helpful discussion, see Parijs, "Difference Principles."

61. Jason Brennan, "Rawls' Paradox"; Samuel Freeman, "Capitalism in the Classical Liberal and High Liberal Traditions."

62. When discussing property-owning democracy, Rawls says, "We certainly do not want to rule out Mill's idea of society in a just stationary state where real capital accumulation may cease" (*JF*, 159).

63. This is true whether one accepts Brennan's assumption that increasing wealth in a society that protects basic rights "touches" all classes of citizens, or Freeman's assumption that in a capitalist welfarist society the redistributive programs can effectively deliver material benefits to the poor.

64. Freeman, "Capitalism in the Classical Liberal and High Liberal Traditions," 50.

65. Of course, whether such ownership stakes will result in the empowerment of workers depends on the size of the companies and other factors. Notice that the question of whether the possession of a vote (in the case of worker-owned firms) will result in the empowerment of workers faces parallel concerns.

66. I thank Alex Gourevitch for discussion of some background issues here.

67. There are many variants here, including what Nien-he Hsieh calls "workplace republicanism"; see "Rawlsian Justice and Workplace Republicanism," *Social Theory and Practice* 31, no. 1 (2005).

68. Keynes, more colorfully, writes: "When the accumulation of wealth is no longer of high social importance, there will be great changes in the code of morals. We shall be able to rid ourselves of many of the pseudo-moral principles which have hag-ridden us for two hundred years, by which we have exalted some of the most distasteful of human qualities into the position of highest virtues. . . . All kinds of social customs and economic practices, affecting the distribution of wealth and economic rewards and penalties, which we now maintain at all costs, however distasteful and unjust they may be in themselves, because they are tremendously useful in promoting the accumulation of capital, we shall then be free, at last, to discard." (Keynes implies that among the changes he most looks forward to is a conversion in the social attitudes, and religious convictions, of Jews.) "Economic Possibilities for Our Grandchildren," esp. 6–7.

69. *TJ*/rev., 136. See also *JF*, 99–100.

70. There are also daunting feasibility issues here. Hayek writes: "A plant or industry cannot be conducted in the interest of some permanent distinct body of workers if it is at the same time to serve the interests of consumers. Moreover, effective participation in the direction of an enterprise is a full-time job, and anybody so engaged soon ceases to have the outlook of an employee" (*Constitution*, 242).

71. Hayek argues that extensive transfer programs tend to reduce the material shares held by the working poor over time. Regarding such programs, Hayek writes: "while such an equalizing of the positions in the columns of progress would temporarily

quicken the closing-up of the ranks, it would, before long, slow down the movement of the whole and in the long run hold back those in the rear" (*Constitution*, quoted in the introduction, xii–xiii).

72. I thank Keith Hankins for this formulation of this idea, and for several illuminating discussions of surrounding ideas. While the distinction I make below between treating citizens as "equally free" versus as "freely equal" is my own, that distinction first occurred to me during a conversation with Keith. Also, it was Keith who first encouraged me to illustrate that distinction in terms of "doing" and "action" versus "being" and "status."

73. Waldron, "Theoretical Foundations of Liberalism," 129.

74. Following Derek Parfit, we can distinguish egalitarian views from prioritarian ones. The former emphasize the importance of creating states of equality between citizens; the latter, the importance of improving the condition of the citizens who are worse off. "Equality and Priority," 202–21.

75. I am assuming here that we are working within the boundaries of environmental sustainability. Reasonable people can view the relationship of economic development and environmental sustainability in very different ways (see, for example, Schmidtz and Willott, eds., *Environmental Ethics: What Really Matters, What Really Works*).

76. For an argument of this sort, see G. A. Cohen, *Rescuing Justice and Equality*, esp. chaps. 1 and 2. But see Richard Arneson, "Justice Is Not Equality." Derek Parfit argues that Rawls's view is fundamentally prioritarian, in "Equality or Priority?" ("Appendix: Rawls's View"), in *The Ideal of Equality*, ed. Matthew Clayton and Andrew Williams, 116–21.

77. This exception animates G. A. Cohen's defense of socialism (see Cohen, *Why Not Socialism?*). Keynes also looks to a change in incentives once the age of affluence arrives: "The course of affairs will simply be that there will be ever larger and larger classes and groups of people from whom problems of economic necessity have been practically removed. The critical difference will be realized when this condition has become so general that the nature of one's duty to one's neighbor is changed. For it will remain reasonable to be economically purposive for others after it has ceased to be reasonable for oneself" ("Economic Possibilities for Our Grandchildren," 7).

Chapter 7: Feasibility, Normativity, and Institutional Guarantees

1. Jerry Gaus writes: "Just as the utilitarian fathers of the welfare state anticipated a powerful social science that would allow us to grasp the causes of social problems and predict the effects of our policies on them, so too did they suppose an efficient, public-spirited bureaucracy that would carry out these policies." Gaus, "Why All Welfare States (Including Laissez-Faire Ones) Are Unreasonable," 19.

2. Congressional Budget Office, at http://www.cbo.gov/doc.cfm?index=3521&type=0.

3. As of this writing, the projected date of insolvency is 2041. See http://www.whitehouse.gov/cea/three-quest-soc-sec.pdf.

4. Figures quoted in Veronique de Rugy, "Our Unsustainable Debt."

5. Welfare programs are usually divided into three categories: nationalized insurance programs based upon mandatory contributions (for example, Social Security), noncontributory insurance for people in a particular category of permanent need (programs for the physically disabled, for example), and a variety of means-tested programs, typically for those in temporary need of assistance (welfare, food stamps, housing assistance).

6. According to Frank Field: "Means-tests penalize the very basis upon which a free and prosperous society depends. Means-tests take account of income. They therefore impose a penal tax on working, or on working harder. Means-tests take account of savings. They therefore impose a penal tax on savings. Means-tests depend on answering questions about income and savings. They therefore impose a penal tax on honesty." Field, "What, Then, Was Unthinkable?," 14, 16.

7. J. P. Freire, "Wisconsin Reveals Class War between 'Have-Nots' and 'Have-Yours.'"

8. David Lewis Schaefer reports that the estate of Joseph Kennedy was worth between $300 and $500 million; yet the family paid only $134,330.09 in taxes because the money was placed in "an intricate web of trusts and private foundations" (*Illiberal Justice*, 117, quoting Michael Jensen, "Managing the Kennedy Millions," *New York Times*, June 12, 1977).

9. "Understanding the Tax Gap" (FS-2005-14, March 2005), Internal Revenue Service, at http://www.irs.gov/newsroom/article/0,,id=137246,00.html.

10. Jude Wanniski, "Taxes, Revenues, and the 'Laffer Curve.'"

11. Speaking to the Economics Club of New York in 1963, President John F. Kennedy (D) said: "It is a paradoxical truth that tax rates today are too high, and tax revenues are too low and the soundest way to raise the revenues in the long run is to cut the rate of taxes" (quoted in Laffer, Moore, and Tanous, *The End of Prosperity*, 51).

12. Larry Bartels argues that under Democratic presidencies, the relative material holdings of the poor improved more *and* real GDP growth had been higher than under Republican presidencies. *Unequal Democracy: The Political Economy of the New Gilded Age*.

13. President Bill Clinton, 1996. See also Nina Easton, "Will Fear of Big Government End Obama's Audacity?" *Time*, December 14, 2009. See also "Stop!: The Size and Power of the State Is Growing, and Discontent Is on the Rise," *The Economist*, January 23, 2010, 11–12.

14. I am indebted to Jason Brennan for conversations about these ideas.

15. Mancur Olson, *The Logic of Collective Action: Public Goods and the Theory of Groups*, 28.

16. Gordon Tullock, "The Welfare Costs of Tariffs, Monopolies, and Theft," 224–32. The term "rent seeking" was introduced by A. O. Krueger, "The Political Economy of the Rent-Seeking Society," 291–303. There is a voluminous literature on rent seeking and log rolling. For an overview, see Gordon Tullock, Arthur Seldon, and Gordon L. Brady, *Government Failure: A Primer in Public Choice*.

17. Anthony Downs, *An Economic Theory of Democracy*; Gordon Tullock, *Towards a Mathematics of Politics*.

18. Bryan Caplan, *The Myth of the Rational Voter: Why Democracies Choose Bad Policies*.

19. Caplan presents his idea of voter irrationality as a conceptual alternative to the classical public choice idea of rational ignorance. Note that even if this is right, conceptual alternatives can work together to explain different tendencies within the same electoral system. I think of the theories of voter irrationality and voter ignorance as working together in that way. For a fascinating exploration of these ideas, see Jason Brennan, *The Ethics of Voting*.

20. Diana Mutz, *Hearing the Other Side: Deliberative versus Participatory Democracy*, 147.

21. John Roemer, *Equal Shares*, 37.

22. Miller, *Principles of Social Justice*, 246. For Miller's own analysis of this charge, however, see 254–56.

23. Actual economies, unlike the ideal of a perfectly competitive market, typically labor under constraints of suboptimal competitiveness, as well as constraints related to the incomplete and/or incorrect information held by market actors.

24. I am indebted to Carlos Ormachea for first focusing my attention on this idea of identification and, especially, to David Estlund for a number of illuminating discussions.

25. Rawls writes, "The problem here is that the limits of the possible are not given by the actual, for we can to a greater or lesser extent change political and social institutions and much else." He continues, "Hence we have to rely on conjecture and speculation, arguing as best we can that the social world we envision is feasible and might actually exist, if not now then at some future time under happier circumstances." *LP*, 12.

26. See Rawls, part IV of *JF*.

27. "Why Stakeholding?" in Ackerman, Alstott, and van Parijs, *Redesigning Distribution*, 55.

28. Amartya Sen, *The Idea of Justice*, ix.

29. Ibid., 15.

30. Miller, "Political Philosophy for Earthlings," in David Leopold and Marc Stears, eds., *Political Theory: Methods and Approaches*, 31.

31. There is a rich literature here from a variety of ideological perspectives. In particular, see Robert Goodin, "Political Ideals and Political Practice," *British Journal of Political Science* 25 (1995): 37–56; Tamar Shapiro, "Compliance, Complicity, and the Nature of Nonideal Conditions," *Journal of Philosophy* (2003): 329–55; Andrew Mason, "Just Constraints," *British Journal of Political Science* 34 (2004): 251–68; Michael Freeden, "What Should the 'Political' in Political Theory Explore," *Journal of Political Philosophy* 13 (2005): 113–34; Geoffrey Brennan and Philip Pettit, "The Feasibility Constraint," in *The Oxford Handbook of Contemporary Philosophy*, ed. Frank Jackson and Michael Smith (New York: Oxford University Press, 2005), 258–79; Colin Farrelly, "Justice in Ideal Theory: A Refutation," *Political Studies* 55, no 4 (2007): 844–64; Adam Swift and Stuart White, "Political Theory, Social Science, and Real Politics," in *Political Theory: Methods and Approaches*, ed. David Leopold and Marc Stears (Oxford: Oxford University Press, 2008); Zofia Stemplowska "What's Ideal about Ideal Theory?" *Social Theory and Practice*, special issue (July 2008); Charles Larmore, "What Is Political Philosophy?" (working manuscript, December 2010).

32. G. A. Cohen, *Rescuing Justice and Equality*, 21.

33. Cohen's argument has been met with a great deal of criticism from left liberals. Richard Arneson argues that Cohen's metaethical view about justice does not imply his thoroughgoing egalitarianism; Thomas Pogge rejects Cohen's view of the proper role of idealization in political philosophy. See Richard Arneson, "Justice Is Not Equality," 371–91; and Thomas Pogge, "Cohen to the Rescue!," 454–75. See also Miller, "Political Philosophy for Earthlings"; and Larmore, "What Is Political Philosophy?"

34. Krause, "Review Essay: Beyond Capitalism?," 887.

35. Schmidtz, *Rational Choice and Moral Agency*, 183. I am indebted to Kevin Vallier for discussion of this point. See also David Schmidtz, "Nonideal Theory: What It Is and What It Needs To Be," *Ethics* 121 (2011).

36. Lomasky, "Libertarianism at Twin Harvard," 191. Richard Epstein makes a similar argument: "Rawls Remembered," *National Review*, National Review Online, November 27, 2002, at http://old.nationalreview.com/comment/comment-epstein112702.asp.

37. Brennan, "Rawls' Paradox," 288.

38. For a critique that the commitment to the abstractions of ideal theory effectively displaces a practical concern for the poor, see also David Lewis Schaefer, *Illiberal Justice*. For arguments that classical liberal institutions are more likely to satisfy the difference principle / justice as fairness than are social democratic ones, see also Daniel Shapiro, "Liberalism, Basic Rights, and Free Exchange," 103–26, and "Why Rawlsian Liberals Should Support Free Market Capitalism." For an assessment of institutional alternatives, see Tyler Cowen, "Does the Welfare State Help the Poor?"

39. Gaus, "Liberal Neutrality: A Compelling and Radical Principle," chap. 10 of *Perfectionism and Neutrality: Essays in Liberal Theory*, ed. Steven Wall and George Klosko, 137–65 (Lanham, MD: Rowman and Littlefield, 2003); Gaus, "On Justifying the Moral Rights of the Moderns: A Case of Old Wine in New Bottles," esp. 89–99. Gaus's comprehensive statement is *The Order of Public Reason: A Theory of Freedom and Morality in a Diverse and Bounded World*.

40. See Gaus, "On Justifying the Moral Rights of the Moderns: A Case of Old Wine in New Bottles." Gaus describes how contemporary "social justice" liberalism is worked out at a high level of abstraction, whereas even earlier "high liberal" views were worked out at a more empirically sensitive, public policy level.

41. Ibid., 275. Even Rawls's close admirers have criticized his tendency to advance institutional recommendations with insufficient, or unpersuasive, argumentative support. For example, Thomas Pogge, *Realizing Rawls*, 153–55.

42. At http://www.themoneyillusion.com/?p=5164.

43. See David Estlund, *Democratic Authority: A Philosophical Framework*, chap. 14, "Utopophobia: Concession and Aspiration in Democratic Theory," 258–75. Estlund develops these ideas in his book manuscript, *Utopophobia* (working manuscript, forthcoming Princeton University Press, 2012).

44. According to Rawls, "political philosophy is realistically utopian when it extends what are ordinarily thought to be the limits of practical political possibility and, in doing so, reconciles us to our political and social condition" (*LP*, 11).

45. Estlund, *Democratic Authority*, 263.

46. Ibid.

47. Ibid. *Utopophobia* working manuscript, 2.

48. *Utopophobia* working manuscript, 3.

49. Ibid, 22.

50. Martha Nussbaum writes: "Philosophy seems best at articulating basic political principles at a rather high level of abstraction, leaving it to other disciplines to think how, as institutions and their configurations change, those principles can be made reality" (*Frontiers of Justice*, 306–7).

51. I am not suggesting that Rawls or Estlund deny the importance of more empirical questions. After explaining why he puts aside a variety of feasibility questions in order to evaluate institutions on the level of ideal theory, Rawls adds: "This recognizes that the other questions still have to be faced" (*JF*, 137). Estlund says: "There is a place for non-hopeless theory, but it is not somehow privileged. Non-hopeless theory is what we want when we want to know what we should do, in practice, given what people and institutions are actually likely to do. It is obviously an important inquiry" (*Utopophobia*, 6–7).

52. Rawls, *JF*, part IV.

53. People in the construction trades measure insulation in terms of R-value, a common measure of thermal resistance.

54. I am not suggesting that the relationship of liberalism to theocracy need always take this simple form. For a sophisticated treatment, see Lucas Swaine, *The Liberal Conscience: Politics and Principle in a World of Religious Pluralism*.

55. My description of Liberal ChickenWingdom is adapted from an example that David Estlund suggested in one of our many conversations on these topics.

56. Kant writes: "The idea that something which has hitherto been unsuccessful will never be successful does not justify anyone in abandoning even a pragmatic or technical aim. . . . This applies even to moral aims, which, so long as it is not demonstrably impossible to fulfill them, amount to duties" ("On the Common Saying: 'This May be True in Theory, but It Does not Apply in Practice'" [1793], p. 89; quoted in Beitz, *Political Theory and International Relations*, 156).

57. Freeman comments: "the difference principle is not designed to be taken into consideration and directly applied by consumers or firms as they make specific economic decisions. . . . Consumers do not have the kind of information needed to apply the difference principle in their individual economic choices. Rarely can any individual ever know whether his economic choice is more or less beneficial to the less advantaged" (*Rawls*, 100).

58. Elster, "Comments on Krouse and McPherson,"148.

59. As Samuel Freeman puts it, the institutional strategy must be "realistically possible" (*Rawls*, 132). This is similar to what Steven Wall calls the "realism constraint" on counterexamples: "a legitimate example for testing a principle of justice must be one that could occur in the real world" ("Just Savings and the Difference Principle," 79–102, 203, at 83).

60. David Schmidtz, "Guarantees," in *Person, Polis, Planet: Essays in Applied Philosophy*, 182. For striking historical examples, see James C. Scott, *Seeing Like a State: How Certain Schemes to Improve the Human Condition have Failed*, esp. chap. 6, "Soviet Collectivism, Capitalist Dreams," 193–222.

61. When we operate at the level of ideal theory, Rawls emphasizes that we must compare like to like, ideal to ideal (*JF*, 178). There is room for debate about how consistently Rawls's work satisfies this standard of impartiality.

Chapter 8: Free Market Fairness

1. Freeman comments: under the DP, "the rich may not gain unless it benefits the least advantaged, but not vice versa; moreover, it is to benefit the least advantaged maximally, or better than any other arrangement" (*Rawls*, 191).

2. Rawls: "It is sometimes objected to the difference principle as a principle of distributive justice that it contains no restriction on the overall nature of permissible distributions. It is concerned, the objection runs, solely with the least advantaged. But this objection is incorrect: it overlooks the fact that the parts of the two principles are designed to work in tandem and apply as a unit. The requirements of prior principles have important distributive effects. . . . We cannot possibly take the difference principle seriously so long as we think of it by itself, apart from its setting within prior principles" (*JF*, 46n10).

3. The idea of the DP, Rawls suggests, is to regulate economic and social inequalities by a principle of mutuality (e.g., *JF*, 138).

4. For example, *JF*, 162.

5. For example, *TJ*, sect. 43.

6. For discussion of "trickle down," see Freeman, *Rawls*, 222–23.

7. Dworkin, "Liberalism," in *A Matter of Principle*.

8. Economic growth does not *always* benefit the working poor. But an impressive body of literature suggests that growth, in combination with protection of property rights and rule of law, often does benefit the members of the class. See Douglass North, *Institutions, Institutional Change, and Economic Performance*, and Hernando de Soto, *The Mystery of Capital*.

9. Brennan, "Rawls' Paradox," 287–99, dates adjusted.

10. Rawls writes: "A feature of the difference principle is that it does not *require* continual economic growth over generations to maximize upward indefinitely the expectations of the least advantaged measures in terms of income and wealth. . . . That would not be a reasonable conception of justice" (*JF*, 159, emphasis mine). By the same token, it would not be reasonable to *rule out* a system that seeks to maximize the expectations of the least advantaged by a policy of continued economic growth, whether to some future point or even "indefinitely." Rawls continues: "We certainly do not want to rule out Mill's idea of a society in a just stationary state where (real) capital accumulation may cease." One might reasonably wonder whether a society could be maintained at such a state without violation of citizens' basic rights (e.g., their right freely to associate and to communicate their ideas and ambitions to one another). But if we are not to rule out the no-growth society, then we have no reason to rule out the progrowth one.

11. *TJ*, 267. Rawls offers this formulation as part of his discussion of "the second priority rule" (regarding the priority of justice over efficiency). Also: "The role of the

principle of fair opportunity is to insure that the system of cooperation is one of pure procedural justice. Unless it is satisfied, distributive justice could not be left to take care of itself" (*TJ*, 87/76 rev.). As we have seen, Rawls glosses his formal statement of this principle by saying that people of roughly equal talents should have roughly equal chances of winning desired positions. Thus a just regime type must ensure "roughly equal prospects of culture and achievement for citizens equally talented and motivated" (*TJ*, 73). This raises difficult issues about what counts as a "talent" and what social institutions might best allow us to measure talent so conceived. I am indebted to Carlos Ormachea and Keith Hankins for discussion of these issues.

12. On James Meade's formulation, the inheritance tax policy of property-owning democracy is intended to encourage wealthy individuals to make many small bequests, with the hope that this would lead to a wide dispersion of property ownership. See Meade, *Efficiency, Equality, and the Ownership of Property*. Richard Krouse and Michael McPherson, whose work on property-owning democracy Rawls cites, follow Meade in describing the aim and method of a steeply progressive taxation system of property-owning democracy this way. See "A 'Mixed'-Property Regime: Equality and Liberty in a Market Economy." Jon Elster has sharply criticized this feature of property-owning democracy on grounds of feasibility ("Comments on Krouse and McPherson," 146–53, at 148).

13. J. S. Mill, who was famously homeschooled, wrote: "If the government would make up its mind to require for every child a good education, it might save itself the trouble of providing one. It might leave to parents to obtain the education where and how they pleased" (*On Liberty*, 62). Still, it is curious that Rawls wants to keep open the possibility of a semiprivate, voucher-based system of education. Perhaps this is an acknowledgment of the feasibility problems that plague state-based schooling in actual liberal societies. If feasibility considerations require an openness to market-based systems in the area of education, however, those same considerations would seem to require an openness to such systems with respect to a range of other social goals—health care, middle-class retirement and savings plans, and more.

14. A good starting place is Amy Gutmann, *Democratic Education*. An important work is Stephen Macedo, *Diversity and Distrust: Civic Education in a Multicultural Democracy*, esp. 229–74.

15. See Norman Daniels, *Just Health Care*, esp. chap. 3.

16. A number of rationales might support this policy position. For example, advocates of the laissez-faire approach might claim that state-based programs that require people to hire or make loans to visible racial groups, however well intended, actually exacerbate racial tensions. If so, such policies would be objectionable because they retard the development and exercise of the moral powers of citizens.

17. Like social democratic regime types, market democratic regime types also likely would include principles of rectificatory justice. Such principles might justify status-sensitive legal policies such as "affirmative action"—at least under carefully constrained circumstances and as a temporary, ameliorative measure.

18. Hayek, for example, recognizes that the self-respect of citizens often depends upon their having opportunities to develop their talents that they think are at least roughly like those available to their fellow citizens. "Perhaps the acutest sense of

grievance about injustice inflicted on one, not by particular persons but by the 'system,' is that about being deprived of opportunities for developing one's abilities which others enjoy" (*Mirage*, 87). In part for this reason, Hayek advocates public support of schooling: "There is much to be said in favor of the government providing on an equal basis the means for the schooling of minors who are not yet fully responsible citizens . . ." (*Mirage*, 84).

19. Within social democracies, civic virtue is largely or even wholly a matter of people performing the responsibilities set out for them as public citizens. Civic virtue, in market democracies, largely concerns the manner in which individual citizens navigate the intersection of their public and nonpublic identities. Making room for many different forms of social construction, market democracies recognize a much wider range of attitudes and activities as properly "civic." I develop these ideas in *Liberalism Beyond Justice: Citizens, Society, and the Boundaries of Political Theory*.

20. See Terry Moe and John Chubb, *Liberating Learning: Technology, Politics, and the Future of American Education*.

21. Milton Friedman, *Capitalism and Freedom*; and Milton Friedman and Rose Friedman, *Free to Choose: A Personal Statement*.

22. John E. Chubb and Terry M. Moe, *Politics, Markets, and America's Schools*. The Chubb and Moe plan, like that of Friedman, treats education as a marketable good. Unlike Friedman, though, Chubb and Moe explicitly aim at equalizing education (for example, they suggest that states should allocate funding to districts according to need-based criteria, p. 220). Moe and Chubb have recently described the de-centered educational opportunities that are becoming available in the era of what I have a called the personalized economy. See Moe and Chubb, *Liberating Learning: Technology, Politics, and the Future of American Education*.

23. An important statement of this market-based approach is Daniel Shapiro, *Is the Welfare State Justified?* See also Frank Field, *Making Welfare Work: Reconstructing Welfare for the Millennium*, esp. 152–87.

24. Scholarly reviews of Daniel Shapiro's book follow this ideological pattern. For example, Mark Hyde, and John Dixon, "Book Review of Shapiro's *Is the Welfare State Justified?*" *Poverty & Public Policy* 1, no. 1 (2009): article 7.

25. *PL*, 327–28. Recall that our general formulation of justice as fairness gives no special weight to the political liberties. While my formulation of free market fairness follows Rawls in assigning special weight, one might argue that this is merely an accretion to justice as fairness that would be better left off. For a probing discussion, see Steven Wall, "Rawls and the Status of Political Liberty," 245–70.

26. See Krouse and McPherson, "A 'Mixed'-Property Regime: Equality and Liberty in a Market Economy," 86.

27. *TJ*, 225.

28. Krouse and McPherson, "A 'Mixed'-Property Regime: Equality and Liberty in a Market Economy"; see also Freeman, *Rawls*, 116, esp. 131–32. Notice that if, as I suggest, we read social democrats as interpreting the difference principle to be more concerned with democratic powers and positions of authority than with the personal control of wealth and income, this alleged redundancy dissolves.

29. An illuminating discussion of this point is Guido Pincione "The Constitution of Nondomination," esp. 267.

30. For example, James Buchanan criticizes current legislative practice in the United States for allowing expenditure bills and revenue bills to be treated separately. This practice impoverishes political discourse by allowing difficult debates about priorities to be avoided. See "Taxation in Fiscal Exchange," in *The Collected Works of James M. Buchanan*, vol. 1, *The Logical Foundations of Constitutional Liberty*.

31. On Rawls's account, the just savings principle is lexically prior to the difference principle, *TJ*, 287/255 rev. For critical discussion, see Steven Wall, "Just Savings and the Difference Principle," 79–102.

32. On classical liberal approaches to banking, see Lawrence White, *The Theory of Monetary Institutions*.

33. In his exposition of the just saving principle in the original version of *TJ*, Rawls suggests that parties in the original position would have emotional ties to their children and grandchildren and so could be expected to want to save for them (sect. 44). In later work, though, Rawls says, "While this not an unreasonable stipulation, it has certain difficulties . . ." (*JF*, 160n). Freeman suggests that Rawls made this change "perhaps reflecting here upon our current indifference regarding the costs of our consumption patterns on future generations" (*Rawls*, 139).

34. See Leopold, "The Land Ethic," in *A Sand County Almanac*.

35. Peter S. Wenz, *Environmental Justice*, esp. 248–49. I thank Joshua Bernard for calling my attention to Wenz's work and, more generally, for discussion of these environmental issues.

36. Rawls defines this good variously as "culture," "civilization," and a suitable amount of "real capital accumulation" (*TJ*/rev., 252, see also *TJ*/rev., 256). The suggestion that environmental assets be included is my own.

37. Garret Hardin, "The Tragedy of the Commons," 1243–48.

38. Peter M. Vitousek, et al., "Human Domination of Earth's Ecosystems."

39. Hayek argues in favor of tax revenues being used for such purposes, provided that voters are made fully aware of the financial costs involved before voting for such measures. See *Constitution*, 324.

40. Hardin, "The Tragedy of the Commons," 1245.

41. David Schmidtz, "The Institution of Property," in *The Common Law and the Environment*, 117. See also Schmidtz "When Is Original Appropriation 'Required'?," 504–18.

42. Terry Anderson and Donald Leal, *Free Market Environmentalism*.

43. See William Galston, *Ethical Dimensions of Global Development*.

44. See especially Charles Beitz, *Political Theory and International Relations*; Brian Barry, *Theories of Justice*; Thomas Pogge, "An Egalitarian Law of Peoples," 195–224; and K. C. Tan, *Justice without Borders*. By contrast, see Thomas Nagel, "The Problem of Global Justice," *Philosophy & Public Affairs* 33 (2005): 113–47. For a refreshing reinterpretation of Rawls's project, see Christopher Wellman, "Reinterpreting Rawls's *The Law of the Peoples*," *Social Philosophy & Policy* (forthcoming 2011).

45. Rawls suggests that this duty of assistance shares roots with the duty to save: both duties aim "to secure a social world that makes possible a worthwhile life for all" (*LP*, 107).

46. Freeman, *Rawls*, 441.

47. Tobin originally proposed a tax on short-term currency transactions in 1972 as a method for managing exchange-rate volatility. More recently, the Tobin tax is typi-

cally advocated as a way of meeting duties of international aid. See, e.g., Pete Stark, "We Need a Tobin Tax to Fund Development" (online edition).

48. A rich and thoughtful essay is Loren Lomasky and Kyle Swan, "Wealth and Poverty in the Liberal Tradition," *Independent Review* 13, no. 4 (2009): 493–510, esp. 505–9.

49. For a discussion of the moral issues, see Tom Palmer, *Realizing Freedom: Libertarian Theory, History and Practice*, 85–129.

50. See Lant Pritchett, *Let Their People Come: Breaking the Gridlock on Global Labor Mobility*.

51. The literature on the failures of western aid programs is vast. To begin, see William Easterly, *The White Man's Burden: Why the West's Efforts to Aid the Rest Have Done So Much Ill and So Little Good*; Dambisa Moyo, *Dead Aid: Why Aid Is Not Working and Why There Is a Better Way for Africa*.

52. Hayek, *The Road to Serfdom: Fiftieth Anniversary Edition*, with an introduction by Milton Friedman, 241.

53. Ibid., 257–60. Von Mises, going further, advocates a world state to secure the economic freedom and (formal) equality of individuals everywhere. I discuss these issues in "Sovereignty, Commerce, and Cosmopolitanism: Lessons from Early America for the Future of the World," 223–46.

54. Washington: "The great rule of conduct for us in regard to foreign nations is in extending our commercial relations, to have with them as little political connection as possible" ("Avalon Project—Washington's Farewell Address 1796," Yale Law School, at http://avalon.law.yale.edu/18th_century/washing.asp). Madison: "Each generation should be made to bear the burden of its own wars, instead of carrying them on at the expense of other generations" ("Universal Peace," in *The Writings of James Madison*, ed. Gaillard Hunt, vol. 6, *1790–1802* [New York: Putnam Press, 1907], 91). See also John Tomasi, "Governance beyond the Nation State: James Madison on Foreign Policy and 'Universal Peace,'" 213–29.

Bibliography

Ackerman, Bruce. "What Is Neutral about Neutrality?" *Ethics* 93, no. 2 (January 1983): 372–90.

Ackerman, Bruce, Anne Alstott, and Philippe van Parijs. *Redesigning Distribution: Basic Income and Stakeholder Grants as Cornerstones for an Egalitarian Capitalism*. Edited and introduced by Erik Olin Wright. New York: Verso, 2006.

Adams, James Truslow. *The Epic of America*. Boston: Little, Brown, 1931.

Anderson, Terry L., and Donald R. Leal. *Free Market Environmentalism*. San Francisco: Pacific Research Institute for Public Policy, 1991.

Appleby, Joyce. *Capitalism and a New Social Order: The Republican Vision of the 1790s*. New York: New York University Press, 1984.

Armitage, David. *The Declaration of Independence: A Global History*. Cambridge, MA: Harvard University Press, 2007.

Arneson, R. J. "Equality and Equal Opportunity for Welfare." *Philosophical Studies* 56, no. 1 (1988): 77–93.

———. "Justice Is Not Equality." *Ratio* 21, no. 4 (2008).

———. "Luck Egalitarianism: An Interpretation and Defense." *Philosophical Topics* 32, nos. 1 & 2 (2004): 1–20.

Ashton, Thomas S. *The Industrial Revolution, 1760–1830*. New York: Oxford University Press, 1964.

Ashworth, John. "The Jeffersonians," *Journal of American Studies* 18 (1984): 425–35.

Bardhan, Pranab, and John E. Roemer, eds. *Market Socialism: The Current Debate*. New York: Oxford University Press, 1993.

Barry, Brian. *Theories of Justice*. Berkeley: University of California Press, 1989.

Bartels, Larry M. *Unequal Democracy: the Political Economy of the New Gilded Age*. New York: Russell Sage Foundation, 2008.

Becker, Lawrence. *Property Rights: Philosophical Foundations*. Boston: Routledge & Kegan Paul, 1977.

Beito, David. *From Mutual Aid to the Welfare State: Fraternal Societies and Social Services, 1890–1967*. Chapel Hill: University of North Carolina Press, 2000.

Beitz, Charles R. *Political Theory and International Relations*. Princeton, NJ: Princeton University Press, 1979.

Bell, Daniel. *The Coming of Post-Industrial Society: A Venture in Social Forecasting*. New York: Basic Books, 1973.

Bentham, Jeremy. *Jeremy Bentham's Economic Writings*. Vol. 2. London: Allen & Unwin, 1952.

Berlin, Isaiah. "Two Concepts of Liberty." In *Four Essays on Liberty*. Oxford and New York: Oxford University Press, 1969.

Berman, Harold. *Law and Revolution: The Formation of the Western Legal Tradition*. Cambridge, MA: Harvard University Press, 1983.

Bloch, Marc. *Feudal Society*. Translated by L. A. Manyon. New York: Routledge, 1989.

Block, Walter. "Towards a Libertarian Theory of Inalienability." *Journal of Libertarian Studies* 17, no. 2 (2003): 39–85.

Bootle, Roger. *Money for Nothing: Real Wealth, Financial Fantasies, and the Economy of the Future*. London: Nicholas Brealey, 2004.

Bowles, Samuel, and Herbert Gintis. "The Inheritance of Inequality." *Journal of Economic Perspectives* 16, no. 3 (2002): 3-30.

Bremmer, Ian. *The End of the Free Market: Who Wins the War between States and Corporations?* New York: Portfolio, 2010.

Brennan, Geoffrey. "The Myth of Ownership: Liam Murphy and Thomas Nagel." *Constitutional Political Economy* 16, no. 2 (2005): 207–19.

Brennan, Geoffrey, and Philip Pettit. "The Feasibility Issue." In *The Oxford Handbook of Contemporary Philosophy*, edited by Frank Jackson and Michael Smith, 258–79. New York: Oxford University Press, 2005.

Brennan, Jason. *The Ethics of Voting*. Princeton, NJ: Princeton University Press, 2011.

———. "Polluting the Polls: When Citizens Should Not Vote." *Australasian Journal of Philosophy* 87 (2009): 535–49.

———. "Rawls' Paradox." *Constitutional Political Economy* 18, no. 4 (2007): 287–99.

Brennan, Jason, and John Tomasi. "Classical Liberalism." In *Oxford Handbook in Political Philosophy*, edited by David Estlund. New York: Oxford University Press, 2012.

Brettschneider, Corey. *Democratic Rights: The Substance of Self-Government*. Princeton, NJ: Princeton University Press, 2007.

Buchanan, James. "Taxation in Fiscal Exchange." In *The Collected Works of James M. Buchanan*. Vol. 1, *The Logical Foundations of Constitutional Liberty*, 133–49. Indianapolis, IN: Liberty Fund, 1999.

Caplan, Bryan. *The Myth of the Rational Voter: Why Democracies Choose Bad Policies*. Princeton. NJ: Princeton University Press, 2007.

CBSnews.com. "Death (Tax) Takes a Holiday: But Nearly Everyone Wants It Repealed." At http://www.cbsnews.com/stories/2001/03/14/politics/main278884.shtml, March 14, 2001.

Chandler, Alfred. *The Visible Hand: The Managerial Revolution in American Business*. Cambridge, MA: Belknap Press of Harvard University Press, 1977.

Chubb, John E., and Terry M. Moe. *Politics, Markets, and America's Schools*. Washington, DC: Brookings Institution Press, 1990.

Clark, Don. "Gem Formation." International Gem Society. November 4, 2008. At http://www.gemsociety.org /info/igem17.htm.

Clayton, Matthew, and Andrew Williams, eds. *The Ideal of Equality*. London: Palgrave Macmillan, 2002.

Cockett, Richard. *Thinking the Unthinkable: Think-Tanks and the Economic Counter-Revolution, 1931–1983*. London: HarperCollins, 1994.

Cohen, G. A. "Facts and Principles." *Philosophy & Public Affairs* 31, no. 3 (2003).

———. *Rescuing Justice and Equality*. Cambridge, MA: Harvard University Press, 2008.

———. *Why Not Socialism?* Princeton, NJ: Princeton University Press, 2009.

Congressional Budget Office. At http://www.cbo.gov/doc.cfm?index=3521& type=0.

Cowen, Tyler. *Create Your Own Economy: The Path to Prosperity in a Disordered World*. New York: Penguin, 2009.

———. *Creative Destruction: How Globalization Is Changing the World's Cultures*. Princeton, NJ: Princeton University Press, 2004.

———. "Does the Welfare State Help the Poor?" *Social Philosophy & Policy* 19 (2002).

Coyle, Diane. *The Weightless World: Strategies for Managing the Digital Economy*. Cambridge, MA: MIT Press, 1997.

Daniels, Norman. *Just Health Care*. New York: Cambridge University Press, 1985.

De Rugy, Veronique. "Our Unsustainable Debt." *Reason*, June 2010.

DiQuattro, Arthur. "Rawls versus Hayek." *Political Theory* 14, no. 2 (1986): 307–10.

Doctorow, Cory. *Down and Out in the Magic Kingdom*. New York: Tor Books, 2003.

Doherty, Brian. *Radicals for Capitalism: A Freewheeling History of the Modern American Libertarian Movement*. New York: Perseus, 2007.

Dollar, David, and Aart Kraay. "Growth Is Good for the Poor." *Journal of Economic Growth* 7 (2001).

Downs, Anthony. *An Economic Theory of Democracy*. New York: Harper and Row, 1957.

Dworkin, Ronald. "Equality, Luck, and Hierarchy." *Philosophy & Public Affairs* 31 (2003): 190–98.

———. *Justice for Hedgehogs*. Cambridge, MA: Harvard University Press, 2011.

———. *A Matter of Principle*. Cambridge, MA: Harvard University Press, 1985.

———. *Sovereign Virtue*. Cambridge, MA: Harvard University Press, 2000.

———. *Taking Rights Seriously*. Cambridge, MA: Harvard University Press, 1977.

Easterly, William. *The White Man's Burden: Why the West's Efforts to Aid the Rest Have Done So Much Ill and So Little Good*. New York: Penguin Press, 2006.

Easton, Nina. "Will Fear of Big Government End Obama's Audacity?" *Time*, December 14, 2009.

Eckholm, Erik. "Prolonged Aid to Unemployed Is Running Out." *New York Times*, August 2, 2009.

Edsall, Thomas. "Rich Dem, Poor Dem: Class War in Obamaland." *The New Republic*, September 30, 2009.

Elster, Jon. "Comments on Krouse and McPherson." *Ethics* 97, no. 1 (1986): 146–53.

Ely, James W. *The Guardian of Every Other Right: A Constitutional History of Property Rights.* New York: Oxford University Press, 1998.

Epstein, Richard. *How Progressives Rewrote the Constitution.* Washington DC: Cato Institute, 2006.

———. *Skepticism and Freedom: A Modern Case for Classical Liberalism.* Chicago: University of Chicago Press, 2003.

———. *Takings: Private Property and the Power of Eminent Domain.* Cambridge, MA: Harvard University Press, 2005.

Espada, João Carlos. 1996. *Social Citizenship Rights: A Critique of F. A. Hayek and Raymond Plant.* St. Antony's Series. New York: St. Martin's Press, 1996.

Estlund, David. *Democratic Authority: A Philosophical Framework.* Princeton, NJ: Princeton University Press, 2008.

"Fanfare for the Common Man: Is Economic Populism on the Rise in the Democratic Party?" *The Economist*, November 23, 2006.

Farrelly, Colin. "Justice in Ideal Theory: A Refutation." *Political Studies* 55, no. 4 (2007): 844–64.

Ferguson, Adam. *An Essay on the History of Civil Society.* Edinburgh: Printed for A. Millar and T. Caddel, 1767, pt. 3.2.

Feser, Edward, ed. *The Cambridge Companion to Hayek.* New York: Cambridge University Press, 2006.

———. "Hayek, Social Justice, and the Market: Reply to Johnston." *Critical Review* 12, no. 3 (1998): 269–81.

———. "Hayek on Social Justice: Reply to Lukes and Johnston." *Critical Review* 2, no. 4 (1997): 581–606.

Field, Frank. *Making Welfare Work: Reconstructing Welfare for the Millennium.* New Brunswick, NJ: Transaction Publishers, 2001.

———. "What, Then, Was Unthinkable?" In *Crucible*. London: Board for Social Responsibility, Church House, Westminster, 1998.

Filmer, Robert. *Patriarcha and Other Writings.* Cambridge Texts in the History of Political Thought. 1680. Cambridge: Cambridge University Press, 1991.

Fleischacker, Samuel. *A Short History of Distributive Justice.* Cambridge, MA: Harvard University Press, 2004.

Freeden, Michael. *The New Liberalism: An Ideology of Social Reform.* New York: Oxford University Press, 1986.

———. "What Should the 'Political' in Political Theory Explore." *Journal of Political Philosophy* 13 (2005): 113–34.

Freeman, Samuel. *The Cambridge Companion to Rawls.* New York: Cambridge University Press, 2003.

———. "Capitalism in the Classical Liberal and High Liberal Traditions." *Social Philosophy & Policy* 28, no. 2 (2011).

———. "Illiberal Libertarians: Why Libertarianism Is Not a Liberal View." *Philosophy & Public Affairs* 30, no. 2 (2001).

———. *Rawls.* New York: Routledge, 2007.

Freire, J. P. "Wisconsin Reveals Class War between 'Have-Nots' and 'Have-Yours.'" Washingtonexaminer.com, February 22, 2011.

Fried, Barbara. "Left Libertarianism: A Review Essay." *Philosophy & Public Affairs* 32 (2004): 66–92.

Friedman, Milton. *Capitalism and Freedom*. Chicago: University of Chicago Press, 1962.

Friedman, Milton, and Rose Friedman. *Free to Choose: A Personal Statement*. San Diego: Harcourt, Brace, 1980.

Furstenberg, François. 2003. "Beyond Freedom and Slavery: Autonomy, Virtue, and Resistance in Early American Political Discourse." *Journal of American History* 89, no. 4 (2003): 1295–330.

Galeotti, Anna Elisabetta. "Individualism, Social Rules, Tradition: The Case of Friedrich A. Hayek." *Political Theory* 15, no. 2 (1987): 163–81.

Galston, William A. *Ethical Dimensions of Global Development*. Lanham, MD: Rowman and Littlefield, 2006.

Gaus, Gerald F. "Coercion, Ownership, and the Redistributive State: Justificatory Liberalism's Classical Tilt." *Social Philosophy & Policy* 27 (2010): 233–75.

———. *Contemporary Theories of Liberalism: Public Reason as a Post-Enlightenment Project*. London: Sage Publications, 2003.

———. *Justificatory Liberalism: An Essay on Epistemology and Political Theory*. New York: Oxford University Press, 1996.

———. *The Modern Liberal Theory of Man*. New York: St. Martin's Press, 1983.

———. "On Justifying the Moral Rights of the Moderns: A Case of Old Wine in New Bottles." *Social Philosophy & Policy* 24, no. 1 (2007): 84–119.

———. *The Order of Public Reason: A Theory of Freedom and Morality in a Diverse and Bounded World*. New York: Cambridge University Press, 2010.

———. "Reasonable Pluralism and the Domain of the Political: How the Weakness of John Rawls's Political Liberalism Can Be Overcome by a Justificatory Liberalism." *Inquiry* 42 (1999): 229–58.

———. *Social Philosophy*. Armonk, NY: M. E. Sharpe, 1999.

———. "Why All Welfare States (Including Laissez-Faire Ones) Are Unreasonable." *Social Philosophy & Policy* 15, no. 2 (1998).

Gauthier, David. *Morals by Agreement*. Oxford University Press, 1987.

Gibson, Alan. *Interpreting the Founding*. 2nd ed. Lawrence: University Press of Kansas, 2009.

Goldberg, Samuel. *Probability: An Introduction*. New York: Dover Publications, 1986.

Golway, Terry. *Ronald Reagan's America: His Voice, His Dreams, and His Vision of Tomorrow*. Naperville, IL: Sourcebooks MediaFusion, 2008.

Goodin, Robert. "Political Ideals and Political Practice." *British Journal of Political Science* 25 (1995): 37–56.

Gourevitch, Victor, ed. *Discourse on the Origin and Foundation of Inequality among Men, by Jean-Jacques Rousseau*. Cambridge: Cambridge University Press, 1997.

Graetz, Michael J., and Ian Shapiro. *Death by a Thousand Cuts: The Fight over Taxing Inherited Wealth*. Princeton, NJ: Princeton University Press, 2005.

Grant, Ruth. *John Locke's Liberalism*. Chicago: University of Chicago Press, 1987.

Gray, John. *Hayek on Liberty*. New York: Routledge, 1984.

———. *Post-Liberalism: Studies in Political Thought*. New York: Routledge, 1996.

Greif, Avner. *Institutions and the Path to the Modern Economy: Lessons from Medieval Trade*. New York: Cambridge University Press, 2006.

Gutmann, Amy. *Democratic Education*. Princeton, NJ: Princeton University Press, 1987.

Gutmann, Amy, ed. *Democracy and the Welfare State*. Princeton, NJ: Princeton University Press, 1988.

Hamowy, Ronald. *The Scottish Enlightenment and the Theory of Spontaneous Order*. Carbondale: Southern Illinois University Press, 1987.

Hardin, Garret. "The Tragedy of the Commons." *Science* 162 (December 13, 1968).

Hardin, Russell. "From Bodo Ethics to Distributive Justice." *Ethical Theory and Moral Practice* 2, no. 4 (1999).

Hayek, F. A. *The Constitution of Liberty*. Chicago: University of Chicago Press, 1978.

———. *The Fatal Conceit: The Errors of Socialism*. Chicago: University of Chicago Press, 1988.

———. "History and Politics." In *Capitalism and the Historians*, edited by F. A. Hayek. Chicago: University of New Mexico Press, 1984.

———. *Law, Legislation, and Liberty*. Vol. 1, *Rules and Order*. Chicago: University of Chicago Press, 1973.

———. *Law, Legislation, and Liberty*. Vol. 2, *The Mirage of Social Justice*. Chicago: University of Chicago Press, 1977.

———. *New Studies in Philosophy, Politics, Economics, and the History of Ideas*. Chicago: University of Chicago Press, 1985.

———. *The Road to Serfdom: Fiftieth Anniversary Edition*. With an introduction by Milton Friedman. Chicago: University of Chicago Press, 1994.

———. *The Trend of Economic Thinking*. Chicago: University of Chicago Press, 1991.

———. "The Use of Knowledge in Society." *American Economic Review* 35, no. 4 (1945): 519.

Hayek, F. A., ed. *Collectivist Economic Planning*. London: George Routledge & Sons, 1935.

Hayek, F. A., with Leif Wenar and Stephen Kresge, eds. *Hayek on Hayek: An Autobiographical Dialogue*. Chicago: University of Chicago Press, 2008.

Hegel, G.W.F. *Outlines of the Philosophy of Right*. New York: Oxford University Press, 2008.

Higgs, Robert. *Crisis and Leviathan: Critical Episodes in the Growth of American Government*. New York: Oxford University Press, 1987.

Hill, Christopher. *The Century of Revolution, 1603–1714*. 2nd ed. New York: W. W. Norton, 1982.

Hohfeld, Wesley Newcomb. *Fundamental Legal Conceptions as Applied in Judicial Reasoning*. New Haven, CT: Yale University Press, 1964.

Hogue, Arthur R. *Origins of the Common Law*. Indianapolis, IN: Liberty Fund, 1986.

Holmes, Stephen. *Passions and Constraint: On the Liberal Theory of Democracy*. Chicago: University of Chicago Press, 1995.

Holmgren, Margaret. "Justifying Desert Claims: Desert and Opportunity." *Journal of Value Inquiry* 20 (1986): 265–78.

Honoré, T. M. "Ownership." In *Oxford Essays in Jurisprudence*, edited by A. G. Guest, 107–47. London: Oxford University Press, 1961.

Hume, David. *An Enquiry concerning the Principles of Morals*. Whitefish, MT: Kessinger Publishing, 2004.

———. *A Treatise of Human Nature*. 1740. Oxford: Oxford University Press, 1960.

Hunt, Gaillard, ed. *The Writings of James Madison*. Vol. 9, *1819–1836*. New York: G. P. Putnam's Sons, 1910.

Ibsen, Henrik. *A Doll's House*. New York: E. P. Dutton, 1910.

Indiviglio, Daniel. "National Unemployment Rate Unchanged at 10.0% in December." *The Atlantic*, January 8, 2010.

Jacobson, Daniel. "Mill on Liberty, Speech, and the Free Society." *Philosophy & Public Affairs* 29, no. 3 (2000): 276–309.

Jain, Himanshu, and Isha H. Jain. "Learning the Principles of Glass Science and Technology from Candy Making," 2001. At http://www.lehigh.edu/~inmatsci/faculty/jain/candy_making.pdf, November 2008 and May 2011.

Johnston, David. "Hayek's Attack on Social Justice." *Critical Review* 11, no. 1 (1997): 81–100.

———. "Is the Idea of Social Justice Meaningful?" *Critical Review* 11, no. 4 (1997): 607–14.

Judt, Tony. "What Is Living and What Is Dead in Social Democracy?" *New York Review of Books*, December 17, 2009.

Kant, Immanuel. *Doctrine of Right*. New York: Cambridge University Press, 1999.

Keynes, John Maynard. "Economic Possibilities for Our Grandchildren." 1930. At http://www.econ.yale.edu/smith/econ116a/keynes1.pdf, 6.

———. "The General Theory of Employment, Interest and Money." At http://www.marxists.org/reference/subject/economics/keynes/general-theory/ch24.htm.

Kling, Arnold, and Nick Schulz. *From Poverty to Prosperity: Intangible Assets, Hidden Liabilities, and the Lasting Triumph over Scarcity*. New York: Encounter Books, 2009.

Koch, Richard, and Chris Smith. *Suicide of the West*. New York: Continuum International, 2007.

Koyama, Mark. "Evading the Taint of Usury: The Usury Prohibition as a Barrier to Entry." *Explorations in Economic History* 47, no. 4 (2010): 420–42.

———. "The Political Economy of Expulsion: The Regulation of Jewish Moneylending in Medieval England." *Constitutional Political Economy* 21, no. 4 (2010): 374–406.

Krause, Sharon. "Review Essay: Beyond Capitalism?" *Political Theory* 38 (2010): 884–90.

Krouse, Richard, and Michael McPherson. "A 'Mixed'-Property Regime: Equality and Liberty in a Market Economy." *Ethics* 97, no. 1 (1986): 119.

Krueger, A. O. "The Political Economy of the Rent-Seeking Society," *American Economic Review* 64 (1974): 291–303.

Kukathas, Chandran. *Hayek and Modern Liberalism*. New York: Oxford University Press, 1989.

Kymlicka, Will. *Contemporary Political Philosophy: An Introduction*. New York: Oxford University Press, 1990.

Laffer, Arthur B., Stephen Moore, and Peter Tanous. *The End of Prosperity: How Higher Taxes Will Doom the Economy—If We Let It Happen*. New York: Threshold Editions, 2008.

Lange, Oskar. *On the Economic Theory of Socialism*. New York: McGraw-Hill, 1964.

Larmore, Charles. "What Is Political Philosophy?" Working draft presented at Brown University's Political Philosophy Workshop, spring 2010.

Lavoie, Don. "Computations, Incentives, and Discovery: The Cognitive Function of Socialism." *Annals of the American Academy of Political and Social Science* 507 (January 1990).

Lee, Patrick G., "Food Stamp Discount for Buying Produce." *Boston Globe*, August 19, 2010, B.1 Metro.

Leopold, Aldo. *A Sand County Almanac*. New York: Oxford University Press, 1949.

Leopold, David, and Marc Stears, eds. *Political Theory: Methods and Approaches*. Oxford: Oxford University Press, 2008.

Lindsey, Brink. "Liberaltarians." *The New Republic*, December 11, 2006. At http://www.tnr.com/article/politics/liberaltarians.

Locke, John. "Some Considerations of the Consequences of the Lowering of Interest and the Raising the Value of Money." 1691. At http://socserv.mcmaster.ca/econ/ugcm/3ll3/locke/consid.txt, November 4, 2008.

Locke, John. *Two Treatises of Government*. Edited by Peter Laslett. Cambridge: Cambridge University Press, 1988.

Lomasky, Loren. "Libertarianism at Twin Harvard." *Social Philosophy & Policy*, 23, no. 1 (2005).

———. *Persons, Rights, and the Moral Community*. New York: Oxford University Press, 1990.

Lukes, Steven. "Social Justice: The Hayekian Challenge." *Critical Review* 11, no. 1 (1997): 65–80.

Macedo, Stephen. *Diversity and Distrust: Civic Education in a Multicultural Democracy*. Cambridge, MA: Harvard University Press, 2003.

Macey, Jonathan. "Some Causes and Consequences of the Bifurcated Treatment of Economic Rights and 'Other' Rights under the United States Constitution." In *Economic Rights*, edited by Ellen Frankel Paul, Fred D. Miller, and Jeffrey Paul, 141–70. New York: Cambridge University Press, 1992.

Mack, Erick. "Self-Ownership, Marxism, and Egalitarianism: Part II: Challenges to the Self-Ownership Thesis." *Politics, Philosophy, and Economics* 1, no. 2 (2002).

Maddison, Angus. *Contours of the World Economy, 1–2030 AD: Essays in Macro-Economic History*. New York: Oxford University Press, 2007.

Madison, James. "Universal Peace." In *The Writings of James Madison*, edited by Gaillard Hunt, 88–91. New York: Putnam Press, 1907.

Mandeville, Bernard. "The Grumbling Hive or, Knaves Turn'd Honest." In *The Fable of the Bees; or, Private Vices, Public Benefits*. 1732 ed. Vol. 1. Indianapolis, IN: Liberty Fund, 1988.

Marx, Karl, and Friedrich Engels. *Karl Marx, Frederick Engels: Marx and Engels Collected Works, vol. 11*. London: Lawrence & Wishart, 1979.

Mason, Andrew. "Just Constraints." *British Journal of Political Science* 34 (2004): 251–68.

Massey, Douglas S. *Return of the L-Word: A Liberal Vision for the New Century*. Princeton, NJ: Princeton University Press, 2005.

McCloskey, Deirdre. "Growth, Quality, Happiness, and the Poor." Munich University Library, 2009. At http://mpra.ub.uni-muenchen.de/17967/.

McElroy, Wendy, ed. *Freedom, Feminism, and the State: An Overview of Individualist Feminism*. Washington, DC: Cato Institute, 1982.

———. *Individualist Feminism of the Nineteenth Century: Collected Writings and Biographical Profiles*. Jefferson, NC: McFarland, 2001.

McKinley, Jesse. "A Tax on Nips and Tucks Angers Patients, Surgeons." *New York Times*, November 30, 2009.

Meade, James. *Efficiency, Equality, and the Ownership of Property*. London: Allen and Unwin, 1964.

MeasuringWorth.com. At http://measuringworth.com/USwages.

Meyers, Marvin, ed. *The Mind of the Founder: Sources of the Political Thought of James Madison*. 1973. Rev. ed.: Waltham, MA: Brandeis University Press, 1981.

Milgate, Murray, and Shannon C. Stimson. *After Adam Smith: A Century of Transformation in Politics and Political Economy*. Princeton, NJ: Princeton University Press, 2009.

Mill, John Stuart. *On Liberty*. London: Longmans, Green, 1921.

———. "On the Probable Futurity of the Labouring Classes." In *Principles of Political Economy*. 1st ed. Boston: Little, Brown, 1848.

———. *Principles of Political Economy*. Amherst, NY: Prometheus Books, 2004.

Miller, David. *Market, State, and Community: Theoretical Foundations of Market Socialism*. New York: Oxford University Press, 1991.

———. "Political Philosophy for Earthlings." In *Political Theory: Methods and Approaches*, edited by David Leopold and Marc Stears, 29–48. New York: Oxford University Press, 2008.

Miller, David. *Principles of Social Justice*. Cambridge, MA: Harvard University Press, 1999.

Moe ,Terry, and John Chubb. *Liberating Learning: Technology, Politics, and the Future of American Education*. San Francisco: Jossey-Bass, 2009.

Mokyr, Joel. *The Enlightened Economy: An Economic History of Britain, 1700–1850*. New Haven, CT: Yale University Press, 2010.

Montgomerie, Tim. "Tesco, Purveyors of Jobs, Cheap Food and Social Justice." *The Times*, June 8, 2010.

Morgan, Edmund. *American Slavery, American Freedom: The Ordeal of Colonial Virginia*. New York: W. W. Norton, 1975.

Morrissey, Janet. "Proposed 'Botox Tax' Draws Wide Array of Opponents." *Time*, December 17, 2009.

Moyo, Dambisa. *Dead Aid: Why Aid Is Not Working and Why There Is a Better Way for Africa*. New York: Farrar, Straus and Giroux, 2009.

Munzer, Steven. *A Theory of Property*. Cambridge: Cambridge University Press, 1990.

Murray, Charles. "The Happiness of the People." 2009 Irving Kristol Lecture. Washington, DC: American Enterprise Institute for Public Policy Research, American Enterprise Institute Press, 2009.

———. *In Our Hands: A Plan to Replace the Welfare State*. Washington, DC: American Enterprise Institute Press, 2006.

Mutz, Diana. *Hearing the Other Side: Deliberative versus Participatory Democracy*. New York: Cambridge University Press, 2006.

Nagel, Thomas. "Libertarianism without Foundations." *Yale Law Journal* 85, no. 1 (1975).

———. "The Problem of Global Justice," *Philosophy & Public Affairs* 33 (2005) 113–47.

———. "Rawls and Liberalism." In *The Cambridge Companion to Rawls*, edited by Samuel Freeman. Cambridge: Cambridge University Press, 2002.

———. "What Is It Like to Be a Bat?" *Philosophical Review* 83 (1974): 435–50.

Nagel, Thomas, and Liam Murphy. *The Myth of Ownership: Taxes and Justice*. New York: Oxford University Press, 2002.

Narveson, Jan. *The Libertarian Idea*. Philadelphia: Temple University Press, 1988.

Nedelsky, Jennifer. *Private Property and the Limits of American Constitutionalism: The Madisonian Framework and its Legacy*. Chicago: University of Chicago Press, 1990.

Nickel, James W. "Economic Liberties." In *The Idea of a Political Liberalism: Essays on Rawls*, edited by Victoria Davion and Clark Wolf. Lanham, MD: Rowman and Littlefield, 2000.

Nishiyama, Chiaki, and Kurt Leube, eds. *The Essence of Hayek*. Stanford, CA: Hoover Institution Press, 1984.

North, Douglass. *Institutions, Institutional Change, and Economic Performance*. Cambridge: Cambridge University Press, 1990.

———. *Understanding the Process of Economic Change*. Princeton, NJ: Princeton University Press, 2005.

North, Douglass, and Robert Paul Thomas. *The Rise of the Western World: A New Economic History*. New York: Cambridge University Press, 2006.

Norton, David Fate, and Mary J. Norton, eds. *David Hume: A Treatise of Human Nature*. New York: Oxford University Press. 2007.

Novak, Michael. *Three in One: Essays on Democratic Capitalism, 1976–2000*. Edited by Edward W. Younkins. Lanham, MD: Rowman and Littlefield, 2001.

Novak, William. *People's Welfare: Law and Regulation in Nineteenth-Century America*. Chapel Hill: University of North Carolina Press, 1996.

Nozick, Robert. *Anarchy, State, and Utopia*. New York: Basic Books, 1974.

———. *The Examined Life: Philosophical Meditations*. New York: Simon and Schuster, 1990.

———. *Invariances: The Structure of the Objective World*. Cambridge, MA: Harvard University Press, 2001.

Nussbaum, Martha. *Frontiers of Justice: Disabilities, Nationality, Species Membership*. Cambridge, MA: Belknap Press of Harvard University Press, 2006.

———. "Making Philosophy Matter to Politics." *New York Times*, December 2, 2002.

———. *Women and Human Development: The Capabilities Approach*. Cambridge: Cambridge University Press, 2000.

Oakeshott, Michael. *Rationalism in Politics and Other Essays*. Indianapolis, IN: Liberty Fund, 1991.

Ogden, Christopher, and Frank Melville. "Thatcher: We Are Building a Property-Owning Democracy." *Time*, June 22, 1987.

Olson, Mancur. *The Logic of Collective Action: Public Goods and the Theory of Groups*. Cambridge, MA: Harvard University Press, 1971.

Otsuka, Michael. "Self-Ownership and Equality: A Lockean Reconciliation." *Philosophy & Public Affairs* 27 (1998): 65–92.

Otteson, James R. *Actual Ethics*. New York: Cambridge University Press, 2006.

Paine, Thomas. *Common Sense*. Harvard, MA: Belknap Press of Harvard University Press, 2010.

Palmer, Tom G. *Realizing Freedom: Libertarian Theory, History, and Practice*. Washington, DC: Cato Institute, 2009.

———. "Liberty Is Liberty." In *Cato Unbound*. At http://www.cato-unbound.org/2010/03/12/tom-g-palmer/liberty-is-liberty/.

Parijs, Phillipe van. "Difference Principles." In *The Cambridge Companion to Rawls*, edited by Samuel Freeman, 200–240. New York: Cambridge Universe Press, 2003.

Parfit, Derek. "Equality and Priority." *Ratio* (n.s.) 10, no. 3 (December 1997).

Paul, Jeffrey, ed. *Reading Nozick*. Totowa, NJ: Rowman and Allanheld, 1981.

Pincione, Guido. "The Constitution of Nondomination." *Social Philosophy & Policy* 28, no. 1 (2011): 261–89.

Pipes, Richard. *Property and Freedom*. New York: Vintage Books, 2000.

Pogge, Thomas W. "Cohen to the Rescue!" *Ratio* 21, no. 4 (2008): 454–75.

Pogge, Thomas W. "An Egalitarian Law of Peoples." *Philosophy & Public Affairs* 23 (1994): 195–224.

———. *Realizing Rawls*. Ithaca, NY: Cornell University Press, 1989.

Polanyi, Michael. *The Great Transformation: The Political and Economic Origins of Our Time*. Boston: Beacon Press, 1971.

———. *The Logic of Liberty*. Chicago: University of Chicago Press, 1951.

Pollock, Frederick, and Frederic Maitland. *History of English Law before the Time of Edward I. Vol. 2*. Indianapolis, IN: Liberty Fund, 2009.

Pritchett, Lant. *Let Their People Come: Breaking the Gridlock on Global Labor Mobility*. Washington, DC: Center for Global Development, 2006.

Rand, Ayn. *Atlas Shrugged*. New York: Plume, 1999.

———. *The Virtue of Selfishness: A New Concept of Egoism*. With additional articles by Nathaniel Branden. New York: Signet, 1964.

Raphael, D. D., and A. L. Macfie, eds. *The Theory of the Moral Sentiments*. Indianapolis, IN: Liberty Fund, 1982.

Rasmussen, Dennis. *The Problems and Promise of Commercial Society: Adam Smith's Response to Rousseau*. University Park: Pennsylvania State University Press, 2008.

Rasmussen, Douglas B., and Den Uyl, Douglas. *Norms of Liberty: A Perfectionist Basis for Non-Perfectionist Politics*. University Park: Pennsylvania State University Press, 2005.

Rawls, John. *Justice as Fairness: A Restatement*. Edited by Erin Kelly. Cambridge, MA: Belknap Press of Harvard University Press, 2001.

———. *The Law of Peoples: With "The Idea of Public Reason Revisited."* 1st ed. Cambridge, MA: Harvard University Press, 2001.

———. *Political Liberalism*. New York: Columbia University Press, 2005.

———. *A Theory of Justice*. Cambridge, MA: Belknap Press of Harvard University Press, 1971.

———. *A Theory of Justice*. Rev. ed. Cambridge, MA: Harvard University Press, 1999.

Read, Leonard E. "I, Pencil: My Family Tree as Told to Leonard E. Read." *The Freeman*, December 1958. Irvington-on-Hudson, NY: The Foundation for Economic Education, 1999.

Ripstein, Arthur. *Force and Freedom: Kant's Legal and Political Philosophy*. Cambridge, MA: Harvard University Press, 2009.

Robbins, Lionel. *A History of Economic Thought: The LSE Lectures*. Princeton, NJ: Princeton University Press, 2000.

———. *The Theory of Economic Policy in English Classical Political Economy*. London: Macmillan, 1961.

Roberts, John. *The Modern Firm: Organizational Design for Performance and Growth*. New York: Oxford University Press, 2007.

Rockwell, Llewellyn H. "The State Expands, and Weakens." Speech delivered in Okemos, Michigan, April 16, 2005. At http://www.lewrockwell.com/rockwell/empire-shrinks.html.

Roemer, John. *A Future for Socialism*. Cambridge, MA: Harvard University Press, 1994.

Roemer, John, et al. *Equal Shares: Making Market Socialism Work*. Edited and introduced by Erik Olin Wright. New York: Verso 1996.

Rosenberg, Nathan, and L. E. Birdzell Jr. *How the West Grew Rich: The Economic Transformation of the Industrial World*. New York: Basic Books, 1986.

Ross, Ian Simpson. *The Life of Adam Smith*. New York: Oxford University Press, 1995.

Rothbard, Murray. *For a New Liberty: The Libertarian Manifesto*. Rev. ed. New York: Collier, 1978.

Rousseau, Jean-Jacques. *The Discourses and Other Early Political Writings*. Edited by Victor Gourevitch. Cambridge: Cambridge University Press, 1997.

Sandefur, Timothy. *Cornerstone of Liberty: Property Rights in 21st-Century America*. Washington, DC: Cato Institute, 2006.

Satz, Debra. *Why Some Things Should Not Be for Sale: The Moral Limits of Markets*. New York: Oxford University Press, 2010.

Schaefer, David Lewis. *Illiberal Justice: John Rawls vs. The American Political Tradition*. Columbia: University of Missouri Press, 2007.

Schmidtz, David. *Elements of Justice*. Cambridge: Cambridge University Press, 2006.

———. "The Institution of Property." In *The Common Law and the Environment: Rethinking Statutory Basis for Modern Environmental Law*, edited by Roger E. Meiners and Andrew P. Morriss, 109–29. Lanham, MD: Rowman and Littlefield, 2000.

———. "Nonideal Theory: What It Is and What It Needs To Be." *Ethics* 121 (2011).

———. *Person, Polis, Planet: Essays in Applied Philosophy*. New York: Oxford University Press, 2008.

———. *Rational Choice and Moral Agency*. Princeton NJ: Princeton University Press, 1996.

———. "Review of Debra Satz's *Why Some Things Should Not Be for Sale*." *Journal of Philosophy* (forthcoming 2011).

———. "When Is Original Appropriation 'Required'?" *The Monist* 73 (1990): 504–18.

Schmidtz, David, ed. *Robert Nozick*. Cambridge: Cambridge University Press, 2002.

Schmidtz, David, and Jason Brennan. *A Brief History of Liberty*. Malden, MA: Wiley-Blackwell, 2010.

———. "Conceptions of Freedom." *Cato Unbound*. March 10, 2010. At http:// cato-unbound.org/2010/03/10/david-schmidtz-and-jason-brennan.

Schmidtz, David, and Robert E. Goodin. *Social Welfare and Individual Responsibility*. Cambridge: Cambridge University Press, 1998.

Schmidtz, David, and Elizabeth Willott, eds. *Environmental Ethics: What Really Matters, What Really Works*. New York: Oxford University Press, 2002.

Schumpeter, J. A. *History of Economic Analysis*. New York: Oxford University Press, 1994.

Scott, James C. *Seeing Like a State: How Certain Schemes to Improve the Human Condition Have Failed*. New Haven, CT: Yale University Press, 1998.

Sen, Amartya. *The Idea of Justice*. Cambridge, MA: Belknap Press of Harvard University Press, 2009.

———. *Inequality Reexamined*. Cambridge, MA: Harvard University Press, 1992.

———. "Maximization and the Act of Choice." *Economitrica* (1997): 65.

Shapiro, Daniel. *Is the Welfare State Justified?* New York: Cambridge University Press, 2007.

———. "Liberalism, Basic Rights, and Free Exchange." *Journal of Social Philosophy* 26, no. 2 (1995): 103–26.

———. "Why Rawlsian Liberals Should Support Free Market Capitalism," *Journal of Political Philosophy* 3, no. 1 (1995): 58–85.

Shapiro, Tamar. "Compliance, Complicity, and the Nature of Nonideal Conditions." *Journal of Philosophy* (2003): 329–55.

Siegan, Bernard. *Economic Liberties and the Constitution*. 2nd ed. New Brunswick, NJ: Transaction Publishers, 2006.

———. *Property Rights: From Magna Carta to the Fourteenth Amendment*. New Brunswick, NJ: Transaction Publishers, 2001.

Simon, Julian L. "Population Growth, Natural Resources, and Future Generations." From *The Ultimate Resource II: People, Materials, and Environment*, 1998. At http://www.juliansimon.com/writings/Ultimate_Resource/.

Smith, Adam. *An Inquiry into the Nature and Causes of the Wealth of Nations*. Edited by R. H. Campbell, A. S. Skinner, and W. B. Todd. Oxford: Clarendon Press, 1976.

———. *An Inquiry into the Nature and Causes of the Wealth of Nations*. London: Oxford University Press, 2008.

———. *Lectures on Jurisprudence*. Edited by R. L. Meek, and D. D. Raphael, and P. G. Stein. New York: Oxford University Press, 1978.

———. *The Wealth of Nations*. Petersfield: Harriman House, 2007.

Smith, Adam. *Adam Smith: The Theory of Moral Sentiments*. Edited by Knud Haakonssen. Cambridge: Cambridge University Press, 2002.

Soto, Hernando de. *The Mystery of Capital*. New York: Basic Books, 2000.

Spencer, Herbert. *The Man versus the State*. London: Williams and Norgate, 1884.

———. *Social Statics or the Conditions Essential to Human Happiness Specified and the First of Them Developed*. BibilioLife, 2009.

Spragens, Thomas A. *Getting the Left Right: The Transformation, Decline, and Reformation of American Liberalism*. Lawrence: University Press of Kansas, 2009.

Sreenivasan, Gopal. *The Limits of Lockean Rights in Property*. New York: Oxford University Press, 1995.

Stark, Pete. "We Need a Tobin Tax to Fund Development." *Financial Times*, September 23, 2010.

Steiner, Hillel. *An Essay on Rights*. Oxford: Blackwell, 1994.

Stemplowska, Zofia. "What's Ideal about Ideal Theory?" *Social Theory and Practice*, special issue (July 2008).

Sunstein, Cass. *The Second Bill of Rights: FDR's Unfinished Revolution and Why We Need It More Than Ever*. New York: Basic Books, 2004.

Swadley, Jason. "Economic Liberties and the High Liberal Tradition." Working manuscript by Brown University PhD candidate, 2010.

Swaine, Lucas. *The Liberal Conscience: Politics and Principle in a World of Religious Pluralism*. New York: Columbia University Press, 2006.

Swift, Adam. "Social Justice: Why Does It Matter What the People Think?" In *Forms of Justice: Critical Perspectives on David Miller's Political Philosophy*, edited by Daniel Bell and Avner de-Shalit. Lanham, MD: Rowman and Littlefield, 2003.

Swift, Adam, and Stuart White. "Political Theory, Social Science, and Real Politics." In *Political Theory: Methods and Approaches*, edited by David Leopold and Marc Stears. Oxford: Oxford University Press, 2008.

Tan, K. C. *Justice without Borders*. New York: Cambridge University Press, 2004.

Tempkin, Larry. "Egalitarianism Defended." *Ethics* 113, no. 4 (2003): 764–82.

Tocqueville, Alexis de. *Democracy in America*. Chicago: University of Chicago Press, 2002.

Tomasi, John. "Can Feminism Be Liberated from Governmentalism?" In *Toward a Humanist Justice: The Political Philosophy of Susan Moller Okin*, edited by Robert Reich and Debra Satz. New York: Oxford University Press, 2009.

———. "Governance beyond the Nation State: James Madison on Foreign Policy and 'Universal Peace.'" In *James Madison and the Future of Limited Government*, edited by John Samples. Washington, DC: Cato Institute, 2002.

———. "Hayek on Spontaneous Order and the Mirage of Social Justice." Bradley Lecture monograph, American Enterprise Institute, 2008.

———. "Individual Rights and Community Virtues." *Ethics* 101, no. 3 (1991).

———. "Justice." In *The Oxford Companion to American Law*, edited by K. Hall, J. Elly, J. Grossman, and N. Hull. New York: Oxford University Press, 2002.

———. "The Key to Locke's Proviso." *British Journal for the History of Philosophy* 6, no. 3 (1998): 447–54.

———. *Liberalism beyond Justice: Citizens, Society, and the Boundaries of Political Theory*. Princeton, NJ: Princeton University Press, 2001.

———. "Should Political Liberals Be Compassionate Conservatives?: Philosophical Foundations of the Faith-Based Initiative." In *Morality and Politics*, edited by Jeffrey Paul. New York: Cambridge University Press, 2004.

———. "Sovereignty, Commerce, and Cosmopolitanism: Lessons from Early America for the Future of the World." In *After Socialism*, edited by Ellen Frankl Paul. New York: Cambridge University Press, 2003.

Tucker, Robert C., ed. *The Marx-Engels Reader*. W.W. Norton, 1978.

Tullock, Gordon. *Towards a Mathematics of Politics*. Ann Arbor: University of Michigan Press, 1967.

———. "The Welfare Costs of Tariffs, Monopolies, and Theft," *Western Economic Journal* 5 (1967): 224–32.

Tullock, Gordon, Arthur Seldon, and Gordon L. Brady. *Government Failure: A Primer in Public Choice*. Washington, DC: Cato Institute, 2002.

"Understanding the Tax Gap" (FS-2005-14, March 2005), Internal Revenue Service. At http://www.irs.gov/newsroom/article/0,,id=137246,00.html.

Uzgalis, William. "John Locke," substantive revision 2007. *Stanford Encyclopedia of Philosophy*. Fall 2008 ed. At http://plato.stanford.edu/archives/fall2008/entries/locke. Accessed September 24, 2008.

Vallentyne, Peter, and Hillel Steiner, eds. *Left-Libertarianism and Its Critics: The Contemporary Debate*. New York: Palgrave, 2000.

Vaughn, Karen. "John Locke's Theory of Property." *Literature of Liberty: A Review of Contemporary Liberal Thought* (Spring 1980): 5–37.

Vitousek, Peter M., et al. "Human Domination of Earth's Ecosystems." *Science* 277 (July 25, 1997).

Von Mises, Ludwig. *Economic Calculation in the Socialist Commonwealth*. Auburn, AL: Ludwig Von Mises Institute, 1990.

———. *Human Action: A Treatise on Economics*. Indianapolis, IN: Liberty Fund, 2007.

———. *Liberalism: In the Classical Tradition*. New York: The Foundation for Economic Education, 1985.

Vonnegut, Kurt. "Harrison Bergeron." In *Welcome to the Monkey House*. New York: Dial Press, 1998.

Waldron, Jeremy. "Enough and as Good Left for Others." *Philosophical Quarterly* 29, no. 117 (1979): 319–28.

———. *The Right to Private Property*. Oxford: Clarendon Press, 1988.

———. "Socioeconomic Rights and Theories of Justice." Working manuscript, electronic copy available at http/ssrn.com/abstract=1699898, p. 3, 2010.

———. "Theoretical Foundations of Liberalism." *Philosophical Quarterly* 37, no. 147 (1987): 127–50.

Wall, Steven. "Just Savings and the Difference Principle." *Philosophical Studies* 116 (2003): 79–102.

———. "Rawls and the Status of Political Liberty," *Pacific Philosophical Quarterly* 87, no. 2 (2006): 245–70.

Wall, Steven and George Klosko, eds. *Perfectionism and Neutrality: Essays in Liberal Theory*. Lanham, MD: Rowman and Littlefield, 2003.

Wanniski, Jude. "Taxes, Revenues, and the 'Laffer Curve.'" *The Public Interest* 50 (1978): 3–16.

Wenar, Leif. "Political Liberalism: An Internal Critique." *Ethics* 106, no. 1 (1995).

Wenz, Peter S. *Environmental Justice*. Albany: State University of New York Press, 1988.

White, Lawrence. *The Theory of Monetary Institutions*. Malden, MA: Blackwell Publishers, 1999.

White, Stuart. "The Citizen's Stake and Paternalism." In *Redesigning Distribution*, edited by Erik Olin Wright. New York: Verso, 2006.

Whitehouse.gov. At http://www.whitehouse.gov/cea/three-quest-soc-sec .pdf.

Whitney, Gleaves, ed. *The American Cause*. Wilmington, DE: Intercollegiate Studies Institute Books, 2009.

Wolfe, Alan. *The Future of Liberalism*. New York: Alfred A. Knopf, 2009.

Wood, Gordon. *Empire of Liberty: The History of the Early Republic, 1789–1815*. New York: Oxford University Press, 2009.

———. *The Radicalism of the American Revolution*. New York: A. A. Knopf, 1992.

Yale Law School. "The Avalon Project: Washington's Farewell Address 1796." At http://avalon.law.yale.edu/18th_century/washing.asp.

Zuckert, Michael. *Launching Liberalism: On Lockean Political Philosophy*. Lawrence: University Press of Kansas, 2002.

Zwolinski, Matt. "Classical Liberalism and the Basic Income." *Basic Income Studies* (forthcoming).

———. "Libertarianism," *The Internet Encyclopedia of Philosophy*. http://www.iep.utm.edu/libertar/, 2008.

Index